Psychological Testing

Psychological Testing

A Practical Approach to Design and Evaluation

Theresa J.B. Kline
University of Calgary

SAGE Publications
Thousand Oaks ▪ London ▪ New Delhi

For information:

Sage Publications, Inc.
2455 Teller Road
Thousand Oaks, California 91320
E-mail: order@sagepub.com

Sage Publications Ltd.
1 Oliver's Yard
55 City Road
London, EC1Y 1SP
United Kingdom

Sage Publications India Pvt. Ltd.
B-42, Panchsheel Enclave
Post Box 4109
New Delhi 110 017 India

Printed in the United States of America on acid-free paper.

Library of Congress Cataloging-in-Publication Data

Kline, Theresa, 1960-
Psychological testing: a practical approach to design and evaluation / Theresa J.B. Kline.
    p. cm.
Includes bibliographical references and index.
ISBN 1-4129-0544-3 (hardcover)
  1. Psychological tests. I. Title.
BF176.K583 2005
150′.28′7—dc22

                              2004022907

05 06 07 08 09 10 9 8 7 6 5 4 3 2 1

Acquiring Editor:	Lisa Cuevas Shaw
Editorial Assistant:	Margo Crouppen
Project Editor:	Claudia A. Hoffman
Copy Editor:	Brenda Weight
Typesetter:	C&M Digitals (P) Ltd.
Indexer:	Will Ragsdale
Cover Designer:	Janet Foulger

Contents

Preface

Test development and test use are two common activities of those who work with people. Tests are used in academic, employment, clinical, and research settings. The purpose of this book is to present readers with a sound basis from which to develop tests for their own use and also to be able to evaluate tests, whether these are their own developed instruments or instruments developed by others. The process of developing and evaluating a test is not a mysterious one. It is very methodical and deliberate. It takes time and effort. Fortunately, the way has been paved with many standard procedures and general protocols. Unfortunately, these procedures and protocols have been scattered in various textbooks, guidelines, and research articles. Up to this point, there has been no one resource that can be used as a guide for the test development and evaluation process. This book aims to fill that gap.

The book is laid out in a stepwise manner, as though one were going to embark on developing and evaluating a test. Chapter 1 begins by reminding the reader of the importance of tests and testing in our everyday lives. There is also a review of highlights in the testing field and some of the statistical procedures used in latter parts of the book. The chapter closes with a brief introduction to the first step in test construction—that of defining the test construct. Chapter 2 moves on with the testing construct by describing how items are developed and written to operationalize the construct. Sources of information and writing styles are described. Chapter 3 covers the topic of what type of response is required by the test taker and how that should be decided based on the test construct and use. Tests of achievement, attitudes, and behaviors all require different approaches to response design. They are all covered in this chapter. Chapter 4 reviews the processes and issues associated with securing samples of individuals to complete a test. Types of random and nonrandom samples are described. Response rates and missing data are also discussed.

At this point, the text shifts from the more conceptual to the more statistical. That is, statistical analyses are a primary feature of Chapters 5–10. Chapter 5 reviews the tenets of classical test theory and begins the empirical assessment of tests via item analyses. These include item difficulty and discrimination indices. In addition, differential item weighting is covered. Chapter 6 focuses on modern test theory and the extensive item analyses available via this framework. Dichotomous and multiple-response models are described and analyses shown. Estimation procedures for items and test takers are described, as are the types of fit indices for modern test theory. The chapter closes by discussing the strengths and limitations of modern test theory and providing citations of some computer programs available for use in modern test theory. Chapters 7 and 8 are devoted to the techniques used to assess various aspects of test and rater reliability. Chapter 7 covers test-retest, alternative forms, and internal consistency measures of reliability. Chapter 8 describes several different types of rater consistency measures and what is meant by reliability generalization. Chapters 9 and 10 discuss the various ways one can infer validity of test scores. Chapter 9 focuses on the content and criterion methods of establishing test score validity, and Chapter 10 primarily describes analyses that use factor-analytic approaches to establishing validity.

The final two chapters take a turn once more with less emphasis on statistical analyses. Chapter 11 covers the important ethical and professional issues that individuals must be aware of and keep abreast of if they are to be competent in the testing area. These include professional standards, legal challenges, integrity testing, computer testing, and test translation. Chapter 12 goes over some of the resources that can be accessed to find test reviews; provides short reviews of eight commonly used tests in the areas of intelligence, achievement, structured personality, and career choice; and, finally, summarizes the main points covered in the book.

At the end of this experience of reading about testing and assessment techniques, learners should be able to do two things. The first is to effectively appraise any test they come across in terms of why and how it was developed and come to a decision about whether or not it meets the standards of testing and their needs. The other is to effectively design and evaluate tests. This book was written to meet these learning objectives.

To develop a book from the idea stage to publication requires the time and effort of many individuals. I want to thank them for their unique and necessary contributions. First, I am indebted to Lisa Cuevas Shaw, Acquisitions Editor at Sage Publications, for her support and suggestions to ensure that this book would be of interest to a wide audience. Second, thanks to the anonymous reviewers for their extensive time and effort; their comments greatly improved this book. Finally, I am indebted to the individuals who were instrumental in highlighting for me the important role of measurement in behavioral science throughout my career. These include my undergraduate psychological testing instructor, Dr. Wilbur Scoville; my graduate education supervisors, Drs. Guy Rowland and Edwin Boyd; and my colleague Dr. Lorne Sulsky.

CHAPTER 1

The Assessment of Individuals

The Critical Role and Fundamentals of Measurement

The importance of measurement in our daily lives and in research in education and the social sciences cannot be overstated. How well a construct is measured is critical in so many different ways. Consider the importance of measuring the height and weight of a newborn baby. These are general indicators of the health of the baby. If a measurement is unusual, then actions are taken to bring the measurement more in line with what is considered typical. Consider any college or university course taken. Achievement tests to determine how much students have mastered the course content are the norm. If the test is flawed in some way, this may have a negative impact on GPA, which would have further consequences. Consider tests of ability that are used for streaming junior high school students into a university-bound or non-university-bound set of courses in high school. Based on the test score, a student's life is affected. Consider a job interview where a panel of judges rates applicant responses to interview questions. Based at least partly on their ratings (measurement of applicant performance in the interview), a job offer may or may not be forthcoming. Consider how carefully politicians pay attention to popularity polls. Their future careers rest on how this information is collected and portrayed.

On the research side of things, if the measures used in the study that is being carried out are questionable, the research is not going to be published. If a poor measure of job satisfaction is used, then the likelihood of it being related to other variables of interest to the researcher (such as intentions to quit the organization) is also poor; the analyses are less likely to be able to detect the relationships hypothesized. The measure that is being used in research should exactly measure the construct of interest. For example, in a measure of job satisfaction, there may be a couple of items that actually measure knowledge of organizational policies. If this is the case, then that measure is impure or contaminated.

Measurement is used all the time in our daily lives and it is an integral part of the research process. Knowledge about measurement—how to correctly assess constructs, how to critically examine others' use of measures, and how to be a smart consumer of published tests—is an important skill of a social scientist. This book is written for that reason. At the end, you should know how to construct a test, how to evaluate a test, and how much faith you can put in the scores of any given instrument.

Measurement in the Physical Sciences

Those of us in the social sciences are often envious of the precision with which physical scientists are able to measure their constructs. There is not a lot of quarreling about the temperature, speed, height, weight, luminance level, or color of a given substance or event. The instruments that have been designed to measure such constructs have been built to be reliable and are usually calibrated on a regular basis to ensure the accuracy of the values that they produce. As long as the individual using the instrument knows how to use it and knows how to interpret the values, there is no problem in the measurement aspect of the work.

Measurement in the Social Sciences

On the other hand, social scientists are often dealing with ambiguous constructs such as political activism, delinquency, leadership, intelligence, personality, creativity, depression, anxiety, and so forth. Not only is there disagreement on how these are measured but also, in many cases, there is no overall agreement on what is meant by the construct itself. Thus, social scientists battle on two fronts. The first thing to do when preparing to develop or use a test is to be absolutely clear about what it is that you want to measure. This is called the conceptual definition of the construct. For example, if you want to measure creativity, you must first define for yourself, and therefore for all who will read your work, what you mean by creativity. As a creativity test consumer, you will first want to determine how much you agree with how the test author defined creativity. If you don't agree, then don't purchase the test.

Even after leaping the first hurdle of getting an audience to agree with a conceptual definition, social scientists must then convince them that how that construct is measured is an accurate representation of the construct. That is, translating the conceptual definition into an operational definition (in measurement, this usually means creating items to assess the construct) requires careful and methodical work. Two chapters are devoted to this exercise—one to creating items and the other to creating responses to those items.

Thus, measurement in the social sciences is fraught with pitfalls and yet is such a critical skill that it is well worth cultivating. Before moving on to introduce the topic of construct definition, a review of some of the highlights in the history of individual difference measurement, or, more technically, psychometrics, is presented.

Historical Highlights of Measurement

Assessment of individual differences has a very long history. The Chinese civil service in 2200 B.C. was the first recorded group to use formal testing procedures for selection and performance appraisal (Bowman, 1989). This system was the model for British, French, and German governments in the 19th century. The ancient Greeks also used individual difference testing (Doyle, 1974).

Measurement and testing, however, received a great boost in the 19th century due to the rising interest in several countries about various aspects of individual differences. The controversial and revolutionary writings of the English naturalist Charles Darwin; the work in the experimental psychology laboratories of Wundt, Ebbinghaus, and Fechner in Germany; the study of intelligence in France by Binet and Simon; the work of English biologists Galton and Pearson; and the American experimental psychologist Cattell all contributed in tangential or direct ways to the testing movement.

A seminal event in testing occurred when Alfred Binet, a French psychologist, and Theodore Simon were commissioned by the Parisian minister of public education in 1904 to develop a process to identify schoolchildren who would not benefit from instruction in the regular school system. Their work on the first formal intelligence test resulted in the assessment of children aged 3 to 13.

Work on other tests of intelligence, achievement, personality, and interests took place in the early 20th century. The advent of the First World War, and the need to test intelligence for large numbers of people in group settings, rendered the individually administered tests that had been developed to date too resource intensive. The result was the development by Otis in 1917 of the Army Alpha (for literate respondents) and Army Beta (for illiterate respondents) group-administered intelligence tests. The current Armed Services Vocational Aptitude Battery is based on Otis's early work.

The need for matching the vocational skills and interests of the many new immigrants to North America was answered by the development of interest inventories. As the standard of living for many living in North America climbed, more young adults wanted to enter colleges, universities, and graduate schools. The need for tests of achievement that assessed students and allowed for comparison with others across the continent (i.e., standardized testing) influenced the creation and use of the Scholastic Aptitude Test, the Graduate Record Examination, and many others.

It was during World War II that, for the first time, the capabilities of machines outpaced the capabilities of humans. The need to develop careful tests of psychomotor skills was answered. In the 1930s and 1940s, the interest in personality as a construct was widely discussed, with Freud's and Jung's writings capturing the imaginations of laypeople and professionals alike. Today, measures of various aspects of personality are commonplace.

Testing has become normative in schools and workplaces. However, some identifiable demographic groups have been disadvantaged by traditional paper-and-pencil tests. With the civil rights movement and the passage of Title VII in the United States, the testing enterprise went on the defensive. Specifically, the onus of the "validity of a test" was on the test administrator. Litigation abounded and many organizations became wary of using test scores for making personnel decisions.

The 1980s saw an exponential rise in the use of computers. Computer-based testing and computer-adaptive testing have become more regular features of the testing terrain. New tests are coming on the scene every day, revisions to older tests recur on a regular basis, and the public is increasingly knowledgeable about tests and their rights with regard to the use of test scores. All of these advances testify to the need for social scientists to be skilled in test development and evaluation methods.

Statistics Background

Before continuing, it will be useful to freshen up on some statistics basics. As this book proceeds, some fairly advanced statistical information will be introduced. This book assumes that the reader has taken (and passed) a basic statistics course in college or university. Topics that will be reviewed here are scales of measurement, characteristics of the normal distribution, p values, and statistical significance. In addition, a quick refresher on sampling distributions, correlation, and regression is in order. Finally, linear conversion of raw scores is presented, as this is used extensively in the measurement literature.

Scales of Measurement. In the measurement process, data are collected and numbers assigned to them. Depending on the type of data collected, those numbers carry different meanings. These meanings are based on the scale of measurement used.

The most rudimentary scale of measurement is the nominal scale. Here, the numbers are simply ways to code categorical information. For example, data may be collected on men and women and, for sake of expediency, all cases that are men are coded with a 1 and all cases that are women are coded with a 2. If data are collected on a college campus, college major may be coded numerically (e.g., science = 1, social science = 2, humanities = 3, etc.). In all instances, these nominal numbers reflect nothing other than a category. The numerical values in nominal scores do not represent an assessment of more or less of any particular value.

The next, more complex, level of measurement is ordinal. In ordinal measurement, the numbers assigned have meaning in that they demonstrate a rank order of the cases. For example, if members of a class are rank ordered from highest to lowest based on their test scores, the rank ordering indicates who did better than whom. However, ordinal measures do not indicate an absolute level of performance. For example, if the finishers of a race are rank ordered from first to last, this indicates who ran faster than whom but does not indicate anything about the runners' absolute speed in completing the race.

Interval is the next most sophisticated level of measurement. Here, the numbers are rank ordered, but now more information is contained in the numbers. Specifically, the differences between the numbers are equivalent. That is, the difference between 2 and 3 can be assumed to be the same as the difference between 3 and 4. For example, temperature is measured at the interval level. If it is 20 degrees on Day 1, 25 degrees on Day 2, and 30 degrees on Day 3, the temperature change from Day 1 to Day 2 is exactly the same as that from Day 2 to Day 3.

For interval-level data, each case has an absolute value associated with it. However, there is no fixed zero point with these types of scales. The result of no fixed zero is best demonstrated through an example. Let's say we want to measure individuals' "need for achievement" with a particular scale. With an interval level of measurement, the scores can be interpreted to mean that someone with a score of 15 is as different from someone with a score of 20 as is someone with a score of 20 compared to someone with a score of 25. The scale provides us with interval-level information. However, there is no universally accepted level of "zero need for achievement." Therefore, we cannot conclude that someone with a score of 20 has half the need for achievement as does a person with a score of 40. In order to make that claim, we would need to have an absolute zero point on the scale.

Ratio level of measurement provides the most information about the numbers because it has all the characteristics of interval-level measurement, plus there is an absolute zero point. Scales measured at the ratio level would include height, weight, speed, time, and distance. If person A is six feet tall and person B is three feet tall, it is true to say that person A is twice as tall as person B. If person A runs 10 kilometers in 40 minutes and person B runs 5 kilometers in 40 minutes, it is true to say that person B ran half as fast as person A.

The reason for the review of this topic is that the appropriate statistical procedure to use in any data set depends on the level of measurement used. Most data that social scientists collect are at the nominal, ordinal, or interval level. In scale development and use, we often aspire to measure at the interval level, but we can often only achieve the ordinal level.

The Normal Distribution. A common assumption about any measured individual difference, whether it is a personality characteristic, cognitive skill, motor skill, social skill, or other attribute, is that this difference is normally distributed in the population. The normal distribution is a symmetrical, bell-shaped curve (see Figure 1.1). The shape shows that more of the area under the curve is in the center of the distribution, and, as one moves toward the "tails" of the distribution, the area under the curve becomes less and less.

Using height as an example of a normally distributed characteristic, everyone's height in a country could be measured. It would be the case that there are a few short people and a few tall people, but most people's heights would fall somewhere in the midrange. The more extreme the height (shorter or taller), the fewer the number of people who would have that height. The normal distribution serves to determine if a particular value is extreme or not when conducting statistical analyses. Values at the extreme ends of the distribution are unusual and the exact "extremeness" of any value can be quantified based on probability, which we turn to next.

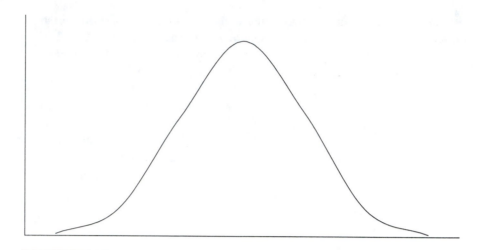

Figure 1.1   Normal Distribution

Probability and Statistical Significance. Prior to beginning this section, recall that when probability is mentioned, science is a conservative endeavor. This means that when scientists ask a question such as, Are girls more likely than boys to sign up for a high school auto mechanics class? they are likely to say that the question is empirical and that data should be collected to answer the question.

So a sample of high schools in the city is selected, and the percentages of girls and boys enrolled in auto mechanics classes are compared. Suppose it is found that, out of the 1,000 enrollments in the high school auto mechanics classes for the fall term, 55% were boys and 45% were girls. Would it be justifiable to claim that more boys than girls signed up for auto mechanics? What if the percentages were 60% to 40%? What if the percentages were 75% to 25%? What if the percentages were 90% to 10%? At what point would the scientists be willing to say that there is a "statistically significant difference in the proportion of boys versus girls taking auto mechanics"?

The answer is known as the adopted *alpha level* (α). It reports that the difference found in the sample of boys versus girls would happen by chance alone X number of times out of 100. So what does X equal? Usually it equals 1 or 5. This means that the difference in percentages found in the sample would have to be large enough to only occur by chance 1 out of 100 times ($\alpha = 0.01$); or, less conservatively, 5 out of 100 times ($\alpha = 0.05$); or, even less conservatively, 10 out of 100 times ($\alpha = 0.10$).

These α levels correspond to *p values,* or sometimes *p levels,* on statistical printouts. The p value stands for the probability level. If the p value for a particular statistical test (whether it is a correlation, t test, chi-square, etc.) is equal to 0.03, then this is interpreted to mean that the finding from the particular sample would occur by chance alone 3 times out of 100. If the p value was equal to 0.30, then this is interpreted to mean that the finding from the particular sample would occur by chance alone 30 times out of 100. If the p value was equal to 0.006, then this is interpreted to mean that the finding from the particular sample would occur by chance alone 6 times out of 1,000. In the social sciences, the usual α level adopted for making decisions about statistical significance is 0.05 or 0.01.

Sampling Distributions. There is a difference between sample distributions and sampling distributions. An example of a sample distribution would be a distribution of a set of scores on a history test by a class of 6th-grade students. This distribution would show the mean score of the class, variance of the class scores, lowest and highest scores, and so forth. Sampling distributions, however, are theoretical distributions and are used in making statistical decisions. Like sample distributions, sampling distributions have means and variances. Multiple sampling distributions are associated with inferential statistics, such as t tests, F tests, chi-square tests, correlation tests, and so forth. The shape of each sampling distribution is based on different sample sizes and the number of variables in the analysis. Sampling distributions are used to set the α level for a particular statistical test and used to decide whether or not to reject the null hypothesis.

For example, if we were interested in the difference between need for achievement scores for men and women and we had a sample of 10 men and 10 women, we would test for the differences between the means of the sample scores and have a t statistic generated. We would then use a t table that reports the critical value the calculated t value needs to exceed in order for it be considered *statistically significant*. That is, the t value calculated has to be extreme enough to be considered highly unusual and not likely to occur by chance alone.

Sample sizes are important because they tell which sampling distribution to use to test whether or not the calculated statistic is significant or not. What is common about all sampling distributions is that as the sample size on which the statistic is calculated increases, the *critical value* the statistic needs to exceed to be considered significant (i.e., extreme) decreases. Take, for example, our 10 men and 10 women and their hypothesized difference in need for achievement scores. If we had used a two-tailed test and adopted an α level of 0.05, then the critical t value the calculated t value needs to exceed is 2.101. All else remaining constant, if we had 15 men and 15 women in our sample, the t value to exceed is 2.048. Thus, it is easier to find a significant difference using the larger sample than with the smaller sample.

Correlation. Correlation describes the strength and direction of the linear relationship between two variables. Data for a correlational analysis are put into two columns (vectors) of numbers, where X represents values on one variable and Y represents values on the other variable. These columns would be set up like the following:

X	Y

If the *X* variable was the number of hours studied, the *Y* variable might represent grades on an exam on that material as follows:

X	Y
5	80
6	87
7	89
9	95

A general pattern in the four pairs of scores emerges: as the number of hours of study goes up, the grade on the exam goes up. That is, the pairs vary together in a linear, positive manner. Let's take another example. What if the *X* variable was a measure of job satisfaction (where higher scores mean higher levels of satisfaction) and *Y* was a measure of intentions to quit? Then the pairs of numbers might look like the following:

X	Y
10	3
8	5
7	7
2	10

In this example, a general pattern in the four pairs of scores also emerges. However, this time, as the job satisfaction values go down, intentions to quit values go up. So in this example, the pairs vary together in a linear, negative manner.

The statistic that summarizes the strength and direction of the relationship between two vectors of variables is called the *Pearson product-moment correlation coefficient,* or *correlation coefficient* for short. Values of the correlation coefficient vary from −1.00 to +1.00. The more the pairs of values vary together, the stronger the relationship and the farther from 0.00 (whether a positive or negative value) the correlation coefficient will be. That is, a correlation coefficient of −0.80 indicates that there is a strong negative relationship between the pairs of values. A correlation coefficient of 0.40 indicates that there is a moderate positive relationship between the pairs of values.

Table 1.1 shows a set of four scores: *A, B, X,* and *Y.* In Box 1.1, the correlation between *A* and *B* is calculated to review the procedure. However, given the common availability of many of these calculations in computer programs, this book takes the approach that interpreting the information on the outputs provided by such programs is worthy of discussion. Therefore, the correlation program in SPSS will be used to first assess the correlation between *A* and *B,* and then again between *X* and *Y.* The relevant sections of the printout are shown in Box 1.2.

Table 1.1   Data for Two Examples of Pearson Correlations

Case	A	B	X	Y
1	6	45	10	1
2	7	120	9	3
3	8	100	8	2
4	9	101	7	4
5	2	76	6	3
6	3	55	5	5
7	4	80	4	3
8	5	76	3	4
9	6	90	2	5
10	7	110	1	5
11	8	115	10	6
12	9	120	9	3
13	1	52	8	2
14	2	40	7	4
15	3	43	6	1
16	4	20	5	6
17	5	86	4	5
18	5	80	3	4
19	6	15	2	1
20	7	87	1	2

Box 1.1   Computation of the Pearson Correlation of Columns *A* and *B* in Table 1.1

The Pearson Correlation for two variables (bivariate) computational formula is as follows:

$$(1\text{--}1) \quad r = [N\Sigma AB - (\Sigma A)(\Sigma B)]/\sqrt{[N(\Sigma A^2) - (\Sigma A)^2][N(\Sigma B^2) - (\Sigma B)^2]}$$

This formula is used to calculate the correlation of the data in columns *A* and *B* in Table 1.1. First, the values in columns *A* and *B* are squared and then *A* and *B* are cross-multiplied. The results are shown in Table 1.2.

(Continued)

Box 1.1 (Continued)

Table 1.2   Bivariate Pearson Correlation Computation Example Data Set

Case	A	B	A^2	B^2	AB
1	6	45	36	2025	270
2	7	120	49	14400	840
3	8	100	64	10000	800
4	9	101	81	10201	909
5	2	76	4	5776	152
6	3	55	9	3025	165
7	4	80	16	6400	320
8	5	76	25	5776	380
9	6	90	36	8100	540
10	7	110	49	12100	770
11	8	115	64	13225	920
12	9	120	81	14400	1080
13	1	52	1	2704	52
14	2	40	4	1600	80
15	3	43	9	1849	129
16	4	20	16	400	80
17	5	86	25	7396	430
18	5	80	25	6400	400
19	6	15	36	225	90
20	7	87	49	7569	609
SUM (Σ)	107	1511	679	133571	9016

$r = [(20 \times 9016) - (107)(1511)]/\sqrt{[20(679) - (107)^2][20(133571) - (1511)^2]}$

$= (180320 - 161677)/\sqrt{[(13580) - (11449)][(2671420) - (2283121)]}$

$= (18643)/\sqrt{(2131)(383299)}$

$= 18643/28766$

$= 0.684$

The results from the printout show that the correlation coefficient calculated between *A* and *B* is equal to 0.648. The significance level (or *p* value) of 0.002 indicates that the chance of us finding the magnitude of relationship between these

---

Box 1.2   Output from the SPSS Pearson Bivariate Correlational Analyses of Columns *A* and *B* and Columns *X* and *Y* in Table 1.1

Pearson Correlation between *A* and *B*: 0.648[a]
Sig. (two-tailed): 0.002; *N* = 20
a. Correlation is significant ($p < 0.01$; two-tailed)

Pearson Correlation between *X* and *Y*: −0.150[a]
Sig. (two-tailed): 0.527; *N* = 20
a. Correlation is not significant ($p > 0.05$; two-tailed)

---

20 pairs of numbers by chance alone is 2 in 1000 times. This is even less common (i.e., the finding of 0.648 is a value that would be found at the very extreme upper end of the sampling distribution) than the usual threshold of 0.01 or 0.05, and so it can be concluded that there is a significant positive relationship between *A* and *B*. The two-tailed test is the default for SPSS for testing correlation coefficients. This means that the direction of the relationship between *A* and *B* was not specified in advance. If the direction was specified to be either positive or negative, the option "one-tailed" in the SPSS program could be selected.

The correlation coefficient calculated for *X* and *Y* is equal to −0.150. It is negative in value and has a significance level of 0.527. This indicates that the chances of finding the calculated magnitude of relationship between these 20 pairs of numbers by chance is 527 in 1000 times. This is much higher than the usual threshold of 0.01 or 0.05 (i.e., the finding of −0.150 is a value that would be found in the middle of the sampling distribution), and so it must be concluded that there is no relationship between *X* and *Y*. That is, unless the significance level is smaller than 0.05 or 0.01 (whichever is adopted), it is assumed that the calculated value is not significantly different from 0.00 (the value at the exact middle of the sampling distribution).

Sometimes the question is raised as to how many cases one needs to calculate a correlation coefficient. The answer is, at a bare minimum, three. This is because there need to be at least three cases for the correlation significance level to be calculated. However, three cases are hardly enough to be confident about the calculated value of the correlation coefficient. Exactly how many cases are needed can be directly assessed, depending on the strength of the expected relationship, through something called a power analysis (e.g., Cohen, 1988). However, a good rough rule of thumb is to have 10 cases per variable. Because correlation uses two variables, 20 cases are usually sufficient to be able to draw some conclusions about the sample data if a moderate relationship between them is expected.

Linear Regression. Regression, as in correlation, is an analysis of linear relationships between variables. However, a major difference is that regression requires the researcher to indicate that one variable is dependent (criterion) on the other(s) (predictor[s]). In the linear regression examples in this book, there will always be only one criterion variable. In some cases there will be one predictor (simple or bivariate regression) and in other cases more than one predictor (multiple regression).

A regression analysis produces a series of results that will take a bit of time to review. As in correlation, assume that there are vectors (or columns) of numbers: each column represents a variable and each row represents a case, or a subject's scores on each of the variables. First, a case of simple regression will be reviewed, where there is only one predictor, followed by an example of multiple regression, with two predictors.

Assume the criterion is "starting salary" in $1000 dollars and the predictor is "university GPA." Another predictor, "cognitive ability," will be added in the second analysis. The data are set up as in Table 1.3 and the computational calculations of the bivariate regression are presented in Box 1.3. The SPSS output for the bivariate analysis is shown in Box 1.4.

Text continues on page 17

Table 1.3   Data for Bivariate (Simple) and Multiple Linear Regression Analyses

	Starting Salary ($1,000)	University GPA	Cognitive Ability
Case 1	20	2.0	100
Case 2	21	2.1	120
Case 3	22	2.0	110
Case 4	23	2.3	104
Case 5	24	2.1	90
Case 6	25	3.5	95
Case 7	26	3.0	115
Case 8	27	2.9	112
Case 9	28	3.4	115
Case 10	29	2.8	98
Case 11	30	3.0	120
Case 12	31	3.3	100
Case 13	32	3.4	110
Case 14	33	2.9	115
Case 15	34	2.8	100
Case 16	35	3.5	102
Case 17	36	3.4	108
Case 18	37	3.3	110
Case 19	38	3.2	116
Case 20	39	3.0	118

Simple Regression Output:

Model Summary			
R	R-Square	Adjusted R-Square	Std. Error of Estimate
0.70	0.49	0.46	4.3378

ANOVA					
	Sums of Squares	df	Mean Square	F	Sig.
Regression	326.23	1	326.30	17.34	0.001
Residual	338.70	18	18.82		
Total	665.00	19			

Coefficients					
Model	Unstandardized b	Standard Error	Standardized (Beta)	t	Sig.
Constant	6.54	5.60		1.17	0.258
GPA	7.93	1.90	0.70	4.16	0.001

Multiple Regression Output:

Model Summary			
R	R-Square	Adjusted R-Square	Std. Error of Estimate
0.72	0.52	0.46	4.3559

ANOVA					
	Sums of Squares	df	Mean Square	F	Sig.
Regression	342.44	2	171.30	9.02	0.002
Residual	322.56	17	18.97		
Total	665.00	19			

Coefficients					
Model	Unstandardized b	Standard Error	Standardized (Beta)	t	Sig.
Constant	−4.25	12.99		−0.33	0.747
GPA	7.72	1.93	0.68	4.01	0.001
Cognitive	0.11	0.12	0.16	0.92	0.369

Box 1.3 Computational Calculations of a Bivariate Regression Analysis

Using the data in Table 1.3, computational formulae are used to generate the regression line and other statistics for the bivariate regression of salary on GPA (see Table 1.4).

The predicted salary scores (using the regression line formula calculated), and squared deviation scores can then be calculated. These are needed for the calculation of the R^2 and standard error of estimate.

Presented next are the predictor scores, the predictor scores less the mean of the predictor scores, and the squares of the difference of those terms. These are needed for the calculation of the standard error of the regression coefficient (b).

Table 1.4 Data for Use in Calculating the Bivariate Regression Line

Case	Salary	GPA	GPA²	GPA × Salary
1	20	2	4	40
2	21	2.1	4.41	44.1
3	22	2	4	44
4	23	2.3	5.29	52.9
5	24	2.1	4.41	50.4
6	25	3.5	12.25	87.5
7	26	3	9	78
8	27	2.9	8.41	78.3
9	28	3.4	11.56	95.2
10	29	2.8	7.84	81.2
11	30	3	9	90
12	31	3.3	10.89	102.3
13	32	3.4	11.56	108.8
14	33	2.9	8.41	95.7
15	34	2.8	7.84	95.2
16	35	3.5	12.25	122.5
17	36	3.4	11.56	122.4
18	37	3.3	10.89	122.1
19	38	3.2	10.24	121.6
20	39	3	9	117
Sum (Σ)	590	57.9	172.81	1749.2
Mean	29.5	2.895		

Predicted Salary	(Actual − Predicted)^2	(Actual − $\bar{Y}$)^2	(Predicted − $\bar{Y}$)^2
22.4	5.76	90.25	50.41
23.193	4.809249	72.25	39.778249
22.4	0.16	56.25	50.41
24.779	3.164841	42.25	22.287841
23.193	0.651249	30.25	39.778249
34.295	86.397025	20.25	22.992025
30.33	18.7489	12.25	0.6889
29.537	6.436369	6.25	0.001369
33.502	30.272004	2.25	16.016004
28.744	0.065536	0.25	0.571536
30.33	0.1089	0.25	0.6889
32.709	2.920681	2.25	10.297681
33.502	2.256004	6.25	16.016004
29.537	11.992369	12.25	0.001369
28.744	27.625536	20.25	0.571536
34.295	0.497025	30.25	22.992025
33.502	6.240004	42.25	16.016004
32.709	18.412681	56.25	10.297681
31.916	37.015056	72.25	5.837056
30.33	75.1689	90.25	0.6889
	Σ338.70[a]	Σ665	Σ326.34[b]

a. This is also known as the residual sums of squares.

b. This is also known as the regression sums of squares. Note there is a slight discrepancy from the printout version due to rounding error in generating the predicted scores.

(Continued)

Box 1.3 (Continued)

GPA	GPA – Mean GPA	(GPA – Mean GPA)^2
2	−0.895	0.801025
2.1	−0.795	0.632025
2	−0.895	0.801025
2.3	−0.595	0.354025
2.1	−0.795	0.632025
3.5	0.605	0.366025
3	0.105	0.011025
2.9	0.005	2.5E-05
3.4	0.505	0.255025
2.8	−0.095	0.009025
3	0.105	0.011025
3.3	0.405	0.164025
3.4	0.505	0.255025
2.9	0.005	2.5E-05
2.8	−0.095	0.009025
3.5	0.605	0.366025
3.4	0.505	0.255025
3.3	0.405	0.164025
3.2	0.305	0.093025
3	0.105	0.011025
$\bar{X} = 2.895$		

Bivariate regression coefficient computational formula:

(1–2) $b = [N \times \Sigma XY - (\Sigma X)(\Sigma Y)]/[N\Sigma X^2 - (\Sigma X)^2]$.

Bivariate regression constant computational formula:

(1–3) $a = \bar{Y} - b\bar{X}$.

To solve for b,

$b = [(20)(1749.2) - (57.9)(590)]/[20(172.81) - (57.9)^2]$,

  $= (34984 - 34161)/(3456.2 - 3352.41)$,

  $= 823/103.79$,

  $= 7.93$.

To solve for a, then,

$a = \bar{Y} - b\bar{X}$,

  $= 29.5 - (7.93)(2.895)$,

  $= 29.5 - 22.96$,

  $= 6.54$.

Regression line: predicted salary $= 6.54 + 7.93(GPA)$

Calculating the R^2 value:

(1–4) $R^2 = S\ \Sigma(\bar{Y} - \bar{Y})^2/\Sigma(\bar{Y} - \bar{Y})^2$,

$= 326.34/665$,

$= 0.49$.

Calculating the adjusted R^2 value:

(1–5) Adjusted $R^2 = 1 - (1 - R^2)[(N - 1)/(N - k - 1)]$,

$= 1 - (1 - 0.49)\ [(20 - 1)/(20 - 1 - 1)]$,

$= 1 - (0.51)(19/18)$,

$= 1 - (0.51)(1.06)$,

$= 1 - 0.54$,

$= 0.46$.

Calculating the standard error of estimate:

(1–6) $SE = \sqrt{\Sigma(Y - Y')^2/(N - k - 1)}$,

where Y = actual scores, Y' = predicted scores, N = sample size, and k = number of predictors,

$SE = \sqrt{338.70/(20 - 1 - 1)}$,

$SE = 4.34$.

Calculating the F:

(1–7) F = (Regression Sums of Squares/df)/(Residual Sums of Squares/df),

$= (326.34/1)/(338.70/18)$,

$= 326.34/18.82$,

$= 17.34\ (1,18\ \text{degrees of freedom})$.

Calculating the standard error of b:

(1–8) $Sb = \sqrt{(SE)^2/(\text{Sum of Squared Deviations of } X)}$,

$= \sqrt{(4.34)^2/5.19}$,

$= \sqrt{18.84/5.19}$,

$= 1.90$.

Calculating the t:

(1–9) $t = b/Sb$,

$= 7.93/1.90$,

$= 4.17$. (This value is the same as that found in the computer printout within rounding error.)

Referring to the information in Box 1.4, there are three tables in the output of an SPSS regression analysis: the model summary, the ANOVA table, and the coefficient table. The model summary and ANOVA tables indicate whether or not *all* of predictors, as a unit, account for a significant amount of variance in the criterion. In the case of simple regression, there is only one predictor, so "all of them as a unit" means only GPA. In the model summary, the R value is the multiple correlation between the predictor and criterion. For this example, the value is 0.70 and it is actually calculated

Box 1.4   Bivariate (Simple) Regression Output From SPSS

Model Summary			
R	R-Square	Adjusted R-Square	Std. Error of Estimate
0.70	0.49	0.46	4.3378

ANOVA					
	Sums of Squares	df	Mean Square	F	Sig.
Regression	326.23	1	326.30	17.34	0.001
Residual	338.70	18	18.82		
Total	665.00	19			

Coefficients					
Model	Unstandardized b	Standard Error	Standardized (Beta)	t	Sig.
Constant	6.54	5.60		1.17	0.258
GPA	7.93	1.90	0.70	4.16	0.001

based on the R-square value that indicates how much variance in the criterion (salary) can be predicted with the predictor (GPA). In this example, it is 0.49, or 49%.

The adjusted R-square value provides an estimate of what to expect the R-square value to be if the study was conducted again with a new sample of 20 cases. In this case, the value is 0.46, indicating that some shrinkage in the R-square value is expected (i.e., reduced from 0.49 to 0.46). Although the adjusted R-square value is always smaller than the R-square value, the less shrinkage between the calculated R-square and adjusted R-square the better. When the difference between them is small, one can be more confident about the robustness of the R-square value. Next, the standard error is reported. This is the error associated with predicting scores on the criterion. Larger values indicate more error in prediction than do smaller values.

Whether or not the R-square value is significant is determined in the ANOVA table, using an F test. It can be seen that the F associated with the amount of variance accounted for in starting salary by GPA is 17.34 (with 1 and 18 degrees of freedom), which is significant at 0.001 (i.e., this extreme a value would occur by chance alone only 1 time out of 1,000). Therefore, concluding that university GPA accounts for a significant amount of variance in starting salary is justified.

One of the more important calculations from the analysis is the regression line. The summary of those calculations is in the coefficients table. The regression line is a mathematical function that relates the predictor to the criterion variable. It is calculated so that the line minimizes the squared distances of each point from the line. In simple regression, the regression line is written with the following formula:

(1–10) $$Y' = a + bX,$$

where Y' = the predicted Y score for a given value of X, b = the regression coefficient (also called the *slope*), a = the intercept (or constant), where the regression line crosses the y-axis, and X = the obtained values on X.

To interpret the information in the coefficients table, use the unstandardized constant and GPA coefficients (6.54 and 7.93, respectively). The regression line then can be written as follows:

$$Y' = 6.55 + 7.93(\text{GPA}).$$

For someone with a GPA of 4.0, the predicted starting salary would be

$$Y' = 6.55 + 7.93(4.0),$$

or 36.11 ($36,110, as salary level was coded in $1,000 units).

A scatterplot of the two variables is shown in Figure 1.2 as well as the regression line.

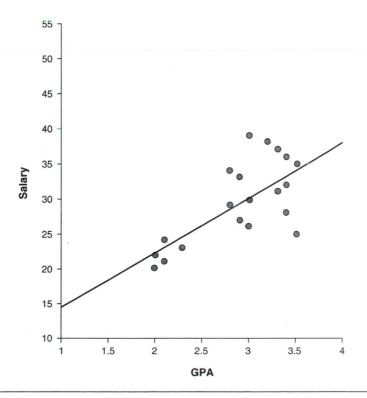

Figure 1.2   Regression Line of Starting Salary on GPA

In addition to obtaining the information for the regression line, the coefficients table reports the "unique" contributions of each predictor and whether the unique contribution is significantly different from zero. If the unstandardized coefficient value is divided by its respective standard error, a t value for the predictor is obtained. In this example, there is one predictor (i.e., GPA) and it has a t value of 4.16 (7.93/1.90), which is significant at 0.001. When there is only one predictor, the F value in the ANOVA table is equal to the square of the t value ($4.16^2 = 17.34$). The beta value, or standardized coefficient, is simply the standardized value of the unstandardized coefficient. That is, if standard scores rather than raw scores had been used in this analysis, the beta value would be 0.70. Beta values are like correlations insofar as they range in value from −1.00 to 0.00 to a high of 1.00. A score of 0.00 shows no relationship between the predictor and criterion. Its use will become more apparent in multiple regression, which we will turn to next.

As an example of a multiple regression analysis, cognitive ability scores will be added as a predictor (see Box 1.5). Because cognitive ability is added *after* GPA, a *hierarchical* approach is used in entering the variables into the equation. If both GPA and cognitive ability were entered into the equation at the same time, this would have been a *simultaneous,* or *direct,* entry of the predictors. If the computer selected which variable to enter first into the regression analysis based on a statistical criterion, it would be called a statistically driven entry, the most common of which is *stepwise.* In a stepwise regression analysis, the predictor with the highest zero-order correlation with the criterion is entered into the equation first. Then the predictor with the highest correlation with the criterion, after the effects of the first predictor are taken into account, is entered on the next step. Subsequent steps continue until there are no more variables left that account for a significant amount of the variance in the criterion.

Notice that the R-square value in this analysis is 0.52. By adding cognitive ability into the mix, an additional 3% of the variance in starting salary can be accounted for. The overall value of 52% is significant ($F = 9.02$, significant at 0.002), indicating that together GPA and cognitive ability account for a significant amount of variance in starting salary. The adjusted R-square is 0.46, indicating that the shrinkage estimate is calculated to be 6% (0.52 − 0.46). This shrinkage is larger than in the previous example with one predictor (recall that it was 3%). This is in part due to the increase in the number of predictors with no commensurate increase in the number of cases.

The regression line is $Y' = -4.25 + 7.72(\text{GPA}) + 0.11(\text{cognitive ability})$. The printout shows that the t value for GPA is significant ($t = 4.01$, significance of 0.001), but for cognitive ability is not ($t = 0.92$, significance of 0.369). This means that GPA predicts starting salary above and beyond what cognitive ability does, but cognitive ability does not predict starting salary above and beyond GPA.

In addition, the beta values confirm that the predictive value of cognitive ability is questionable. That is, the relative strength of GPA (0.68) is quite high compared to that of cognitive ability (0.16). Thus, with this data set it would be concluded that the measure of cognitive ability does not enhance the prediction of starting salary, whereas GPA does.

Box 1.5   Multiple Regression Output from SPSS

Model Summary			
R	R-Square	Adjusted R-Square	Std. Error of Estimate
0.72	0.52	0.46	4.3559

ANOVA					
	Sums of Squares	df	Mean Square	F	Sig.
Regression	342.44	2	171.30	9.02	0.002
Residual	322.56	17	18.97		
Total	665.00	19			

Coefficients					
Model	Unstandardized b	Standard Error	Standardized (Beta)	t	Sig.
Constant	−4.25	12.99		−0.33	0.747
GPA	7.72	1.93	0.68	4.01	0.001
Cognitive	0.11	0.12	0.16	0.92	0.369

There is a sample size problem here. Recall that there should be about 10 cases per variable in the equation. Because there are three variables, there should be about 30 cases but there are only 20 in this analysis. It is not that the regression program won't run—it will. It is up to the researchers to indicate that a lower than desirable sample size was used in the analysis and that, therefore, caution needs to be exercised so that the results are not overinterpreted. As scientists, it is convention to err on the side of being conservative in knowledge claims.

Correlation and regression will be used frequently in the coming chapters and thus a cursory review was deemed warranted at this point. If this brief overview was not sufficient, please see any number of introductory statistics textbooks to refresh more fully these topics.

Score Meaning. Raw scores on tests need to be interpreted. The numbers attached to raw scores are only meaningful in the context of a referent group of scores. For example, if I say, "I got a 15 on my history exam!" you don't know what that means—did I do well or poorly? This comparative information is called *normative* information. It is determined by knowledge about the referent group; in this case, you need to know how well the rest of the history class did on the exam to make my 15 meaningful.

Normative information is important for making sure that correct interpretations of scores are made. The larger and more representative the reference group to which a single score is compared, the more confidence can be placed in the interpretation of that score's meaning. For example, it would be better to compare my history exam mark of 15 with 1,000 students' marks over the last 10 years than to compare it with the marks of three classmates sitting around me.

This is why, for the more popular published tests, norm tables are provided. These tables have been created over many years by collecting large samples of data from many different test takers. These tables are sometimes broken down by demographic variables such as gender or age. This is so the test score interpreter can make a comparison of a score with the most appropriate demographic group. These normative samples are both very large and representative of the demographic characteristics of the group. An assumption in using norm tables is that the same test was used and administered under the same conditions as in the normative sample. Thus, it is up to test administrators to familiarize themselves with the administration protocol.

To make any raw score meaningful, it can be transformed into a distribution of meaningful, familiar values. The distribution most commonly known to social scientists is the standard normal distribution discussed earlier. It has a mean of 0.0 and a standard deviation of 1.0. This distribution is used because most individual differences are assumed to be normally distributed in the population. However, it is important to examine the degree to which this assumption is met in any sample data set. Luckily, most of the statistical procedures used in this text are robust (yield similar results to those found in normal distributions) to deviations of normality.

Converting a raw score (X) to a standard score (z score) based on the normal distribution is done via a simple transformation:

(1–11) $$z \text{ score} = (X - \bar{X})/SD \text{ (standard deviation)},$$

where the $\bar{X}$ and standard deviations are based on the sample.

Let's reconsider my history exam score of 15. If the mean of the class was 13 and the standard deviation was 2, then my raw score converts to a standard score of

$$z \text{ score} = (15 - 13)/2,$$

$$z \text{ score} = 1.0.$$

This means that if I look up my score of 1.0 in a distribution of normal scores, I see that I did better than about 84% of the class. Once I determine my z score, I can convert it to any other distribution where the mean and standard deviations are known. Some well-known distributions are the T score distribution with a mean of 50 and standard deviation of 10, or the Graduate Record Exam (GRE) distribution with a mean of 500 and standard deviation of 100. To make the conversions, simply use the following equation:

(1–12) New distribution score = (z score × SD new) + Mean new.

Assume someone has a *z* score of 0.43 on the GRE. The new GRE distribution score would be

$$GRE = (0.43 \times 100) + 500,$$
$$= (43) + 500,$$
$$= 543.$$

Assume someone has a *z* score of −1.5 on a test that will be converted to a *T* score. The new *T* distribution score would be

$$T \text{ score} = (-1.5 \times 10) + 50,$$
$$= (-15) + 50,$$
$$= 35.$$

Figure 1.3 shows the normal distribution and the *T* score equivalents of some of the major values on the distributions. Thus, it can be seen that transforming scores simply means taking the values on one distribution and changing the values to reflect another distribution.

Another common conversion of raw scores is to percentile ranks. This is the percentage of individuals in the reference group earning a lower score than the score obtained. So, for example, if a score of 153 on a test is obtained and this is superior to 67% of the reference group, then the percentile rank is 67%. To calculate the percentile rank, the raw scores of the sample must be known as well as the number of individuals in the sample. Percentiles are not as commonly used as are standardized scores.

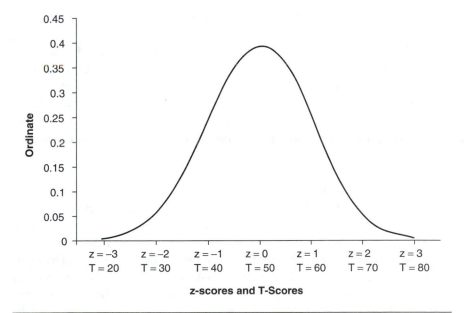

Figure 1.3   Normal Distribution Showing Selected *z* and *T* Scores

Quite a bit of time has been taken to review some of the information needed before embarking on the actual construction of a test. It is now time to make the transition to beginning the test development process. The first of these steps is to be clear on the construct to be measured. The rest of this chapter is devoted to that issue.

The First Step: Identifying the Construct

The first step in building any type of tool to assess individual differences is to identify the construct. The Webster's dictionary (Guralnik, 1976) defines a construct as "An idea or perception resulting from a synthesis of sense impressions." This is a useful definition, because it intimates that constructs are amorphous things; they are "ideas" and these ideas are a synthesis about a series of impressions. In other words, constructs are self-defined. The onus is on the test developer to convince the test user that the construct that is being measured is a reasonable assimilation and synthesis of ideas. Arguments are commonplace in the social sciences about "what we mean by construct *X*." One person's definition may not be the same as another's. If I ask an entire class to write down a definition of *success,* I will get as many different responses as there are students in the class. This means that it is unlikely that I will be able to create a test to assess success that will meet the expectations of all the students.

What is expected with a scale that is developed or used is that the individuals who respond to the items will provide information that will allow inferences to be made about the construct. Let's assume, for example, that we want to define the construct of being a team player in an organizational setting. Eventually, we will create a set of items that will, it's hoped, operationalize the construct of being a team player. For the moment, however, we'll concern ourselves with the issues of defining the construct itself.

It is helpful to have a list of what should be included and excluded from the construct. For example, in our assessment of being a team player, we'll restrict the construct to work settings; being a team player in sports, personal relationships, and so forth are not to be included in the domain of interest. Other aspects of what we want to include and what we want to exclude are also noted (see Table 1.5). This process makes explicit, for both the test developer and others as test consumers, what the measure will try to encompass and what it will not.

Links Between Constructs. For many tests, the goal is not just to test for the sake of testing. Instead, making inferences about the scores obtained on those tests is of interest. For example, the GRE is often used to make inferences about how well a test taker will do in graduate school. An assumption here is that the GRE assesses some cognitive skills that are needed to be successful in graduate school. The validity of this inference about GRE scores, then, is dependent on two things: the actual link between cognitive skills in graduate school and how well the GRE measures cognitive skills. In order to test this inference, actual numbers (data) must be

Table 1.5   Included and Excluded Aspects of Being a Team Player

Included	Excluded
Workplace examples	Sports examples
School projects	Personal relationships
Past experiences	Present circumstances
Outcomes	Personality conflicts
Progress to ends	Non-Western cultures
Effort expended	
Evaluation of results	

collected and will include GRE scores and some measure of success in graduate school. The strength of this link will be calculated using the actual data collected. Keep in mind, however, that the real purpose of the testing enterprise is to make inferences about the "true" link of cognitive skill and success in graduate school.

Figure 1.4 shows an example of what we may be likely to try to do with our scale of team performance. That is, we may want to predict an outcome, such as team effectiveness, and we want to use the amount of "team playerness" in teams as a predictor of that outcome. Recognize at the outset that a direct assessment of the true relationship between the amount of team playerness and team effectiveness is not possible (noted as the *hypothesis question* relationship in Figure 1.4). Instead, a *calculated value* between two measures of the constructs will be obtained. The measures of the constructs are ideally going to be accurate assessments of being a team player and team effectiveness. While the desired relationship is aimed for, calculated relationships inevitably fall quite short of that mark. An example will assist in making this clear.

Let's say we are in an organization that creates computer software. We want to know if being a good team player is related to team performance. There are an infinite number of ways to assess how much being a team player is part of the work group. One of the measures of the effectiveness of the team's work could be the number of errors that have to be debugged in the computer program. This is obviously only one of many potential ways to assess team effectiveness, but it will be helpful to keep things simple for the time being.

Now, information is collected about being a team player using a team player measure and about team effectiveness using a measure of the number of errors. We now have numbers to calculate the relationship between the two measured variables. It is apparent that the tighter the measurement linkages between the ideal constructs (shown in circles in Figure 1.4) and the measured variables (shown as squares in Figure 1.4), the better. *Better* in this context means more confidence in the inferences and knowledge claims about the link between being a team player and team effectiveness based on a calculated relationship between two measures.

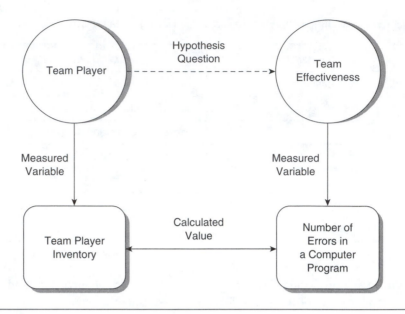

Figure 1.4   Linkages Between Hypothesized and Measured Relationships

Construct Cleanliness. Constructs are "clean" when they evaluate what they are supposed to; that is, the measurement links shown in Figure 1.4 are perfect insofar as the measured variables correspond 100% to the idea constructs. If a variable perfectly represents the construct, then measurement issues are not a concern. The trouble is that measured variables inevitably represent the idea construct imperfectly.

These imperfections come in two types: deficiency and contamination. A variable is deficient to the extent that the domain of interest is not covered. If I want to assess the extent that someone is likely to be a team player and I do not ask about that person's past experiences working on teams, my variable is likely to be deficient. If a group of 4th-graders is told that they will have a test on basic math skills but they are only given subtraction problems, the test is deficient in that addition, multiplication, and division problems have not been included.

Contamination of a construct by a measured variable is when the measure contains information that should not be part of the construct. If the team player assessment tool is administered to a team and they all fill it out together so that they all see each other's responses, "socially desirable" responses are more likely to occur rather than true responses. If a 4th-grade class is told that that they will be having a test on division but addition items are included, then the test is contaminated.

Contamination is easier to detect than is deficiency in any variable using various statistical procedures. Deficiency, however, has to be demonstrated rationally. If a construct seems to be missing something, finding that missing something usually comes from reviewing the existing theories and research or from practical knowledge about the construct.

Single Versus Multiple Constructs. An extremely important consideration in scale development and assessment is the extent to which the scale measures single or multiple constructs. This is not a simple matter. For example, volumes of writing and much work have gone into taking sides in the debate about whether or not intelligence is a multifaceted construct or a single construct. The evidence that both sides produce is logical and statistically sophisticated. The question, though, remains unanswered.

Some who have created scales to measure certain constructs have called a truce on this issue. For example, there are scales that measure facets of job satisfaction (e.g., satisfaction with pay, promotion, supervisor, etc.) and others that measure overall job satisfaction. Both are useful in different contexts. If an organization wants to assess if a new promotion system has had an effect on job satisfaction, then assessing "satisfaction with promotional opportunities" is more relevant than measuring other facets of job satisfaction (such as satisfaction with coworkers) or overall job satisfaction. On the other hand, if a new leadership team makes large structural changes in the organization, the members may be interested in the effects this might have on overall job satisfaction and therefore the overall measure would be more appropriate.

There is no right answer in the development of constructs as to whether the construct is unitary or multiple. It is better that a scale is developed with a clear idea first about whether one or multiple constructs are to be measured. Multiple constructs are more difficult to measure because, in addition to measuring them individually, how the constructs work together and relate to one another must be understood. This layer of complexity is best handled methodologically and statistically if it is posited to exist in advance of collecting any data.

Summary and Next Step

In this introductory chapter we have

a. reviewed why measurement is critical for science and why the problems associated with measurement in the social sciences pose unique problems,

b. provided a brief summary of some of the historical highlights of measurement,

c. reviewed the nomenclature around scales of measurement,

d. reviewed some of the basic premises of statistical analyses,

e. presented some of the common statistical procedures we'll be using in this text,

f. showed how scores are made meaningful by transforming them, and

g. presented the first step in developing any scale—defining the construct of interest.

The next step in the process of developing an instrument is to convert a construct into a series of stimuli (items) on which numerical information can be collected. This is the operationalization phase. It is time-consuming but, if done correctly, will save hours and days of time later on in the process.

Problems and Exercises

1. Recall a time when a test score had an impact on your life or on the life of someone you know. Describe what was measured, how it was measured, and how the score was used. Indicate the degree to which you felt that the test score was used appropriately and why.

2. An α level of 0.05 means what? What about an α level of 0.01, 0.001, 0.10, or 0.20?

3. Calculate the correlation coefficient by hand for the X and Y variables in Table 1.1.

4. Calculate the bivariate regression line of salary regressed on cognitive ability (data in Table 1.3). If you had a cognitive skill of 110, what would be your predicted starting salary level? Calculate the R-squared, adjusted R-squared, F, Sb, and t when regressing starting salary on cognitive ability. Interpret your findings.

5. At what level would the following variables be measured?
   a. Distances between towns
   b. Intelligence measured by an IQ test
   c. The rank ordering of members of a class based on height
   d. The numbering of those with blue eyes 1, brown eyes 2, green eyes 3, and other colors 4

6. If I obtain a score of 100 on a test that has a mean of 120 and a standard deviation of 10, what is my standard score? What would be my T score (mean of 50 and standard deviation of 10)?

7. Choose a construct that you are interested in finding more about. Here are a few examples to get you started thinking: civic-minded, athletic, studious, and humorous. Once you have selected your topic, create a chart like the one in Table 1.5. Share your ideas with your classmates.

CHAPTER 2

Designing and Writing Items

Once the construct (or constructs) to be assessed is clarified, the next step is to get on with the business of writing items that assess various aspects of the construct. The approaches to designing items have been compartmentalized into three general categories: empirical, theoretical, and rational. However, this compartmentalization is somewhat artificial, as the three approaches often overlap.

Empirical, Theoretical, and Rational Approaches to Item Construction

Empirically generated items are those that "do the job" but the test developer either does not know and/or does not care why the item is relevant. As an example, items for the Minnesota Multiphasic Personality Inventory (MMPI), developed and published by Hathaway and McKinley in 1943, were designed and retained because they were able to distinguish between two groups of individuals. These groups could be "normal" versus "paranoid" or "depressed" versus "schizophrenic" and so forth. Because the purpose of the scale was to distinguish between normal and psychiatrically disturbed individuals, the criterion for retaining an item was the degree to which it was able to make the distinctions required, regardless of the item's content. The MMPI comprises a total of 550 statements, to which the respondent indicates "yes," "no," or "cannot say." There were nine clinical scales and four validity scales in the original MMPI. Other scales have been added since it was created. This "dust bowl" empirical approach characterized many scales that were developed in the middle of the 20th century.

A different tactic used to design test items is a theory-driven approach. An example of such a scale is the Wechsler Adult Intelligence Scale-III (WAIS-III;

Tulsky, Zhu, & Ledbetter, 1997). In 1939, David Wechsler designed and published a test of intelligence aimed at the adult population. There have been several revisions to the test, the most recent in 1997. His theory of intelligence was that it had different facets, each of which should be assessed with different methods. For example, the Information subtest is made up of general information questions that can be answered in a few words. The Picture Completion subscale shows pictures on cards, each with a missing part, and the test taker must identify the missing part. The Digit Span subtest asks the test taker to repeat strings of digits forward and backward. Other subtests on the WAIS-III include Picture Arrangement, Vocabulary, Block Design, Arithmetic, Object Assembly, Comprehension, Digit Symbol, Similarities, Letter-Number Sequencing, Matrix Reasoning, and Symbol Search. You can see that Wechsler had a theory about intelligence (that it was multifaceted), created items to assess each aspect of that facet of intelligence, and asked the test taker to make responses that he believed were relevant to each facet of intelligence.

Rationally developed scales use a combination of theory and empirical work to guide the item construction and retention. A good example of a rational scale is the Jackson Vocational Interest Survey (JVIS; Jackson, 1977). Jackson initially created hundreds of items for his survey. The items were based on the vocational literature, and he used various statistical procedures to whittle the items down to the ones that he found to be most useful. In the end, he generated a scale that is praised as being one of the most carefully constructed scales available. The JVIS measures 34 basic interest scales, 26 work role scales, and 8 work style scales. Most scales that are developed now use a rational model; they are not likely to be purely empirically based nor purely theoretically based.

Literature Search. The science side of item development provides a pretty clear roadmap of what is expected in this phase. The first thing to do when creating a scale is to go to the theoretical and empirical literature that will have an impact on the scale's development. Using the team player construct described in Chapter 1, for example, how other researchers have defined (both conceptually as well as operationally) being a team player as well as potentially related constructs has to be examined. In this instance, journals that deal with workplace issues—such as *Journal of Applied Psychology, Journal of Occupational and Organizational Behavior, Academy of Management Journal,* and *Administrative Science Quarterly*—will be reviewed to see which articles include the words *teams* or *team player.* Journals that contain articles about groups and personality in broader settings, such as *Journal of Personality and Social Psychology, Journal of Small Group Research,* and *Journal for Specialists in Group Work,* are also potential sources of information. Journals that specialize in scale development and assessment, such as *Assessment, Educational and Psychological Measurement, Psychological Assessment, International Journal of Testing, Journal of Psychoeducational Assessment,* and *Journal of Educational Measurement,* may also provide ideas about how others have attempted to measure the construct.

Books on teams in organizations abound. Some have an empirical approach, some are more theoretical in orientation, and some have an anecdotal flavor.

Regardless of their approach, they need to be examined for how the authors have defined the construct of being a team player.

The World Wide Web provides links to several test locator services. Searching these sites for existing instruments is a very fast and potentially fruitful activity. The following websites can be helpful: www.unl.edu/buros and www.ets.org

If there is existing research where the authors already have gone to the trouble of developing items for such a construct, consider using that research rather than developing new items. This will depend on how close a match there is between the construct that you want to assess and what the developed scale assesses, how carefully the items were developed for those instruments, and the results of the analyses that assess the instrument's psychometric properties. It is always easier to use an existing scale or even modify an existing one than it is to create a new scale.

If you do decide to modify a scale by deleting items, rewording items, changing the response format, or making any other change, the psychometric properties of the new scale based on analyses with the new sample will need to be reported.

Subject Matter Experts. The next place to go for information about your construct is to subject matter experts (SMEs). SMEs come from a variety of settings. One obvious group is made up of those individuals who study the phenomenon that you are interested in measuring. These individuals will be easily located after having completed the literature search. Names of some researchers will keep recurring, and these are the people you will want to contact. They are usually found in university and college settings.

They are often very helpful and willing to assist in the construction of your scales, particularly if you've done your homework and found out a lot about the subject matter through your literature search. You may want to interview these SMEs in person, by phone, or electronically to ask them about the construct you want to measure. They will often refer you to new sources that you may not have come across. They may refer you to other researchers and/or graduate students working in the same area, thus providing you with access to more and more individuals who know about the construct.

Another group of SMEs would be laypersons who have specific knowledge about the construct you are interested in assessing. For example, if we want to find out information about what is important to being a team player in a work setting, we would likely want to speak with individuals who work on or with teams. Interviews with people who work on teams, manage teams, and facilitate teams in work environments will provide a perspective that the researchers cannot on what it means to be a team player. Again, interviews with these SMEs are invaluable to understand as clearly as possible what it is you want to measure.

A familiar question in terms of interviewing SMEs is, How many should I interview? The answer is, As many as it takes until no new perspective or information is obtained. Those who use qualitative data collection procedures on a regular basis call this point the *saturation of themes*. Let's suppose I interview some top researchers in the "team" literature and I find that in my fifth interview, I no longer get any new information on what it means to be a team player. I decide to carry out another two interviews just to make sure that I don't miss anything important.

If the sixth and seventh interviews also yield no new information, it is likely that my themes are saturated.

Then I would turn to my practitioner SMEs and interview people who work on different types of teams in different organizations, people who are managers of work teams, and people who are called in to work with teams when they are experiencing difficulty. If I use the same criterion of theme saturation, I may find, at the end of my theme saturation approach, that I have interviewed 10 people who work on teams, 9 team managers, and 8 team facilitators. Box 2.1 shows an example of how theme saturation would work.

In my own experience in developing scales used in research (e.g., Kline, 1994; Kline & McGrath, 1998; Kline, 1999; Kline, 2001; Kline, 2003) as well as in practice (e.g., Kline & Brown, 1994; Kline & Brown, 1995; Rogers, Finley, & Kline, 2001), I have found that after about seven interviews, I don't usually get any new information. The important consideration here, though, is that the seven interviews are with only one constituent group. So, for example, if I want to develop an instrument to assess teacher effectiveness in a psychological testing course, several constituent groups would have perspectives to contribute: students, instructors, teaching facilitators, and administrators. It is likely that I'll need to conduct 7–10 interviews with each constituent group.

Sometimes the constituent groups don't add any real new information, but need to be included for political reasons. For example, I was involved in developing a scale to assess the stress of city bus drivers (Angus Reid Group, 1991). The project team interviewed bus drivers of varying seniority, dispatchers, managers, bus riders, and members of the city council. For the report to be believable and the recommendations acted on, the constituent groups wanted to see that their perspectives were heard and incorporated into the survey.

Once the themes for a construct have been identified, items need to be created that transform the construct into something that can be measured with a number attached to the level of the construct. The next part of this chapter is devoted to how to go about that task.

Writing Items: Guiding Rules. Continuing with the team player example, we should now have a wealth of information about what it means to be a team player. This information has been obtained from a variety of sources and thus we can be fairly confident that, in Western-culture organizational settings, we know what being a team player means and have a sense of how to operationalize this construct through measurement.

So how are items written? Depending on whether the scale is to assess an attitude, content knowledge, ability, or personality trait, the types of issues will be somewhat different. One consideration is to determine whether the items should be questions or declarative statements. Regardless of what type of item is chosen, stick with the pattern for the entire instrument. For example, do not shift from declarative to interrogative statements.

The overall issue in item writing is one of clarity—be as clear as possible in asking respondents the questions. The more clear the question, the more confident

Box 2.1   An Example of Theme Saturation Process for an Aspect of Team Player Predisposition

One question that would likely be asked of SMEs about their experiences working on teams is, Give me an example of a time when a team you were on was a positive experience. Here are some examples of some responses you might get to such a question.

SME 1: I was a member of a soccer team as a kid. Whether we won or lost, the coach always had something good to say about each and every player and pointed out something for each of us to work on for the next time. This made us all feel like she cared about us as individual players.

SME 2: When I was in high school, I was in a school play. We rehearsed for weeks and everyone appreciated everyone else's accomplishments and input into the play. We all knew that, down to the ticket takers, the play would not be a success unless we all pulled together. On opening night, it was a really wonderful feeling to hear the applause at the end of the show.

SME 3: I worked at a retail clothing store once where the shift on the floor was considered a team. Sales commissions were not given out for each person but for the whole shift on the floor at the time. This worked really well for me because I was not very outgoing and was shy of approaching customers. However, I was always there to help the salesperson assisting the customers to get different sizes and to check them out at the end. This freed up the sales staff that were more outgoing to play to their strengths and approach new customers.

SME 4: I worked on a group project in a college English course where the assignment was to review how a number of different writers described their experiences immigrating to a new country. We each quickly decided as a group how to analyze the content and style of the writer. Then we decided who would research what writer and how we would integrate the overall conclusions. Everyone pulled their own weight and we learned a lot from each other.

SME 5: My experience as a team member was when I was a flight crew member for an airline. There were five of us including the pilot, copilot, and navigator. All of us would greet the passengers as they boarded the aircraft. The pilots would know all of our names and would treat us with a great deal of respect, even though they had a much higher rank in the organization. Our purpose was clear—we were there to ensure the safety, comfort, and enjoyment of the passengers.

Although usually you would continue to interview others, it is clear already that some of the themes that recur in these answers are the following:

1. Each team member contributes.
2. Each team member recognizes the contributions of other members.
3. Team leaders treat all members of the team as valued contributors and with fairness and respect.
4. The purpose of the team is clear.

These themes can then be converted to items such as the following:

My experiences about being a member of a team include

1. each team member putting forth equal effort,
2. each team member knowing the teams' purpose,
3. team leadership that was respectful,
4. team leadership that was fair, and
5. team members appreciating the efforts of all members.

you'll be that the respondents have provided the information desired. There are some guiding principles that are quite obvious but often not attended to in writing items. These principles are based on the guides cited in Ghiselli, Campbell, and Zedek (1981) and Nunnally and Bernstein (1994).

1. Deal with only *one* central thought in each item. Those with more than one are called *double-barreled.*

   Poor item: My instructor grades fairly and quickly.

   Better item: My instructor grades fairly.

2. Be precise.

   Poor item: I receive good customer service from XYZ company.

   Better item: A member of the sales staff at XYZ company asked me if he or she could assist me within one minute of entering the store.

3. Be brief.

   Poor item: You go to the corner store and decide you want to buy $10 worth of candy. You see that you have only a $20 bill and so pay with that. How much change would you get back?

   Better item: If you purchase $10 worth of candy and pay with a $20 bill, what change would you receive?

4. Avoid awkward wording or dangling constructs.

   Poor item: Being clear is the overall guiding principle in writing items.

   Better item: The overall guiding principle in writing items is to be clear.

5. Avoid irrelevant information.

   Poor item: Subtractive and additive color mixing processes produce differing results. If blue and yellow are added together using subtractive color mixing, what would be the resulting color?

   Better item: In subtractive color mixing, blue and yellow added together make . . .

6. Present items in positive language.

   Poor item: Which of the following does *not* describe a characteristic of a democracy?

   Better item: Which of the following is a characteristic of a democracy?

7. Avoid double negatives.

   Poor item: For what age group will it not be the case that people disapprove of graded vehicle licensing?

   Better item: What age group is most in favor of graded vehicle licensing?

8. Avoid terms like *all* and *none.*

   Poor item: Which of the following never occurs . . .

   Better item: Which of the following is extremely unlikely to occur . . .

9. Avoid indeterminate terms like *frequently* or *sometimes.*

   Poor item: Higher levels of self-efficacy frequently result after . . .

   Better item: Research shows that significantly higher levels of self-efficacy result after . . .

How Many Items? The question of how many items to include on a scale is simple to answer but difficult to pinpoint. The answer is, As many items as are necessary to properly assess the construct. The number will also be somewhat dependent on what types of analyses will be performed on the scale. It is unlikely that the construct of interest can be captured in a single item. Most analyses require at least 2 and more appropriately 5–10 items to perform analyses that suggest the construct is a reasonable one. Some analyses suggest that no fewer than 20 items for the construct is appropriate. However, 20 items to assess a construct may take a while for participants to complete. How many different constructs are to be assessed and how long it takes to respond to each item will play a role in determining how many items are appropriate for a given context.

Be cognizant of the mundane administrative issues such as how long the scale will take to complete. If it is too long, fewer people will be willing to respond. Those who do may be fatigued by the end and thus provide "garbage" answers. So the decision about how many items to construct and use has to be based on the rational consideration of both statistical needs and administrative concerns.

Attitudinal Items: Early Work in Item Generation

Burgeoning interest by social scientists in attitudinal assessment gave rise to various methods of developing and assessing numerical values for attitudinal items. Some of the assessments provided direct numerical estimates of stimuli differences and some provided indirect estimates. The indirect estimates need to be converted to numerical values.

Paired Comparisons. One of the first ways designed to assess item-to-response links entailed individuals making comparison judgments. Comparison judgments require the respondent to compare two different stimuli and make some sort of judgment about them. Paired comparisons require an individual to compare each stimulus with every other stimulus and make a judgment about their relative relationship. It provides an indirect assessment of the differences between stimuli (whether they be items or persons).

For example, I may have five graduate students that I am responsible for supervising, and I am asked to compare their performance. So, I have to compare Student 1 with Students 2–5, compare Student 2 with Student 1 and Students 3–5, and so forth. In total, I will have to make 10 comparisons. This highlights a drawback of paired comparison methods. That is, the number of comparisons goes up dramatically by adding more stimuli. If I have six students, I will have to make 15 comparisons. Be aware of this when using a paired comparison method as the measurement instrument. The burden on participants becomes quite heavy as the number of stimuli becomes even moderate.

So what can be learned from data that are collected in a paired comparison method? To illustrate, here is an example of a paired comparison question: Is there a preference for a particular flavor out of four types of ice cream? Assume that 500 students are asked to make paired comparisons of the ice cream flavors: vanilla, chocolate, strawberry, and butterscotch. The data are then set up as in Table 2.1, where the proportions of people who preferred one type of ice cream over another are reported. First, note that the diagonal of the table is left blank, as this represents each ice cream flavor compared with itself. Second, note that the opposing proportions always sum to 1.0. That is because, if 0.25 of the students preferred strawberry to chocolate ice cream, then, by default, 0.75 preferred chocolate to strawberry.

The proportions are converted into a final preference scale by first changing the proportions to normal (z) values, summing down the columns, and then taking the averages of each sum. Table 2.2 shows the most preferred flavor is chocolate,

Table 2.1   Proportions of Paired Comparisons for Four Ice Cream Flavors

	Vanilla	Chocolate	Strawberry	Butterscotch
Vanilla		0.90	0.50	0.10
Chocolate	0.10		0.25	0.05
Strawberry	0.50	0.75		0.03
Butterscotch	0.90	0.95	0.97	

Note: The underlined values represent the derived proportions.

Table 2.2   Normal z Values for the Paired Comparisons for Four Ice Cream Flavors

	Vanilla	Chocolate	Strawberry	Butterscotch
Vanilla		1.28	0.00	−1.28
Chocolate	−1.28		−0.67	−1.65
Strawberry	0.00	0.67		−1.88
Butterscotch	1.28	1.65	1.88	
Total	0.00	3.60	1.21	−4.81
Average	0.00	0.90	0.30	−1.20

Note: The underlined values represent the derived proportions.

followed by strawberry, followed by vanilla, and with butterscotch a distant last. The resulting scale is an interval-level assessment of the degree of preference difference for ice cream flavor.

Items in Ranked Categories. One can also take stimuli and ask a number of judges to rank order the stimuli along some dimension. This is a direct estimate of stimuli although the scale is ordinal, not interval. The stimuli can be items in a test ranked on the dimension of "difficulty," they can be items in an attitude scale ranked on the dimension of "demonstrating altruistic behavior," or they can be students ranked on the dimension of "industriousness."

As an example, suppose I am asked to rank order the five graduate students I supervise in terms of which is most industrious and which is least industrious, with an award going to the most deserving. Further, suppose I ask three of my colleagues to do the same. Now I have a matrix of rankings like that shown in Tables 2.3 and 2.4.

Student 2 is rated top, followed by Students 1, 3, 4, and 5, in that order. So the award for industriousness goes to Student 2.

Table 2.3 Ranks of Five Graduate Students by Five Faculty Members on Industriousness

Student	Faculty Member (F) Rankings			
	F1	F2	F3	F4
1	1	2	2	2
2	2	1	1	1
3	3	3	4	3
4	4	5	3	5
5	5	4	5	4

Table 2.4 Mean and Overall Ranks of Five Graduate Students by Five Faculty Members on Industriousness

	Mean Ranking	Overall Rank
Student 1	1.75	2
Student 2	1.25	1
Student 3	3.25	3
Student 4	4.25	4
Student 5	4.5	5

Items in Interval-Level Categories. One can generate both the true interval-level boundaries of the response categories as well as the true interval level of each item's value using an approach called successive intervals (e.g., Ghiselli, Campbell, & Zedek, 1981). This is an indirect method, so it requires some conversions and, therefore, it is best to understand this by going through an example.

First, judges are required to place a number of stimuli (items) into a set number of categories (such as 5 or 10), where each category represents more or less of a particular dimension. For example, I may give 100 workers the following 10 stimuli and ask them to place the statements about their jobs into five different categories on the dimension of "satisfyingness," where 1 is the least satisfying and 5 is the most satisfying.

My job is . . .

1. disgusting

2. fun

3. underpaid

4. rewarding

5. delightful

6. challenging

7. enjoyable

8. revolting

9. interesting

10. meaningful

First, the proportions of the 100 workers who sorted the items into the five categories ranging from least favorable (1) to most favorable (5) are reported. These are shown in Table 2.5. Then a cumulative proportion matrix across the rows, leaving out the 5th column as it will always be 1.00 and does not provide any information, is created (see Table 2.6).

Next, proportions are changed to normal (z) scores, and the average of those z scores across the rows and down the columns are calculated. The column averages indicate the interval-level boundary for each category. Each row (item) average is then subtracted from the *grand mean* of the rows and columns (in our case, -0.17) and thus provides the interval-level stimulus value of each of our items. For example, item 1, "disgusting," has an interval-level value of ($-0.17 - 3.41$), which equals -3.58. Item 2, "fun," has an interval-level value of $[-0.17 - (-1.68)]$, which equals 1.51.

Note a couple of things in this matrix. The first is that the grand mean should be the same whether you generate it by taking the mean of the row averages or the column averages. This is a check on your calculations. Also, the sum of the scale scores for the items should be 0.00. In Table 2.7, these two conditions are met (within rounding error).

Table 2.5   Proportion of Judges Placing Each Statement Into One of Five Categories

	Category				
Item	1 (least satisfying)	2	3	4	5 (most satisfying)
disgusting	0.95	0.05	0.00	0.00	0.00
fun	0.00	0.00	0.50	0.40	0.10
underpaid	0.80	0.15	0.05	0.00	0.00
rewarding	0.00	0.00	0.50	0.25	0.25
delightful	0.00	0.00	0.05	0.05	0.90
challenging	0.00	0.10	0.60	0.20	0.10
enjoyable	0.00	0.10	0.40	0.35	0.15
revolting	0.90	0.10	0.00	0.00	0.00
interesting	0.00	0.05	0.30	0.50	0.15
meaningful	0.00	0.00	0.50	0.40	0.10

Table 2.6   Cumulative Proportion of Judges Placing Each Statement Into One of Five Categories

	Category				
Item	1 (least satisfying)	2	3	4	5 (most satisfying)
disgusting	0.95	1.00	1.00	1.00	1.00
fun	0.00	0.00	0.50	0.90	1.00
underpaid	0.80	0.95	1.00	1.00	1.00
rewarding	0.00	0.00	0.50	0.75	1.00
delightful	0.00	0.00	0.05	0.10	1.00
challenging	0.00	0.10	0.70	0.90	1.00
enjoyable	0.00	0.10	0.50	0.85	1.00
revolting	0.90	1.00	1.00	1.00	1.00
interesting	0.00	0.05	0.35	0.85	1.00
meaningful	0.00	0.00	0.50	0.90	1.00

Table 2.7   Normal Scores of Judges' Statements and Interval Scale and Item Boundary Values

Item	Category 1	2	3	4	Row Average	Scale Score
disgusting	1.65	4.00	4.00	4.00	3.41	−3.58
fun	−4.00	−4.00	0.00	1.28	−1.68	1.51
underpaid	1.28	1.65	4.00	4.00	2.73	−2.90
rewarding	−4.00	−4.00	0.00	0.68	−1.83	1.66
delightful	−4.00	−4.00	−1.65	−1.28	−2.73	2.56
challenging	−4.00	−1.28	0.52	1.28	−0.87	0.70
enjoyable	−4.00	−1.28	0.00	1.04	−1.06	0.89
revolting	1.28	4.00	4.00	4.00	3.32	−3.49
interesting	−4.00	−1.65	−0.39	1.04	−1.25	1.08
meaningful	−4.00	−4.00	0.00	1.28	−1.68	1.51
Column Average	−2.40	−1.06	1.05	1.73	**−0.17**	- - - -

From an interpretation perspective, the least to most satisfying items and their interval-level value can be reported:

1. disgusting (−3.58)

2. revolting (−3.49)

3. underpaid (−2.90)

4. challenging (0.70)

5. enjoyable (0.89)

6. interesting (1.08)

7./8. fun/meaningful (1.51 for both)

9. rewarding (1.66)

10. delightful (2.56)

Note that fun and meaningful have the same level of satisfyingness. So now that these items and the scale scores have been generated, what can be done with them? The items can now be administered to another sample, asking them if each of the items characterizes their jobs. Once their "yes" and "no" responses to each item are obtained, the mean of the scores of the items to which they said "yes" will provide a measure of the desirableness of their jobs. For example, if I say "yes" to items 4, 5, and 6 but "no" to all the others, my job satisfaction would be $[(0.70 + 0.89 + 1.08)/3] = 0.89$. Once job satisfaction scores are generated this way for a sample of individuals, these interval-level scores can be used to (a) correlate with other variables, (b) compare jobs on their satisfaction levels, (c) compare industry satisfaction levels, and so forth.

A way to directly generate interval-level information about items is to use a method of equal-appearing intervals (Thurstone, 1929). To do so requires SMEs to make categorical judgments about a number of stimuli. It is absolutely essential that the item pool is large and encompasses the entire domain of interest. It is also important that the individuals making the judgments are SMEs. The strength of any conclusions will be based on the degree to which each of these criteria is met.

An example will be helpful here as well. Suppose I have 10 SMEs who are the job satisfaction gurus, and I ask them to take my 10 job characteristics and put them into five equal intervals. It is important that my SMEs assume that the intervals are indeed equal. So they do this, and the frequency with which each expert puts each item into each category is recorded. Then the means and standard deviations of these frequencies are calculated. This information is shown in Table 2.8.

In interpreting and using these findings, it can be seen that the "challenging" characteristic has the highest variability with a standard deviation of 1.03. This suggests that this item should perhaps be removed from the pool of items because it will

Table 2.8   Frequencies With Which Subject Matter Experts Placed Each Statement Into One of Five Equal-Interval Categories

	Category						
Item	*1*	*2*	*3*	*4*	*5*	*Row Mean*	*Row S.D.*
disgusting	8	2	0	0	0	1.2	0.42
fun	0	0	4	4	2	3.8	0.79
underpaid	6	3	1	0	0	1.5	0.71
rewarding	0	0	4	6	0	3.6	0.52
delightful	0	0	1	2	7	4.6	0.70
challenging	0	1	1	2	6	4.2	1.03
enjoyable	0	0	0	2	8	4.8	0.42
revolting	9	1	0	0	0	1.1	0.32
interesting	0	0	3	3	4	4.1	0.89
meaningful	0	0	0	7	3	4.3	0.48

have different meanings for different respondents in terms of how representative it is of job satisfaction. Another way to use this type of data is to ensure that items in the final scale that have widely differing levels of the attribute based on their mean scores are included. Therefore, if it is desirable to shorten the scale to three items, it would be appropriate to choose the items "disgusting" (mean of 1.2), "rewarding" (mean of 3.6), and "enjoyable" (mean of 4.8), as these three are likely to provide the highest range of scores from any subsequent sample of respondents.

Using a combination of the means and standard deviations, choosing between items becomes easier. Let's say that you needed to choose between the items "fun" and "rewarding." Because they are so close in their means (3.5 and 3.6), the standard deviation is examined and it shows that there was more consistency in SME responses on the "rewarding" item ($SD = 0.52$) than on the "fun" item ($SD = 0.79$). This would lead to the selection of "rewarding" over "fun" to represent the upper-middle range of satisfaction.

So, again, what can be done with such a scale? Similar to the indirect approach above, the mean score of each item that is retained in the item pool represents its scale value. Use the scale values to generate a score for each respondent. For example, if I say "yes," my job is characterized by being (a) underpaid (1.5), (b) rewarding (3.6), (c) challenging (4.2), and (d) meaningful (4.3) but not any of the other items, then my job satisfaction score is: $[(1.5 + 3.6 + 4.2 + 4.3)/4] = 3.4$. Once these satisfaction scores are generated for a sample, they can be used for other purposes.

Guttman Scales. A Guttman scale is another way of determining how the items are behaving in relation to one another. In the early history of experimental psychology, where psychophysical measures abounded, Guttman scaling made some sense. In the more amorphous realm of psychological constructs, however, the utility of Guttman scaling has all but disappeared. Interestingly, its theoretical background and rationale has resurfaced in modern test theory and so it is worthwhile to review the Guttman scaling approach.

In a Guttman scale, stimuli (otherwise known as test items) are presented in order of increasing extremeness. Knowing where the participants fall on the extremeness scale allows one to know what their responses were to all of the items—not just to the most extreme one. An example should help clarify this process. Let's assume we want to measure the construct of "veganness"—the degree to which an individual espouses being a vegan (someone who avoids using or consuming animal products). So we ask the following six questions; each is answered "yes" or "no":

1. I have restrictions on the type of food I eat.

2. I do not eat red meats.

3. I do not eat red meats or fowl.

4. I do not eat red meats, fowl, or fish.

5. I do not eat red meats, fowl, fish, or eggs.

6. I do not eat red meats, fowl, fish, eggs, or dairy products.

If someone responded to Item 6 with a "yes," he or she should have also have answered "yes" to Items 1–5. This individual would be on one extreme of the vegan scale. If an individual answered "no" to Item 1, he or she should also have answered "no" to Items 2–5. This person is at the other extreme of the vegan scale. The point where the individual shifts from saying "yes" to saying "no" determines his or her veganness.

The extent to which the items match a Guttman scale can be assessed by examining the pattern of responses. The more triangular the shape (like a staircase), the more Guttman-like the scale is acting. An example of seven people responding to the six vegan items is shown in Table 2.9. Person 7 is the most carnivorous and Person 1 is the most vegan. The others fall somewhere in between.

In the psychophysical realm, it is likely that the researcher is able to control the specific levels for a given stimuli, such as motion rates or luminance levels for visual stimuli or volume for auditory stimuli, and do so in a very fine-grained manner. Asking participants to respond with a "yes" or a "no" to "I see that" or "I hear that" will likely provide the researcher with a Guttman scale where increased steps in the stimuli correspond nicely to increased likelihood of participants seeing or hearing the stimuli. Those who see or hear the fainter stimuli are highly likely to see or hear the stronger stimuli.

Items for most psychological constructs, however, cannot easily be placed into a Guttman scale. For example, take the construct of leadership; how would one create items that would accurately reflect a simple staircase? What would a stimulus be that, if a person responded "yes" to it, would assure that that same person would have responded "yes" to all the other items representing less leadership? It simply does not make a lot of sense.

Sometimes individuals make the claim that items that form a Guttman scale response pattern make up a single construct (Guttman, 1947). However, this is not necessarily the case, even in a fairly straightforward example such as in an

Table 2.9   Guttman Scale Triangular Pattern for Seven Participants in Their Veganness

Item	Person						
	1	*2*	*3*	*4*	*5*	*6*	*7*
1	X						
2	X	X					
3	X	X	X				
4	X	X	X	X			
5	X	X	X	X	X		
6	X	X	X	X	X	X	

Note: X indicates a "yes" response.

achievement test. For example, suppose the following items are given to a sample ranging in age from 5 to 18:

1. What is the first letter in the alphabet?

2. What is the sum of 4 and 6?

3. What is the product of 7 and 9?

4. What is the capital of Great Britain?

5. What is the temperature for absolute zero?

It is very likely that the Guttman triangular form would fit responses to these questions perfectly. If a person gets the last item correct, he or she is likely to have gotten all of the rest correct. However, the items range from science to geography to math to verbal skills. In other words, responses that fall into a Guttman triangular form is not sufficient evidence to make the claim that the items form a single underlying construct.

The example above was created to demonstrate that it is important to consider the population or populations that will be responding to the scale, as well as the items, when developing a scale. A Guttman scalogram analysis would more likely proceed in the following manner. Let's use the example of being a team player in an organizational setting. There are four items in the scale of increasing extremeness in terms of whether or not moving to a team-based work environment would be beneficial to the organization. A sample of 10 workers is asked to respond to these items, and the data will be used to demonstrate that the team player construct is indeed a single construct. The items are as follows:

1. Teams might be helpful in this organization.

2. Teams would likely be helpful in this organization.

3. Teams would definitely be helpful in this organization.

4. Teams will be critical to the survival of this organization.

The pattern of responding "yes" to the items is shown in Table 2.10, with an X indicating agreement. It is anticipated that if individuals respond "yes" to item 4, they will have responded "yes" to the first three items as well. Conversely, if they do not respond "yes" to item 1, they will likely not respond "yes" to item 2. The number of times that unexpected responses, called reversal errors, occur provides an index of the degree of non-unidimensionality in the set of items.

Reversal errors can be used to assess the reproducibility or consistency of the scale items. The formula for calculating the *reproducibility coefficient* is

(2–1)   Reproducibility = [1 – (total errors/total responses)] × 100.

In this example, it is observed that Person D said "yes" to Items 3 and 4 but not to Items 1 and 2. Person I said "yes" to Items 2 and 3 but not to Item 1. Person J said

Table 2.10   Guttman Scalogram for 10 Respondents to Four Team Player Items

Person	Item 1	Item 2	Item 3	Item 4	Errors
A	X	X	X	X	0
B	X	X			0
C	X	X	X		0
D			X	X	2
E	X	X	X	X	0
F	X	X	X		0
G					0
H	X	X			0
I		X	X		1
J		X		X	2

Note: X indicates a "yes" response

"yes" to Items 2 and 4 but not to Items 1 and 3. This gives a total of 5 errors out of a total of 40 responses (each of 10 participants responded to 4 items). The reproducibility index then is

$$\text{Reproducibility} = [1 - (5/40)] \times 100,$$
$$= (1 - 0.125) \times 100,$$
$$= 0.875 \times 100 = 87.5\%.$$

Reproducibility indices less than 85% are low and indicate a need for items to be rewritten or deleted.

The difficulty in creating items that would generate a Guttman triangular form for the more amorphous psychological constructs (which are often of most interest) has made the Guttman scale generally not very practical. Furthermore, the notion of assessing the degree to which individuals possess an underlying trait (such as veganness or leadership) has moved forward with great strides in modern test theory, which leaves Guttman scaling somewhat obsolete.

Assessing Behaviors

How attitude measurement has developed over the past several decades has been covered in some depth. The assessment of behaviors rather than attitudes uses a somewhat different approach. In creating behavior-based scale items, the process is similar to that of any other scale development. The focus of the literature search and SME interviews would include clearly identifying the target behaviors and defining them in a way that is accepted. Because the focus of many behavioral scales is their use in assessing behavioral change, it is critical to identify the antecedent conditions that trigger the behavior as well as the consequences of the behavior (both positive and negative).

Critical Incident Technique. A popular approach to developing items for behaviorally based scales is the critical incident technique (Flanagan, 1954). An illustration will be better than a verbal description, and the Behavioral Observation Scale (BOS) development (Latham & Wexley, 1977) provides a good example. BOSs are used in the context of rating employee performance. The critical incidents in the job performance area are those behaviors that are critical in determining good and poor performance. Over a period of time—say a month—supervisors carefully monitor the performance of the employees who report to them. The supervisors then rate the frequency with which the behaviors are demonstrated by the employees. For example, if the behavior to be rated is "greets the customer within 30 seconds of the customer entering the store," the supervisor would rate how often each employee does so over a fixed period of time.

After the allotted time period, ratings on each item are correlated to the total score across items. The ones with the highest correlations are presumed to be the most important for job performance and are retained for the final scale. As noted, the BOS is just one application of the critical incident technique, and it can be applied in a wide variety of settings.

Pilot Testing

There is no way to overemphasize the need to pilot test scale items. Asking colleagues, friends, family members, small groups of potential samples, and so forth to complete the scale is a critical step in the process of its development. Ask them to time how long it takes to complete the scale. Ask them to note where they have questions or clarity problems. Ask them to point out typos, grammatical errors, or anything else they can spot as they go through the scale. Ask them if items are too difficult (in achievement or ability tests).

A pilot test (or more than one pilot test) will provide feedback on all of these issues and serve an invaluable purpose. Issues raised by your pilot subjects can be taken care of before time and resources are wasted collecting useless data.

Summary and Next Step

In this chapter, the long process of creating a set of items and a scale to provide an index about an individual has been described. Specifically reviewed were

a. the empirical, theoretical, and rational approaches to item creation;

b. how to go about doing a thorough literature search and appropriate use of subject matter experts;

c. the principles in writing clear items;

d. the criteria to use in determining the appropriate number of items for a scale;

e. the history of creating attitude items;

f. what behavioral items should cover;

g. how to use the critical incident technique in creating behaviorally based items; and

h. the importance of pilot testing any scale.

The next step in creating a scale is to make several decisions about the types of responses that are to be obtained from those who answer the items on the scale. This is the topic of Chapter 3.

Problems and Exercises

1. An empirically developed set of test items are designed to do what?

2. Items developed theoretically have what characteristics?

3. Rationally developed tests use what techniques for item development and retention?

4. Using the construct you worked on for the Exercise in chapter 1, go to the existing literature and report how others have tried to develop the construct. What are their definitions? Use similar constructs to develop your own in more detail.

5. Rewrite each of the following items to improve them:
    a. My instructor presents material in an organized and enthusiastic manner.
    b. My instructor can be heard by everyone in the class.
    c. My instructor believes in what she or he is teaching.
    d. My instructor always provides feedback in a supportive manner.
    e. My instructor likes to use a variety of ways and materials to present information, such as videos, group discussions, projects, and outside speakers, so that the students have the opportunity to learn in a way most appropriate for their learning style.

6. Design five (5) items that will assess your construct of interest. Be sure to use SMEs, critical incidents, and existing information to generate some items.

7. Using the items you've designed, ask at least four colleagues to make paired comparisons of which item is most extreme in assessing your construct. With five items, you will have 10 paired comparisons. Set the data up as in Table 2.1, with your five items across the first row and down the first column. Put the proportion of people who rated the item as more extreme than the other item in the appropriate cell in the upper triangle of the table. Put 1 minus

this proportion in the opposing cell. Change the proportions to normalized z values as in Table 2.2, sum the columns, and then take the averages of those sums. Now you have a good idea as to the relative extremeness of your items in terms of how well they capture the construct.

8. Now ask another group of four colleagues to rank order the items from least (1) to most extreme (5). Record their rankings and then average the ranks. You now have another assessment of how extreme your items are in assessing the construct. Take your five items that you now have some confidence in regarding their rank-order of extremeness and put them in order of least extreme to most extreme. Now ask another group of four colleagues to respond "yes" or "no" to the items. Set up your data as in Table 2.9, with items in the first column, participants as the first row, and participant ratings of "yes" marked as an X in each cell. See if your scale follows a Guttman scalogram pattern. Calculate the reproducibility index for your scale.

CHAPTER 3

Designing and Scoring Responses

After working to have a solid conceptual definition of the construct, and then sweating over the operationalization of the construct by creating items, it is time to move on to the next step in the scale construction process by creating a response scale. This step calls for making decisions about what type of response you want from your test takers as well as the format of those responses. These issues may sound straightforward, but there are tradeoffs regardless of your choice.

Open-Ended Responses

The first major decision to make is whether open-ended responses or closed-ended responses are the most appropriate for the assessment situation. Open-ended items can be unstructured or structured. An example of a structured open-ended response would be to ask everyone in a class to write down their favorite prime-time television show on Sunday evenings. Then the frequency with which each response occurs can be counted, tabulated, and so forth. On the other hand, this type of response will not provide the test administrator with a lot of information about what motivates people to watch particular types of television shows. If a less structured, open-ended question is asked, such as, "Write down your favorite prime-time television show on Sunday evenings and *why* it is your favorite," then the administrator is likely to get some insight as to television-show-watching motives. However, wading through the responses and categorizing them into coherent groupings will take a lot of time.

Lots of detailed information is an advantage of responses to open-ended questions. Often open-ended questions are used in the early stages of theory development, or when an area of research provides conflicting findings. The open-ended approach can assist in clarifying what might be important to consider in including in theoretical frameworks. For example, there is considerable evidence that workplace stress is linked to cardiovascular problems (e.g., Cartwright & Cooper, 1997). However, the link is not consistent across individuals. Some researchers hypothesize that the link is moderated by such things as personality, gender, family history, social support, financial concerns, and so forth. Identifying these potentially moderating variables is greatly facilitated by responses of participants to open-ended questions such as, "What is most stressful about your work?" and "What types of things can you identify that alleviate workplace stress?"

The downside of open-ended questions is that they are very time-consuming to administer and interpret. The more open-ended questions asked, the more depth of information obtained, the more time it will take for respondents to complete the questions and the more time will be spent categorizing, analyzing, and trying to make sense of the responses. In fact, collecting and analyzing the qualitative responses from open-ended questions is a very detailed process that requires a strict methodology to ensure that researcher biases are minimized. Strategies to collect qualitative data include interviews, observation, the use of archival information such as notes and transcripts, and ethnography, to name but a few. The data collected provide rich and highly descriptive information that is very useful for understanding a phenomenon from a particular point of view in a particular context.

The qualitative data are content analyzed using a variety of techniques that include grounded theory, interrogative hypothesis testing, and case studies. Because the focus of this text is on quantitative measurement rather than on qualitative approaches, these techniques will not be pursued further. References that do an excellent job in describing how to collect and analyze qualitative data include Berg (1989), Creswell (1998), Denzin and Lincoln (2000), and Strauss and Corbin (1998).

Closed-Ended Questions

Closed-ended questions require a single response. The biggest drawback of closed-ended questions, in comparison to open-ended ones, is that the depth and richness of response is not captured. On the other hand, analyzing responses to these types of items is a relatively straightforward process. Frequencies of responses to closed-ended questions can be numerically coded and then depicted graphically. For example, bar or pie charts can be used to highlight different response categories for different groups. If relevant, the data might be shown in line graphs to show trends across time.

Closed-ended responses can also be analyzed and provide statistical evidence for making decisions (e.g., responses to a plebiscite on whether to widen a section of roadway in a city). A couple of examples of some simple analyses of responses to closed-ended questions will demonstrate how to use such data. Specifically, frequency analysis will be used to make some determinations about whether a particular type of television show is more or less common for the particular sample.

Table 3.1   Frequency Distribution for 30 Students and Their Television Preferences

Show Type	Comedy	Drama	Life Situation
Number (Percent) Preferring	17 (56.7%)	8 (26.7%)	5 (16.7%)

Example 1: Proportional Differences for a Single Variable.

Assume students in a class are asked to indicate which type of show they prefer most: situation comedies, dramas, or life situations. Of the 30 students, 17 prefer situation comedies, 8 prefer dramas, and the other 5 prefer life-situation shows. They indicate their show preferences as in Table 3.1.

To determine if the proportions are statistically different from that which would be expected in the population by chance alone (in this case, we would expect 33.3% of the cases to be in each category), a test of proportions is conducted. The formula for doing so is

$$(3\text{--}1) \qquad (X - NP)/\sqrt{(N)\,(P)\,(1{-}P)},$$

where X = number of responses in a category, N = total sample size, and P = expected proportion in the category.

So, in the example for situation comedies, $X = 17$, $N = 30$, and $P = 0.333$.

$$[17 - (30 \times 0.333)]/\sqrt{[(30)\,(0.333)\,(1 - 0.333)]},$$

$$(17 - 9.99)/\sqrt{(9.999)\,(0.667)},$$

$$7.01/2.58,$$

$$2.72.$$

The calculated value (2.72) is distributed approximately as a normal (z) distribution. Using the standard significance level of 0.05, the critical value to exceed to be considered statistically significant is 1.96 (using a two-tailed test). So, it can be seen that the ratio of 17 of 30 people watching situation comedies is statistically significant. Thus it can be concluded in this sample that a statistically significant proportion preferred comedy to the other two types of shows.

Example 2: Proportional Differences for Two Variables.

A somewhat more complicated question can also be asked of such data: Do men and women have similar or dissimilar tastes in Sunday prime-time television show viewing (using the same three categories of situation comedies, dramas, or life situations)? Assume there are 15 men and 15 women in the class and they indicate their show preferences as in Table 3.2.

Table 3.2   Frequency Distribution for 30 Students and Their Television Preferences by Gender

Gender	Comedy	Drama	Life Situation
Men	11	1	3
Women	4	9	2

The response pattern indicates that the men seem to have a higher than expected preference for comedy and the women seem to have a higher than expected preference for drama. An analysis of the data using the Pearson chi-square gives a value of 9.867. Box 3.1 shows the computation of the Pearson chi-square and Box 3.2 shows the SPSS cross-tabulation output that reports the Pearson chi-square.

The chi-square is calculated by examining the extent to which the expected cell frequencies deviate from the observed cell frequencies. If the deviations are significant, then it is concluded that the cell frequencies are dependent on the variables. In this example, the interest was in determining if show preference is dependent on gender.

Box 3.1   Computation of the Pearson chi-Square (χ^2) Using the Data From Table 3.2

The formula for calculating the Pearson chi-square statistic is

(3–2) χ^2 (Degrees of freedom of [(rows − 1) × (columns − 1)] = $\Sigma[(O_{ij} − E_{ij})^2/E_{ij}]$,

where O_{ij} = the observed frequencies for each cell and E_{ij} = the expected frequencies for each cell. That is, each cell's expected frequency is subtracted from the cell's observed frequency. These differences are squared, and then divided by the cell's expected frequency. Then the obtained values are summed across each cell.

The information from Table 3.2 is reproduced here as well as the row and column totals and row percentages (Table 3.3).

Table 3.3   Frequency Distribution for 30 Students and Their Television Preferences by Gender, Row and Column Totals, and Row Percentages

Gender	Comedy	Drama	Life Situation	Row total	Row %
Men	11	1	3	15	50%
Women	4	9	2	15	50%
Column total	15	10	5	30	100%

The first task is to generate the expected frequencies for each cell. To do this, we take the percentage of men and percentage of women and multiply each of these by the column totals to generate the expected cell frequencies. We see that men make up 50% of our sample. If the cells in the Men row were distributed as expected by chance alone, then we would have 50% of 15, or 7.5; 50% of 10, or 5; and 50% of 5, or 2.5 in the Men row. We would also have the same set of expected frequencies for the Women row.

These expected frequencies are noted in brackets along with the observed frequencies below (Table 3.4).

Table 3.4   Observed and Expected Frequencies (in Brackets) for a Distribution of 30 Students and Their Television Preferences by Gender

Gender	Comedy	Drama	Life Situation
Men	11 (7.5)	1 (5)	3 (2.5)
Women	4 (7.5)	9 (5)	2 (2.5)

Now, using our formula, we can calculate the Pearson χ^2:

$\chi^2(1 \times 2)$

$= \sum [(11 - 7.5)^2/7.5] + [(1 - 5)^2/5] + [(3 - 2.5)^2/2.5] + [(4 - 7.5)^2/7.5]$

$\quad + [(9 - 5)^2/5] + [(2 - 2.5)^2/2.5]$

$= 1.63 + 3.2 + 0.1 + 1.63 + 3.2 + 0.1$

$\chi^2(2) = 9.86$

The computer output indicates that with two degrees of freedom [(no. of rows – 1) × (no. of columns – 1)], the obtained chi-square is statistically significant (0.007). This means that the pattern in the rows and columns is not what would be expected by chance alone (i.e., the rows and columns are not independent). The meaning of this finding would be interpreted by going back to the table to determine where the pattern seems to be unusual. In this case, 11/15 (73%) of the men preferred the comedy shows and 9/15 (60%) of the women preferred drama. These percentages are highly unlikely to occur simply by chance alone.

There is another statistic provided in the output that is called the *likelihood ratio chi-square statistic* (denoted as G^2). Like the Pearson chi-square, it has two degrees of freedom. However, the calculated value is 10.960 and its significance level is 0.004. The likelihood ratio is used more than any other statistic in multiway frequency table analyses. Although we have used only a simple two-way table here in

Box 3.2   SPSS Cross-Tabulation Output of the Data From Table 3.2

Chi-Square Tests				
	Value	df	Sig. (two-sided)	
Pearson Chi-Square	9.867	2	2	0.007
Likelihood Ratio	10.960	2	0.004	
N of Valid Cases	30			
Symmetric Measures				
	Value	Approx. Sig.		
Phi	0.573	0.007		
Cramer's V	0.573	0.007		
Contingency Coefficient	0.497	0.007		
N of Valid Cases	30			

this example, when tables become three-way, four-way, and so forth, the likelihood ratio is reported more often than the Pearson chi-square. We will not review the hand calculation for the likelihood ratio chi-square statistic in this text.

In addition to these chi-square statistics, there are summary measures of symmetry reported in the output. The ones of relevance are the *phi coefficient* (0.573), *Cramer's V* (0.573), and the *contingency coefficient* (0.497). The phi coefficient is simply a variation on the Pearson product-moment correlation coefficient. Pearson correlations are usually produced when correlating two continuous variables (like GPA and salary earnings as shown in Chapter 1). When the two variables are dichotomous, then the phi coefficient is calculated. A significant value indicates that there is a dependency in the data set; that is, if the value of one of the variables is known, there is a better than chance odds at guessing what the value of the other variable will be.

In our example, if it is known that the person is a man, it is likely that his preferred television show type on Sunday night at prime time is comedy. If it is known that the individual in question prefers drama television shows on Sunday nights at prime time, then it is likely that individual is a woman. Like any other correlation coefficient, the phi can take on positive or negative values. So, by noting the coefficient's sign and knowing how the nominal variables were coded, one is able to interpret how the relationships in the table are manifesting themselves.

Cramer's V is based on the calculated chi-square value and is a measure of the strength of a relationship between the variables. Because it is based on the chi-square value, it can only take on positive values. It is found via the following formula:

(3–3)
$$V = \sqrt{\chi^2/[(N)(n-1)]},$$

where N = sample size and n = the number of rows or columns, whichever is smaller. In this case,

$$V = \sqrt{9.867/[(30)(2-1)]},$$
$$= 0.573.$$

The contingency coefficient is normalized slightly differently from phi and Cramer's V. Like the Cramer's V, it can only take on positive values (from 0–1).

These examples have demonstrated that when the responses to questions are categorized into frequencies, one can ask various research questions about the data. Simple one- and two-way frequencies have been reviewed here. However, it is possible to have more complicated designs where three or more variables are set up in frequency tables. These types of tables require multiway frequency analyses. Although they will not be reviewed here, a good source for information about these analyses is Rudas (1997).

Dichotomous Responses. Dichotomous responses are closed-ended questions that are most often coded with a 0 or a 1. They are frequently used when the item has a correct or incorrect response. For example, in this item, "Is the answer to $2 + 2 = 4$ true or false?" the response is a dichotomous one. If the respondent answers "false," the code is 0 and if the respondent answers "true," the code is 1. This item response is a true dichotomy. With this particular item, the respondent has a 50/50 chance of getting the item correct just by guessing. Thus, care should then be taken in deciding if a dichotomous format with the potential for guessing is appropriate.

Another issue to consider is whether or not the item should actually require a dichotomous response. Consider the following item: "Do you feel happy today?" with response option of "yes" or "no." This dichotomy is somewhat limiting, and the response options to this question might be better asked on a continuum. This item response is thus called a false dichotomy. For example, the question can be rephrased to ask, "On a scale of 1–10, with 1 being extremely unhappy and 10 being extremely happy, how happy do you feel today?" While dichotomous responses force individuals to make a choice (i.e., yes or no) and this might suit the needs of the researcher or test administrator (e.g., quick to administer and easy to score), test takers may be reluctant to provide such responses. Because a dichotomous response format does not allow test takers the flexibility to show gradation in their attitudes, they may become frustrated and refuse to continue to complete the test or, if they do so, they may provide inaccurate information.

Dichotomous responses are also called for in responses to adjective checklists. A checklist presents a list of adjectives to respondents and they are asked to indicate whether they think the adjective describes some stimulus (like oneself, a friend, coworker, spouse, etc.). For example, here is a list of adjectives and the respondent is directed to "check off the ones that characterize you":

1. quiet

2. sincere

3. happy

4. selfish

5. ambitious

Each response is then coded as a 1 if it is checked off and a 0 if it is not.

Multiple-Choice Tests. Multiple-choice tests are also called objective tests, and the items are scored as correct or incorrect. Thus, responses to these types of items are dichotomous. These types of tests are widely used and a number of issues arise when constructing, administering, and scoring them. These will be discussed next.

Distractors. One of the important aspects to multiple-choice test item creation is that the *distractors* (the options that are not correct) are just as important as the *target*, or correct response. Look at this item, "What is the sum of 15 + 365?" with the following four options provided: (a) 386, (b) 350, (c) 1478, and (d) 380. Which of the distractors is really not useful? The answer selected should be *c.* The first distractor would indicate that the person might be guessing, the second that he or she did an incorrect operation, and the fourth is correct. The third distractor is so outrageous that no one would likely pick that as a response. There are several guides to developing distractors, as there were with developing items. As before, these are based on Ghiselli, Campbell, and Zedek (1981) and Nunnally and Bernstein (1994).

1. Create distractors that are plausible, but not so plausible as to easily confuse the correct with the incorrect response.

2. Make all of the alternatives parallel in length and grammatical structure. If they are not, the correct response becomes more apparent.

3. Keep the alternatives short, putting as much of the information in the item stem as possible.

4. Don't write distractors that mean the same thing. The testwise student will know to eliminate them both as not correct.

5. Alternate the position of the correct answer within the distractors. Testwise students will figure out that, if the correct response is usually in the C position, then on an item to which they don't know the answer, a guess of C is better than chance.

6. Use the alternatives "all of the above" and "none of the above" as little as possible.

7. Make sure each alternative agrees with the stem. If it does not, then this is again a clue to the testwise student that the alternative is a distractor.

Analysis of distractor responding is usually done in a couple of ways. One is to see how many individuals selected each distractor. If a multiple-choice test has four options, then one would examine the percentage of the respondents choosing each distractor. If 5% or fewer respondents select the distractor, consider rewriting the distractor as it is not serving its intended purpose. Second, a sense of who is responding to the distractors can be obtained by carrying out chi-square analyses.

For example, suppose it is of interest to see if men or women are more likely to select a particular distractor to an item than would be expected by chance alone. A multiple-choice item is administered to 100 individuals (50 men and 50 women) and there are three response alternatives. Assume that response B is the correct response. The data collected can be shown in a table like that in Table 3.5. The computer output of the cross-tabulation analysis is shown there as well.

Table 3.5   Response Choice to an Item Cross-Classified by Gender and SPSS Cross-Tabulation Output

Gender	A (distractor)	B (correct)	C (distractor)
Men	10	30	10
Women	3	25	22

Chi-Square Tests			
	Value	df	Sig. (two-sided)
Pearson Chi-Square	8.724	2	0.013
Likelihood Ratio	9.044	2	0.011
N of Valid Cases	100		
Symmetric Measures			
	Value	Approx. Sig.	
Phi	0.295	0.013	
Cramer's V	0.295	0.013	
Contingency Coefficient	0.283	0.013	
N of Valid Cases	100		

Most of the participants (55%) answered the question correctly. The men were equally as likely to select Distractor A as Distractor C. The women, however, seemed much more likely to select Distractor C than Distractor A when they got the item incorrect. A 2×3 chi-square analysis run on this table indicates that, indeed, there is a significant dependency in the data; women are more likely to select Distractor C (22/50) than A (3/50). To determine if this is significant, the expected versus observed difference in proportions using Formula 3–1 can be applied.

In this example, for Distractor A, $X = 3$, $N = 25$ (25 women were incorrect), and $P = 0.50$ (it is expected by chance that 50% of the women selecting an incorrect answer would select Distractor A).

$$[3 - (25)(0.5)]/\sqrt{(25)(0.5)(1 - 0.5)},$$

$$(3 - 12.5)/\sqrt{(12.5)(0.5)},$$

$$-9.5/2.5,$$

$$-3.8.$$

Recall that the calculated value is distributed approximately as a normal (z) distribution and the critical value to exceed to be considered statistically significant is 1.96. The value of -3.8 indicates that Distractor A is significantly less likely to be selected than is Distractor C by the women.

Now that it has been demonstrated that Distractor A is selected disproportionately as a distractor, what can be done? The item writer must go back to the distractors and examine them closely. The task is to determine what it is about the content of the distractor that makes it more likely for women not getting the item correct to choose Distractor C. Test designers try to make the distractors consistent across demographic variables. This example used gender to check for demographic differences, but any type of grouping variable such as education level, race, high versus low test scorers, and so forth can be used to assess disproportionate distractor selection rates. Information based on gender or racial differences may point out potential problems with the item from a bias perspective.

Examining differences in distractor selection by those who did well on the test overall versus those who did more poorly provides information about whether distractors are useful for discriminating between better and worse performers, as well as whether or not the distractor might be confusing. Consider the situation where the best performers on the test overall all seem to get the answer to one item incorrect. Further assume that they all chose a particular distractor. On the other hand, the poorer performers did not select this distractor with any greater frequency than they selected another. This indicates that the item is tripping up the best students and the distractor might need to be rewritten.

Guessing. An issue in multiple-choice or true-false tests is that the respondent can guess the correct answer. For a true-false test, the respondent has a 50% chance of getting the answer correct without knowing the answer. For a four-option multiple-choice test, the respondent has a 25% chance of getting the answer correct by guessing. Some tests factor a guessing penalty into computing the total score on a test to take this guessing component into account. The formula for doing so is

(3–4)   Guessing corrected score $= C - [I/(n-1)]$,

where $C =$ the number of correct responses, $I =$ the number of incorrect responses, and $n =$ the number of alternatives available for each item.

For example, assume a test has 100 multiple-choice items with five potential alternatives for each item. A test taker manages to complete 90 items. Of the 90 items, the test taker gets 70 correct.

$$\text{Corrected score} = 70 - (20/4),$$
$$= 70 - 5,$$
$$= 65.$$

Note that if the test taker had gotten none of the answered items incorrect, then the corrected score would not be lowered by a guessing correction. The more items the respondent gets incorrect, the more the person will be penalized for guessing on the correct responses. The assumption underlying this equation is that, if test takers get items incorrect, they are likely to be guessing.

It is extremely important as a test taker to know if a test has a penalty for guessing built into generating the total score. If there is no penalty for guessing and there is one minute left to complete the test but 20 questions left to answer, then the test taker should quickly choose any response to the rest of the items. However, if there is a penalty for guessing, test takers would not want to use this approach as it would be detrimental to their scores. The exception is if there are at least four alternatives and the test taker is able to narrow down the answer to two options; in this case, a guess provides a slight statistical advantage in the correction formula.

Speeded and Power Tests. Power tests assess individual differences without any effects of imposed time limits changing scores. Power tests often are made up of items that vary in their level of difficulty. Although pure power tests are not usual, most tests of achievement are designed so that 90% of the individuals taking the test can complete all of the items in a specified period of time (Nunnally & Bernstein, 1994). That is, most power tests of achievement have an arbitrary time frame (such as the length of a class period) as an administrative constraint. The power test designer should ensure that the test is long enough to cover the content domain, but not so long that there is not enough time available for most people to complete the test.

Pure speeded tests are composed of easy items where the variation in scores from individual to individual is based simply on how many correct items are completed. For example, a test in grade school where students are asked to complete as many multiplication facts as possible in two minutes is an example of a pure speeded test. Pure speeded tests are not useful unless the underlying construct being measured is one where speed is important (e.g., a typing task).

One issue in speeded tests that is somewhat different than that in a power test is the test length. Given the ease with which speeded test items can be constructed, it is usually not a problem to create new items if more are needed. The only way to get variance on the test scores for a group of test takers on a speeded test is to control the amount of time given to the test taker. Variability of test scores is a strong determinant of a test's reliability, so the time limit should be set to ensure maximum variance in the test scores. This can be determined empirically simply by having individuals complete as many items as possible in 1 minute, 2 minutes, 3 minutes, and so forth. The standard deviation can then be plotted against the time interval and a determination of the time limit when the highest variance in scores occurs is then selected. Figure 3.1 shows that the most variability for the items on the test in question occurs at 8 minutes. This, then, would be the optimal time limit on the test.

Some speeded tests often take into account the individual difference of age. It is a well-established empirical finding that as individuals age, their response times to stimuli slow (e.g., Birren & Schaie, 2001). Older individuals simply take longer to complete tasks than do younger individuals. When administering a speeded test, ensure that the test manual has addressed the issue of age. Usually this is done by adding a constant to scores of individuals within certain age bands. For example, individuals between 30–39 years of age taking the Wonderlic Personnel Test (1999) add one point to their raw score. Similar adjustments to raw scores are made for each decade up to 60 years of age and over.

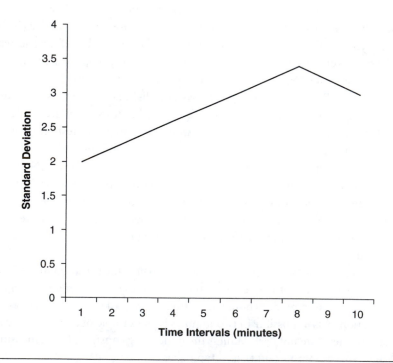

Figure 3.1   Speeded Test Standard Deviations

Omitted and Partial Credit. The terms *omitted* and *partial credit* are used in analyzing correct/incorrect test data and are particularly important in speeded tests. Omitted items are items that the respondent skips over. Sometimes it is appropriate to assign the omitted items a value of $1/A$, where A is equal to the number of alternatives. So if a respondent does not make a response to item 20 in a 25-item test with four alternatives, but completes items 1–19 and 21–25, the person would get a score of 0.25 on item 20. In effect, this gives the person a "guessed" value correct for the omitted items and improves the accuracy of score estimation (Lord, 1980). The formula for correcting for omitted items is

(3–5) $$\text{Omitted corrected score} = 1/A \times O + \text{total,}$$

where $A =$ the number of alternatives available, $O =$ the number of omitted items, and total $=$ the total number of items correct.

It may also be desirable to give partial credit for items where parts of the answer can be scored correctly and other parts incorrectly. It is important when using the partial credit approach that the difficulty of each of the parts of the question is known. For example, take an item such as the following:

$$\sqrt{25} + 2 = ?.$$

The answer to the first part ($\sqrt{25}$) requires more sophisticated math ability than does the second part ($+\,2$). Therefore, any partial credit strategy should be able to take into account differences in difficulty for the parts of the question. When the parts are of equal difficulty, then simply creating separate items out of each part would be appropriate. For example, in the following item:

$$(2 + 3) - 4 = ?,$$

the individual would get one point for solving the first part ($2 + 3$) correctly and one point for solving the second part ($5 - 4$) correctly. Test administrators should know in advance how omitted and partial credit are to be dealt with rather than trying to decide after the test takers have completed the items.

Continuous Responses

Up to this point, issues associated with responses that have only two primary options (dichotomous) have been reviewed. Many scales, however, are developed with responses that have more than two options for responding. One of the most popular of these types is the summated-rating scale based on the work of Likert.

Summated-Rating Scales. In the previous chapter, various ways to assess attitudinal items were presented. However, many of the procedures may have seemed long and tedious. Why can't a simple question such as, "What is your satisfaction with your coworkers?" be asked with the response being one of five options: very unsatisfied,

unsatisfied, neither satisfied nor unsatisfied, satisfied, and very satisfied? There are a couple of reasons why some care should be made in creating such items.

One assumption of items such as this is that the construct under investigation—in this case satisfaction with one's coworkers—can be placed into ordered categories where higher values can be inferred to mean higher satisfaction. Another assumption is that each of the response categories will have a normal distribution of responses around it in the population.

Recall that in the paired comparison approach example, 500 students were asked to make six paired comparisons between flavors of ice cream. Alternatively, those 500 students could have been asked to rate each of the four flavors of ice cream on a five-point scale, such as the following: "horrible, bad, okay, good, delicious." The problem with the latter approach is that there is no basis for determining the relative difference between "horrible" and "bad," nor is there any basis for determining whether the difference between "horrible" and "bad" is the same as that between "okay" and "good" (or for any other combination). Fortunately, a critical piece of empirical work was conducted such that confidence in the assumptions of these continuum-based response scales is now appropriate. The researcher who conducted the work was Rensis Likert.

In many ways, Likert revolutionized how attitudes are assessed and scaled. Prior to his work, the attitude scale assessment and scoring occurred as described in Chapter 2. In 1932, Likert published his method for scaling response categories that were separate from the items. He evaluated many attitude statements using five response categories: 1 = strongly approve, 2 = approve, 3 = undecided, 4 = disapprove, and 5 = strongly disapprove. As was shown in the previous chapter, these attitude items resulted in scale scores. What he found was that the simple categories 1, 2, 3, 4, and 5 that were labeled "strongly approve" to "strongly disapprove" correlated so highly with the more tediously determined scale scores that one could readily use the categories 1 through 5 rather than the item's scaled values.

This did two very important things. The first was to enable test developers to not be so dependent on the labor intensive generation of scale scores for each item. That is, it was no longer necessary to know "how much" stimuli was present in each item. The second was that the purpose of Likert's approach was not to scale items but to scale participants. One could obtain an assessment of an individual's strength of an attitude by simply summing across each of the response categories for each person.

So if respondents were presented with the 10 job characteristics that were introduced in Chapter 2, instead of having to respond "yes" or "no" as to whether each characterized their jobs, they could agree with the statement to a varying extent. They would do so by indicating their agreement level regarding how much each descriptor (such as "challenging") characterized their jobs on a scale anchored with 1 = strongly disagree, 2 = disagree, 3 = undecided, 4 = agree, and 5 = strongly agree.

It is critical to know the *valence* (negativeness or positiveness) of the item's content when calculating total scores on summated rating scales. Items with a negative valence should be *reverse coded* such that the response given is transposed: in the case of a five-point scale, a 1 would be changed to a 5, and a 2 would be changed to a 4, while the 3 would remain the same. Recall that in Chapter 2, three of the items in the job description scale had negative scale scores: disgusting, underpaid, and revolting.

The job descriptors, a sample respondent's ratings of agreement, the item scale score values, and the ratings with reverse coding are shown in Table 3.6. Because of the reverse coding for the three items, the respondent's total score would be based on the last column of the table rather than the second column. In this case, the person's job satisfaction score would be 35. This 35 is an indication of the attitude of the respondent toward his or her job. This number can be compared to the scores of other job incumbents and used to make a decision such as whether or not the respondent should stay with the organization, or for other purposes. If a number of job incumbents complete the scale, the whole group's score on job attitude could be correlated with other variables, such as intentions to quit, organizational commitment, and so forth.

Likert designed his response approach to assess individual differences in attitudes. Scales today that use a five-point format like the one described are called Likert scales. Variations on the traditional Likert scale are called summated rating scales or Likert-type scales. These variations pose some issues that are explained next.

Variations and Issues With Likert Scales. Variations in the category descriptors seems to be the least problematic concern. While Likert used "strongly approve" to

Table 3.6   Likert Scaled Responses to Job Characteristics Items

Item	1–5 Rating	Scale Score	Reverse Coded Responses
disgusting	1[a]	−3.58	5
fun	2	1.51	2
underpaid	3[a]	−2.90	3
rewarding	4	1.66	4
delightful	2	2.56	2
challenging	4	0.70	4
enjoyable	3	0.89	3
revolting	1[a]	−3.49	5
interesting	3	1.08	3
meaningful	4	1.51	4
			$\Sigma = 35$

a. Negative valence items that are reverse coded.

"strongly disapprove" as his original descriptors, many scales use "strongly agree" to "strongly disagree" or "extremely difficult" to "extremely easy," and so forth. There is an assumption that the response categories of these variants are "equal interval" as Likert had demonstrated so many years ago. This assumption is not always correct. However, work by Bass, Cascio, and O'Connor (1974) as well as Spector (1976) suggest that most attitude surveys using Likert's general approach do have categories of approximately equal intervals.

The number of categories has also been a subject of much debate in the psychometric literature. Should there be 3, 5, 7, 9, or 26 categories, or does it matter at all? Symonds (1924) argued that 7 categories is the optimal number and Champney and Marshall (1939) indicated it is best to have 20 or so categories. Anderson (1991) found that for most rating tasks, 10 categories provides as much discrimination as is needed. Rather than pick a number of categories to be used based on empirical information, however, a more theoretical approach seems reasonable.

That is, what are the data going to be used for? Assume that a series of items with responses on a 1–5 scale with 1 = strongly disagree and 5 = strongly agree is posed. If categories 1 and 2 (strongly disagree and disagree) and categories 4 and 5 (agree and strongly agree) are going to be collapsed into single categories, then a three-point scale would have been sufficient. For example, in a performance appraisal rating task, a supervisor may be asked to rate the performance of an employee on a number of dimensions (punctuality, customer service, quality of work output, etc.). If the required information about the employee is "does not meet expectations," "meets expectations," and "exceeds expectations," then three categories are sufficient. Requiring the supervisor to rate the person on a 10-point scale might be stretching that person's capacity to make that fine a set of discriminations. On the other hand, if the sample of supervisors who will be the ultimate users of such a rating scale is used to having a 7-point scale for rating their employees, it may be difficult for them to adjust to a 3-point scale and they would not be comfortable using the 3-point scale.

So one should use the number of categories that provides as much discrimination as is reasonable to expect from the respondents combined with the number of categories to be used in any analysis and interpretation of results. It is most likely that a number between three and nine will be selected. Regardless of the number of categories selected, it is very helpful to have clear descriptors for each of the categories. This is particularly important for the end-point categories, as the respondent should know what an extreme score represents.

Midpoints on summated-rating scales also seem to cause a great deal of concern for some scale developers. A scale with a defined midpoint is one such as the following.

Strongly Disagree	Disagree	Undecided	Agree	Strongly Agree
1	2	3	4	5

A scale without a defined midpoint would read like the following.

Strongly Disagree	Disagree	Agree	Strongly Agree
1	2	3	4

There are no strong arguments from a statistical perspective for one type of response scale over the other. The issue that I have found to be most relevant is how the respondents will deal with no midpoint. With no midpoint, the effect is to force respondents to choose to agree or disagree with a statement about which they may be truly ambivalent. I have had the experience where respondents became frustrated with no midpoint and refused to complete the scale or refused to answer the item. Sound advice on this issue is to make a rational decision as best you can. If most people completing the scale will have feelings of agreement or disagreement about virtually all of the items, then no midpoint will stop those who "sit on the fence" from circling the midpoint all the time. If at least some of the respondents are expected to be undecided about some of the items, then it is better to provide a midpoint as it is a more accurate reflection of their attitudes, and they will be more likely to complete the scale.

Another of the questions about response scales is whether to include a "don't know" or "not enough information to make a judgment" type of response. Some would argue that these should not be included because it gives respondents an "out." Others argue that if respondents really do not know the answer, they should be allowed to indicate that on the scale. For example, suppose a group of workers is asked to rate their agreement with the following item: "My organization's goals are aligned with my own values." If the workers don't know the organization's goals, how will they know if the goals are aligned with their values? In this case, a "don't know" response is very useful. In item construction, try not to include items to which individuals will not know the response. When it is anticipated there may be some "don't knows," adding the option is a wise move.

Another issue that comes up more in research in the field than in lab-based research is use of items with a negative valence. These are the items that need to be reverse coded before summing across the items. For example, items with a positive valence about job satisfaction might include "my job is an exciting one," "my supervisor listens to my suggestions," and "my coworkers are supportive." Then the scale developers throw in an item such as, "I have no commitment to my organization." If all of these were to be responded to on a five-point Likert-type scale with responses ranging from strongly disagree to strongly agree, high scores on the first three items would mean higher levels of satisfaction. High scores on the fourth item would indicate low levels of satisfaction.

In scale construction, it is frequently advised to include items that are negative in valence to ensure that the respondent is paying attention to the items. It prevents respondents from always selecting a particular response category without really attending to the item. While these are logical reasons for including negative valence items, they are also problematic. Specifically, I have found two issues arise. The first is that respondents who are not students in university classes don't like these types of items. It has been reported back to me that the negatively worded items are confusing. In addition, on more than one occasion, I have had to delete the items because analyses of responding patterns suggested that the respondents made mistakes on these items. I am not alone in these observations (e.g., DeVellis, 2003; Netemeyer, Bearden, & Sharma, 2003).

Therefore, it is advisable to use negatively worded items with caution. Be deliberate in making the decision of including such items. If the sample of respondents is under time pressure to complete the surveys, not used to completing surveys regularly, or might be easily confused, then don't use them. If it is decided to use such items, include many of them. That is, don't write 19 positively worded items and then add one that is negatively worded. Instead, write 10 positively worded and 10 negatively worded items so that the respondents become used to the fact that negatively worded items are a usual occurrence on the survey. Finally, make sure that the negatively worded items are interspersed throughout the survey and not all at the beginning or end.

Response categories should also allow for an even distribution of negative and positive attitudes or else they will negatively or positively skew the interpretation. Here is a typical example: A marketing representative calls me and asks me about the customer service I received when I took my car in for service. I'm asked to rate the service on the following scale: "unsatisfied, satisfied, very satisfied, or extremely satisfied." The problem here is that only one of the four options allows me to express a negative attitude; the other three are levels of satisfaction. Be suspicious of companies that say they have a 90% customer satisfaction rating. To interpret this statistic, it would be necessary to see the questions *and* the response options.

Other Types of Continuous Response Scales. Visual analogue scales are a variant on the multicategorical approach to responses. In these scales, the respondent is presented with an item and asked to make a mark on a line, and the score for that item is the number of millimeters from one end point. Although there are no inherent statistical problems with this approach, it is quite time consuming to score. Visual analogue scales are common in assessments of health and stress. Figure 3.2 shows a response of this nature.

If a respondent was asked to mark an X on this scale to show the level of stress he or she was currently feeling and marked it as shown, the score on this item would be the distance from the left end point to the X. Higher scores would correspond to higher levels of stress.

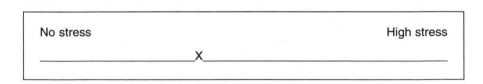

Figure 3.2   Visual Analogue Scale

Figure 3.3   Facial Scale

Another response format is pictorial. These are particularly useful for respondents who do not have strong verbal skills, such as young children, people without language proficiency in the language in which the test was constructed, those with low literacy, and so forth. The items can be read out loud by the test administrator and test takers respond to the items by selecting the facial expression that best captures their attitudes. Figure 3.3 shows an example of a three-alternative facial response format. A question might be posed to the individual: "How do you feel about your psychometrics class?" The individual then would be expected to choose the facial expression that most closely matches his or her affective reaction to the psychometrics class.

Adjective rating scales are another way to obtain continuous responses. In these scales, the ends of the scale are anchored with presumed polar opposites. These are called *polar adjective* rating scales. An example of one follows:

1. quiet	___	___	___	___	___	loud
2. sincere	___	___	___	___	___	insincere
3. happy	___	___	___	___	___	sad
4. selfish	___	___	___	___	___	selfless
5. ambitious	___	___	___	___	___	lazy

An X that is placed on the line in between each polar pair is the respondent's scale value for that item. If a respondent placed an X on the third line for Item 1, it would indicate that the individual thought he was neither quiet nor loud but right in the middle.

Some of the scales that have been created this way make assumptions about the oppositeness of the adjectives. A good example is in the above list. While most people would agree that loud and quiet are opposites, as are happy and sad, it is not as clear that ambitious and lazy are necessarily opposites. Thus, when using or creating scales like these, it is critical that the decisions made to create the opposing pairs are defensible.

Another important contribution to the continuous scaling process has been in the design of category descriptors. These are often referred to as *anchors*. As with the Behavioral Observation Scale (BOS) scaling process discussed in Chapter 2, the behaviorally anchored rating scales (BARS) process also uses a critical incident technique and can be used to create the anchors for such scales. One of the most frequent uses of BARS is in the assessment of employee performance, but it can easily be used in a number of other settings.

The process for developing anchors for BARS in a work performance setting would be to first have subject matter experts (SMEs) generate a list of critical behaviors that result in good and poor performance. For example, good performance for a sales staff employee might include approaching customers coming into the store within 30 seconds, smiling and saying hello to customers, asking customers if there is anything in particular that they are looking for, and so forth. Poor performance for a sales staff employee might include waiting for customers to approach the staff member to secure assistance, not smiling at customers, not offering to assist customers to find what they need, and so forth. All of these behaviors are associated with customer service. Other domains of behaviors would also be generated for such things as assisting other sales staff, punctuality, flexibility in scheduling, solving customer service problems, and so forth.

Next, the behaviors are clustered together into their domain content areas. For example, all the good and poor behaviors generated that were associated with customer service would be grouped together. All the good and poor behaviors that were associated with helping other sales staff would be grouped together, and so on. To check whether the behaviors were correctly grouped into their domain content area, all of the behaviors for all of the domains would be gathered and mixed up, and another sample of SMEs would be asked to sort them into their domain areas (e.g., customer service, assisting other sales staff, etc.). These new SMEs would be expected to show consistency in grouping the behaviors into the same domain areas as the first set of experts.

An agreement percentage is set in advance to determine if a particular behavior is confusing. For example, if a behavior such as "approach customers coming into the store within 30 seconds" is re-sorted by 90% of the new SMEs into its original domain of customer service, then that behavior would be said to be consistent. On the other hand, if a behavior such as "counts out correct change for the customer" is re-sorted by 50% of the new experts into its original domain (e.g., completes sale accurately) and 50% into another domain (e.g., customer service), then that behavior would be said to be inconsistent, and would likely not be used in the final scale. The percentage agreement level the scale developer sets is really up to him or her. Previous research in the same area, as well as common sense, is useful as a guide in selecting a percentage agreement rate that is appropriate.

Next, each SME is asked to rate the effectiveness of the behaviors that survived the sorting process in terms of the job performance domain (usually on a five-, seven-, or nine-point scale). Behaviors that have high variability in the ratings are dropped. For example, if a behavior such as "approaches customers within 30 seconds of entering the store" is rated as a 6 or a 7 (i.e., highly effective) on a seven-point scale by all of the SMEs, then the behavior is consistent. If half of the experts rate the behavior as a 3 and the other half as a 7, then the variability of the ratings is quite high. This item, then, would likely not be retained. The specific level of variation selected as the cutoff is up to the scale developer, but should be consistent with previously developed scales in the area. Finally, the scale is developed so that the domain of "customer service" can be assessed on a three-, five-, or seven-point Likert-type scale with behavioral descriptors anchoring various parts of the scale. It is not necessary to anchor all of the points on the scale; however, the end points and the center point of the rating scale must be clearly anchored.

Intensity Versus Frequency Likert-Type Scales. One general issue that does arise in creating Likert or Likert-type scales is whether to ask the respondent for intensity information, such as levels of agreement, liking, or satisfaction, or whether to ask the respondent for frequency information, such as, "How often or how frequently do you experience headaches?" or "How often do you observe your coworker coming in to work late?"

The following is an example of an item asked in an intensity manner. "Rate your level of agreement (on a 1–5 scale) with the following statement: I am happy most of the time." The item could also be asked in a frequency manner such as the following: "How often do you feel happy?" The respondent has to read the category descriptors carefully to see which one is most appropriate. Assume the response options are "never," "sometimes," "frequently," and "almost always." The problem is that what the test developer meant by *sometimes* may very well not be what the respondent means by *sometimes*. In fact, each and every respondent may have a different interpretation of *sometimes*.

Clearly, there are times when frequency is an important measure. For example, rating the frequencies of behaviors or symptoms is often of great import in both diagnosing a disorder/disease and assessing the effectiveness of treatments. This would be the case for physical and psychological symptoms, behavior problems, and so forth. Frequencies are also of import in less life-affecting areas, but ones where frequency measurement is appropriate—for example, assessing an aspect of employee performance by counting the number of errors made, or assessing safe driving behavior by counting the frequency of carrying out safe actions.

However, it is critical that the category descriptors for such scales are carefully constructed. An appropriate set of category descriptors for the question "How often do you feel happy?" might be the following: "less than once a week, once a week, two to three times a week, four to five times a week, or more than five times a week." Test constructors must know the construct under investigation quite well in order to create the correct category descriptions. That is, for any given item, they need to know the typical frequency, very low and very high frequencies, and moderately low and moderately high frequencies. These, then, become the anchors for the points on the scale.

Ipsative Versus Normative Scales

Up to this point, the focus of scale development has been on normative scales. In normative scales, there is one measurement scale for every construct of interest—whether that be an attitude, personality measure, interest, or ability. The usual normative scaling development and use procedure is to create a scale, ask a number of different individuals to complete the scale, compute each respective score, and then use the scores for direct interpretation (e.g., comparing one to another, one to a group, one group versus another) or in relating the scores to other variables of interest. This is also referred to as *nomothetic assessment.*

It is assumed in normative scales that the scores underlying the construct being assessed are normally distributed in the population. Thus, normative scores are used with normative scales to compare *across* individuals. In ipsative scales, there is a separate scale for each individual respondent, and the population of that individual's trait scores is distributed about the mean of that individual's scores. Thus, the purpose in ipsative scoring is to make comparisons about different constructs *within* each individual. This is also referred to as *idiographic assessment.*

The following are some examples of ipsative items:

1. Rank order the following ice cream flavors (vanilla, chocolate, strawberry, butterscotch), with 1 being the most tasty and 4 being the least tasty. (If the first three flavors of ice cream are ranked, then it is known by default what the fourth ranking is going to be.)

2. Which of the two items best describes your interests: "I like to arrange flowers" or "I like to solve computer software problems"? (If flower arranging is selected as the interest, then it is known that the respondent is less interested in solving computer software problems.)

3. Rank order the four statements as to their description of your supervisor, with 1 being most like and 4 being least like your supervisor:

   "My supervisor always asks for my opinion on matters that affect my work,"

   "My supervisor frequently asks for my opinion on matters that affect my work,"

   "My supervisor sometimes asks for my opinion on matters that affect my work," and

   "My supervisor rarely asks for my opinion on matters that affect my work."

   (If rankings for three of the supervisor descriptions are provided, then it is known what the fourth one is going to be.)

All of these items have a similar characteristic—knowledge of the response to one item provides information about what the respondent will (and can) put for another item. This means that the responses are not independent of one another. The lack of item independence makes ipsative data inappropriate for many analyses that make an implicit (and sometimes explicit) assumption about item independence.

Respondents often report a dislike of ipsative measures. This is because they may not be able to accurately make the judgments requested. For example, what if respondents like vanilla and chocolate ice cream to exactly the same degree? By forcing them to rank order the flavors, an accurate assessment of ice cream flavor liking is not possible. What if respondents don't like flower arranging or solving computer software problems? This dislike cannot be captured. What if a respondent's supervisor rarely asks for opinions so this option is ranked 1, but all the rest are equally unlikely? If that is the case, the 1–4 ranking will not capture the reality of the supervisory situation.

From a statistical perspective, many researchers have gone so far as to suggest that purely ipsative measures have such severe limitations that they should not be used (e.g., Cornwell & Dunlap, 1994; Hicks, 1970; Tenopyr, 1988). A special factor analytic approach called the *Q-technique* is needed when scores are ipsative (Guilford, 1952).

There are several reasons for not using ipsative measures; however, there is evidence that ipsative scores are useful in some respects (e.g., Greer & Dunlap, 1997; Ravlin & Maglino, 1987; Saville & Willson, 1991). The primary use is when intraindividual assessment is the goal of the testing situation. For example, if an individual desires information about his or her most appropriate career options, forcing the respondent to choose between activities associated with vocational alternatives provides valuable information for that one individual. That is the basis for the Kuder Occupational Interest Survey (Kuder, 1979). Kolb (1985) has been assessing preferred learning styles with his ipsative measure for many years. Assessment of various aspects of personality with ipsative measures has also been conducted—with the Edwards Personal Preference Inventory (Edwards, 1959) and with the Myers-Briggs Type Indicator (Myers, McCaulley, Quenck, & Hammer, 1998).

One variant on the purely ipsative versus purely normative scaling is a particular type of forced-choice item and summing process. In purely ipsative scales, the response choices are pitted against one another so that choosing one option by definition makes the respondent higher on one scale and lower on the other. So, for example, if I choose an option that puts me higher on the extroversion scale, I am by default lower on the introversion scale. Some forced-choice formats are created so that choosing one option does not by default ensure a lower score on the other. That is, respondents are asked to respond using a forced-choice format, but the item responses are independent of one another. An example of this type of scale is the Sensation Seeking Scale (Zuckerman, 1979). It is a 40-item scale that has four subscales, each of which is made up of 10 forced-choice questions. The individual respondent can be high on all four subscales, low on them all, or any combination thereof. These types of forced-choice scales seem not to suffer the statistical problems of the purely ipsative scales.

Another type of approach to generating both normative and ipsative data is with the Q-sort method. This has been used in personality assessment (Block, 1978) and in assessing organizational value congruence (Chatman, 1989). A series of items (say 50) is generated to capture the domain of interest. Next, an individual sorts the items into a specified number of categories (say 10) on the basis of the importance or relevance of the item for the domain. For example, assume that the domain of interest is organizational effectiveness and the purpose of the task is to compare a potential job applicant's values to those of the organization's. If an organizational attribute such as "allows for participation in decision making" is very important to the applicant in the domain of organizational effectiveness, he or she might place that item in the 9 or 10 category. If "competitive pay" is of moderate importance to the respondent in the domain of organizational effectiveness, the item might be placed in the 5 or 6 category. The applicant does this for each of the 50 items. Fewer items are permitted in the extreme categories (e.g., 1, 2, 9, and 10). The result is supposed to be a normal distribution of items such that most are piled up in the more neutral categories and then taper off to the ends. This produces an ipsative set of values for the applicant.

The next step is to have a large number of incumbent employees do the same sorting but with the caveat that they sort on the basis of how important each item is to the organization as it currently operates. These current employees thus provide a distribution of organizational attributes that range from more to less important. These employee-sorted item category assignments are averaged and this produces an average of ipsative data that represents the importance of various organizational attributes.

Now the applicant's profile can be compared with the organizational profile by correlating the item category assignments the applicant made with the category assignments made by the large employee group. The higher the correlation, the more likely the person will "fit" the organization. This correlation provides a normative set of values that can then be compared across individuals.

So, a question remains about what type of scaling is best, ipsative or normative? As with many of the choices that have been posed thus far, there is a need for making a reasonable decision based not on statistical grounds alone, but on rational grounds. The most important issue is what the information will be used for. If a set of items has been carefully developed and shows strong psychometric characteristics in normative samples, revising the items into an ipsative measure can force high degrees of intraindividual variance, which is often useful in describing one person. This type of information is most helpful when the individual appears for assistance (for example, in vocational counseling). If the purpose is to compare across individuals, then clearly a normative scaling scale is most appropriate.

Difference and Change Scores

Another debate that has raged in the psychometric literature is over difference scores. Often it is of interest to researchers and practitioners alike to ask questions such as "How much autonomy do you have in your job?" and "How much autonomy would you like to have in your job?" The respondent rates his or her degree of autonomy for the first at a 3 on a seven-point Likert scale. Then he or she answers 6 to the second item. The difference is 3 points on the scale and would indicate that the person would like more autonomy than is presently experienced. The difference is between two conceptually linked but distinct constructs (called *components* in this literature).

Change scores assess the same individual using the same measure but at two (or more) different times. Researchers and practitioners in the areas of education and evaluation would be likely to use change scores as data points. They are not the same as difference scores, but both change and difference scores have come under fire. The issues with difference scores will be discussed first.

There are problems with simple difference scores, and the three most common will be discussed here. The first concern is that the reliability of difference scores will most likely be lower than each of the component scales that make up the difference score. Another problem is that they do not account for any variance in a criterion above and beyond that accounted for by each of the components. Assume everyone in an organization ($N = 2,000$) indicated on a five-point scale how much they felt the organization valued their contributions (variable X). They are also asked how much they would like their organization to value their contributions on a 1–5 scale (variable Y). Next, the difference between these two values for all 2,000 employees is calculated (variable Z). A criterion variable such as job performance is then collected on all of the employees as well. Opponents of using the difference score argue that if the job performance measure is regressed on X and Y, Z will not add any additional information above and beyond that provided by X and Y separately.

The third criticism of difference scores is a conceptual concern rather than a statistical one—just what is it that the difference measures? Researchers and practitioners using difference scores must pay close attention to what they are measuring. For instance, difference scores have been calculated in various ways: algebraic differences (this means that the signs of the differences are left intact), absolute differences, and squared differences are the most common. In many instances, the rationale for using one over the other is not made. Sometimes it is critical that the sign, or direction of the difference, is part of the construct. At other times, the magnitude of the difference, regardless of direction, is important.

If difference scores are used, addressing the psychometric concerns that have been expressed is necessary. The component scales must have good reliability and there should be high variability on each of them. In addition, the components should *not* be highly correlated with one another. In the unusual instance when the component scores are negatively correlated, the reliability of the difference score will actually be higher than the reliability of the two component scales. Component scales that use multiple items and/or are completed by two different sources (e.g., employees and managers) are more likely to have more reliable difference scores than component scales that use single items and/or are both completed by the same person. Be thoughtful about how difference scores are constructed and what they will mean. Make sure that they add incremental information above that contained in the component scores. Be aware of the arguments for and against using difference scores by reading some articles on the subject matter and make a case for why they are being used. Some excellent articles on this issue include Edwards (1993), Edwards (1994), Edwards (1995), Edwards and Cooper (1990), Johns (1981), and Tisak and Smith, (1994).

Change scores, as noted earlier, are the same measure used on the same individuals taken at different times. For example, suppose a sample of students is measured at the beginning of a typing course on the number of words typed correctly per minute. The students are then sent through 6 weeks of typing training. After the course, they are measured on the number of words typed correctly per minute. The difference between the two measures is a change score, or gain score, as it is sometimes called.

The reliability problem alluded to in the difference score literature is the same in the change score literature. In fact, this is the crux of the argument about why not to use change scores. Much research and argument abounds in the psychometric literature about change scores. References that are highly useful in understanding the arguments include Collins (1996); Cronbach and Furby (1970); Humphreys (1996); Rogosa and Willett (1983); Williams and Zimmerman (1996a); Williams and Zimmerman (1996b); and Zumbo (1999). Other readings are more helpful in that they provide alternative approaches to the simple change score, and these include Collins and Sayer (2001); Cribbie and Jamieson (2000); Rogosa, Brandt, and Zimowski (1982); and Tisak and Tisak (1996). One particularly helpful approach has been clearly described by Zuckerman, Gagne, Nafshi, Knee, and Kieffer (2002). They make a compelling argument that one can defensibly create a difference score using measures of the same construct (e.g., two different measures of need for achievement). However, if the difference score is generated from two different constructs (e.g., the difference between actual and ideal organizational attributes), then an interaction term should be created from the two component measures first. Then, any relationship of the interaction with a criterion should first take into account the two component measures.

Change scores on a typing test are based on psychomotor skills and are problematic from a reliability standpoint. Change scores that use attitude measures are problematic for another reason; they sensitize the test taker to the issue at hand. For example, suppose a measure of employee job satisfaction is taken at one time, then an intervention is introduced (e.g., managers are trained to be more sensitive to employee needs), and then employee job satisfaction is measured at a later time. The employee scores are likely to change from the first to the second administration of the job satisfaction measure. However, employees have been sensitized to the issue simply by having completed the first job satisfaction measure. Employees may have had a heightened sensitivity to any changes in the job environment and these may have artificially inflated their job satisfaction scores at a later time. This issue of sensitization needs to be taken into account when interpreting change scores.

It is worthwhile to be familiar with the change and difference score literature when using a change score research design. Williams and Zimmerman (1996a) note that there are assumptions in the attack on change score reliability that may not be met. Specifically, the attack assumes the worst-case scenario, where the variances of the pretest and posttest are equivalent and where the correlation between the pretest and posttest are high. The reliability of a change score increases as (a) the correlation between the pretest and posttest decreases and (b) the ratio of the variances of the pretest and posttest deviate from 1.0. If the data show that the pretest and posttests are highly correlated and they have similar variances, consider an alternative to using the change scores.

Summary and Next Step

In this chapter, the many issues facing scale designers in structuring the type of response desired were covered. These included

a. deciding whether to use an open- or closed-ended format;

b. when choosing a closed-ended format where there is a "correct" answer, settling on the number of alternatives, carefully crafting distractors, determining if there will be a penalty for guessing, choosing whether or not to use a power or a speeded test, and deciding what will be done with omitted responses and partial credit;

c. introducing the revolutionary work of Rensis Likert in attitude assessment;

d. in attitude assessment, discussing the purpose of the instrument, decisions about the type of scale to use (frequency versus intensity, ipsative versus normative), the number of alternatives to use, and the anchors/descriptors for the categories; and

e. reviewing issues that have arisen based on calculating difference and change scores and the fact that the pitfalls associated with these are worth attending to before trying to publish the scale and work associated with the scale.

Most of the literature on scale development focuses on the issues of creating samples of items from the population of items and, to this point, this has been the focus. However, sampling issues as they pertain to respondent populations are just as important, so in the next chapter issues of respondent samples are covered.

Problems and Exercises

1. Write an open-ended question asking your colleagues for information about their work experience. Ask a few of them to respond to the items.

2. Write some closed-ended questions about your colleagues' work experience. Ask a few of them to respond to the items.

3. Assume you ask 50 students to indicate where they have had the majority of their work experience. You get the following numbers: retail = 25, food service = 15, financial sector = 7, and other = 3. Calculate if there is a proportional difference in the data.

4. Assume you have the same data as in Problem 3, but now you break it down by age (those 25 years and under and those 26 years and older). You obtain the following table of data (Table 3.7). Calculate the chi-square statistic and Cramer's V for this table. Interpret your results.

Table 3.7 Cross-Tabulation of Age and Employment Frequencies, Row and Column Totals, and Row Percentages

	25 and Under	26 and Older	Row Total	Row %
Retail	16	8	24	48%
Food Service	10	2	12	24%
Financial	3	8	11	22%
Other	1	2	3	6%
Column Total	30	20		

5. Indicate if the following are true or false dichotomies (as measured in brackets):

a. Gender (male/female)

b. Age (under 30 years/over 30 years)

    c. Marital status (married/not married)

    d. Job attitude (satisfied/not satisfied)

    e. Organization (organized/disorganized)

    f. Student status (registered student/nonregistered student)

    g. Speed (over the speed limit/under the speed limit)

    h. Incarceration (in jail/not in jail)

6. Take a subject material (stimuli) such as a pizza. Generate an adjective checklist associated with that stimulus. Ask four of your colleagues to check off the items they think characterize the stimulus.

7. Using the material in the first three chapters of this book, write a multiple-choice test item with three alternatives (one correct and the other two incorrect). Ask your classmates to complete the test item. Generate a table of responses to the item. Using the test of single proportions, calculate whether the correct answer or one of the "foils" was more likely to be selected.

8. What would be the "corrected for guessing score" for someone who answered 45 questions out of 50 correct on a true/false test? What would be the "corrected for guessing score" on a multiple-choice test with four alternatives to each item?

9. What are the differences between power and speeded tests?

10. Assume I take a 100-item multiple-choice test that has three alternatives for each item. I get 80 correct, but skip five of the items. If my instructor gives omitted credit for the five items, what would be my score?

11. Using the construct you have been developing thus far, create five Likert-type items labeling your response categories.

12. What is an item with a negative valence? What are the arguments for including and arguments for not including such items?

13. What is a visual analogue scale and how is it scored?

14. Why are pictures used sometimes as responses?

15. Create a polar-adjective scale for your stimuli from Problem 6. Try to generate at least five pairs of polar opposites.

16. What is the utility of a behaviorally anchored rating scale?

17. Using the construct "healthy lifestyle," generate five items that ask for frequency responses on a Likert-type scale.

18. What is the difference between normative and ipsative test items? Why would one use one type versus the other?

19. What is a difference score and what are the arguments that have been leveled against using such scores?

CHAPTER 4

Collecting Data

Sampling and Screening

Once a set of items is prepared and ready to be responded to, the next step is to gather data from a group of respondents. In fact, this will not be done just once, but many times. This is because the process of developing a coherent and useful measure of a construct is an iterative one. That is, the test is given to a group of respondents. The response data are analyzed and, as a result of the analysis, items may be dropped or refined, or new ones may be added. Then the new instrument is administered to another group of respondents and the process repeats itself. Tests are often revised in their initial stages of development. As a test becomes more established, it may undergo revision only periodically.

Unless you happen to be in the enviable position of being able to collect data on an entire population, a sample will have to be drawn from that population. The expectation for making inferences based on samples is that the sample will be representative of the population from which it has been drawn. If this is the case, there will be no systematic bias in the data collected from that sample, and generalizations about the population based on the sample are appropriate (Goldenberg, 1992).

There are two general types of samples: probability and nonprobability. In probability sampling, each element has a known probability of being sampled. For probability samples, the error due to sampling can be closely estimated based on probability theory. In nonprobability samples, each element has an unknown probability of being sampled and thus sampling error cannot be estimated.

Probability Sampling

A simple random sample is a probability sample. A simple random sample requires (a) a complete listing of all of the elements, (b) an equal chance for each element to be selected, and (c) a selection process whereby the selection of one element has no effect on the chances of selecting another element. These conditions are largely met in telephone survey sampling, where a computer can be programmed to dial a number at random. However, this is not usually the case in most other types of data collection efforts—where the population is not even clearly defined.

Another type of probability sampling technique is stratified random sampling. In this method, the population of elements is classified into non-overlapping subpopulations (called *strata*) such as age groups or geographic locations, after which usually a simple random sample from each of the strata is taken. If random samples of similar size are taken across strata, regardless of their proportion in the population, then this is called *disproportionate stratified random sampling*. If samples of differing sizes (based on their population proportions) are taken across strata, then this is called *proportionate stratified random sampling*.

Disproportionate stratified random sampling is the more common of the two, as the purpose of stratifying is usually to ensure that reasonable sample sizes of varying groups are included. To stratify and then proportionately sample defeats this purpose, and a simple random sample would have provided a similar set of demographic characteristics. An example should clarify this distinction. For example, assume that there is a liberal arts college with a full-time student population of 10,000. A teacher effectiveness survey is to be sent to a sample of them. Assume that there are nine majors in the college, and the students are distributed across them as in column 2 of Table 4.1.

To ensure that comparisons across the groups could be made by having a large enough sample size for each major, it would be desirable to survey 1.25% of some groups and 20% of other groups (column 3 of Table 4.1). This is disproportionate

Table 4.1   Disproportionate and Proportionate Stratified Random Sampling

Major	Actual N-size of Majors	N-size and % Sampled	N-size with 5% Sampling
Psychology	4,000	50 (1.25%)	200
Sociology	2,000	50 (2.5%)	100
Economics	1,000	50 (5%)	50
Political Science	1,000	50 (5%)	50
History	500	50 (10%)	25
Philosophy	500	50 (10%)	25
Geography	500	50 (10%)	25
Fine Arts	250	50 (20%)	12.5
English Literature	250	50 (20%)	12.5

sampling. If, instead, the approach was to sample 5% of each major, this would be sampling proportionately (column 4 of Table 4.1), and the resulting numbers of each major would have likely been obtained using a simple random sampling process.

Systematic sampling can also be a probability random sampling technique if certain conditions are met. In a systematic sample, there needs to be a list of the population. This list must be in a nonbiased order. Therefore, lists of students by the first letter of their last names, or by grade point averages, or by income levels, and so forth, are considered biased. Instead, the list must be in random order. A starting point in the list is randomly selected. Then, every 10th name (or 20th name, etc.) is selected to be in the sample.

Finally, multistage, or cluster, sampling occurs when random samples are selected within other random samples. For example, if we wanted to survey some aspects of 3rd-grade elementary school classrooms, first a random sample of a number of counties from across the country would be selected. Next, within each selected county, a random selection of a certain number of school districts would be made. Then, within the selected school districts, a random selection of a certain number of elementary schools would be made. Finally, within each elementary school a random selection of a certain number of 3rd-grade classrooms would be made. Because each level is randomly sampled, the final sample is random.

Nonprobability Sampling

Often, there does not exist a list of the population to which one wishes to gener-alize one's findings. In this case, nonprobability sampling occurs. One type of nonprobability sample is a quota sample. In this case, relevant demographic char-acteristics of the general population might be known. For example, let's say that, in general, 50% of assistant professors are men and 50% are women, 60% of associate professors are men and 40% are women, and 70% of full professors are men and 30% are women. Further assume that the professorial ranks are distributed as fol-lows: 30% assistant, 50% associate, and 20% full. A quota sample based on a total sample of 100 would be made up of numbers that reflect these demographic differences: 15 men and 15 women assistant professors, 30 men and 20 women associate professors, and 14 men and 6 women full professors. If a sample of 100 professors with these demographic characteristics is surveyed, with no random sampling technique involved, then they do not represent a probability sample.

A *snowball sample* is also nonprobability and begins by the collection of data on one or more contacts usually known to the person collecting the data. At the end of the data collection process (e.g., questionnaire, survey, or interview), the data col-lector asks the respondent to provide contact information for other potential respondents. These potential respondents are contacted and provide more contacts. Snowball sampling is most useful when there are very few methods to secure a list of the population or when the population is unknowable.

Convenience samples are just that—they are made up of those people most conveniently located to the data collector and who are willing to participate. Other terms used for convenience samples are *accidental, fortuitous,* and *opportunity.* Convenience sampling is very common in research based on undergraduate students. Often, students are given course credit for participating or are required to participate in research projects as part of a course requirement. They are not a random sample.

Theoretical or *purposive sampling* is used in theory building or, as it is often called, *grounded theory* work (Glaser & Strauss, 1967). This approach to sampling looks a bit like snowball sampling but is quite different. The data collector might choose to interview or survey an individual about a certain phenomenon, let's say the experience of being laid off from a job. After speaking with this first respondent (a single professional man), the data collector decides that she or he needs to know more about people who are laid off and have a large number of dependents. The collector thus makes a conscious decision that the next interview or survey should be with a married woman with three children who was laid off from a clerical position. Based on the new information from the second respondent, the data collector may find that speaking with a woman from a professional background with few dependents would be useful in understanding the phenomenon of being laid off. All of these interviews would contribute to the generation of a theory about the phenomenon of being laid off. As the data collector speaks with more and more informants, she or he becomes more and more familiar with the various aspects of the phenomenon of being laid off. The sampling stops when no new information is obtained (i.e., theme saturation).

One of the newer techniques available for securing responses to items is via the Internet. Questionnaire data are now often collected using surveys that can be accessed via the World Wide Web. Several issues have been raised regarding this type of data collection process. Specifically, as this is clearly a nonprobability sample, how confident can the researcher be that the data are representative? Gosling, Vazire, Srivastava, and John (2004) examined the strength of six criticisms directed at Web-based studies: (a) Internet samples are not demographically diverse, (b) Internet participants are maladjusted, socially isolated, or depressed, (c) Internet data do not generalize across presentation formats, (d) Internet participants are unmotivated, (e) Internet data are compromised by anonymity of participants, and (f) Internet-based findings differ from those obtained with other methods. They show clearly that five of the six issues are not problematic. The one that is an issue is that Internet data are compromised by anonymity of participants. That is, an individual may respond more than once to the survey. Gosling et al. go on to describe a couple of methods for trying to deal with this concern. Multiple responders can be identified by using the Internet protocol (IP) addresses that the Web server records for each completed questionnaire. If an IP address appears more than once, this could be due to two or more legitimate responders (i.e., members of a household using the same computer). If multiple responses are found, demographic information about the respondents can be checked for differences and a determination can be made regarding whether or not the responses came from one or more individuals. In addition, simply asking respondents if they have already responded to the questionnaire and asking them not to do so more than once has been useful.

All nonprobability samples suffer from the lack of being able to generalize results based on the findings from the sample to a population. Nonprobability samples are fully capable of producing relationships between variables. The computer program used to analyze the data does not know whether or not they came from a random sample. The reasonableness of generalizing results from nonprobability samples to other populations rests on the ability of the writer to convince the reader that the conditions under which the sample was obtained are indeed representative of the population of interest. The strength of the theoretical underpinnings of the relationships and the degree to which the writer is able to rule out alternative explanations of the findings will assist the writer in convincing the reader that the findings can indeed be generalized.

Sample Sizes

One of the most important issues in any statistical procedure or measurement development approach is sample size. This is because tests of statistical significance are affected dramatically by the size of the sample. In turn, the assessment of the psychometric properties of measurement instruments relies heavily on statistical procedures. It is important to be clear at the outset of this section that sample size and sample representativeness are two separate issues. The sampling technique determines how representative a sample is of the population it is supposed to represent. A larger sample may or may not be more representative than a smaller sample. Let's say the population of full-time students at College X is 10,000. You sample 5,000 of them. This is quite large, but what if the sample contained only females although the student body was 50% men and 50% women? Clearly, the size of the sample was not related to its representativeness. The two are different issues.

One of the most common questions in sampling is how large a sample do we need? The answers provided here assume that there is a probability sample to begin with, so be cautious in interpreting the information presented. To answer this question, one must first know the *alpha level, effect size,* and *power.* Some of these may be new terms, so a review of them is warranted. The alpha is straightforward; this is the same alpha from Chapter 1 that corresponds to the willingness to live with a certain amount of error. The usual alpha level in science is 0.05 or 0.01.

The effect size is less easily determined. For some relationships, the effect size in the population can be readily estimated (usually from previous research). For example, in the employee selection literature, the correlation between cognitive ability and job performance is usually around 0.30. Effect size can also be determined from previous experience with measuring a phenomenon in the population. For example, assume that for a 20-item depression-screening instrument in the population, the mean score for nondepressed people is 5 and for depressed people is 15. Because the mean difference is quite large, there is large effect size. The effect size, then, is "the degree to which a phenomenon is present in the population or the degree to which the null hypothesis is false" (Cohen, 1988, pp. 9–10). Cohen makes suggestions for rules of thumb about effect sizes as well (see Table 4.2 for some examples).

Table 4.2   Some Effect Size Conventions

Test Type	Small	Medium	Large
Independent t test (d) $d = \|\bar{X}_1 - \bar{X}_2\|/\sigma$, where σ can be from either group 1 or group 2 as they are assumed to be equal, or, alternatively, a pooled σ can be used	0.20	0.50	0.80
Correlation coefficient (r)	0.10	0.30	0.50
Proportion is 0.50 (g) $g = \|P - 0.50\|$	0.05	0.15	0.25
Chi-square (w) $w = \sqrt{\chi^2/N}$	0.10	0.30	0.50
One-way ANOVA (f) $f = \sqrt{\eta^2/(1 - h^2)}$ where $\eta^2 = SS_{effect}/SS_{total}$	0.10	0.25	0.40

The power level is even more vague, but it is equal to the probability of rejecting the null hypothesis. In other words, the power of a procedure is the degree to which it can be expected that the hypothesis of interest can be supported. A fairly high degree of power is desirable in hypothesis testing, so power in the range of 0.80 is quite typical. However, technical tables often provide examples of power as low as 0.25 and as high as 0.99.

There is a dependency between the alpha level, effect size, power, and sample size. Because researchers have the greatest control over sample size, they are usually most concerned with the requirements for a sample size. So, once the alpha, power, and effect sizes are known, using tables provided in texts such as Cohen (1988) is very straightforward in determining the sample size needed.

For example, suppose we want to examine the correlation between need for achievement and salary. The alpha is set to 0.05, it is known that a medium effect size (0.30) is expected, and the desired power is 0.80. Based on these numbers, one of Cohen's tables could be used to determine that a sample size of 85 is needed to be likely to detect a medium effect with that level of power (see Table 4.3). If the desired power is reduced to 0.75, only 75 participants would be needed. If the expected effect size is large (0.50) and the power is to remain at 0.80, a much smaller sample size ($N = 28$) would be needed. Thus, alpha, power, effect, and sample sizes are intertwined.

While these tables are useful in most instances, some analyses are not as straightforward because sampling distributions of the statistics are not known, and multiple effects (moderated and meditated), also, are not easily captured in the tables. Therefore, some helpful rules of thumb have been developed and used in much of the literature. For example, as noted before, in correlation and regression analyses, about 10 cases per variable is a reasonable expectation. Goldenberg (1992) suggests that in analysis of categorical (i.e., nominal) data, about 20 cases per cell is a reasonable rule of thumb.

Table 4.3   A Power Table of the *N*-Size Needed in a Correlational Analysis

Power Level	$a_2 = 0.05$ $(a_1 = 0.025)$ Effect Size								
	0.10	0.20	0.30	0.40	0.50	0.60	0.70	0.80	0.90
0.25	167	42	20	12	8	6	5	4	3
0.50	385	96	42	24	15	10	7	6	4
0.60	490	122	53	29	18	12	9	6	5
02/3	570	142	63	34	21	14	10	7	5
0.70	616	153	67	37	23	15	10	7	5
0.75	692	172	75	41	25	17	11	8	6
0.80	783	194	85	46	28	18	12	9	6
0.85	895	221	97	52	32	21	14	10	6
0.90	1047	259	113	62	37	24	16	11	7
0.95	1294	319	139	75	46	30	19	13	8
0.99	1828	450	195	105	64	40	27	18	11

Note: Cell entries equal the sample sizes. Table 3.4.1 Panel 5, reprinted with permission (Cohen, 1988, p. 102).

For example, suppose a study of gender, industry type, and need for achievement is conducted, but the data for the need for achievement scores are not normally distributed. It may be wise to categorize the need for achievement scores into three groups: high, medium, and low. The gender variable has two levels (male and female) and industry type has three levels (retail, professional, and managerial). In total, then, there are 18 cells ($3 \times 2 \times 3$). If there should be 20 cases per cell, then 360 cases are needed (18×20). Rules of thumb are not exact; they do, however, provide you with some confidence about the stability of the findings. That is, if the study is replicated with a sample of similar size and characteristics, a similar pattern of results is likely to be found.

Response Rates

Mailed-out surveys, e-mailed-out surveys, and the ever more common Web-based surveys have response rates—that is, fewer are completed than sent out. Because no one knows how many potential respondents came across the survey and did not complete it, the response rate for Web-based surveys is unknowable. Thus, results based on surveys or questionnaires that have been posted at various web sites for data collection should carry a cautionary note about this in the report of findings. One of the things to look for, then, in Web-based survey results, is whether the most appropriate sites were used to access the sample.

A good discussion of the biases associated with nonrespondents when the respondent population is known is provided in Jolliffe (1986). What follows is a brief summary of his general argument. Given a population (N), there will be respondents (Y) and nonrespondents (Z), where $Y + Z = N$. A sample is drawn from N (n), and the number of respondents in this sample is y. The response rate is determined by y/n. The nonrespondents in the sample ($n - y$) come from the nonrespondents in the population (Z). The degree to which the sample of respondents is not representative of the population will bias the statistics associated with the sample. Assume the calculated mean in a respondent group is $\bar{Y}$. The bias is equal to

(4–1) $$\text{Bias} = (Z/N) \times (\bar{Y} - \bar{Z}).$$

The bias is only zero if (a) there are no nonrespondents (i.e., $Z = 0$) or (b) the mean of the population of respondents is equal to the mean of the population of nonrespondents (i.e., $\bar{Y} - \bar{Z} = 0$). This is not likely to be the case (e.g., Fairclough, 1977). Clearly, it is desirable to have as few nonresponses as possible and to have the sample drawn be as representative of the population as is humanly possible.

In surface mail, e-mail, and telephone surveys, there are going to be nonrespondents. It is not possible to say exactly what the response rate will be to any one survey. The literature that has used similar surveys or instruments and similar sampling strategies will give some idea as to what the typical response rate is for a given population to a given type of survey. For example, employee satisfaction surveys often have response rates of about 30%. Response rates to national surveys usually have a much higher rate, in the order of 70%–95% (Madow, Nisselson, & Olkin, 1983).

One common question is, If the usual response rate is known, how many surveys should be sent out to ensure a sample size that is large enough to conduct the analyses? If a power analysis has been done, the number of participants needed is also known. The number of surveys to send is calculated simply by dividing the number needed by the response rate. For example, if a sample size of 150 is needed and the expected response rate is 30%, then 500 surveys (150/0.30 = 500) should be sent out.

In some survey situations, it might be of interest to simply know what percentage of the population has a particular characteristic. For example, it is quite common for municipalities to conduct telephone polls of their constituent groups on an issue. To figure out how many calls need to be made to generate a reasonable sample size, some pieces of information are required: the margin of error willing to be tolerated (the alpha level), the z value associated with that margin of error, and the expected response rate.

Let's suppose we want to find out what proportion of people are for or against closing a daycare facility in a neighborhood, and a telephone poll of the constituents is going to be conducted. Further assume the poll is to be accurate 19 times out of 20 (margin of error or alpha level of 0.05). The z value associated with this level is 1.96. Note that if a more conservative accuracy level was desired (alpha of 0.01), the z value would be 2.58, or if a more liberal accuracy level was desired (alpha of 0.10), the z value would be 1.65. To determine the sample size needed, the proportion that is likely to show the characteristic (p) and not show the characteristic ($1 - p$ or q) must be estimated. In this case, the estimates are the proportion that is likely to be in favor of closing the daycare (p) and the proportion that is likely to be against closing the daycare (q). The most conservative estimate is always provided by $p = 0.50$, and thus it should be used if no information about the expected proportions is known.

The sample size would need to be

(4–2)
$$N = (z^2 \times p \times q)/(\alpha^2). \text{ In this case, then,}$$

$$N = (1.96^2 \times 0.50 \times 0.50)/(0.05^2),$$

$$N = (3.84 \times 0.25)/0.0025,$$

$$N = 0.96/0.0025,$$

$$N = 384.$$

If the p and q values deviate from 0.50, the sample size needed will decrease.

In addition, if the population size is known, a correction factor can be used that will also shrink the sample size needed. Let's say we know that there are 1,500 households in the neighborhood, and this is the population. The correction factor (CF) is

(4–3)
$$CF = [\text{population}/(N + \text{population})]. \text{ So, for this example,}$$

$$CF = [1500/(384 + 1500)],$$

$$CF = [1500/1884],$$

$$CF = 0.80.$$

When the correction factor is applied to the sample size needed, the result is $384 \times 0.80 = 307.2$ (which is then rounded up to 308). So now, rather than 384 households, only 308 households need to be surveyed. This correction factor will have a direct impact on the resources required to conduct the poll. If the population is not known, then the uncorrected sample size must be used.

If it is also known from previous experience that 70% of the households polled will respond, then the number of calls that will have to be made is 440 (308/0.70). After all these calculations have been made, it is possible to plan for how many calls and how much time will be needed to conduct the survey. It is not until this point that the resources needed to carry out the poll can be accurately estimated.

This whole process assumes a simple random sampling process. That is, the 440 households must be sampled at random. The more deviation there is from random sampling, the less confidence that the results will be reflective of the population's attitudes toward closing the daycare.

Missing Data

Missing data are simply a fact of social science life. There are all sorts of reasons data sets are incomplete, and thus how to deal appropriately with missing data has been a source of interest and debate among social scientists. Fortunately, some clear recommendations are well accepted.

Incomplete data result from undercoverage, nonresponses, and item nonresponses. Undercoverage missing data are those data points missing because potential respondents were excluded from a sampling frame when they should not have been. Nonresponse missing data occur when respondents do not provide the requested information or provide information that is not usable. Data that are not usable occur for many reasons: the respondent may not have understood the question, may have been illiterate, or may have just lied. Missing data may be due to respondents mistakenly or on purpose providing no response.

Undercoverage is difficult to detect and thus difficult to remedy. The best advice here is to carefully examine the sampling frame and be as inclusive as possible. For the other types of missing data, one of the most common questions asked is how much can be tolerated. There is no strict rule, although Madow, Nisselson, and Olkin (1983) suggest that few surveys can achieve less than a 5% nonresponse rate, and to expect better is not reasonable. Nonresponses and, if possible, the reasons they occurred must be reported overall.

Madow, Nisselson, and Olkin (1983) also make several recommendations about nonrespondents. First, make the survey as short and effortless as possible. Next, make as many callbacks and follow-ups as resources allow. Plan for nonresponses by training interviewers and surveying early so that time for callbacks is built into the overall survey timeline. Devote part of the survey to capturing information about nonresponses, so that they can be analyzed for effects that might be due to demographics, geographics, time of day, and so forth. Provide incentives for responding and guarantees of privacy so that the potential respondent is more likely to participate. Ensure that the codes for missing and nonresponse data are set up in the database.

In *repeated measures designs* (measures that are taken at two or more times), missing data in second and consecutive follow-ups is due to attrition. There are many reasons for attrition: respondents may move and not leave forwarding contact information, die, refuse to continue to participate, and so forth. Thus, in these types of designs, oversampling in the early stages will help avoid having too few cases for analysis in later stages of the study.

Tabachnick and Fidell (2001) suggest several ways to deal with item nonresponses. They indicate that the pattern of the missing data indicates the relative seriousness of the problem. For example, if 5% of the data points are missing and are scattered randomly throughout the data set, this does not pose a serious problem. The safe approach is to check to ensure that it is random. When a single variable has more than 5% of its data missing, check to see if the cases where the data are missing are different in some important respect (e.g., gender, ethnicity) from cases without the missing data. To do this, just set up an extra column that might be called "missing on variable X" and code the cases 1 for missing and 2 for nonmissing. Then, carry out t tests using the missing variable as the grouping variable on any variable of interest. If there are differences, running the analyses separately for the missing and nonmissing cases might be appropriate.

A draconian approach to missing data is to delete all cases that have any missing data (called *listwise* deletion). This is highly undesirable, as data collection takes a lot of time, effort, and resources. Another option is to delete a single variable entirely from the data set if it has an unusually large number of missing data points. This would be appropriate if the variable is not of theoretical interest. Alternatively, if, for example, 50% of the respondents did not report their marital status, then even if the variable was of interest, it would likely not be included in any analyses.

Another option is to leave the missing data in and run the various analyses only on those cases with all of the data for those analyses (called *pairwise* deletion). So, for example, if data are missing for a case on one variable (say age), but the variable is not being used in a particular analysis (for example, comparing male and female scores on achievement need), then the case would be included for that analysis. However, the case would not be included if males and females were compared on age. This approach may pose problems when trying to equate the results from one analysis to another analysis because the results are, in effect, based on different samples.

Another option is to replace the missing values with estimates. Replacement can take a variety of forms. One of the most common is a *mean substitution*. For example, if one case was missing data on age, the mean age of all the cases in the data set could be determined. The mean value is substituted for the case that was missing data on age. This is quite conservative, as mean values reduce the variability of the variable. However, it does allow the case to be retained. If something is known about the case, a mean score based on that knowledge would be less conservative. For example, if the missing data point for age was a female case, the mean age for the rest of the females in the data set would be substituted rather than the mean age of the men and women combined.

Mean substitution for multi-item measures can be done within the case as opposed to across cases. Let's suppose I have a 20-item scale to assess being a team player. Case number 43 in the data set does not answer Item 6 on the scale. Case 43's average of the other items (1–5, 7–20) can then be used as a best guess for what that case would have responded for the missing Item 6. This approach is more reasonable than taking the average response to Item 6 from all the other respondents. When only a few data points are missing and there are a reasonably large number of items in the scale by which to estimate the missing value, this is a useful approach. For example, this approach would not be appropriate for Case 43 if it was missing data on five items rather than just one. In that instance, it might be more prudent to not include the case in the analysis.

Another estimation procedure is to use prior expert knowledge to estimate the missing data point. This is a valid approach only if the consumer of the analyses findings can be convinced that whoever provided the missing data value is an expert in the field.

Other, more statistically sophisticated, approaches have been developed for handling missing data. These include regression, expectation minimization, multiple imputation, and hot decking. They require specific software to be run, and are useful particularly when there is a pattern to the missing data.

It is advisable to run the analyses with and without the missing data and/or with and without estimated values. Compare the findings and, if the results are similar, more confidence can be placed in them. Indeed, the consumers of such findings will also be more comfortable with any knowledge claims if the results are similar.

Preparing to Analyze Your Data

The first thing to do before analyzing any data is to ensure that the variables are entered properly and that the codes (e.g., 1 = male, 2 = female) are correct. This is particularly important when using archival data that was input by someone else. In addition, I have found it useful to keep outputs of analyses recorded in binders or folders. This is extremely useful if a data set has to be reanalyzed at a later date. Ethical codes require that researchers keep electronic copies of data sets for 5 years for other researchers to peruse as well as for other purposes (e.g., a meta-analysis).

The next thing to do is examine the univariate distributions of the variables. If there is restriction of range or high skew on some variables, subsequent analyses will likely be adversely affected. Some analyses require that the assumptions of homoscedasticity, homogeneity of variance, and homogeneity of variance-covariance (sphericity) are met. When they are not, transforming the variable (square root, logarithm, inverse, etc.) is sometimes recommended. It is not recommended, however, when the variable being used is commonly known and just by fluke it happens that the data set is very strange. However, for scores that are based on arbitrary scales just developed for use, it is legitimate to make such changes.

It is worthwhile to examine scatterplots of correlations to see if the relationships between the variables that had been anticipated to be linear are actually curvilinear, or U-shaped. If this turns out to be the case, linear correlation or linear regression are inappropriate analyses.

It is also important to check the variables for *multicollinearity*. Variables are multicollinear when they are highly correlated (0.90 or above). For example, age and job tenure are highly related variables. It may be most appropriate to use one or the other, but not both, in any analysis. Ensure that the data matrix is not singular. A singular matrix occurs most often when a total score has been created from a set of subscores that are also in the matrix. For example, assume that three subscales of intelligence (spatial intelligence, verbal intelligence, and emotional intelligence) are assessed and that the subscales are summed to provide a general intelligence score. Then, all four of these variables are used in an analysis. In this case, there is a *linear dependency* in the data set (i.e., the general score is completely dependent on the other scores). This occurs with ipsative scores as shown in an earlier chapter, rendering the matrix of such scores inappropriate for many inferential statistical procedures.

Take care in creating new variables. For example, summing across a number of items to get a total score on a test or measure is quite common. Make sure that items are not counted two times for different subscales or for different measures. If they are, then there will be a spuriously high correlation between them. Ensure that reverse-coded items are actually reversed before analyzing the data or creating new variables.

Variables that are dichotomous should be roughly equal in their proportions. For example, in the employee turnover literature, unequal splits in the dichotomous variable of "turned over" (say 10%) versus "remained" (say 90%) are not uncommon. It is much more difficult to detect significant relationships when the data are skewed like this.

Outliers (unusually high or low scores) must be dealt with. Make sure that the outlier is not simply a data entry error. To do this, the original data has to be reexamined to ensure that it was entered correctly. Sometimes, if the data collector can recall the particular respondent, he or she may have noted if the person seemed inattentive or distracted, or was simply goofing off. If this was the case, it would be reasonable to delete the case from the data set. On the other hand, if there is nothing apparently wrong with the case's data, exercise great caution in deleting an outlier. Regardless, examine data for outliers and make some decisions that can be ethically defended in terms of including or not including them in the analyses.

If data are grouped (e.g., a set of data for science majors and a set of data for humanities majors), be sure to check for whether or not collapsing across the groups for analysis or conducting separate analyses for each of them is most appropriate. In some instances, there may be interest in the group differences, but often collapsing across some demographic differences is most efficient. Before doing so, ensure that the means and standard deviations of the groups are not significantly different. Ensure that the relationships with other variables are also comparable. For example, if, for one group, there is a significant and negative relationship between two variables and, for the other, the relationship is significant and positive, collapsing across them will yield a nonsignificant correlation.

Once all the steps involved in collecting and screening data are completed, analyses can begin. It is not unusual to spend several days screening the data, dealing with missing data, making appropriate transformations, and so forth. However, if the analyses are performed without first coming to terms with these important issues, all it means is that the analyses will need to be rerun and time is wasted. Worse, conclusions may be drawn that are inappropriate and will not stand up to scrutiny. So, despite the lengthy process, it is well worth the time and effort to be completely familiar with the data and be prepared to defend any decision made with the data.

Summary and Next Step

This chapter was devoted to issues about data collection: samples, sampling, and data management. The topics covered included

a. the types of samples—particularly the difference between probability and nonprobability samples,

b. issues of sample sizes and response rates,

c. appropriate decision making and handling of missing data, and

d. issues surrounding preparing the data.

The next chapter begins the analysis of data associated with test items. However, before the analysis begins, the theoretical framework of classical test theory will be discussed. This theory has guided test development for the past 150 years.

Problems and Exercises

1. What does a simple random sample mean?

2. What is stratified random sampling and why would one use this approach?

3. What is the difference between proportionate and disproportionate stratified random sampling?

4. What is multistage, or cluster, sampling?

5. What are some types of nonprobability sampling techniques?

6. What is the problem with all nonprobability samples?

7. How could you have a large sample that was not representative?

8. Using Table 4.3 (alpha assumed to be 0.05), what is the sample size needed when the effect size is expected to be 0.10 (small) and the power desired is moderate (0.60)? What is the sample size needed when the effect size is expected to be 0.50 (moderate) and the power desired is high (0.90)?

9. If I know that the usual response rate is 20% to an e-mail survey, and I know I need 100 respondents for my analyses, how many email surveys should I send out?

10. Assume I want to conduct a plebiscite of an entire town about whether or not the citizens want to have their water fluoridated or not. I want to conduct a survey first. If we want our margin of error on the survey to be accurate 9 times out of 10, and do not know what to expect with regard to "yes" or "no," what sample size will we need? What would the sample size be if we knew that the voter population is 5,000? If we knew that people in this community are vocal about their opinions and therefore likely to respond to the survey (e.g., 85%), how many voters will we need to canvass to get the sample size we need?

11. What is undercoverage and why is it a problem?

12. If you have missing information in your data set, how would you determine if it is problematic? What options do you have to deal with the missing data?

13. What are some things to look for in your data set prior to analyzing it?

CHAPTER 5

Classical Test Theory

*Assumptions, Equations,
Limitations, and Item Analyses*

Classical test theory (CTT) has been the foundation for measurement theory for over 80 years. The conceptual foundations, assumptions, and extensions of the basic premises of CTT have allowed for the development of some excellent psychometrically sound scales. This chapter outlines the basic concepts of CTT as well as highlights its strengths and limitations.

Because total test scores are most frequently used to make decisions or relate to other variables of interest, sifting through item-level statistics may seem tedious and boring. However, the total score is only as good as the sum of its parts, and that means its items. Several analyses are available to assess item characteristics. The approaches discussed in this chapter have stemmed from CTT.

Classical Test Theory

Classical test *theory* is a bit of a misnomer; there are actually several types of CTTs. The foundation for them all rests on aspects of a total test score made up of multiple items. Most classical approaches assume that the raw score (X) obtained by any one individual is made up of a true component (T) and a random error (E) component:

$$(5–1) \qquad X = T + E.$$

The true score of a person can be found by taking the mean score that the person would get on the same test if they had an infinite number of testing sessions.

Because it is not possible to obtain an infinite number of test scores, T is a hypothetical, yet central, aspect of CTTs.

Domain sampling theory assumes that the items that have been selected for any one test are just a sample of items from an infinite domain of potential items. Domain sampling is the most common CTT used for practical purposes. The parallel test theory assumes that two or more tests with different domains sampled (i.e., each is made up of different but parallel items) will give similar true scores but have different error scores.

Regardless of the theory used, classical approaches to test theory (and subsequently test assessment) give rise to a number of assumptions and rules. In addition, the overriding concern of CTTs is to cope effectively with the random error portion (E) of the raw score. The less random error in the measure, the more the raw score reflects the true score. Thus, tests that have been developed and improved over the years have adhered to one or another of the classical theory approaches. By and large, these tests are well developed and quite worthy of the time and effort that have gone into them. There are, however, some drawbacks to CTTs and these will be outlined in this chapter as well.

Theory of True and Error Scores: Description and Assumptions

The theory of true and error scores has several assumptions; the first, as was already noted, is that the raw score (X) is made up of a true score (T) plus random error (E). Let's say I was to administer the Team Player Inventory (TPI; Kline, 1999) to myself every day for two years. Sometimes my score would be higher and sometimes lower. The average of my raw scores ($\bar{X}$), however, would be the best estimate of my true score (T).

It is also expected that the random errors around my true score would be normally distributed. That is, sometimes when I took the TPI my scores would be higher (maybe I was in a good mood or had just completed a fantastic team project that day), and sometimes when I took the TPI my scores would be lower (maybe I was tired, distracted, or had just completed a team project that was a flop). Because the random errors are normally distributed, the expected value of the error (i.e., the mean of the distribution of errors over an infinite number of trials) is 0. In addition, those random errors are uncorrelated with each other; that is, there is no systematic pattern to why my scores would fluctuate from time to time. Finally, those random errors are also uncorrelated to the true score, T, in that is there is no systematic relationship between a true score (T) and whether or not that person will have positive or negative errors. All of these assumptions about the random errors form the foundations of CTT.

The standard deviation of the distribution of random errors around the true score is called the *standard error of measurement*. The lower it is, the more tightly packed around the true score the random errors will be. Therefore, one index of the degree of usefulness of the TPI will be its standard error of measurement. Now, you may be thinking, why on earth would anyone want to take the TPI every day for two years? Good question. This is to simulate the notion of taking a test an infinite number of times (50 times, even, would seem pretty infinite!).

An extremely important shift in this approach came when psychometricians demonstrated that the theory of true and error scores developed over *multiple samplings* of the *same person* (i.e., taking the TPI myself 1,000 times) holds over to a *single administration* of an instrument over *multiple persons* (i.e., administering the TPI to a group of 1,000 different people once). The mathematical proofs for this will not be reviewed but can be found in some psychometrics texts (e.g., Allen & Yen, 1979). This new approach speeds things up dramatically, because through the proofs it is possible to collect data once (single administration) on a sample of individuals (multiple persons). The same CTT and assumptions of the true and error scores can now be applied to this sample of TPI scores.

In the latter scenario, of interest is the variance of the raw scores, true scores, and random error across the sample. So instead of taking the TPI for two years to get an estimate of the standard error for one person (e.g., me), I can give it once to 1,000 people and get the same standard error of measurement that will generalize to the population. The equation for this process is as follows:

(5–2)
$$VAR(X) = VAR(T) + VAR(E).$$

Given this, it can be shown that the variance of the observed scores $VAR(X)$ that is due to true score variance $VAR(T)$ provides the reliability index of the test (Equation 5–3).

(5–3)
$$VAR(T)/VAR(X) = R.$$

When the variance of true scores is high relative to the variance of the observed scores, the reliability (R) of the measure will be high (e.g., $50/60 = 0.83$), whereas if the variance of true scores is low relative to the variance of the observed scores, the reliability (R) of the measure will be low (e.g., $20/60 = 0.33$). Reliability values range from 0.00 to 1.00. Rearranging the terms from the above equations, it can be shown that

(5–4)
$$R = 1 - [VAR(E)/VAR(X)].$$

That is, the reliability is equal to 1 – the ratio of random error variance to total score variance. Further, there are analyses that allow for an estimation of R (reliability), and, of course, calculating the observed variance of a set of scores is a straightforward process. Because R and $VAR(X)$ can be calculated, $VAR(T)$ can be solved for with the following equation:

(5–5)
$$VAR(T) = VAR(X) \times R.$$

It is worth reiterating here that CTTs are largely interested in modeling the random error component of a raw score. Some error is *not* random; it is systematic.

Much time and effort has been spent to identify and deal with systematic error in the context of test validity. However, it remains largely undetermined in CTT. As such, systematic errors (such as changes in scores over time due to learning, growth, training, or aging) are not handled well in CTT.

Ramifications and Limitations of Classical Test Theory Assumptions

Embretson and Reise (2000) review the ramifications (or "rules," as they call them) of CTTs. The first is that the standard error of measurement of a test is consistent across an entire population. That is, the standard error does not differ from person to person but is instead generated by large numbers of individuals taking the test, and it is subsequently generalized to the population of potential test takers. In addition, regardless of the raw test score (high, medium, or low), the standard error for each score is the same.

Another ramification is that as tests become longer, they become increasingly reliable. Recall that in domain sampling, the sample of test items that makes up a single test comes from an infinite population of items. Also recall that larger numbers of subjects make the statistics generated by that sample more representative of the population of people than would a smaller sample. These statistics are also more stable than those based on a small sample. The same logic holds in CTT. Larger numbers of items better sample the universe of items and statistics generated by them (such as mean test scores) are more stable if they are based on more items.

Multiple forms of a test (e.g., Form A and Form B) are considered to be parallel only after much effort has been expended to demonstrate their equality (Gulliksen, 1950). Not only do the means have to be equal but also the variances and reliabilities, as well as the relationships of the test scores to other variables. Another ramification is that the important statistics about test items (e.g., their difficulty) depend on the sample of respondents being representative of the population. As noted earlier, the interpretation of a test score is meaningless without the context of normative information. The same holds true in CTT, where statistics generated from the sample can only be confidently generalized to the population from which the sample was drawn.

True scores in the population are assumed to be (a) measured at the interval level and (b) normally distributed. When these assumptions are not met, test developers convert scores, combine scales, and do a variety of other things to the data to ensure that this assumption is met. In CTT, if item responses are changed (e.g., a test that had a 4-point Likert-type rating scale for responses now uses a 10-point Likert-type rating scale for responses), then the properties of the test also change. Therefore, it is unwise to change the scales from their original format because the properties of the new instrument are not known.

The issues around problems with difference and change scores that were discussed in an earlier chapter have their roots in CTT. The problem is that the changes in scores from time one to time two are not likely to be of the same magnitude at all initial levels of scores at time one. For example, suppose at time one, a test of math skills is given (a math pretest) to a group of 100 students. They then have four weeks of math training, after which they are given a posttest. It is likely that there will be more gain for those students who were lower on the test at time one than for those who were higher at time one.

In addition, if item responses are dichotomous, CTT suggests that they should not be subjected to factor analysis. This poses problems in establishing the validity for many tests of cognitive ability, where answers are coded as correct or incorrect.

Finally, once the item stems are created and subjected to content analysis by the experts, they often disappear from the analytical process. Individuals may claim that a particular item stem is biased or unclear, but no statistical procedures allow for comparisons of the item content, or stimulus, in CTT.

Item Analysis Within Classical Test Theory: Approaches, Statistical Analyses, and Interpretation

The next part of this chapter is devoted to the assessment of test items. The approaches presented here have been developed within the theoretical framework of CTT. At the outset, it will be assumed that a test is composed of a number of items and has been administered to a sample of respondents. Once the respondents have completed the test, the analyses can begin. There are several pieces of information that can be used to determine if an item is useful and/or how it performs in relation to the other items on the test.

Descriptive Statistics. Whenever a data set is examined, descriptive statistics come first, and the most common of these are the mean and variance. The same is true for test items. The means and standard deviations of items can provide clues about which items will be useful and which ones will not. For example, if the variance of an item is low, this means that there is little variability on the item and it may not be useful. If the mean response to an item is 4.5 on a 5-point scale, then the item is negatively skewed and may not provide the kind of information needed. Thus, while it is not common to examine item-level descriptive statistics in most research applications, in creating and validating tests it is a crucial first step. Generally, the higher the variability of the item and the more the mean of the item is at the center point of the distribution, the better the item will perform.

Means and variances for items scored on a continuum (such as a five-point Likert-type scale) are calculated simply the way other means and variances are calculated. For dichotomous items, they can be calculated in the same way, but there are derivations that provide much simpler formulae.

The mean of a dichotomous item is equal to the proportion of individuals who endorsed/passed the item (denoted p). The variance of a dichotomous item is calculated by multiplying $p \times q$ (where q is the proportion of individuals who failed, or did not endorse, the item). The standard deviation, then, of dichotomous items is simply the square root of $p \times q$. So, for example, if 500 individuals respond to a yes/no item and 200 respond "yes," then the p value for that item is 200/500, or 0.40. The q is 0.60 ($1.0 - 0.40 = 0.60$). The variance of the item is 0.24 ($0.40 \times 0.60 = 0.24$) and the standard deviation is the square root of 0.24, or 0.49.

Difficulty Level. As noted above, the proportion of individuals who endorse or pass a dichotomous item is termed its p value. This might be somewhat confusing because p has also been used to denote the probability level for a calculated statistic given a particular sample size. To keep them separated, it will be important to keep in mind the context in which p is being used. For this section of the book on item difficulty, p will mean the proportion of individual respondents in a sample that pass/endorse an item.

It is intuitive to grasp that on an achievement test, one can pass an item. It is also the case that many tests of individual differences ask the respondent to agree or disagree with a statement. For example, I might want to assess extroversion by asking the respondent a series of questions that can be answered with a yes (equivalent to a pass on an achievement test) or no (equivalent to a fail on an achievement test). An example of such an item would be, "I enjoy being in social situations where I do not know anyone." The respondent then responds yes or no to each of these types of items. A total score for extroversion is obtained by summing the number of yes responses.

While p is useful as a descriptive statistic, it is also called the item's difficulty level in CTT. Items with high p values are easy items and those with low p values are difficult items. This carries very useful information for designing tests of ability or achievement. When items of varying p values are added up across all items, the total (also called composite) score for any individual will be based on how many items she or he endorsed, or passed.

So what is the optimal p level for a series of items? Items that have p levels of 1.00 or 0.00 are useless because they do not differentiate between individuals. That is, if everyone passes an item, it acts the same as does adding a constant of 1 to everyone's total score. If everyone fails an item, then a constant of 0 is added to everyone's score. The time taken to write the item, produce it, respond to it, and score it is wasted.

Items with p values of 0.50—that is, 50% of the group passes the item—provide the highest levels of differentiation between individuals in a group. For example, if there are 100 individuals taking a test and an item has a p value of 0.50, then there will be 50×50 (2,500) differentiations made by that item, as each person who passed is differentiated from each person who failed the item. An item with a p value of 0.20 will make 20×80 (1,600) differentiations among the 100 test takers. Thus, the closer the p value is to 0.50, the more useful the item is at differentiating among test takers.

The one caveat about the p value of 0.50 being the best occurs when items are highly intercorrelated. If this is the case, then the same 50% of respondents will pass all of the items and one item, rather than the entire test, would have sufficed to differentiate the test takers into two groups. For example, assume I have a class of 20 people and give them a 10-item test comprised of very homogeneous items. Further assume that the p value for all 10 items is 0.50. The same 50% of the 20 students would pass all of the items as would pass only one item. Therefore, this test of 10 items is not any better than a test of one item at differentiating the top and bottom 50% of the class. It is because of this characteristic that test designers usually attempt to create items of varying difficulty with an average p value across the items of 0.50 (Ghiselli, Campbell, & Zedek, 1981).

Some tests are designed deliberately to get progressively more difficult. That is, easy questions are placed at the beginning of a test and the items become more and more difficult. The individual taking the test completes as many items as possible. These adaptive tests are used often in individual testing situations such as in the Wechsler Adult Intelligence Scale (Wechsler, 1981) and in settings where it can be of value to assess an individual quickly by determining where that person's cutoff point is for passing items. Rather than giving the person the entire test with items of varying levels of difficulty interspersed throughout, whether or not the person passes an item determines the difficulty of the next item presented.

Sometimes instructors deliberately put a few easy items at the beginning of a test to get students relaxed and confident so that they continue on and do as well as possible. Most of us have had the negative experience of being daunted by the first question on a test and the lowered motivation and heightened anxiety this can bring. Thus, instructors should be quite conscious of the difficulty level of items presented early on in a testing situation.

Discrimination Index. Using the p values (difficulty indices), discrimination indices (D) can be calculated for each dichotomous item. The higher the D, the more the item discriminates. Items with p levels in the midrange usually have the best D values and, as will be demonstrated shortly, the opportunity for D to be highest occurs when the p level for the item is at 0.50.

The extreme group method is used to calculate D. There are three simple steps to calculating D. First, those who have the highest and lowest overall test scores are grouped into upper and lower groups. The upper group is made up of the 25%–33% who are the best performers (have the highest overall test scores), and the lower group is made up of the bottom 25%–33% who are the poorest performers (have the lowest overall test scores). The most appropriate percentage to use in creating these extreme groups is to use the top and bottom 27% of the distribution, as this is the critical ratio that separates the tail from the mean of the standard normal distribution of response error (Cureton, 1957).

Step two is to examine each item and determine the p levels for the upper and lower groups, respectively. Step three is to subtract the p levels of the two groups; this provides the D. Table 5.1 shows an example for a set of four items. Assume that these data are based on 500 individuals taking a test that is 50 items in length. The highest scoring 135 individuals (500×0.27) for the entire test and lowest scoring 135 individuals for the entire test now make up our upper and lower extreme groups. For Item 1, the upper group has a p level of 0.80 and the lower group has a p level of 0.30. The D, then, is $0.80 - 0.30 = 0.50$. For Item 2, the D is 0.80; for Item 3, it is 0.05; and for Item 4, it is -0.60.

Table 5.1   Example of Item Discrimination Indices

Item	p Level for Upper Group	p Level for Lower Group	D
1	0.80	0.20	0.60
2	0.90	0.10	0.80
3	0.60	0.55	0.05
4	0.10	0.70	−0.60

Items 1 and 2 have reasonable discrimination indices. The values indicate that those who had the highest test scores were more likely to pass the items than individuals with low overall scores. Item 3 is very poor at discriminating; although 60% of those in the upper group passed the item, almost as many (55%) in the lower group passed the item. Item 4 is interesting—it has a negative D value. In tests of achievement or ability, this would indicate a poor item in that those who scored most highly on the test overall were not likely to pass the item, whereas those with low overall scores were likely to pass the item. However, in assessment tools of personality, interests, or attitudes, this negative D is not problematic. In these types of tests, it is often of interest to differentiate between types or groups, and items with high D values (positive or negative) will help in differentiating those groups.

Using p Levels to Plot Item Curves. A technique of item analysis that foreshadowed modern test theory was developed in 1960. The Danish researcher Rasch plotted total test scores against pass rates for items on cognitive tests. These curves summarized how an individual at an overall performance level on the test did on any single item. Item curves using p levels provided more fine-grained information about the item than just the p level overall or the discrimination index did.

Figure 5.1 shows examples of item curves for four separate items. Assume that the entire test was 50 items in length and that 200 students took the test. Then the 200 students were separated into percentiles with cutoffs placed at the 10th, 20th, and so forth to the 99th percentile performance for the entire test. Each of the percentiles is plotted against the p level associated with that item for that percentile.

Note that for Item 1, as the performance of the students on the test increased (i.e., they are in the higher percentile groups), the performance on the item increased. However, at the 50th percentile, the increased p levels slowed. This indicates that up to the 50th percentile level, as overall test performance increased, the pass rate increased in a monotonic linear fashion. After the 50th percentile, as test performance increased, so did the pass rate for the item. However, the curve is not as steep, and thus the item did not discriminate between individuals as well at the upper end of the overall test distribution as it did for those at the lower end.

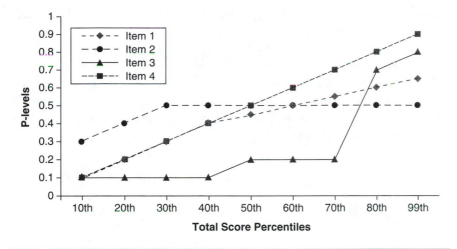

Figure 5.1   Item Curves Based on *p* Levels

Item 2 starts off with more difficulty because the *p* level for the lowest group is 0.30. The slope moves up over the next two percentile levels but after that, the line is flat. This indicates a relatively poorly discriminating item at the lower end of the performance continuum and a nondiscriminating item at the mid- to upper-performance levels.

Item 3 shows relatively little difference in *p* level until one gets to the 80th percentile level. At this point, there is a sharp spike, indicating that the item is particularly good at discriminating between the 70th and 80th percentile students. Finally, Item 4 is a straight line. As the overall performance increases (i.e., percentile) the *p* level increases at a steady rate.

Item-to-Total Correlations. Another assessment of items related to its discrimination index is the Pearson product-moment item-to-total correlation coefficient. For dichotomous items, the Pearson point-biserial or Pearson biserial correlation coefficients are available. The underlying question addressed by each coefficient is the same: How do responses to an item relate to the total test score?

For all three statistics, the relationships between how individuals responded to each item are correlated with the *corrected* total score on the test. The correction is made insofar as the total score does not include the response to the item in question. This is an appropriate correction because total scores that have the item in question embedded within them will have a spuriously higher relationship (i.e., correlation) than total scores made up of only the other items in the test. This correction is particularly important when there are only a few test items—say five or six. However, if a test has 100 items, the influence of any one item on the total score is minimal. There is no rule for how many items should be included before the item has little influence, so it is better to be conservative in the estimates and use the corrected score.

Which version of the Pearson is appropriate? Assume there are 10 items in a scale and each is responded to on a seven-point Likert-type scale. Responses to each item are then correlated to the corrected total scores for each test taker. This is the same as having two continuous variables, and the Pearson product-moment correlation is the right one to use. Table 5.2 shows an example of the vector for one item that is responded to on a four-point Likert-type scale (strongly disagree = 1, disagree = 2, agree = 3, and strongly agree = 4) and a vector of the corrected total scores on a 10-item test across 20 participants.

Table 5.2   Two Continuous Variables Used in Calculating Item-to-Total Correlations for Item 1 of a 10-Item Test

Participant	Four-Point Likert-Type Response	Total Score[a]
1	3	34
2	4	30
3	4	32
4	2	15
5	3	20
6	3	27
7	4	31
8	1	12
9	4	23
10	3	25
11	2	18
12	1	11
13	1	15
14	3	27
15	2	20
16	2	19
17	2	20
18	1	16
19	4	25
20	1	32

a. The total score is corrected so that it does not include the score from Item 1.

One of the hand calculations for the Pearson product-moment correlation coefficient when the variance of the variables is readily at hand is

(5–6)
$$r = [\Sigma XY/n - (\bar{X})(\bar{Y})]/(\sigma_x \times \sigma_y),$$

where $\Sigma XY/n$ = the mean of the sum of cross-products of variable X (item score) and variable Y (total score), $\bar{X}$ = the mean of the scores on the X variable, $\bar{Y}$ = the mean of the scores on the Y variable, σ_x = the standard deviation of scores on the X variable, and σ_y = the standard deviation of scores on the Y variable.

Substituting the appropriate values from Table 5.2, we get the following equation:

$$r = [61.65 - (2.5)(22.6)]/(1.15 \times 7.04),$$
$$= 5.15/8.10,$$
$$= 0.64.$$

Thus, the item-to-total correlation for this item is 0.64.

If the responses represent a true dichotomy (e.g., yes/no; agree/disagree; pass/fail), then this means there is a vector of 1s and 0s for each of the items and a continuous score for the total score on the test. A true dichotomy is one where the categorization really has only two possible alternatives for a single item (e.g., male/female; married/single; yes/no; pass/fail). In this case, the Pearson point-biserial item-to-total correlation coefficient is the appropriate statistic.

If the responses represent a false dichotomy, then there will still be a vector of 1s and 0s for each of the items and a continuous score for the total score on the test. In this instance, however, the Pearson biserial item-to-total correlation coefficient is the appropriate statistic. A false dichotomy is one where an arbitrary decision has been made to force a continuous variable into a dichotomous one. For example, if someone passes or fails a test, the test taker does so because she or he has made or not made it past a particular cutoff score. That cutoff score is arbitrarily set. Similarly, if scores on a four-point Likert-type scale (strongly disagree, disagree, agree, and strongly agree) are grouped into two categories (strongly agree and agree = 1; disagree and strongly disagree = 0), this is a false dichotomy.

It is important to note that computer programs will *not* recognize the difference between 1s and 0s that represent a true dichotomy and those that represent a false dichotomy. It is up to the researcher to know the difference and specify the correct analysis. If the point-biserial equation is used when the biserial was supposed to be, it will underestimate the true strength of the relationship. This is because the biserial correlation takes into account that underlying the 1s and 0s is a normal distribution of scores. One popular computer program (SPSS) does not calculate biserial correlation coefficients. However, the hand calculations of the point-biserial and biserial correlations are not difficult. An example of how to carry them out is shown next.

Table 5.3 shows a vector of dichotomous item responses and a vector of the corrected total scores on a 10-item test across 20 participants. First, assume that the responses are 1 = yes and 0 = no; thus, we have a true dichotomy and use the point-biserial correlation coefficient.

The hand-calculation formula for the point-biserial correlation coefficient is

(5–7)
$$r_{pbis} = [(\overline{Y}_1 - \overline{Y})/\sigma_y] \times \sqrt{p_x/q_x}$$

where $\overline{Y}_1$ = the mean of the total test scores for those whose dichotomous response was 1, $\overline{Y}$ = the mean of the total test scores for the whole sample, σ_y = the standard deviation of all scores on the total test, p_x = the proportion of individuals whose dichotomous response was 1, and q_x = the proportion of individuals whose dichotomous response was 0.

Table 5.3   One Dichotomous and One Continuous Variable Used in Calculating Item-to-Total Correlations for Item 1 of a 10-Item Test

Participant	Dichotomous Response	Total Score[a]
1	1	9
2	1	8
3	1	7
4	0	5
5	1	6
6	1	4
7	1	7
8	0	2
9	1	5
10	1	8
11	0	3
12	0	2
13	0	4
14	1	5
15	0	1
16	0	3
17	0	2
18	0	4
19	1	9
20	0	2

a. The total score is corrected so that it does not include the score from Item 1.

Substituting the correct values into the equation,

$$r_{pbis} = [(6.8 - 4.8)/2.53] \times \sqrt{0.5/0.5},$$
$$= (2/2.53) \times \sqrt{1},$$
$$= 0.79 \times 1,$$
$$= 0.79. \text{ Thus, the item-to-total correlation for this item is } 0.79.$$

Now assume that the responses to the "dichotomous" item have been converted from the responses in Table 5.2, where a 1 or 2 = 0 and a 3 or 4 = 1. This is the *same* data that was used to calculate the point-biserial, but the data represent a false dichotomy, so the biserial correlation coefficient is needed. The hand-calculation formula for the biserial correlation coefficient is

(5–8) $$r_{bis} = [(\bar{Y}_1 - \bar{Y})/\sigma_y)] \times (p_x/\text{ordinate}),$$

where $\bar{Y}_1$ = the mean of the total test scores for those whose dichotomous response was 1, $\bar{Y}$ = the mean of the total test scores for the whole sample, σ_y = the standard deviation of scores for the whole sample on the total test, p_x = the proportion of individuals whose dichotomous response was 1, and ordinate = the ordinate (y-axis value) of the normal distribution at the z value above which p_x cases fall.

In this case, the p_x is equal to 0.50. The corresponding z value above which 50% of the distribution lies is 0.00. The ordinate value (height of the curve on the y-axis) associated with a z value of 0.00 is 0.3989. So, substituting into the formula,

$$r_{bis} = [(6.8 - 4.8)/2.53] \times (0.50/0.3989),$$
$$= 0.79 \times 1.25,$$
$$= 0.99.$$

Thus, the item-to-total correlation for this item is 0.99. Notice that the biserial correlation with the exact same data is much higher (0.99) than the point-biserial value (0.79).

Item assessment interpretation using any of the Pearson correlation coefficients is similar to the usual interpretation of this statistic. For all three versions, the values range from −1.00 to +1.00. Negative values indicate that the item is negatively related to the other items in the test. This is not usually desirable as most tests try to assess a single construct or ability. Items with low correlations indicate that they do not correlate, or "go with," the rest of the items in the data set. In addition, be forewarned that items that have very high or very low p levels have a restriction of range and thus will also have low item-to-total correlations. It is best to have midrange to high item-to-total correlations (say 0.50 and above).

Item-to-Criterion Correlations. Another index of item utility is to examine its relationship with other variables of interest. For example, suppose an item on an interest inventory asks the respondent to indicate yes or no to the following item: "I enjoy studying biology," and this item is administered to a group of high school seniors. Their responses (1 = yes and 0 = no) are correlated with scores on the same item answered by a group of physicians. If the correlation is high, then the item is said to discriminate between individuals who have similar interests to physicians and those who do not. If the correlation is low, then the item is said not to discriminate between individuals who have similar interests to physicians and those who do not.

As another example, consider an item on an employee selection instrument (e.g., "I always complete my work on time") and correlate it with an aspect of job performance (e.g., "completes jobs assigned in a timely manner"). If the correlation is high, then the item relates well to that aspect of job performance. If the correlation is low, then the item does not relate well to that aspect of job performance.

Inter-Item and Item-to-Criterion Paradox. There is an unusual paradox in scale development and use around the notions of inter-item correlations and correlations between items and external (criterion) variables. That is, if a scale is created that is highly homogeneous, then the items will have high intercorrelations. If a scale is created deliberately to capture heterogeneous constructs so that the items can be related to scores on a multifaceted criterion such as job performance, then the items will have low inter-item correlations but the total score is likely to relate well to the multifaceted criterion. Always be conscious of exactly what the scores on a test are to be used for. When they are used in a manner not consistent with the design of the scale, unusual findings may result.

Here is a concrete example. Suppose you design a test of cognitive reading ability and it is designed to be homogeneous. This test is then used to select graduate students into a program. The criterion measure used is supervisor ratings of overall student performance. When the two are correlated, the relationship between them is small (say 0.15). The problem is not necessarily with the test; the problem is that the criterion is multifaceted and this was not taken into account. Specifically, overall student performance ratings would likely encompass diligence in working on research, performance in statistics as well as verbally loaded courses, teaching ability, ability to get along with others, volunteering for tasks, and so forth. Cognitive reading ability (i.e., your test) would be better related to performance in verbally loaded courses and none of the other tasks.

Differential Item Weighting. Differential item weighting occurs when items are given more or less weight when being combined into a total score. This is in contrast to unit-weighting items, where each item has a weight of 1.0 (i.e., effectively contributing equally to the total score). There are several different options for assigning weights to items (e.g., Ghiselli, Campbell, & Zedek, 1981). The first group of techniques is based on statistical grounds. For example, the reliability of items can be calculated and then the reliabilities can be used to assign different weights to the items. Items with higher reliabilities carry more weight in the total score. Another option would be to use a criterion measure and regress the criterion on the items and use the resulting regression weights as the basis for item weighting. Again, those with higher weights are, in turn, weighted more heavily in generating the total score. Another way to decide on weights is to run a factor analysis and use the factor loadings to assign weights to the items. Finally, item-to-total correlation coefficients can be used to weight the items.

Alternatively, theory or application may drive the decision making, and items that are deemed by some decision rule (e.g., majority or consensus) to be more important or meaningful are given more weight. For example, if there is a 10-item assessment of instruction for a course, and "organization" and "fairness" are perceived by stakeholders to be more important than "punctuality" or "oral skills," then the items can be weighted accordingly when obtaining a total score on teaching effectiveness.

While much effort goes into discussing and determining differential item weights, Ghiselli, Campbell, and Zedek (1981) are persuasive in arguing that differential item weighting has virtually no effect on the reliability and validity of the overall total scores. Specifically, they say that "empirical evidence indicates that reliability and validity are usually not increased when nominal differential weights are used" (p. 438). The reason for this is that differential weighting has its greatest impact when there (a) is a wide variation in the weighting values, (b) is little intercorrelation between the items, and (c) are only a few items. All three are usually the opposite of what is likely to occur in test development. That is, if the test is developed to assess a single construct, then if the developer has done the job properly, items will be intercorrelated. As a result, the weights assigned to one item over another are likely to be relatively small. In addition, tests are often 15 or more items in length, thus rendering the effects of differential weighting to be minimized. Finally, the correlation between weighted and unit-weighted test scores is almost 1.0. Thus, the take-home message is pretty simple—don't bother to differentially weight items. It is not worth the effort.

Summary

This chapter reviewed the basic tenets of classical test theory and also the types of analyses that can be used to assess items within classical test theory. The chapter covered

a. the assumptions, ramifications, and limitations of classical test theory;

b. interpretations of item descriptive statistics and discrimination indices;

c. plots of item curves using pass rates;

d. correlations between items and the total test score and between items and external criteria; and

e. a brief description and comment on the utility of differential item weighting.

In the next chapter, modern test theory is presented as well as item analyses associated with that theoretical framework.

Problems and Exercises

1. What are the components in the equation $X = T + E$ and what do they mean?

2. What are the components in the equation $R = 1 - [\text{VAR}(E)/\text{VAR}(X)]$ and what do they mean?

3. What are the components in the equation $VAR(T) = VAR(X) \times R$, what do they mean, and why is this equation so important?

4. What is meant by the term *random error* in classical test theory?

5. How is the standard error of measurement of a test interpreted across multiple individuals' test scores in classical test theory?

6. How does the "law of large numbers" regarding test length manifest itself in classical test theory?

7. Calculate the mean, variance, and standard deviation of a test item where there were 200 respondents and 50 passed the item.

8. What is the p level of a dichotomous item and at what value does it make the highest discrimination?

9. How many discriminations in a sample of 500 test takers will an item with a p level of 0.40 make?

10. Calculate the discrimination index for an item with the lowest group having a p level of 0.10 and the highest group having a p level of 0.80.

11. What is "corrected" in an item-to-total correlation coefficient?

12. What is the difference between a point-biserial and a biserial correlation coefficient?

13. Calculate the point-biserial (assuming a true dichotomy) and biserial (assuming a false dichotomy) correlations for an item with the following statistics:

    Mean of the continuous variable using all test taker scores = 10

    Standard deviation of the continuous variable using all test taker scores = 7

    Mean of the continuous variable for those who passed the items = 13

    Proportion of those who passed the item = 0.80

    Proportion of those who failed the item = 0.20

    Ordinate of the z value for 40% = 0.3867

14. If an item on a pretest correlates with overall score of 0.70 (and is significant) in a course, how would one interpret this?

CHAPTER 6

Modern Test Theory

*Assumptions, Equations,
Limitations, and Item Analyses*

T his chapter continues the assessment of tests at the item level. However, a new theoretical approach will be used in this chapter called modern test theory. While classical test theory (CTT) approaches to item analyses are still pervasively used today, the additional utility of modern test theory—referred to as item response theory (IRT)—principles and practices cannot be overstated.

Interestingly, IRT has been around since the mid-twentieth century. However, it has not been until relatively recently (i.e., the past 15 years) that IRT computer programs have made IRT analysis and interpretation possible for most test developers or users. This chapter will outline the basic concepts of modern test theory as well as highlighting its strengths and limitations. In addition, several models of test item assessment are presented.

Modern Test Theory

Although CTT has brought testing a long way, there are clear shortcomings in the various models. Modern test theory developed in part to address some of them. Modern test theory really got underway with the seminal work by Lord and Novik (1968). They provided the impetus for a new way of conceptualizing testing as well as the approach to the assessment of tests and items called IRT. Another 20 years elapsed before IRT was popularized by the spread of computer programs needed to do the extraordinarily large number of computations for these analyses. IRT programs are still much more traditional and "user-unfriendly" than many commercially available statistical packages. As they become more accessible, the use of IRT will likely increase.

The focus of CTT is most often on the single score that one obtains on a test. It treats all items as though they were parallel. The focus of IRT is on the pattern of responses that the respondent makes to the set of items, and it does not assume that all items on the test are parallel. Thus, CTT and IRT provide different and complementary ways to examine responses to a series of items. Both techniques are useful in test and item design and assessment.

The fundamental assumption in IRT is that there is a linkage between a response to any item on a test and the characteristic being assessed by the test. The characteristic is called a *latent trait* and it is denoted by the symbol theta (Θ). The linkage is that the probability of a positive response to any single item on a test is a function of the individual's Θ level. That is, if I have a high Θ in math ability, then I will have a high probability of getting a math item correct. Conversely, if I have a low Θ in math ability, then I will have a low probability of getting a math item correct. Similarly, if I am a great team player, then I will have a high probability of endorsing a team player item.

The critical feature that is analyzed in IRT models is the entire pattern of responses to all test items by an individual. Many parameters are estimated simultaneously, and so IRT usually requires a large sample of items (20 or more) per test as well as a large sample of respondents (usually a few hundred) for results to be stable.

Because IRT is focused on patterns of item responses, it is substantially different from CTT that focuses on the raw score of the test as a whole. IRT allows for the assessment of measurement error at any level of Θ. This is different from CTT that assumes that the error of measurement is the same at every level of test score. Because of this approach, IRT can assist in developing a test where there is empirically demonstrated consistency in measurement error across all Θ levels. In addition, through IRT analyses, *peaked* tests, or tests that maximally discriminate at specific levels of Θ, can be constructed.

One of the more interesting features of IRT is that neutral response categories (e.g., the "neither agree nor disagree" alternative in a Likert-type scale) can be determined to be actually a neutral choice or, instead, a category individuals use randomly. IRT allows for accurate assessments of item bias against or for selected subgroups. It allows for accurate assessment of how well new items mimic older items in a test and how well new forms equate with older forms. Unusual response patterns by test takers are easy to identify in IRT models; for example, inattentiveness or faking is much easier to detect in IRT than with CTT.

IRT has found tremendous use in computer adaptive testing, where an item of moderate difficulty is presented to the respondent. Whether the respondent answers correctly or not determines the difficulty of the next item presented. This shortens the test-taking time considerably by presenting items that are in the respondent's capability range and allows for a more accurate estimate of the respondent's Θ.

Models

It will be best here to begin to model some items and afterward to review the assumptions, ramifications, and limitations of IRT, as many of the terms used will require the reader to be familiar with the models first. Response categories for IRT can be dichotomous (two response categories), polytomous (more than two ordered response categories—like Likert-type scales), nominal (more than two nonordered response categories such as in a multiple-choice test), partially credited (scored giving partial credit for correct responses), and multidimensional.

Most modern test theory applications assume unidimensionality (the test assesses a single construct) and so the models presented here do so as well. While multidimensional models are possible, they are much less frequently used.

One-Parameter Logistic Model. The most basic model in IRT is the one-parameter logistic model (1PL). This is sometimes referred to as the Rasch model in deference to the Danish mathematician who developed it (1960). The item parameter that is estimated in 1PL models is the *difficulty* (also known as the *location* or *threshold*) parameter, labeled *b*. The *b* is scaled using a distribution with a mean of 0.0 and standard deviation of 1.0. Note that Θ is also scaled on a normal distribution so that the mean is 0.00 and standard deviation is 1.00. Therefore, items with higher *b* values are "more difficult" insofar as the respondent must have a higher level of Θ to pass or endorse the item than items with low *b* values. For example, if there are two items, one with a *b* value of 1.0 and one with a *b* value of −1.0, the probability that someone with slightly above average ability ($\Theta = 0.20$) will pass the items can be calculated. The formula used to solve the problems is

(6–1) $$P_i(\Theta) = 1/\{1 + \exp[-D(\Theta - b_i)]\},$$

where $P_i(\Theta)$ = the probability for a person with a defined level of Θ to pass the item, $D = 1.702$ (a constant that converts the logistic item curve to a normal give [S-shaped] curve), $\exp(x)$ = the expotentiate (an irrational constant [2.718] that is raised to a given power—the value calculated in braces []), *b* is the item difficulty parameter, and Θ = the ability level for the respondent.

Here are a couple of examples. First, substitute when the item parameter *b* value is 1.0 (a difficult item) and $\Theta = 0.20$:

$$P_i(0.20) = 1/\{1 + \exp[-1.702(2 - 1.0)]\},$$
$$P_i(0.20) = 1/\{1 + \exp[-1.702(-0.8)]\},$$
$$P_i(0.20) = 1/(1 + \exp[1.3616]),$$
$$P_i(0.20) = 1/(1 + 3.902),$$
$$P_i(0.20) = 1/4.902,$$
$$P_i(0.20) = 0.20.$$

Next, substitute when the item parameter *b* value is −1.0 (an easy item) and $\Theta = 0.20$:

$$P_i(0.20) = 1/\{1 + \exp[-1.702(2 - 1.0)]\},$$
$$P_i(0.20) = 1/\{1 + \exp[-1.702(120)]\},$$
$$P_i(0.20) = 1/(1 + \exp[-2.0424]),$$
$$P_i(0.20) = 1/(1 + 0.1297),$$
$$P_i(0.20) = 1/1.1297,$$
$$P_i(0.20) = 0.89.$$

Thus, a person with an above-average ability ($\Theta = 0.20$), will have a 20% chance of passing the difficult item ($b = 1.0$) and an 89% chance of passing the easy item ($b = -1.0$).

Figure 6.1 shows three item characteristic curves created using the 1PL model, with three b levels (-1.0, 0.0, and $+1.0$). Note several things about these curves. First, they are normal ogive (S-shaped) curves. This means that the upper and lower asymptotes (ends) never reach the highest and lowest points on the graph. The y-axis indicates the probability of passing the item. The lowest point is 0.00 and the highest is 1.00. The x-axis shows the latent trait, or Θ level, and usually ranges from +3.00, although +4.00 is possible. Note, also, that the slopes or steepness of the curves are all equivalent (slopes = 1.0). This is because the 1PL model assumes equal slopes for all items.

For 1PL models, the point at which the slope is most steep is at the point of the b value parameter. This means that the item is most informative for individuals who have Θ levels right around the b value. At this point in the curve, very small increments in Θ result in very large changes in the probability of passing the item. At the flatter ends of the curve, large changes in Θ are needed to change the probability of passing the item to any meaningful extent. Also, in the 1PL model, the b parameter is the point at which an individual with an average Θ level (0.00) will have a 50% chance of passing the item.

Two-Parameter Logistic Model. The next, more complicated, model is the two-parameter logistic (2PL) model. In this model, all items are not assumed to have equal

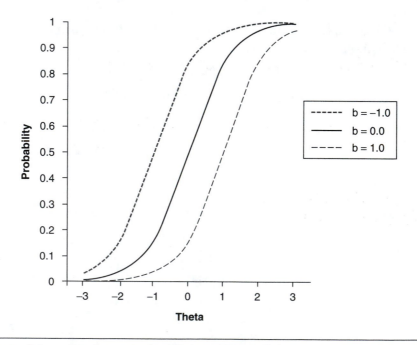

Figure 6.1   One-Parameter Logistic Item Characteristic Curves

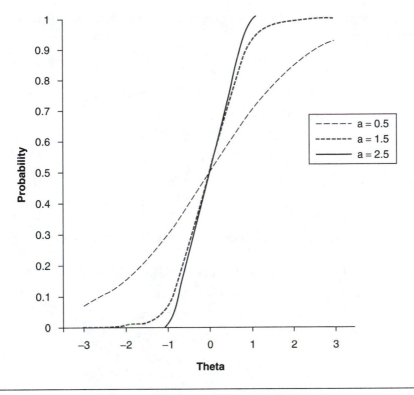

Figure 6.2   Two-Parameter Logistic Item Characteristic Curves

slopes. In fact, the slope is a critical feature of any item insofar as it indicates the discrimination level of the item, and it is denoted *a*. Items with higher *a* values have steeper slopes and discriminate more in the middle of the Θ level range. Items with lower *a* values have flatter slopes and discriminate more at the ends of the Θ level range. The usual range of *a* values is from 0.5 to 2.5. Figure 6.2 shows three item characteristic curves with equal *b* levels (0.0) but with different *a* values (0.5, 1.5, and 2.5).

As with the 1PL model, the *b* parameter in the 2PL model is the point at which an individual with an average Θ level (0.00) will have a 50% chance of passing the item.

In addition, if we know the Θ level for an individual and know the *a* value and *b* value parameters for an item, we can calculate the probability that the person will pass the item. The formula for the 2PL model is very similar to the 1PL model, with the exception that $-D$ is multiplied by the *a* value parameter for the given item:

(6–2) $$P_i(\Theta) = 1/\{1 + \exp[-Da_i(\Theta - b_i)]\}.$$

Note that when the *a* value is equal to 1.0, it has the effect of reducing the equation to be the same as that for the 1PL model. Again, let's work through a couple of examples to highlight the role of the *a* value. First, substitute when the item parameters are $b = 0.15$ and $a = 1.8$, assuming a slightly below Θ level for a respondent (i.e., -0.20):

$$P_i(-0.2) = 1/\{1 + \exp[(-1.702 \times 1.8)(-0.2 - 0.15)]\},$$
$$P_i(-0.2) = 1/\{1 + \exp[(-1.702 \times 1.8)(-0.35)]\},$$
$$P_i(-0.2) = 1/\{1 + \exp[(-3.0636)(-0.35)]\},$$
$$P_i(-0.2) = 1/[1 + \exp(1.07226)],$$
$$P_i(-0.2) = 1/(1 + 2.922),$$
$$P_i(-0.2) = 1/3.922,$$
$$P_i(-0.2) = 0.25.$$

Here is another example using a less discriminating item ($a = 0.5$):

$$P_i(-0.2) = 1/\{1 + \exp[(-1.702 \times 0.5)(-0.2 - 0.15)]\};$$
$$P_i(-0.2) = 1/\{1 + \exp[(-1.702 \times 0.5)(-0.35)]\};$$
$$P_i(-0.2) = 1/\{1 + \exp[(-0.851)(-0.35)]\};$$
$$P_i(-0.2) = 1/[1 + \exp(0.29785)];$$
$$P_i(-0.2) = 1/(1 + 1.347);$$
$$P_i(-0.2) = 1/2.347;$$
$$P_i(-0.2) = 0.43.$$

Thus, a person with a slightly below average ability level ($\Theta = -0.20$) will have a 25% chance of passing a slightly difficult item ($b = 0.15$) when the discrimination index is relatively high ($a = 1.8$). This same person, with an item of the same difficulty, will have a 43% chance of passing when the discrimination index is low ($a = 0.5$). It should be clear from this example that the discrimination index does provide a lot of information about an item.

In fact, a set of items that varies only in its difficulty parameters, *not* in its discrimination parameters, provides no more information about an individual's ability than simply using the total number of items correct on the test as a whole.

Three-Parameter Logistic Model. The three-parameter logistic (3PL) model is the most complex of the dichotomous response models and adds a c parameter. The c value is a guessing parameter. This parameter is useful when items are constructed so that guessing the correct answer is possible, even at very low Θ levels. For multiple-choice and true-false item formats, the 3PL model needs to be used. The 3PL model is also helpful in determining if a response style such as social desirability or faking good is occurring. In these instances, individuals with low Θ levels would still be expected to endorse (pass) certain items (those susceptible to response-style bias).

Guessing parameters can be set to a particular value in advance of the analysis. For example, in a multiple-choice test with four alternatives per item, the estimate

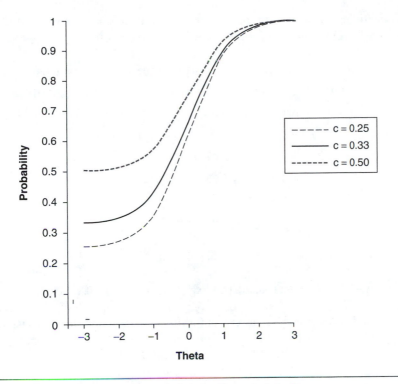

Figure 6.3   Three-Parameter Logistic Item Characteristic Curves

of the c value parameter would be 1/4, or 0.25. Some computer programs demand that the c value parameter be fixed to such a value and remain at that level for all items. For other programs, this is just used as the starting value for the parameter estimation and the final values for each item are allowed to differ. Figure 6.3 shows three item characteristic curves with equal b levels (0.0) and a values (1.0) but different c values (0.25, 0.33, and 0.50).

Notice that the 50% probability for passing the item is higher than at an average Θ level (i.e., 0.0). That is, item difficulty has a different meaning for 3PL models than for 1PL and 2PL models. Item difficulty still occurs at the inflection point of the item characteristic curve, but it is *not* at the Θ level where the respondent has a 50% probability of passing the item. The difficulty is shifted based on the new, lower asymptote (c value). In addition, you might notice that those with high Θ levels are disadvantaged by c level parameters greater than zero. The upper asymptote is not reached as quickly for any of these curves as they are for those in Figures 6.1 and 6.2.

As with the 1PL and 2PL models, if we know the Θ level for an individual and know the a, b, and c value parameters for an item, the probability that the person will pass the item can be calculated. The formula is very similar to the 2PL model, with the exception that the c value is incorporated:

(6–3) $$P_i(\Theta) = c_i + (1 - c_i)/\{1 + \exp[-Da_i(\Theta - b_i)]\}.$$

Substituting when the item parameters are $b = 0.05$, $a = 1.1$, and $c = 0.33$ and assuming a slightly below Θ level for a respondent (i.e., -0.10),

$$P_i(-0.1) = 0.33 + (1 - 0.33)/\{1 + \exp[(-1.702 \times 1.1)(-0.1 - 0.05)]\},$$
$$P_i(-0.1) = 0.33 + (0.67)/\{1 + \exp[(-1.702 \times 1.1)(-0.1 - 0.05)]\},$$
$$P_i(-0.1) = 0.33 + (0.67)/\{1 + \exp[(-1.8722)(-0.1 - 0.05)]\},$$
$$P_i(-0.1) = 0.33 + (0.67)/[1 + \exp(0.28083)],$$
$$P_i(-0.1) = 0.33 + (0.67)/(1 + 1.324),$$
$$P_i(-0.1) = 0.33 + (0.67)/(2.324),$$
$$P_i(-0.1) = 0.33 + 0.288,$$
$$P_i(-0.1) = 0.62.$$

Substituting a lower guessing parameter, $c = 0.25$,

$$P_i(-0.1) = 0.25 + (1 - 0.25)/\{1 + \exp[(-1.702 \times 1.1)(-0.1 - 0.05)]\},$$

and everything remains the same except for the numerator and the added value, so

$$P_i(-0.11) = 0.25 + (0.75)/(2.324),$$
$$P_i(-0.1) = 0.25 + 0.323,$$
$$P_i(-0.1) = 0.57.$$

Using the first set of parameter values, the individual would have a 62% probability of passing the item. With a lower guessing value, the probability decreases to 57%.

Output from 1PL, 2PL, and 3PL models are presented in Box 6.1 using a simulated data set of 500 respondents answering a 20-item test where items are scored as correct (1) or incorrect (0). The item analyses were carried out using the BILOG-MG 3 program (Zimowski, Muraki, Mislevy, & Bock, 2003).

Multiple-Response IRT Models. In addition to the 1PL, 2PL, and 3PL models of dichotomous items, there are other types of IRT models where there are three or more potential responses (polytomous models). The most important for our consideration are those that (a) have nominal response categories, such as in multiple-choice tests, (b) have graded responses, such as Likert-type scale responses, and (c) allow for partial credit to be given to a multipart question. Each of these will be described in turn, and analyses using each type will be presented and interpreted using various IRT computer programs.

Nominal Responses. In 1972, Bock proposed a model for analyzing nominal responses, or responses that do not assume an ordering of responses. The initial impetus for doing so was to allow characteristic curves for all responses to a multiple-choice item to be modeled. However, more recently, the nominal response model has found uses in other domains such as personality and attitude assessment (Thissen & Steinberg, 1988).

(Text continues on page 126)

Box 6.1   Output from 1PL, 2PL, and 3PL Models Using BILOG-MG$_3$

For the one-, two-, and three-parameter logistic model examples, a simulated data set of 500 respondents to 20 history test items is analyzed. The data were analyzed with the BILOG-MG$_3$ program. Only selected portions of the outputs provided by the program are reproduced here for pedagogical purposes.

One-Parameter Logistic Model

The BILOG-MG$_3$ program runs the analyses in three phases. Phase 1 provides classical item statistics. It is a good idea to check the output of this phase to ensure that the correct number of items and cases are included in the analyses. Only the first and last three items are shown in Table 6.1.

Table 6.1   Classical Item Statistics for Six Items in a One-Parameter Logistic Model

Item	Name	# Tried	# Right	Pct	Logit/1.7	Item × Test Correlation	
						Pearson	*Biserial*
1	Item 1	500.0	428.0	85.6	−1.05	0.459	0.710
2	Item 2	500.0	308.0	61.6	−0.28	0.531	0.676
3	Item 3	500.0	365.0	73.0	−0.59	0.496	0.666
18	Item 18	500.0	408.0	81.6	−0.88	0.398	0.579
19	Item 19	500.0	272.0	54.4	−0.10	0.179	0.225
20	Item 20	500.0	472.0	94.4	−1.66	0.254	0.517

Note that the table above shows several classical item statistics. After each item, the #Tried column indicates how many test takers attempted the item. The #Right is simply the number of test takers who got the item correct. Dividing the #Right by #Tried, we get the percentage of the sample getting the item correct. Moving the decimal two places to the left, we get the classical p level for the item. The Logit/1.7 column refers to a conversion of the z value associated with the percentage correct into log units divided by 1.7 to normal metric units. The Pearson Item × Test Correlation is the Pearson item-to-total correlation and the Biserial is the biserial item-to-total correlation. Both are given because, although the items are dichotomously scored, they may be true or false dichotomies. The biserial is less biased when *p* levels are extreme.

Notice that Item 20 is the easiest item and Item 19 is the most difficult. Item 19 also has low Pearson and biserial correlations.

Phase 2 of the BILOG-MG$_3$ program calculates the item parameters. In our example, we have specified first that a one-parameter logistic model be run, followed by a two- and then a three- parameter model. The estimation process is marginal maximum likelihood using the E-M algorithm followed by Newton-Raphson steps. This process is used to improve the parameter estimates.

E-M Cycles (Maximum Of 20)

Followed By Newton-Raphson Steps (Maximum Of 2)

(Continued)

Box 6.1 (Continued)

The "prior" distribution is the normal distribution and is separated into 15 different ability levels. This is the starting distribution the program works with to estimate the difficulty parameters (*bs*) for each item (see Table 6.2).

Table 6.2   15 Quadrature Point Distribution for a One-Parameter Logistic Model

Quadrature Points and Prior Weights					
	1	*2*	*3*	*4*	*5*
POINT	−0.4000E+01	−0.3429E+01	−0.2857E+01	−0.2286E+01	−0.1714E+01
WEIGHT	0.7648E−04	0.6387E−03	0.3848E−02	0.1673E−01	0.5245E−01
	6	*7*	*8*	*9*	*10*
POINT	−0.1143E+01	−0.5714E+00	−0.8882E−15	0.5714E+00	0.1143E+01
WEIGHT	0.1186E+00	0.1936E+00	0.2280E+00	0.1936E+00	0.1186E+00
	11	*12*	*13*	*14*	*15*
POINT	0.1714E+01	0.2286E+01	0.2857E+01	0.3429E+01	0.4000E+01
WEIGHT	0.5245E−01	0.1673E−01	0.3848E−02	0.6387E−03	0.7648E−04

[E-M Cycles]

−2 Log Likelihood = 10557.362

Cycle 1; Largest Change = 0.02776

−2 Log Likelihood = 10551.466

Cycle 2; Largest Change = 0.01520

−2 Log Likelihood = 10549.909

Cycle 3; Largest Change = 0.00927

[Newton Cycles]

−2 Log Likelihood: 10549.3361

Cycle 4; Largest Change = 0.00704

Note that the program found the best-fitting parameters after four cycles, or iterations. The −2 log likelihood value for this model is about 10549. We'll need to keep this value in mind when we test more complex models to determine if the extra parameters estimated are "worth it" in terms of the number of degrees of freedom lost.

Note that the theta distribution for our 500 cases is divided into nine groups (see Table 6.3). The program places 33 cases at the lowest level, 71 cases in the medium level and 29 at the highest level. The mean theta values for each of these nine ability levels are also shown in Table 6.3.

(Continued)

Table 6.3   Interval Counts and Mean Theta Values for Nine Ability Levels for a One-Parameter Logistic Model

Interval Counts for Computation of Item Chi-Squares									
	33.	16.	21.	52.	71	122.	129.	27.	29.
Interval Average Thetas									
	−2.437	−1.703	−1.209	−0.775	−0.264	0.209	0.684	1.137	1.644

In Table 6.4 are the estimated item parameters. The item *intercept* and the *standard error (S.E.)* refer to the logit and its standard error for the item and is equal to −slope × threshold. We will not be interpreting this column. The *slopes* for all items have been constrained to be equal and are 0.575. The *thresholds* and their S.E.'s refer to the item difficulty parameters. These are the parameters of most interest in a 1PL model. Item 20 is clearly the easiest ($b = -3.335$), and Item 19 the most difficult ($b = -0.197$). The *loading* refers to the "loading" of the item in a one-factor factor analysis. It is calculated by slope/($\sqrt{1 + \text{slope}^2}$). Because the slopes are constrained to be equal, the loadings for all items are equal as well. The *asymptote* is the c, or guessing parameter, that we did not model in this program. Therefore, all c values are constrained to be 0.0. The *chisq* indicates the fit of the item. Significant (*prob* less than 0.05) chisq values indicate items that do not fit the model very well. In this case, Item 2, Item 3, and Item 19 are all potentially problematic. Recall that the chisq is a very conservative test, however, and should not be the sole basis on which to base a decision about an item.

Table 6.4   Estimated Item Parameters for a One-Parameter Logistic Model (Six Items Reported Only)

Subtest History; Item Parameters After Cycle: 4							
Item	Intercept	Slope	Threshold	Loading	Asymptote	Chisq	df
	S.E.	S.E.	S.E.	S.E.	S.E.	(Prob)	
Item 1	1.233	0.575	−2.145	0.498	0.000	13.3	7.0
	0.087*	0.018*	0.151*	0.016*	0.000*	(0.657)	
Item 2	0.323	0.575	−0.562	0.498	0.000	32.8	6.0
	0.066*	0.018*	0.114*	0.016*	0.000*	(0.0000)	
Item 3	0.690	0.575	−1.201	0.498	0.000	16.8	7.0
	0.070*	0.018*	0.122*	0.016*	0.000*	(0.0187)	

(Continued)

Box 6.1 (Continued)

Table 6.4 (Continued)

Item	Intercept	Slope	Threshold	Loading	Asymptote	Chisq	df
			Subtest History; Item Parameters After Cycle: 4				
	S.E.	S.E.	S.E.	S.E.	S.E.	(Prob)	
Item 18	1.033	0.575	−1.797	0.498	0.000	8.8	5.0
	0.077*	0.018*	0.134*	0.016*	0.000*	(0.2660)	
Item 19	0.133	0.575	−0.197	0.498	0.000	19.1	9.0
	0.055*	0.018*	0.096*	0.016*	0.000*	(0.0246)	
Item 20	1.917	0.575	−3.335	0.498	0.000	4.5	6.0
	0.122*	0.018*	0.211*	0.016*	0.000*	(0.6063)	

Parameter	Mean	Stn. Dev.
Threshold	−1.061	1.012

The overall mean of the thresholds (−1.061) suggests that as a whole, these items are fairly easy.

Finally, the posterior, or resultant theta distribution, based on the sample, is presented using again 15 cut-points (see Table 6.5). Note that the mean and standard deviations of this distribution are 0.0 and 1.0 respectively.

Table 6.5   Posteriori Theta Distribution for a One-Parameter Logistic Model

	1	2	3	4	5
	Quadrature Points, Posterior Weights, Mean, and S.D.				
Point	−0.4041E+01	−0.3465E+01	−0.2889E+01	−0.2313E+01	−0.1737E+01
Posterior	0.2404E−03	0.1756E−02	0.8143E−02	0.2511E−01	0.5069E−01
	6	7	8	9	10
Point	−0.1160E+01	−0.5844E+00	−0.8401E−02	0.5676E+00	0.1144E+01
Posterior	0.9235E−01	0.1688E+00	0.2452E+00	0.2247E+00	0.1212E+00
	11	12	13	14	15
Point	0.1720E+01	0.2296E+01	0.2872E+01	0.3448E+01	0.4024E+01
Posterior	0.4507E−01	0.1319E−01	0.3005E−02	0.5024E−03	0.6056E−04

Note: Mean: 0.00000, S.D.: 1.00000

Phase 3 of the program scores participants. Users can specify if they want to keep the scores as is, based on the normal distribution, or if they want to rescale to another type of distribution. The program was set to convert the scores to a distribution with a mean of 50 and standard deviation of 10.

Note that the reliability of the items as a whole is provided here (0.75). This is a summary index based on the average squared standard errors of individual scores divided by the trait score variance, which is then subtracted from 1.0 (see Table 6.6).

Table 6.6   Summary Statistics for the One-Parameter Logistic Model Items as a Whole

Summary Statistics for Score Estimates		
Means, Standard Deviations, and Variances of Score Estimates		
Test	History	
Mean	0.0020	
S.D.	0.8768	
Variance	0.7688	
Root-Mean-Square Posterior Standard Deviations		
Test	History	
Rms	0.5019	
Variance	0.2519	
Empirical Reliability	0.7532	
Rescaling With Respect To Sample Distribution		
Rescaling Constants		
Test	Scale	Location
History	10.000	50.000

Note that the location is 50 and scale is 10. That means the ability levels will be rescaled from a mean of 0.0 and standard deviation of 1.0 to a mean of 50 and standard deviation of 10.

This part of the printout is very long (particularly if you have thousands of cases). Only the first and last three cases are reported in Table 6.7. Note that each entry indicates that person's ability level (theta). Recall that the mean of the distribution is 50. So most of the participants shown here (albeit only six cases) have relatively low ability levels. Each participant has a unique standard error (S.E.) around his/her score. Most are in the five-point range, but there is variability here. The *marginal prob* indicates the probability with which one would expect to observe the response pattern of the participant given the ability level. Very small values indicate caution should be used in interpreting scores. They may indicate that the respondent was answering randomly or inappropriately using the response sheet, or a response bias of some sort. Notice that all participants with equal numbers of items correct receive the same ability level rating. That is because the 1PL model does not have item discrimination information to use in scoring participants who get different items correct/incorrect.

(Continued)

Box 6.1 (Continued)

Table 6.7   Rescaled Ability Level Estimates for Six Subjects for the One-Parameter Logistic Model

Subject	Test	Tried	Right	Marginal			
				Percent	Ability	S.E.	Prob.
1	History	20	14	70.00	50.1553	4.9986	0.000009
2	History	20	14	70.00	50.1553	4.9986	0.000001
3	History	20	15	75.00	52.6063	4.9752	0.000051
498	History	20	19	95.00	63.9444	6.0160	0.004246
499	History	20	17	85.00	57.5966	5.3404	0.000012
500	History	20	17	85.00	57.5966	5.3404	0.000892

Next, the items are rescaled (see Table 6.8). Note that their thresholds are frequently below 50, indicating items that should be answerable by low-ability individual cases. The overall mean of the rescaled items is 39.394, again indicating a relatively easy test.

Table 6.8   Rescaled Item Level Estimates for Six Items Using the One-Parameter Logistic Model

Item	Intercept	Slope	Threshold	Loading	Asymptote
	S.E.	S.E.	S.E.	S.E.	S.E.
Item 1	−1.641	0.057	28.549	0.498	0.000
	0.127*	0.002*	1.512*	0.016*	0.000*
Item 2	−2.551	0.057	44.382	0.498	0.000
	0.113*	0.002*	1.141*	0.016*	0.000*
Item 3	−2.184	0.057	37.991	0.498	0.000
	0.116*	0.002*	1.225*	0.016*	0.000*
Item 18	−1.841	0.057	32.025	0.498	0.000
	0.121*	0.002*	1.345*	0.016*	0.000*
Item 19	−2.761	0.057	48.028	0.498	0.000
	0.108*	0.002*	0.962*	0.016*	0.000*
Item 20	−0.957	0.057	16.650	0.498	0.000
	0.153*	0.002*	2.115*	0.016*	0.000*

Test History; Rescaled Item Parameters

Parameter	Mean	Stn. Dev.
Threshold	39.394	10.120

Table 6.9 shows item information statistics. The *point of maximum information* is the column we are most interested in examining. This is the ability level at which the item provides maximum information about a test taker. Consistent with other information thus far in the output, notice that most of the points are below average (0.0) ability levels, again indicating that this is a relatively easy set of items.

Table 6.9   Item Information Statistics for Six Items Using the One-Parameter Logistic Model

Item Information Statistics				
Item	*Maximum Information*	*Point of Maximum Information*	*Maximum Effectiveness*	*Average Information*
	*Standard Error**	*Standard Error**	*Point of Maximum Effectiveness**	*Index of Reliability**
Item 1	0.2387	−2.1451	0.0000	0.0000
	0.0000*	0.1512*	0.0000*	0.0000*
Item 2	0.2387	−0.5618	0.0000	0.0000
	0.0000*	0.1141*	0.0000*	0.0000*
Item 3	0.2387	−1.2009	0.0000	0.0000
	0.0000*	0.1225*	0.0000*	0.0000*
Item 18	0.2387	−1.7975	0.0000	0.0000
	0.0000*	0.1345*	0.0000*	0.0000*
Item 19	0.2387	−0.1972	0.0000	0.0000
	0.0000*	0.0962*	0.0000*	0.0000*
Item 20	0.2387	−3.3350	0.0000	0.0000
	0.0000*	0.2115*	0.0000*	0.0000*

The test information curve is shown next in Figure 6.4.

(Continued)

Box 6.1 (Continued)

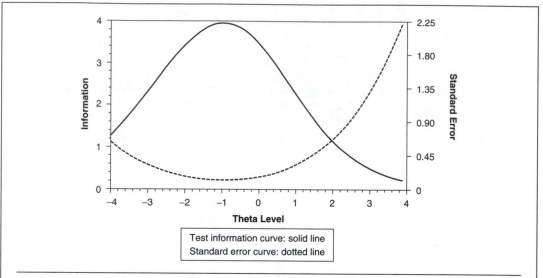

Figure 6.4   BILOG-MG Test Information Curve of a One-Parameter Logistic Model

This test information curve indicates that using all items, the most information is provided for individuals with ability levels of about −1.0. This is where the standard error is lowest and, conversely, the information is highest. This finding is not surprising, as we have already seen that the test should be considered easy. The test is less able to provide discriminations of individuals at higher ability levels.

Two-Parameter Logistic Model

In this next set of outputs, we have allowed the slopes (as, or discriminations) to vary across items (2PL model). Where there are relevant differences between this output and the 1PL output, they will be shown.

> [E-M Cycles]
> −2 Log Likelihood = 10369.108
> Cycle 1; Largest Change = 0.17511
> −2 Log Likelihood: 10354.6120
> Cycle 7; Largest Change = 0.00504

First, note that the −2 log likelihood for the 2PL model is 10355. Recall that for the 1PL model, the −2 log likelihood was equal to 10549. Thus, there is an improvement in fit for the 2PL model over the 1PL model (10549 − 10355 = 194). Again recall that the difference between these values is distributed as a χ^2. In this case, we estimated 20 more parameters (20 items, each with its own slope). The critical value to exceed for a χ^2 with 20 degrees of freedom at an alpha of 0.01 is 37.57. Clearly, the 2PL model fits the data significantly better than the 1PL model.

Note that there are unique slopes now for each item as well as unique loadings for them (see Table 6.10). Recall that the mean threshold for the 1PL model across items was −1.061. In the 2PL model, it is slightly higher (−0.991), suggesting that some of the items may allow for more discrimination at higher ability levels.

Table 6.10   Item Parameters Using a Two-Parameter Logistic Model

Item	Intercept	Slope	Threshold	Loading	Asymptote	Chisq	df
	S.E.	S.E.	S.E.	S.E.	S.E.	(Prob)	
Item 1	1.503	0.968	−1.552	0.696	0.000	3.5	7.0
	0.129*	0.123*	0.141*	0.089*	0.000*	(0.8366)	
Item 2	0.440	1.265	−0.348	0.785	0.000	14.3	5.0
	0.082*	0.170*	0.065*	0.106*	0.000*	(0.0138)	
Item 3	0.889	1.090	−0.815	0.737	0.000	3.6	5.0
	0.093*	0.146*	0.095*	0.099*	0.000*	(0.6103)	
Item 18	1.100	0.697	−1.578	0.572	0.000	8.8	5.0
	0.087*	0.093*	0.191*	0.076*	0.000*	(0.2706)	
Item 19	0.110	0.327	−0.336	0.311	0.000	1.7	9.0
	0.055*	0.057*	0.177*	0.055*	0.000*	(0.9955)	
Item 20	2.025	0.694	−2.915	0.570	0.000	2.2	5.0
	0.164*	0.116*	0.375*	0.096*	0.000*	(0.8140)	

Note that the reliability is slightly higher in the 2PL versus the 1PL model (0.78 versus 0.75). The mean threshold is almost the same in the 2PL as the 1PL model (40 versus 39; see Table 6.11).

Table 6.11   Summary Statistics for the Items as a Whole for a Two-Parameter Logistic Model

Parameter	Mean	Stn. Dev.
Slope	0.068	0.028
Log (Slope)	−2.784	0.462
Threshold	40.085	9.393

Note: Empirical Reliability: 0.7823
The test information curve is shown in Figure 6.5.

(Continued)

Box 6.1 (Continued)

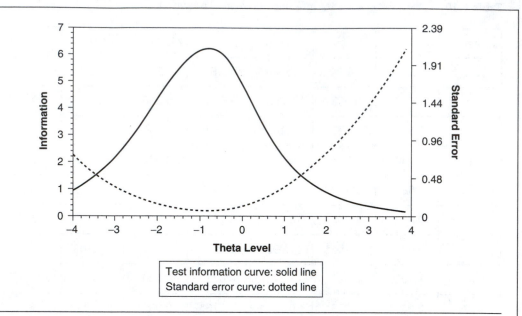

Figure 6.5   BILOG-MG Test Information Curve of a Two-Parameter Logistic Model

Note that there is most information at ability levels of about −0.875, where there is also the lowest standard error. More discrimination is occurring at higher ability levels than what occurs using the 1PL model (−0.875 versus −1.0, respectively).

Three Parameter Logistic Model

In this output, a 3PL model is assessed. That is, a guessing parameter has been estimated for each item. As with the previous output, only relevant differences between the outputs will be shown.

[E-M Cycles]

−2 Log Likelihood = 10919.925

Cycle 1; Largest Change = 3.62985

. . .

−2 Log Likelihood: 10439.5104

Cycle 11; Largest Change = 0.00132

Note that the −2 log likelihood value is higher for the 3PL model (10440) than for the 2PL model (10355), indicating a poorer fit of the model to the data with the 3PL model. However, the 3PL model does provide a better fit than the 1PL model (10549 − 10440 = 109, with 40 degrees of freedom, is significant).

Note that there are unique asymptotes associated with each item (see Table 6.12). These are where the item curve crosses the y-axis, giving an estimate of the guessing to which the item is susceptible. On average, individuals with virtually no ability have a 34% probability of getting the item correct.

Table 6.12   Item Parameters Using a Three-Parameter Logistic Model

Item	Intercept	Slope	Threshold	Loading	Asymptote	Chisq	df
S.E.	S.E.	S.E.	S.E.	S.E.	(Prob)		
Item 1	1.229	1.232	−0.997	0.777	0.363	7.2	7.0
	0.183*	0.232*	0.224*	0.146*	0.088*	(0.4069)	
Item 2	0.152	1.637	−0.093	0.853	0.179	15.0	5.0
	0.145*	0.351*	0.099*	0.183*	0.048*	(0.0102)	
Item 3	0.608	1.251	−0.486	0.781	0.240	17.8	5.0
	0.135*	0.247*	0.153*	0.154*	0.065*	(0.0032)	
Item 18	0.720	0.750	−0.960	0.600	0.359	21.9	7.0
	0.161*	0.145*	0.320*	0.116*	0.092*	(0.0027)	
Item 19	−0.772	0.589	1.311	0.507	0.396	5.9	9.0
	0.332*	0.190*	0.372*	0.163*	0.063*	(0.7518)	
Item 20	1.626	0.802	−2.029	0.625	0.488	4.9	7.0
	0.231*	0.149*	0.412*	0.117*	0.110*	(0.4418)	

Note that the reliability is similar for both the 3PL and 2PL models (0.78; see Table 6.13). Also note that the threshold for the 3PL model is quite a bit higher than for the 2PL or 1PL (49 versus 40 and 39). By modeling in the guessing parameter, that portion of the ability is taken into account when estimating individuals' scores. Thus, the test can be harder as a consequence.

Table 6.13   Summary Statistics for the Items as a Whole for a Three-Parameter Logistic Model

Parameter	Mean	Stn. Dev.
Asymptote	0.340	0.101
Slope	0.092	0.035
Log (Slope)	2.452	0.380
Threshold	49.424	10.995

Note: Empirical Reliability: 0.7778

The test information curve is shown in Figure 6.6.

(Continued)

Box 6.1 (Continued)

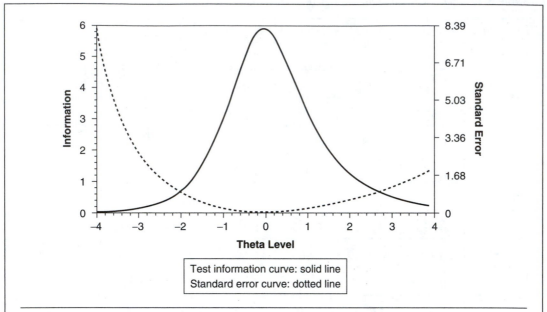

Figure 6.6   BILOG-MG Test Information Curve of a Three-Parameter Logistic Model

This added difficulty, by modeling in the guessing parameter, allows the test to discriminate at higher ability levels (0.0) than either the 2PL (−0.875) or 1PL models (−1.0). The standard error at that point is almost 0.0.

In an analysis of multiple-choice responses to an item where there is a correct response, it is assumed before the analysis begins that all the incorrect responses are equally incorrect. The IRT analysis will show whether or not this assumption is correct; that is, it answers the question, Are individuals with different ability levels more or less likely to select a particular incorrect response? It has been demonstrated that low-ability examinees often tend to select different incorrect alternatives than high-ability examinees (Levine & Drasgow, 1983). Thus, nominal IRT models allow for a more fine-grained analysis of distractor alternatives than lumping all the distractor responses into a single category. The nominal model can also be used to determine group differences in response patterns answering questions such as, Do individuals from collectivist cultures respond differently to an item on political affiliation than respondents from individualist cultures?

The probability of a respondent selecting a particular response category (j) for one item (i) is a ratio of the probability of selecting one option over the sum of the probabilities of selecting any of the options and is written as

$$(6\text{–}4) \qquad P_{ij}(\Theta) = \exp(a_{ij}\,\Theta + c_{ij}) \Big/ \left[\sum_{j=0}^{m} \exp(a_i\Theta + c_{ij}) \right],$$

where a_{ij} = slope for each option, c_{ij} = intercept for each option, j denotes each option, and m denotes the number of categories. The c_{ip} or intercept, term is a transformation using the slope (a), and difficulty (b) parameters; $c_{ij} = (-a_{ij} \times b_{ij})$. The constant D that we saw in the one-, two-, and three-parameter models has been absorbed into the other terms and, as before, Θ is equal to the ability level for the respondent. This equation has to be repeated for every response option. The correct option, if that is the context in which the nominal model is being used, should have the largest a_{ij} value.

Using an example, let's say we ask a group of 600 artists to complete an inventory of their art knowledge and skill. One of the test items asks, "What tone of purple has the most brown in it?" The response options are (a) fuchsia, (b) puce, (c) magenta, and (d) mauve. The a_{ij} and c_{ij} parameters are shown in Table 6.14 and the trace lines (analogous to the item characteristic curves for the binary response models) associated with them in Figure 6.7.

We can see from the shape of the lines that option "fuchsia" and "mauve" are the options most likely to be selected by individuals at very low ability levels, and the probability of selecting this option decreases as ability increases. Option "puce" is

Table 6.14   The a_{ij} and c_{ij} Parameters for One Item on an Artistic Knowledge Test

Response Option	$a_{ij}{}^a$	$c_{ij}{}^b$
fuchsia	−0.40	−1.50
puce (correct)	0.80	−0.50
magenta	−0.10	1.30
mauve	−0.30	0.70

a. The sum of the a_{ij} parameters equals zero.
b. The sum of the c_{ij} parameters equals zero.
As an example, the calculations for the fuchsia trace line will be shown here:

$$P_{ij}(\Theta) = \exp(a_{ij}\Theta + c_{ij}) \bigg/ \left[\sum_{j=0}^{m} \exp(a_i\Theta + c_{ij}) \right]$$

When Θ equals −3, −2, −1, 0, 1, 2, 3:
$\exp(-0.40 \times -3 + -1.5) = 0.74$,
$\exp(-0.40 \times -2 + -1.5) = 0.50$,
$\exp(-0.40 \times -1 + -1.5) = 0.33$,
$\exp(-0.40 \times 0 + -1.5) = 0.22$,
$\exp(-0.40 \times 1 + -1.5) = 0.15$,
$\exp(-0.40 \times 2 + -1.5) = 0.10$,
$\exp(-0.40 \times 3 + -1.5) = 0.07$.
The sum of the expotentiates is $0.74 + 0.50 + 0.33 + 0.15 + 0.22 + 0.10 + 0.07 = 2.11$.
The probability of selecting the fuchsia option at each of seven Θ levels is as follows:
$0.74/2.11 = 0.35$,
$0.50/2.11 = 0.24$,
$0.33/2.11 = 0.16$,
$0.22/2.11 = 0.11$,
$0.15/2.11 = 0.07$,
$0.10/2.11 = 0.05$,
$0.07/2.11 = 0.03$.
Therefore, the option curve for fuchsia can be plotted using the Θ levels on the x-axis and the probabilities for each on the y-axis. The same process is used to calculate each of the other option curves.

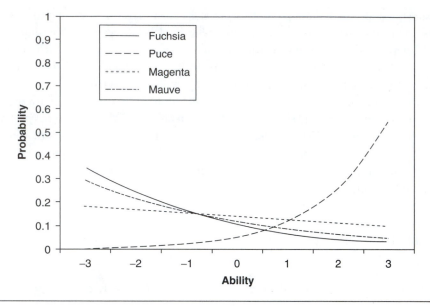

Figure 6.7   Response Curves for a Nominal Item With Four Alternatives

the correct response and is not likely to be selected until ability levels reach 1.5 or more. Past that point, the "puce" curve rises steeply, indicating that this option is increasingly likely to be selected as ability levels increase. Option "magenta" has a flat, low curve, so it is equally likely (in this case not very likely) to be selected by all individuals at all ability levels.

An example of an output and interpretation from a multiple-choice set of test items using the MULTILOG 7 (Thissen, Chen, & Bock, 2002) program is shown in Box 6.2.

Box 6.2   Nominal Response Model: Selected Output from MULTILOG 7

The MULTILOG 7 program was used to analyze simulated data for a 20-item achievement test given to 228 individuals. The test was a multiple-choice examination with four response alternatives for each item. Marginal maximum likelihood was used to generate the item parameters.

In this first item, 2 is the correct response. The entries in Table 6.15 are the slope (A) and intercept (C) parameters associated with each of the four alternatives that have been estimated by the program.

Table 6.15   Item 1: Four Nominal Categories: 2 is Correct

Item 1: Four Nominal Categories, 2 High			
Category(K):	1	2	3	4
A(K)	1.17	0.64	−0.27	0.80
C(K)	−0.51	2.44	0.20	−2.13

Table 6.16 is simply the contrasts or absolute differences between the nominal categories adjacent to one another for the *A* parameters (e.g., |−1.17 − 0.64| = 1.81) and *C* parameters (e.g., |−0.51 − 2.44| = 2.95), as well as their respective standard deviations.

Table 6.16   Contrasts Between Nominal Categories for Item 1

Contrast-Coefficients (Standard Errors)						
For	*A*			*C*		
Contrast	P(#)	Coeff	[Dev.]	P(#)	Coeff	[Dev.]
1	1	1.81	(0.48)	4	2.95	(0.52)
2	2	0.91	(0.53)	5	0.72	(0.61)
3	3	1.98	(1.67)	6	−1.61	(1.24)

Table 6.17 shows the response alternative selections for the 228 respondents. Of the 228, 183 selected 2, or the correct answer. This corresponds to 80.26% of the sample. Given the overall ability levels of the respondents, the expected proportions are also generated.

Table 6.17   Response Alternative Selections of Respondents to Item 1

Observed and Expected Counts/Proportions in:				
Category(K)	*1*	*2*	*3*	*4*
Obs. Freq.	21	183	22	2
Obs. Prop.	0.0921	0.8026	0.0965	0.0088
Exp. Prop.	0.1014	0.7925	0.0975	0.0086

The other 19 items have similar information generated for them. Total test information is also reported as well as the reliability.

Marginal Reliability: 0.6864

The −2 log likelihood value for the model is also reported:

Negative Twice the Log Likelihood = 3560.6

Figure 6.8 presents the item characteristic curve for Item 9. In this case, response alternative 2 is correct. Those with the lowest ability levels are most likely to select option 3, and then option 4, and then option 1. As ability levels increase, there is less likelihood that any of the incorrect alternatives will be selected and that alternative 2 will be selected. This occurs at a low level of ability, suggesting a fairly easy item.

(Continued)

Box 6.2 (Continued)

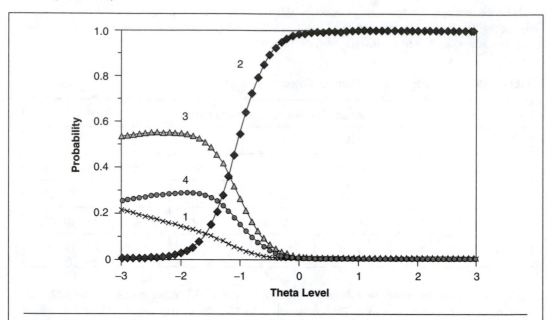

Figure 6.8 Item Characteristic Curve Under a Nominal Response Model

Figure 6.9 shows the information curve for Item 9. It substantiates the findings from the item curves; that is, the item provides most information at low ability levels.

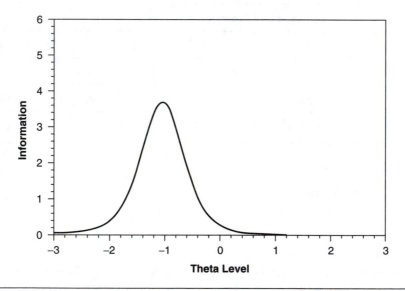

Figure 6.9 Item Information Function Under a Nominal Response Model

Figure 6.10 shows the total test information function. Overall, the test of 20 items provides a lot of information and will estimate those with low ability levels quite well. This is not the case for the upper end of the ability level.

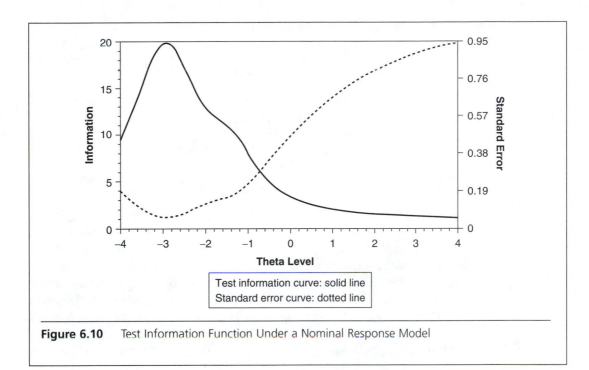

Figure 6.10   Test Information Function Under a Nominal Response Model

Graded Responses. Graded response models are of particular interest to attitude and personality assessment in that Likert-type responses are included in these models. The assumption is that responses lie on an ordered, but categorical, level. Samejima (1969) pioneered this work and thus many programs bear his name. One of the assumptions about Samejima's model is that the item responses do not have to be the same across items (e.g., you can have a three-point Likert-type item, followed by a four-point Likert-type item, followed by a five-point Likert-type item). Muraki (1990) modified Samejima's model to include the restriction that all items in a scale are responded to with the same number of response categories. This restriction characterizes many types of attitude scales and has the advantage of allowing for fewer parameters to be estimated. However, the more general model of Samejima's allows for greater flexibility for data analysis. Note that before analyzing graded responses, it is best to enter the data so that higher values are associated with higher ability or attitude. This makes the final interpretation easier.

Rather than estimating the parameters for each alternative simultaneously, Samejima used a two-step process. First, a series of $k - 1$ ($k =$ number of alternative responses) preliminary item curves (called operating characteristic curves) based on "false dichotomies" are created. These are two-parameter curves calculated in the manner demonstrated for a 2PL model. The false dichotomies are generated by collapsing responses into two groups at various stages along the response continuum. For example, suppose we have the following item from the Team Player Inventory (TPI; Kline, 1999) and response format:

Working in a team gets me to think more creatively.

1	2	3	4	5
strongly disagree	disagree	neither agree nor disagree	agree	strongly agree

Four operating curves (because $k - 1 = 4$) are generated for those scoring (a) above 1 but lower than 2, (b) above 2 but lower than 3, (c) above 3 but lower than 4, and (d) above 4. Therefore, we have four, not five, operating curves. It will always be the case that there will be one fewer operating curves generated than the number of response alternatives for each item. A constraint on the model is that, whereas different b value parameters are generated for each alternative, the a value parameters for all alternatives are equal. Note that the a and b value parameters are not interpreted as difficulty and discrimination parameters as they were in the 1PL, 2PL, and 3PL models. Instead, the b value for each alternative for each item represents the ability level needed to respond above a specific threshold with 50% probability. While the a values indicate slopes, they are not interpreted as discriminations.

The following threshold probabilities for each ability level will be estimated:

a. above 1 but lower than 2 = $P_{i2}(\Theta)$,
b. above 2 but lower than 3 = $P_{i3}(\Theta)$,
c. above 3 but lower than 4 = $P_{i4}(\Theta)$, and
d. above 4 = $P_{i5}(\Theta)$.

Assume that we gave the TPI to a group of 500 employees. The data are subjected to IRT analysis and the a and b value parameters are generated as in Table 6.18 and from them the operating curves (Figure 6.11).

The formula for generating the separate threshold operating curves at various levels of ability (Θ) for each item is

(6–5) $$P_i(\Theta) = \exp[a_i(\Theta - b_{ij})]/\{1 + \exp[a_i(\Theta - b_{ij})]\},$$

where a_i = the slope for each item (i), b_{ij} = the ability level needed to respond above a specific threshold with 50% probability for each alternative (j) of each item. Note that the operating curves for each item all have the same slopes (a values), but, as team player attitude goes up, so does the probability that the individual will select a higher response category.

Step two in the process is to estimate the actual probabilities for each response alternative by subtraction. By definition, the probability of responding at the lowest alternative or above (in this case, 1, 2, 3, 4, or 5) is 1.0; similarly, the probability of responding above the highest alternative (in this case, above 5) is 0.0. The

Table 6.18   The *a* and *b* Threshold Parameters for a Likert-Type Item on the Team Player Inventory

Response Threshold	a	b
P_{i2}	2.0	−1.25
P_{i3}	2.0	−0.75
P_{i4}	2.0	0.75
P_{i5}	2.0	1.25

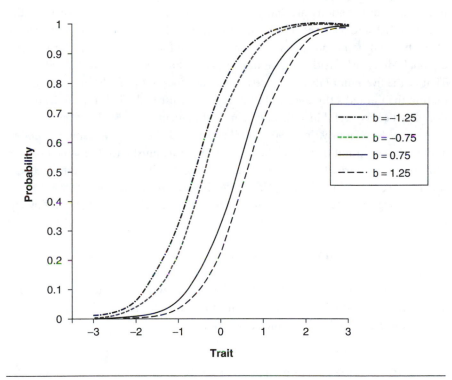

Figure 6.11   Threshold Operating Curves Under a Five-Point Likert-Type Graded Response Model

probabilities can be generated for each alternative in the five-point Likert scale example using the following set of equations:

(6–6)   Alternative 1: $P_{i1}(\Theta) = 1.0 - P_{i2}(\Theta)$

(6–7)   Alternative 2: $P_{i2}(\Theta) = P_{i2}(\Theta) - P_{i3}(\Theta)$

(6–8)   Alternative 3: $P_{i3}(\Theta) = P_{i3}(\Theta) - P_{i4}(\Theta)$

(6–9)   Alternative 4: $P_{i4}(\Theta) = P_{i4}(\Theta) - P_{i5}(\Theta)$

(6–10)   Alternative 5: $P_{i5}(\Theta) = P_{i5}(\Theta) - 0.0$

Using the above formulae, the information in Table 6.19 is generated. These are used in turn to generate what are termed category response curves. Figure 6.12 shows these curves for the team player item. They show that at extremely low levels of the trait ($\Theta = -3$), the individual is almost certainly going to select Category 1. At somewhat higher levels of the trait ($\Theta = -2$), the individual is likely to select from Categories 2 or 3. At somewhat higher levels of the trait ($\Theta = -1$), the individual is most likely to select Category 3. Curves such as these are useful for identifying item response categories that may not function as expected.

This is particularly true for the midpoint category, where it may not be clear whether the respondents use it as a true midpoint or a useless "don't know" category. For the item just plotted, there is not much utility in Category 2 or 4 alternatives. Their distributions are fairly flat and overlap to a large degree with the Category 1, 3, and 5 curves. The midpoint category (3) peaks exactly in the center of the two end-point categories. Thus, not much information is gained other than a global "disagree," "neither agree nor disagree," and "agree" with the statement. That is, the five-point Likert-type response scale does not provide any more information than would a three-point Likert-type response scale. This type of information may be very useful in scale design and refinement.

As noted previously, in 1990, Muraki modified the graded response model, adding the constraint that all of the items in the scale must have the same number of response categories for all items. This is frequently the case in attitude and personality assessment and therefore his model has become quite popular.

Operating characteristic curves are generated for thresholds using the following formula:

(6–11) $$P_i(\Theta) = \exp[a_i(\Theta - b_i + c_j)]/\{1 + \exp[a_i(\Theta - b_i + c_j)]\},$$

where a_i = the slope for each item, b_{ij} = the ability level needed to respond above a specific threshold with 50% probability for each alternative of each item, and c_j = the category threshold parameters for all items.

Table 6.19   Probabilities of Response to Categories for a Likert-Type Item on the Team Player Inventory

Trait Level	1	2	3	4	5
−3	0.99	0.005	0.004	0	0.001
−2	0.94	0.023	0.028	0.004	0.005
−1	0.679	0.098	0.163	0.023	0.037
0	0.223	0.098	0.358	0.098	0.223
1	0.038	0.022	0.163	0.098	0.679
2	0.005	0.003	0.03	0.022	0.940
3	0.001	0	0.004	0.003	0.992

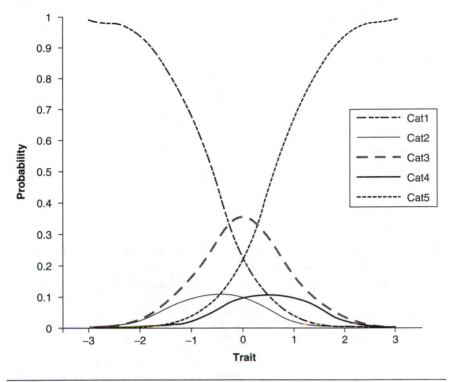

Figure 6.12   Category Response Curves Under a Five-Point Likert-Type Graded Response Model

The same procedure used by Samejima to estimate the probability of responding at a particular category (i.e., subtraction) is used in this model as well.

Only one set of category threshold parameters (c values in the equation) are estimated for the entire scale, whereas recall that in Samejima's model, category thresholds are generated for each item in the scale. One location parameter is estimated for each item (b value), and the restriction of similar slopes (a values) across all items is also in effect in Muraki's model. Because of the additional restrictions, the Muraki model assesses far fewer parameters and is quite efficient.

Another feature of Muraki's model is that, because the b values are associated with complete items, it can be determined which items are more difficult (or more extreme in trait assessment for personality or attitude). Table 6.20 shows the parameters for an item that uses a four-point Likert-type scale, Table 6.21 the probabilities for the four category alternatives, Figure 6.13 the operating curves, and Figure 6.14 the category response curves using Muraki's model.

Interpretation follows the same approach as in Samejima's model. In this case, Category 1 is selected with any degree of probability only by those at the very lowest ability level. Category 2 is selected with highest probability for those of low ability (Θ between −2.25 and −1.5). Category 3 is the most popular category and is selected with reasonably high probability by individuals of moderate to high levels of ability (Θ between 0 and 2.5). Only those of extremely high ability select

Table 6.20   The *a*, *b*, and *c* Threshold Parameters for a Four-Point Likert-Type Response

Response Threshold	a	b	c[a]
P_{i2}	2.5	−1.0	1.8
P_{i3}	2.5	0.0	0.7
P_{i4}	2.5	1.0	−2.2

a. Note that for every item, the c parameters would be the same.

Table 6.21   Probabilities of Response to Categories for an Item With a Four-Point Likert-Type Response Format

Trait Level	1	2	3	4
−3	0.623	0.374	0.003	0
−2	0.119	0.884	0.037	0
−1	0.011	0.668	0.321	0
0	0.001	0.147	0.852	0
1	0.001	0.013	0.982	0.004
2	0	0.001	0.951	0.048
3	0	0	0.623	0.377

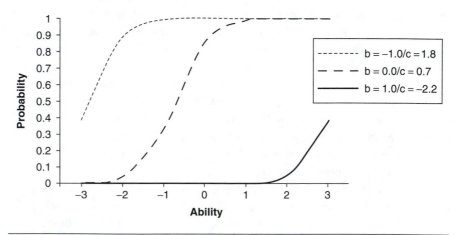

Figure 6.13   Threshold Operating Curves Under a Four-Point Likert-Type Graded Response Model

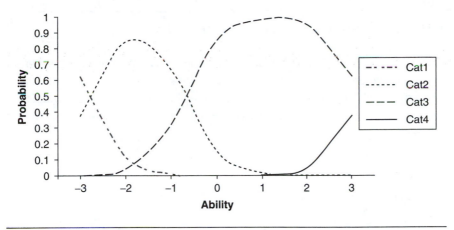

Figure 6.14   Category Response Curves Under a Four-Point Likert-Type Graded
Response Model

Category 4, and those with an ability level of 3 still only have a 40% probability of
selecting that option.

An example of an output and interpretation of a graded response model using
the PARSCALE 4 (Muraki & Bock, 2003) program is shown in Box 6.3.

Partial Credit Responses. Three partial credit models will be described: the
partial credit model proposed by Masters (1982), a more generalized version of
Masters's model proposed by Muraki (1992), and a more restrictive version of
Masters's model proposed earliest by Andrich (1978a, 1978b). These models are frequently used in achievement test situations where test takers complete items with
multiple parts and are given partial credit for answering some sections correctly
even if they do not answer the entire item correctly.

An example of a partial credit item would be if a 4th-grade student is given the
following math item (Item 1): $(63 - 54)/1.5 + 7$. There are three parts to the question, and thus the student can get a score of 0, 1, 2, or 3, depending on the parts
completed correctly. A score of 0 is given if no parts are answered correctly. The first
step (score of 1) is of intermediate difficulty $(63 - 54)$, the second step (score of 2)
is of greater difficulty $(9/1.5)$. The third step is easiest (score of 3) $(6 + 7)$. The next
item (Item 2) is $(2 + 10)/4 \times 0.6$. In this case, the first step is the easiest $(2 + 10)$, the
second step is more difficult $(12/4)$, and the third most difficult (3×0.6). Models
of the scores of a group of 4th-grade students to these items will reflect the fact that
there will be partial credit given.

The partial credit models are in many ways similar to the graded response models because it is assumed that as respondents move higher on the latent trait, the
person will be more likely to correctly respond to all parts of a question. However,
they are similar to the nominal models in that the probability of a particular score,
or response alternative, is an exponential divided by the sum of exponentials.

Masters's (1982) partial credit model assumes that all item slopes are equal. This
results in the slope term not being part of the equation. One-parameter threshold

(Text continues on page 145)

Box 6.3 Graded Response Model: Selected Output from PARSCALE 4

The PARSCALE 4 program was used to analyze simulated data for an eight-item team leadership attitude scale. A five-point Likert-type response format was used for each item, and thus Muraki's modification of Samejima's Graded Response Model was used to analyze the data. The first output phase is Phase 0, where the program provides a check to the programmer about what the data look like and how the analysis is to unfold.

Number of Items: 8

Model Specifications

Normal Ogive-Graded Item Response Model Is Specified.

Scale Constant 1.00 For Slope Parameters.

The Fixed Prior Distribution For Latent Traits

The default for the prior distribution is a normal distribution with a mean of 0.0 and standard deviation of 1.0. This distribution is divided into 30 quadrature points in advance (see Table 6.22).

Table 6.22 Thirty Quadrature Points of the Normal Distribution

Mean: 0.0000				
S.D.: 1.0000				
Quadrature Points And Prior Weights (Program-Generated Normal Approximation)				
	1	2	3	4	5
Point	−0.4000e+01	−0.3724e+01	−0.3448e+01	−0.3172e+01	−0.2897e+01
Weight	0.3692e−04	0.1071e−03	0.2881e−03	0.7181e−03	0.1659e−02
	6	7	8	9	10
Point	−0.2621e+01	−0.2345e+01	−0.2069e+01	−0.1793e+01	−0.1517e+01
Weight	0.3550e−02	0.7042e−02	0.1294e−01	0.2205e−01	0.3481e−01
	11	12	13	14	15
Point	−0.1241e+01	−0.9655e+00	−0.6897e+00	−0.4138e+00	−0.1379e+00
Weight	0.5093e−01	0.6905e−01	0.8676e−01	0.1010e+00	0.1090e+00
	16	17	18	19	20
Point	0.1379e+00	0.4138e+00	0.6897e+00	0.9655e+00	0.1241e+01
Weight	0.1090e+00	0.1010e+00	0.8676e−01	0.6905e−01	0.5093e−01
	21	22	23	24	25
Point	0.1517e+01	0.1793e+01	0.2069e+01	0.2345e+01	0.2621e+01
Weight	0.3481e−01	0.2205e−01	0.1294e−01	0.7042e−02	0.3550e−02
	26	27	28	29	30
Point	0.2897e+01	0.3172e+01	0.3448e+01	0.3724e+01	0.4000e+01
Weight	0.1659e−02	0.7181e−03	0.2881e−03	0.1071e−03	0.3692e−04

Input and Recoded Response of First and Second Observations
As a check, the responses for the first two cases are presented.

Observation #1

Input Responses: 1 3 2 2 1 2 1 1

Observation #2

Input Responses: 4 3 2 4 4 4 4 4

150 Observations Read From File: Graded.Dat

There are 150 cases in the data set.

Phase 1 of the PARSCALE output for the graded response model of eight leadership items is next. It indicates that maximum likelihood is used to estimate the item parameters.

Table 6.23 indicates the number of respondents (frequencies and percentages) who selected each of the 1–5 Likert-type response categories for each of the eight items and an overall summary of the response categories.

Table 6.23   Respondent Frequencies and Percentages for Each Response Category

Item		Total	Not Present	Omit	Categories				
					1	2	3	4	5
0001									
	Freq.	150	0	0	6	25	41	51	27
	Perc.		0.0	0.0	4.0	16.7	27.3	34.0	18.0
0002									
	Freq.	150	0	0	2	13	39	62	34
	Perc.		0.0	0.0	1.3	8.7	26.0	41.3	22.7
0003									
	Freq.	150	0	0	7	19	37	65	22
	Perc.		0.0	0.0	4.7	12.7	24.7	43.3	14.7
0004									
	Freq.	150	0	0	2	2	29	89	28
	Perc.		0.0	0.0	1.3	1.3	19.3	59.3	18.7
0005									
	Freq.	150	0	0	16	15	27	53	39
	Perc.		0.0	0.0	0.7	10.0	18.0	35.3	26.0

(Continued)

Box 6.3 (Continued)

Table 6.23 (Continued)

Item		Total	Not Present	Omit	Categories				
					1	2	3	4	5
0006									
	Freq.	150	0	0	6	33	29	61	21
	Perc.		0.0	0.0	4.0	22.0	19.3	40.7	14.0
0007									
	Freq.	150	0	0	6	10	38	56	40
	Perc.		0.0	0.0	4.0	6.7	25.3	37.3	26.7
0008									
	Freq.	150	0	0	10	26	44	56	14
	Perc.		0.0	0.0	6.7	17.3	29.3	37.3	9.3
Cummul.									
	Freq.				55	143	284	493	225
	Perc.				4.6	11.9	23.7	41.1	18.8

Table 6.24 shows the response mean and standard deviation for each item (using the 1–5 Likert-type format). In addition, the Pearson correlation and polyserial correlation of each item to total score are shown. The polyserial assumes that the response categories are not truly separate and distinct but, instead, are artificially created and are based on an underlying continuum of ability. They are less conservative than the Pearson. The initial slope (a) and location (b) parameters for each item are also calculated based on the correlation coefficients.

Table 6.24   Item Response Descriptive Statistics

Item	Response Mean S.D.*	Total Score Mean S.D.*	Pearson & Polyserial Correlation	Initial Slope	Initial Location
1 0001	3.453	28.600	0.754	1.304	1.378
	1.087*	5.841*	0.794		
2 0002	3.753	28.600	0.593	0.817	−1.117
	0.945*	5.841*	0.633		
3 0003	3.507	28.600	0.652	0.963	0.847
	1.038*	5.841*	0.694		

Item	Response Mean S.D.*	Total Score Mean S.D.*	Pearson & Polyserial Correlation	Initial Slope	Initial Location
4 0004	3.927	28.600	0.591	0.881	−1.889
	0.740*	5.841*	0.661		
5 0005	3.560	28.600	0.773	1.505	1.550
	1.267*	5.841*	0.833		
6 0006	3.387	28.600	0.793	1.564	1.770
	1.094*	5.841*	0.843		
7 0007	3.760	28.600	0.637	0.936	−0.234
	1.044*	5.841*	0.683		
8 0008	3.253	28.600	0.788	1.492	0.537
	1.059*	5.841*	0.831		

Table 6.25 shows the mean and standard deviations for each of the Likert-type categories collapsed across all items.

Table 6.25   Means and Standard Deviations for Each of the Likert-Type Categories Collapsed Across Items

Category	Mean	S.D.	Parameter
1	17.745	3.375	1.568
2	22.629	4.651	0.622
3	26.986	4.477	−0.341
4	30.118	4.090	−1.848
5	33.760	4.132	

The next phase of the PARSCALE output, Phase 2, is where the item calibration occurs. As with the 1PL, 2PL, and 3PL models, iterative E-M cycles and Newton cycles are run with the results after each iteration reported. The −2 log likelihood values after each iteration are reported.

[E-M Cycles] Graded Response Model

Category and Item Parameters After Cycle: 0

Largest Change = 0.000

−2 Log Likelihood = 4330.923

Category and Item Parameters After Cycle: 25

(Continued)

Box 6.3 (Continued)

Largest Change = 0.007 (−1.214−> −1.221) at Location of Item: 4 0004

[Newton Cycles] Graded Response Model

Category and Item Parameters After Cycle: 0

Largest Change = 0.000

−2 Log Likelihood = 2979.352

Category and Item Parameters After Cycle: 5

Largest Change = 0.710 (−0.974−> −1.684) at Location of Item: 4 0004

Presented next are the category threshold parameters for all items on the test. Recall that Muraki's modification allows for the same category thresholds because all items were responded to using the same five-point Likert scale.

Category Parameter	1.724	0.637	−0.411	−1.951
S.E.	0.100	0.058	0.045	0.045

Next, the slopes (a) and intercepts (b) are calculated for each item (see Table 6.26). There is no guessing (c) parameter in the model, so these are all set to 0.0.

Table 6.26   Slopes and Intercepts for Each Item in the Likert-Type Examples

Item	Block	Slope	S.E.	Location	S.E.	Guessing	S.E.
0001	1	1.074	0.089	−0.932	0.144	0.000	0.000
0002	1	0.956	0.099	−1.460	0.185	0.000	0.000
0003	1	0.992	0.083	−0.684	0.159	0.000	0.000
0004	1	1.223	0.115	−1.684	0.161	0.000	0.000
0005	1	0.792	0.070	−0.793	0.167	0.000	0.000
0006	1	1.138	0.109	−0.765	0.140	0.000	0.000
0007	1	0.593	0.068	−1.223	0.172	0.000	0.000
0008	1	1.073	0.114	−0.553	0.143	0.000	0.000

The summary slope and threshold parameters for the test are shown in Table 6.27.

Table 6.27   Summary Slope and Threshold Parameters for the Test

Summary Statistics of Parameter Estimates			
Parameter	Mean	Stn. Dev.	N
Slope	0.980	0.203	8
Log(Slope)	−0.042	0.234	8
Threshold	−1.012	0.402	8
Guessing	0.000	0.000	0

The item fit statistics are presented in Table 6.28. Items with probabilities greater than 0.05 fit the data well. In this example, only Item 3 fits the data well. This is likely due to the small sample size ($N = 150$), where sample sizes of 1,000 or more are expected in applied settings but can be lower (e.g., 250) for research purposes.

Table 6.28   Item Fit Statistics for the Likert-Type Items

Item Fit Statistics				
Block	*Item*	*Chi-Square*	*df*	*Prob.*
LBLOCK	0001	36.63832	11.	0.000
	0002	24.43101	8.	0.002
	0003	16.98425	12.	0.150
	0004	36.01285	8.	0.000
	0005	22.53542	13.	0.047
	0006	36.01197	11.	0.000
	0007	36.23487	12.	0.000
	0008	36.33896	12.	0.000
	TOTAL	245.18767	87.	0.000

Inserted here (Figures 6.15, 6.16, 6.17) are the item characteristic curves and item information functions for one test item (Item 6) and then the test information curve for the test as a whole.

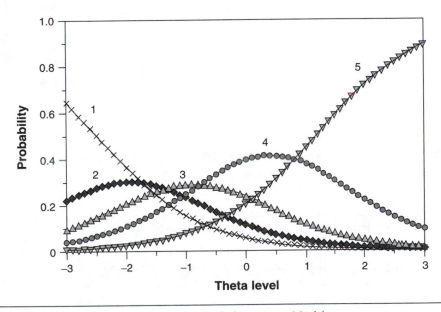

Figure 6.15   Item 6 Characteristic Curve: Graded Response Model

(Continued)

Box 6.3 (Continued)

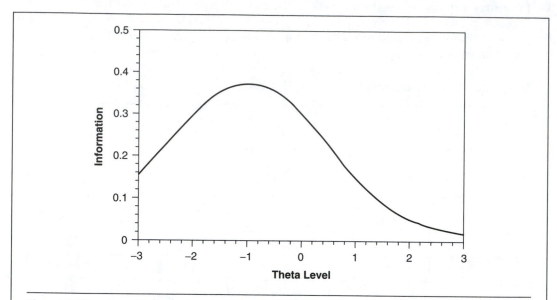

Figure 6.16   Item 6 Information Function: Graded Response Model

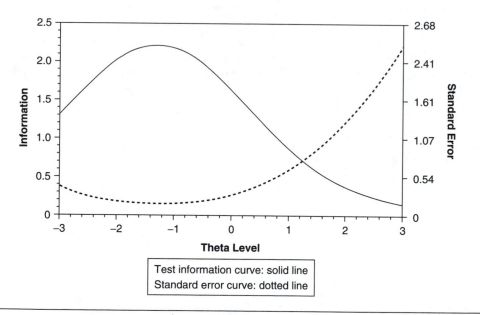

Test information curve: solid line
Standard error curve: dotted line

Figure 6.17   Test Information Function: Graded Response Model

The next phase, Phase 3 of the PARSCALE output, scores the participants in terms of their theta, or trait level, in this case. Scoring can be done using maximum likelihood or EAP. In this case, EAP was used.

Table 6.29   Ability Distribution for Likert-Type Item Example

Means and Standard Deviations of Ability Distributions			
Score Name	Mean	Standard Deviation	Total Frequencies
EAP	−0.268	0.876	150.00

Table 6.29 indicates that, as a whole, these respondents did not rate their leadership in their team at even average levels (mean of −0.268).

Ability and standard error of the estimates are shown in the next table that is produced by the program. However, of the 150 participants, only the first three and last three are shown in Table 6.30.

Table 6.30   Ability Estimates for the First and Last Three Subjects

Score Subject	Name	Group	Weight	Category Mean	Attempts	Ability	S.E.
1	EAP	1	1.00	1.62	1.00	−2.3815	0.4217
2	EAP	1	1.00	3.62	1.00	−0.0140	0.4133
3	EAP	1	1.00	4.12	1.00	0.6000	0.4224
148	EAP	1	1.00	3.75	1.00	0.0399	0.4126
149	EAP	1	1.00	4.50	1.00	1.2238	0.4297
150	EAP	1	1.00	2.62	1.00	−1.2971	0.3999

operating curves for each of the steps (Step 0–Step 1, Step 1–Step 2, and Step 2–Step 3) can be written. These are generated by the 1PL equation used earlier. For the probability of obtaining a score of 1 versus 0, the equation is

(6–12) $$P_1(\Theta) = 1/\{1 + \exp[-D(\Theta - b_1)]\}.$$

For the probability of obtaining a score of 2 versus 1, the equation is

(6–13) $$P_2(\Theta) = 1/\{1 + \exp[-D(\Theta - b_2)]\}.$$

For the probability of obtaining a score of 3 versus 2, the equation is

(6–14) $$P_3(\Theta) = 1/\{1 + \exp[-D(\Theta - b_3)]\}.$$

In the above three equations, the b values correspond to "step difficulties."

Thus, the partial credit model estimates $m - 1$ (where $m =$ the number of possible outcomes) step difficulty parameters to describe the ordered categories. These step difficulties can be graphed as threshold operating curves given one knows the b_1, b_2, and b_3 parameter estimates.

Figures 6.18 and 6.19 show the threshold operating curves of the two math test items for 4th-graders noted above. These curves are analogous to the threshold operating curves in the graded response models. Recall that for Item 1, the first step was of moderate difficulty ($b = 0$), the second step was most difficult ($b = 1$), and the third was easiest ($b = -1$). For Item 2, the first step was easiest ($b = -0.5$), the second step was of intermediate difficulty ($b = 1.5$), and the third was the most difficult ($b = 2.25$).

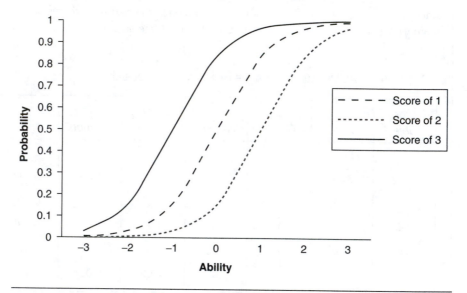

Figure 6.18   Item 1 Threshold Characteristic Curves Under a Partial Credit Model

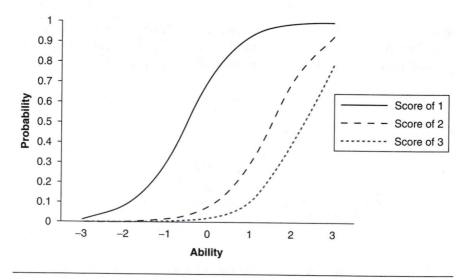

Figure 6.19   Item 2 Threshold Characteristic Curves Under a Partial Credit Model

Notice that for Item 1, there are reversals in that the curve for a score of 1 is in the middle, a score of 2 is to the right of 1, and a score of 3 is leftmost, reflecting their different step difficulty levels. Item 2 is ordered in a more expected manner in that a score of 3 is rightmost, a score of 2 is in the middle, and a score of 1 is leftmost, again reflecting their step difficulty levels.

The equation used to generate the option characteristic curves for each response alternative is a ratio (as was the case for the nominal model): the probability of a particular score, or response alternative for an individual (x) with a particular level of Θ, is an exponential divided by the sum of exponentials.

(6–15)
$$P_{ix}(\Theta) = \exp\left[\sum_{j=0}^{x}(\Theta - \delta_{ij})\right] \Bigg/ \left\{\sum_{k=0}^{m}\left[\exp\sum_{j=0}^{k}(\Theta - \delta_{ij})\right]\right\} \text{ and where } \sum_{j=0}^{0}(\Theta - \delta_{ij}) \equiv 0.$$

The subscripts are as follows: i = the item, j = the categories, and k = the steps. The "where . . . " statement in the equation indicates a restriction in estimating the parameters and means, the sum of the ability levels minus the step difficulty for the first step must be identical to zero. In this case, δ is equal to the step difficulty, not the difficulty of the item. These step difficulties represent the point at which the probability of selecting a lower step response shifts to the next higher step up. That is, they are the relative difficulties between these steps. The option characteristic curves for Items 1 and 2 of the math test are shown in Figures 6.20 and 6.21.

Because the calculations used to generate the data used in creating the figures are quite tedious, option characteristic curve calculations for only math test Item 2 at three different ability levels are shown and described in Table 6.31 for the interested reader.

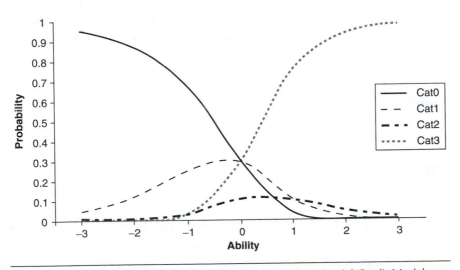

Figure 6.20   Item 1 Option Characteristic Curves Under a Partial Credit Model

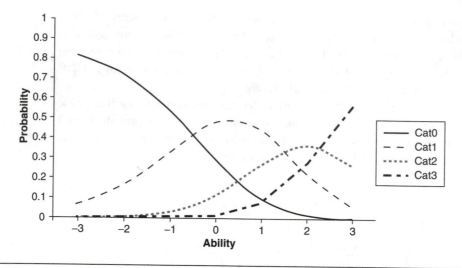

Figure 6.21   Item 2 Option Characteristic Curves Under a Partial Credit Model

More informative and interesting than generating the actual numbers needed to generate the plots is to inspect the shape of the option characteristic curves in Figures 6.20 and 6.21. The problem with Item 1 is quite apparent. Getting no parts of the item correct (a category score of 0) approaches 1.0 at the lowest ability levels. At a moderate ability level ($\Theta = 0$), there is an equal chance (about 30%) of getting a 0 or getting a 3 on the item. Therefore, the interim categories (part 1 correct but not parts 2 or 3, or parts 1 and 2 correct but not part 3) are almost useless.

Category 1 ($b = 0$) is more difficult than Category 3 ($b = -1.0$), and Categories 1 and 3 were less difficult than Category 2 ($b = 1.0$). The curves reflect these reversals. Test takers will almost never get a 2 (i.e., they completed the first two steps but did not complete the third). They are somewhat more likely to get only the first step correct but not the second or third. The most likely pattern, however, is that they will get all steps of the item correct or all of them incorrect. There is minimal additional information provided by Categories 1 or 2. This item, then, could be simply scored as a dichotomous item rather than as one that uses partial credit.

Item 2, however, behaves more like a partial credit item should. Notice that, like Item 1, getting no parts of the item correct (Step 0) approaches 1.0 at the lowest ability levels. As ability goes up, the chances of getting a 1 improve until, at the Step 1 difficulty level (-0.5), the two lines cross and a score of 1 becomes more probable than 0 and stays most probable until the Step 2 difficulty level (1.5), where now a score of 2 becomes more probable than a score of 1. A score of 2 is most probable only over a small number of ability levels until the Step 3 difficulty is encountered (2.25), where now a score of 3 is most probable.

While Masters' model assumed equal slopes across all items in a scale, Muraki (1992, 1993) extended the model to allow for slopes to vary from item to item

Table 6.31 Calculations for Math Item 2 Option Characteristic Curves

Recall that the formula (6–15) is as follows:

$$P_{ix}(\Theta) = \exp\left[\sum_{j=0}^{x}(\Theta - \delta_{ij})\right] \Bigg/ \left\{\sum_{k=0}^{m}\left[\exp\sum_{j=0}^{k}(\Theta - \delta_{ij})\right]\right\} \text{ and where } \sum_{j=0}^{0}(\Theta - \delta_{ij}) \equiv 0.$$

"Unpacking" this formula is demonstrated most easily with examples.

First, calculate the different numerators for ability levels –3, 0, and 3 for options 0, 1, 2, and 3:

Option 0:

$\text{Exp}^{(0)} = 1$ across all ability levels

Option 1:

Ability level –3: $\text{Exp}^{(0) + (-3 - -0.5)} = \text{Exp}^{(-2.5)} = 0.082$

Ability level 0: $\text{Exp}^{(0) + (0 - -0.5)} = \text{Exp}^{(0.5)} = 1.65$

Ability level + 3: $\text{Exp}^{(0) + (3 - -0.5)} = \text{Exp}^{(3.5)} = 33.103$

Option 2:

Ability level –3: $\text{Exp}^{(0) + (-3 - -0.5) + (-3 -1.5)} = \text{Exp}^{(-7)} = 0.0009$

Ability level 0: $\text{Exp}^{(0) + (0 - -0.5) + (0 -1.5)} = \text{Exp}^{(-1)} = 0.368$

Ability level +3: $\text{Exp}^{(0) + (3 - -0.5) + (3 -1.5)} = \text{Exp}^{(5)} = 148.336$

Option 3:

Ability level –3: $\text{Exp}^{(0) + (-3 - -0.5) + (-3 - 1.5) + (-3 -2.25)} = \text{Exp}^{(-12.25)} = 0.000005$

Ability level 0: $\text{Exp}^{(0) + (0 - -0.5) + (0 -1.5) + (0- 2.25)} = \text{Exp}^{(-3.25)} = 0.039$

Ability level +3: $\text{Exp}^{(0) + (3 - -0.5) + (3 -1.5) + (3 -2.25)} = \text{Exp}^{(5.75)} = 314.003$

Next, calculate the denominators for ability levels –3, 0, and 3 that will be used across options:

Ability level –3:

$\text{Exp}(0) + \text{Exp}^{(0) + (-3 - -0.5)} + \text{Exp}^{(0) + (-3 - -0.5) + (-3 -1.5)} + \text{Exp}^{(0) + (-3 - -0.5) + (-3 -1.5) + (-3 -2.25)}$

$= 1 + \text{Exp}^{(-2.5)} + \text{Exp}^{(-7)} + \text{Exp}^{(-12.25)} = 1 + 0.082 + .0009 + .000005$

$= 1.091$

Ability level 0:

$\text{Exp}(0) + \text{Exp}^{(0) + (0 - -0.5)} + \text{Exp}^{(0) + (0 - -0.5) + (0 -1.5)} + \text{Exp}^{(0) + (0 - -0.5) + (0 -1.5) + (0 -2.25)}$

$= 1 + \text{Exp}^{(0.5)} + \text{Exp}^{(-1)} + \text{Exp}^{(-3.5)} = 1 + 1.649 + 0.368 + 0.030$

$= 3.047$

Ability level +3:

$\text{Exp}^{(0)} + \text{Exp}^{(0) + (3 - -0.5)} + \text{Exp}^{(0) + (3 - -0.5) + (3 -1.5)} + \text{Exp}^{(0) + (3 - -0.5) + (3 -1.5) + (3 - 2.25)}$

$= 1 + \text{Exp}^{(3.5)} + \text{Exp}^{(5)} + \text{Exp}^{(5.75)} = 1 + 33.103 + 148.336 + 314.00$

$= 496.44$

Finally, for the ability levels for each option, divide the option–varying numerators by the ability–based denominator:

at ability –3, option 0: 1/1.091 = 0.917

at ability 0, option 0: 1/3.047 = 0.328

at ability 3, option 0: 1/496.44 = 0.002

at ability –3, option 1: 0.082/1.091 = 0.075

at ability 0, option 1: 1.65/3.047 = 0.542

at ability 3, option 1: 33.103/496.44 = 0.067

at ability –3, option 2: 0.0009/1.091 = 0.0008

at ability 0, option 2: 0.368/3.047 = 0.121

at ability 3, option 2: 148.336/496.44 = 0.298

at ability –3, option 3: .000005/1.091 = 0.000

at ability 0, option 3: 0.039/3.047 = 0.013

at ability 3, option 3: 314.003/496.44 = 0.633

Now you can plot ability levels (x– axis) against the probabilities generated in the final step (y– axis). To smooth out the line, you can calculate the probabilities for more ability levels.

within the same scale. In the formula, an *a* value term for each item is incorporated into the previous equation:

(6–16)
$$P_{ix}(\Theta) = \exp\left[\sum_{j=0}^{x} a_i(\Theta - \delta_{ij})\right] \Bigg/$$

$$\left\{\sum_{k=0}^{m}\left[\exp\sum_{j=0}^{k} a_i(\Theta - \delta_{ij})\right]\right\} \text{ and where } \sum_{j=0}^{0} a_i(\Theta - \delta_{ij}) \equiv 0.$$

This equation is more complicated and does require more parameters to be estimated. However, this more generalized model has the potential to provide a better fit to the data where items do in fact have different slopes. Note that the slope does not change within the item, just across different items. In addition, slopes in this model are not interpreted the same as in dichotomous item models. Specifically, they indicate how much categorical responses vary between different items as Θ levels change. Curves with slope parameters less than one are platykurtic (flat) in shape, and curves with slope parameters greater than one are more leptokurtic (peaked) in shape. Because the interpretation of the curves generated is similar to that of Masters's model, an additional example will not be shown.

Finally, the last partial credit model presented is that described by Andrich (1978a, 1978b) and is often called the *rating scale model*. This model is most restrictive in its assumptions. First, it assumes that slopes are equal across all items. In addition, a single parameter is estimated for step difficulties (thresholds), assuming that all items have the same step difficulties. This assumption makes most sense in attitude or personality assessment where Likert-type response formats are used and it is reasonable to assume that the 1 = strongly disagree, 2 = disagree, 3 = neither agree nor disagree, 4 = agree, and 5 = strongly agree differences remain fairly constant across items. This is probably not a reasonable assumption in many achievement tests where steps to complete the problem are likely to vary substantially in their difficulty levels. The formula for this model (Dodd, 1990) is

(6–17)
$$P_x(\Theta) = \exp\left\{\sum_{j=0}^{x}[\Theta - (b_i + t_j)]\right\} \Bigg/$$

$$\sum_{k=0}^{m} \exp\left\{\sum_{j=0}^{k}[\Theta - (b_i + t_j)]\right\} \text{ and where } \sum_{j=0}^{0}[\Theta - (b_i + t_j)] = 0.$$

In this formula, the step difficulties are decomposed into two parts: that associated with the location parameter of the item on the latent trait scale (*b*), and the response threshold parameters (*t*). Again, the interpretations of the curves generated from this model are similar to that of Masters's model. A unique feature of Andrich's model is that the curve shapes do not differ from item to item; they just move left to right along the ability level axis depending on the item difficulty (that is, the *b* parameters).

An example of an output and interpretation of a partial credit model using the PARSCALE 4 (Muraki & Bock, 2003) program is shown in Box 6.4.

Box 6.4   Partial Credit Model: Selected Output from PARSCALE 4

In this simulated data set, there are nine math items to which 400 students responded. Each item can be scored such that partial credit (from 0–3 points) can be given for each item. The PARSCALE 4 program was used to analyze the data using Masters' partial credit model. Phase 0 double-checks the programming syntax and data prior to analysis. As with the other IRT programs, the fixed prior distribution is a normal one with a mean of 0.0 and standard deviation of 1.0. It is divided into 30 quadrature points. In the next section, the number of items are reviewed and the number of cases used is reported. In addition, the actual scores for each item for the first two cases are reported. The program does not allow for 0 to be a score, and thus the scoring was recoded from "0, 1, 2, 3" to "1, 2, 3, 4," respectively.

Number Of Items: 9

Rescale Constant: Mean = 0.00; S.D. = 1.00

Items: 1   2   3   4   5   6   7   8   9

Input and Recoded Response of First and Second

Observations

Observation #1

Input Responses: 2 2 2 2 2 2 2 2 2

Recoded Responses: 3 3 3 3 3 3 3 3 3

Observation #2

Input Responses: 2 2 2 2 2 2 2 2 2

Recoded Responses: 3 3 3 3 3 3 3 3 3

400 Observations Read From File: Partialcredit.Dat

Next is Phase 1 of the partial credit output. It contains the initial information used prior to calibrating the items and generating final parameters. The frequencies of respondent scores in each of the four categories of partial credit for each item are shown in Table 6.32.

Table 6.32   Partial Credit Frequencies and Percentages of Responses for Each Category

Summary Item Statistics

Item		Total	Not Present	Omit	Categories			
					1	*2*	*3*	*4*
0001								
	Freq.	400	0	0	87	75	101	137
	Perc.		0.0	0.0	21.8	18.8	25.2	34.2
0002								
	Freq.	400	0	0	156	99	71	74
	Perc.		0.0	0.0	39.0	24.8	17.8	18.5
0003								
	Freq.	400	0	0	5	6	40	349
	Perc.		0.0	0.0	1.2	1.5	10.0	87.2

(Continued)

Box 6.4 (Continued)

Item		Total	Not Present	Omit	Categories			
					1	2	3	4
0004								
	Freq.	400	0	0	139	117	77	67
	Perc.		0.0	0.0	34.8	29.2	19.2	16.8
0005								
	Freq.	400	0	0	35	71	80	214
	Perc.		0.0	0.0	8.8	17.8	20.0	53.5
0006								
	Freq.	400	0	0	116	59	47	178
	Perc.		0.0	0.0	29.0	14.8	11.8	44.5
0007								
	Freq.	400	0	0	17	35	64	284
	Perc.		0.0	0.0	4.2	8.8	16.0	71.0
0008								
	Freq.	400	0	0	40	128	55	177
	Perc.		0.0	0.0	10.0	32.0	13.8	44.2
0009								
	Freq.	400	0	0	51	83	65	201
	Perc.		0.0	0.0	12.8	20.8	16.2	50.2
Cummul								
	Freq				646	673	600	1681
	Perc				17.9	18.7	16.7	46.7

Table 6.33 reports the mean and standard deviation for each item as well as total score. In addition, the item-to-total Pearson and polyserial correlation coefficients are reported and are used for initial slope (a) and location (b) parameter estimation. The polyserial assumes that the response categories are not truly separate and distinct but instead are artificially created and based on an underlying continuum of ability. The polyserial correlation coefficients are less conservative than the Pearson.

Table 6.33   Partial Credit Descriptive Statistics for Each Item

Block	Item	Response Mean S.D*	Total Score Mean S.D.	Pearson & Polyserial Correlation	Initial Slope	Initial Location
1	0001	2.720	26.290	0.454	0.574	0.696
		1.150*	3.814*	0.498		
2	0002	2.158	26.290	0.517	0.696	1.859
		1.133*	3.814*	0.571		
3	0003	3.833	26.290	0.209	0.358	−5.801
		0.494*	3.814*	0.337		
4	0004	2.180	26.290	0.542	0.734	1.811
		1.085*	3.814*	0.591		
5	0005	3.183	26.290	0.539	0.787	−0.233
		1.014*	3.814*	0.618		
6	0006	2.717	26.290	0.557	0.827	0.890
		1.293*	3.814*	0.637		
7	0007	3.538	26.290	0.374	0.543	−1.982
		0.824*	3.814*	0.477		
8	0008	2.922	26.290	0.283	0.334	−1.523
		1.075*	3.814*	0.316		
9	0009	3.040	26.290	0.123	0.141	−1.602
		1.104*	3.814*	0.139		

Next, the overall test mean and standard deviations for each partial credit category are reported (Table 6.34) as well as the location parameters for the three upper-level partial credit categories.

Table 6.34   Partial Credit Overall Test Descriptive Statistics for Each Category

Category	Scoring	Mean	S.D.	Parameter
1	1.000	23.444	3.820	
2	2.000	25.793	3.493	0.02
3	3.000	26.898	3.462	−0.607
4	4.000	27.365	3.447	0.579

(Continued)

Box 6.4 (Continued)

Phase 2 of the PARSCALE output contains the item calibration and parameter estimation. A generalized partial credit model is used to calculate the parameters with E-M cycles and Newton enhancement procedures.

Step and Item Parameters After Cycle: 25
Largest Change = 3.018 (−15.457–> −18.476) at Location of Item: 3
[Newton Cycles] Partial Credit Model
−2 Log Likelihood = 8323.776
Step And Item Parameters After Cycle: 2
Largest Change = 0.805 (−4.428–> −3.622) at Location of Item: 7

Note that the −2 Log Likelihood value is 8323.776. The "step parameters," as Masters called them, are noted in Table 6.35. Because all were scored using 0, 1, 2, or 3, the step parameters are the same for each item. In addition, the final slope (a) and location (b) parameters are noted in Table 6.35.

Table 6.35   Partial Credit Step Parameters and Final Slope and Location Parameters for Each Item

Scoring Function		1.000	2.000	3.000	4.000		
Step Parameter		0.000	−0.154	−0.655	0.809		
S.E.		0.000	0.136	0.153	0.136		
Item	*Block*	*Slope*	*S.E.*	*Location*	*S.E.*	*Guessing*	*S.E.*
0001	1	0.123	0.036	−0.668	0.026	0.000	0.000
0002	1	0.258	0.041	0.649	0.180	0.000	0.000
0003	1	0.034	0.067	0.000	12.630	0.000	0.000
0004	1	0.222	0.042	0.669	0.192	0.000	0.000
0005	1	0.226	0.039	−1.714	0.262	0.000	0.000
0006	1	0.481	0.052	−0.300	0.088	0.000	0.000
0007	1	0.182	0.039	−3.622	1.204	0.000	0.000
0008	1	0.050	0.036	0.000	2.846	0.000	0.000
0009	1	0.033	0.037	0.000	6.768	0.000	0.000

The overall test summary statistics are reported in Table 6.36.

Table 6.36   Partial Credit Overall Test Summary Statistics

Summary Statistics Of Parameter Estimates			
Parameter	*Mean*	*Stn. Dev.*	*N*
Slope	0.179	0.143	9
Log(Slope)	−2.075	0.969	9
Threshold	−0.554	1.356	9
Guessing	0.000	0.000	0

The item characteristic curve for Item 6 and the information function for Item 6 are shown below (Figures 6.22 and 6.23). In addition, the overall test information curve for all nine items is shown (Figure 6.24).

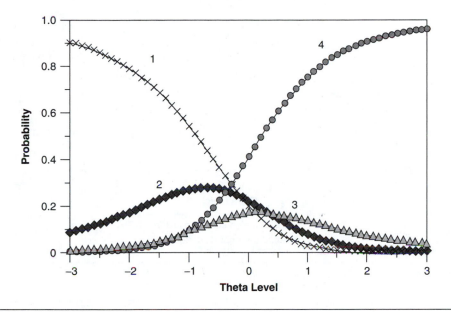

Figure 6.22   Item 6 Characteristic Curves Under a Partial Credit Model

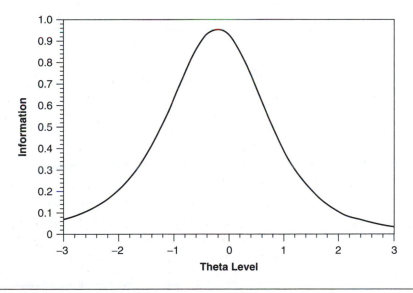

Figure 6.23   Item 6 Information Function Under a Partial Credit Model

(Continued)

Box 6.4 (Continued)

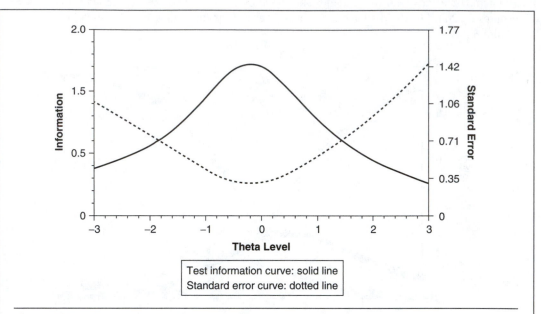

Test information curve: solid line
Standard error curve: dotted line

Figure 6.24   Test Information Function Under a Partial Credit Model

Phase 3 of the PARSCALE program scores participants on their ability levels. EAP scoring is used. The mean of the scores on the ability distribution shows that, on average, individuals scored almost at the mean (0.065).

Means and Standard Deviations of Ability Distributions			
Score Name	Mean	Standard Deviation	Total Frequencies
EAP	0.065	0.766	400.00

Each person's ability level and standard error are reported in the next part of the output. However, only the first and last three entries are reported in Table 6.37.

Table 6.37   Partial Credit Estimated Ability Levels for the First and Last Three Subjects

Subject	Score Name	Group	Weight	Mean	Category Attempt	Ability	S.E.
1	EAP	1	1.00	3.00	1.00	0.3599	0.8575
2	EAP	1	1.00	3.00	1.00	0.3599	0.8575
3	EAP	1	1.00	2.00	1.00	−1.3888	0.8780
398	EAP	1	1.00	3.56	1.00	1.4017	0.9307
399	EAP	1	1.00	3.22	1.00	1.1516	0.9107
400	EAP	1	1.00	3.44	1.00	1.4767	0.9368

Parameter Estimation

In the models described above, the item parameters are estimated. In addition, the latent trait (Θ distribution) is estimated (i.e., a "person parameter" for each case is estimated). These occur simultaneously and iteratively. However, if, for example, the researcher knows the item parameters in advance, these can be noted in the computer program and fixed to those values. Then the estimation is carried out only for person parameters using the fixed item parameter estimates. For our purposes, we'll assume the most normative use of IRT programs—that both person and item parameters are to be estimated. Let's begin with the item parameter estimation (e.g., slopes, difficulties, etc.).

The mathematical equations for solving them are extremely cumbersome and complex. Computers are needed to handle the work efficiently and so hand calculations will not be shown here. Embretson and Reise (2000) provide an excellent description of as much of the analyses that can be done by hand.

Several computer programs are available for these estimations. Each offers different options in this regard, and the pros and cons of each should be understood by the user before proceeding to adopt one. The major differences in these options are reviewed next. Two general categories of item estimation are currently in use and within each are some subcategories. The first category uses maximum likelihood and the second uses Bayesian estimation.

Maximum Likelihood Estimation. Maximum likelihood estimation procedures estimate person and item parameters that are most likely to replicate the response pattern in a set of items. One of the first procedures to be developed in this group was joint maximum likelihood (JML). It is an iterative process that involves sequential estimates of person and item parameters. Whereas JML models have been useful in that they are easy to program and allow for estimation of 1PL, 2PL, and 3PL models, there are drawbacks. The error of person estimates (the calculated Θ levels for each person taking the test) tends to be large with tests of fewer than 50 items, and, in addition, the JML model does not allow for person estimates for individuals that fail or pass all of the items.

These problems led to the development of marginal maximum likelihood (MML) estimation. An assumption in this procedure is that examinees are sampled from a known distribution (usually the normal distribution; Bock & Aitken, 1981). MML provides efficient parameter estimates even for short tests and can estimate parameters for examinees that pass or fail all items. It handles all types of IRT models—even multidimensional ones.

One additional approach in this family is conditional maximum likelihood (CML). In CML, however, a "sufficient statistic" must be available in order for trait levels to be estimated. Because 1PL models are the only ones where raw scores are available as a sufficient statistic, CML is restricted to use in these models.

Bayesian Estimation. In Bayesian estimations, the likelihood function is estimated by multiplying a *prior* distribution to obtain the new *posterior* distribution. Prior distributions use information about what we know about the population of examinees to provide this prior distribution—which is by default in most computer programs the normal distribution. Bayesian estimation is efficient insofar as outlandish possible ability scores (such as −7565.0) are assumed to be far less probable than scores around the midpoint of a normal distribution (± 4.0). The maximum likelihood estimation procedures, on the other hand, assumed all possible scores are equally probable as a starting point.

There are two primary Bayesian approaches: Bayes modal estimation and expected a posteriori (EAP) estimation. The Bayes modal approach maximizes the *modal* values of the posterior distribution, whereas the EAP estimation maximizes the *mean* values of the posterior distribution. Both modes and means are summary scores representing different aspects of a distribution.

Scoring Respondents

Scores for each respondent can be generated using maximum likelihood (ML), maximum a posteriori (MAP), or EAP approaches. While ML is most desirable, it requires large samples of both items and respondents. In addition, respondents with all-incorrect or all-correct response patterns have Θ levels that cannot be estimated. MAP uses a prior distribution, such as a normal distribution, to estimate respondent Θ levels.

Both ML and MAP approaches are iterative; that is, a starting value for the Θ level is generated and changes iteratively until the most likely estimate for Θ is found. EAP also uses prior information, but the Θ levels are estimated noniteratively. Thus, they are much faster to compute. EAP and MAP provide quite similar results. As with the parameter estimation procedures, the pros and cons of each method should be understood before using one over the other. Sometimes the computer program will offer only one option, in which case the user will not have a choice.

Once the latent trait of each respondent is determined, these scores can be transformed into any other scale. The Θ values are interpreted the same as z values. Thus, to transform them to another scale, simply use the same process as that used in Chapter 1. Multiply the Θ value by the standard deviation (SD) of the new scale and add the mean of the new scale. For example, if a respondent has a Θ value of −0.05, and that score is to be transformed to a scale with a mean of 50 and standard deviation of 10, the following formula is used:

$$(6\text{--}18) \qquad \text{new score} = SD(\Theta) + \overline{X},$$

$$\text{new score} = 10(\Theta) + 50,$$

$$\text{new score} = 10(-0.05) + 50,$$

$$\text{new score} = -0.50 + 50,$$

$$\text{new score} = 49.5.$$

Model Fit

Once item and person parameters are estimated, the fit of each can be assessed. A variety of ways to assess item fit have been developed (e.g., Reise, 1990). One way is via the χ^2 statistics provided for each item. If the χ^2 is significant, it indicates that the item does not fit the data well. These tests are most useful in tests of more than 20 items. They are very sensitive to sample size and are particularly conservative if Bayesian rather than maximum likelihood has been used to estimate parameters (Drasgow & Hulin, 1990). Thus, they should not be used as the sole decision-making tool about item fit (McKinley & Mills, 1985).

The χ^2 can also be used to test "nested models." For example, if an IRT program is run on a 20-item test using a 1PL model, a statistic called the -2 log likelihood is generated. Let's assume the value for the -2 log likelihood is 3000. The larger this value is, the worse the fit. Next, a more complex model (2PL) is run on the same data. Again a -2 log likelihood statistic is generated and this one is 2500. It is smaller than the first (3000 versus 2500), indicating a better fit. When there are fewer constraints on the data (i.e., in this case, the constraint of equivalent slopes across all items of the 1PL model is relaxed), the model fits the data better and the -2 log likelihood drops in value. The difference between the two -2 log likelihoods is distributed as a χ^2 (i.e., $3000 - 2500 = 500$). The degrees of freedom to test this χ^2 are the additional parameters estimated in the more complicated model. In this case, there were 20 items and so 20 new parameters were estimated in the more complex model (one slope for each item). Thus, $\chi^2 (20) = 500$ is significant, indicating that the 2PL model fits the data significantly better than the 1PL model. It is worth noting that the χ^2 is a powerful statistic with large sample sizes. Because large samples are often the norm in IRT analyses, even minor deviations in fit will be statistically significant. These deviations, then, may not be of practical utility.

A nonstatistical procedure to assess fit is by examining the plot of standardized residuals. In this approach, examinees' estimated Θ values are utilized. They are sorted from highest to lowest and then grouped into equal-sized categories (say 20). Then, for each item within each of these categories, the actual number of individuals who passed or endorsed the item is calculated. Next, these frequencies are converted to be the proportion of the sample for each level. A plot of the categories (x-axis) against the proportions (y-axis) provides the *empirical item characteristic curve*. This can be compared to the *hypothesized item characteristic curve* that was generated by the IRT analysis. Figure 6.25 shows an example of such curves.

Notice that up to about a Θ level of 0.0, the curves match fairly well. However, past Θ levels of 0.5, the hypothetical curve is higher than the empirical curve. The differences between these curves can be calculated at various points (usually the midpoint for each category) and are called residuals. Large residuals indicate points along the Θ continuum where the model does not fit the data. These residuals can be standardized and examined for values ± 2.0 for ill-fitting areas of the model. Table 6.38 shows such a table that reflects numerically the discrepancies between the curves shown in Figure 6.25.

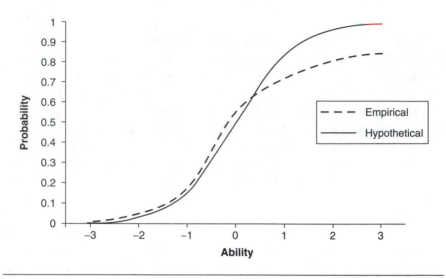

Figure 6.25 Empirical and Hypothetical Curves to Assess Model Fit

Another nonstatistical assessment of fit is by examination of the amount of information each item provides about the latent trait at different values of Θ and is called the standard error of the estimated Θ value. The formula of the standard error for a given item is

(6–19) $$\Theta = 1/\sqrt{I(\Theta)}.$$

The standard error of each item at different levels of Θ will differ. In fact, the item characteristic curves that have been drawn can be transformed directly into item information curves (IICs). These were shown in the box examples.

The IICs are U-shaped, with ability along the x-axis and standard error on the y-axis. At quite specific points along the Θ continuum, the standard error is very small and at other locations is very large. These curves are particularly useful in item design and test revision in that they indicate where along the Θ continuum each item best discriminates. If the test does not discriminate at various areas along the continuum, more or less difficult and/or more discriminating items may need to be written. Items providing minimal information can be replaced with better items.

The IICs can be also be summed across all items in the scale to provide a test information curve:

(6–20) $$TI(\Theta) = \Sigma I(\Theta).$$

The standard error of measurement across all items (i.e., the test as a whole) is given by the standard error for a given test:

(6–21) $$\Theta = 1/\sqrt{TI\Theta}.$$

Table 6.38   Tabular Presentation of Residuals

Mean of the Theta Interval	Standardized Residuals
−3	0.03
−2.75	0.02
−2.5	0.12
−2.25	−0.35
−2	−0.40
−1.75	−0.30
−1.5	−0.20
−1.25	−0.15
−1	−0.35
−0.75	−0.60
−0.5	−0.76
−0.25	−0.85
0.25	0.00
0.5	0.50
0.75	1.00
1	1.51
1.25	1.62
1.5	1.73
1.75	2.03
2	2.24
2.25	2.32
2.5	2.31
2.75	2.45
3	2.33

This can be converted into a test information function where, at specified levels of Θ, the standard error of that estimate can be found. Again, these test information curves were shown in the box examples.

This approach to measurement error is quite different from CTT, where it is assumed that the standard error for all scores on the test is equal. Those who want to use scores based on estimates of Θ for decision making can determine the standard error they are comfortable with in making those decisions.

Person-fit indices suggest the degree to which the trait level estimate for a given respondent is reasonable or not. There are several options for assessing person-fit that will not be reviewed here, as for most of the models no generally accepted fit statistic is superior. The interested reader is referred to Meijer and Sijtsma (2001) and Reise (1990) for reviews.

Assumptions

There are two assumptions in IRT but they are quite restrictive. The first is that the item characteristic curves have a specified form. This means that if the item characteristic curves have been specified to be two-parameter and unidimensional, then this model should fit the item data. Unidimensional (i.e., one underlying construct) models are far and away more common than multidimensional models. Unfortunately, well-accepted and understood assessments of the fit of the data that would suggest that a unidimensional versus a multidimensional model is more appropriate are not yet available. There is research underway, however, to address this issue (e.g., Nandakumar, 1993; Nandakumar, 1994; Nandakumar & Stout, 1993; Stout, 1987; Stout, 1990).

The second assumption, local independence, is actually tied quite closely to the first. Local independence means that the response to one item has no effect on the response to any other item. Items that are blatantly not locally independent would be the answer to $(3 + 5) - 6 = ?$, where the first item would be the answer to $(3 + 5)$, and the second item would be the answer to $8 - 6$. If the answer to the first item is incorrect, then the probability of getting the answer to the second item correct is almost zero. Other situations are less clear, such as in tests that use passages and ask multiple items on the passage. Yen (1993) discusses at length the issue of local independence and suggests a way to assess each item's level of local dependence.

All of the models demonstrated in this chapter have assumed that the latent trait is unidimensional. Multidimensional models have been proposed more recently (e.g., Kelderman & Rijkes, 1994; Muraki & Carlson, 1995). It is beyond the scope of this book to discuss any of the more complex models, but the interested reader should find the cited readings helpful.

Ramifications of the Assumptions of Modern Test Theory

Embretson and Reise (2000) have articulated the rules of modern test theory, just as they did for CTT. It is worth reviewing them. As noted, the standard error of measurement differs at different levels of Θ. Shorter tests can be more reliable than longer ones. As was pointed out, items that are highly discriminating at specific levels of Θ can be presented in a short test but provide a more reliable estimate of Θ than in CTT.

This leads to the next rule that states that different forms (sets of items) are best for respondents of different Θ levels. The more the respondents differ, the more the sets of items presented to them should differ to better assess the particular Θ level of the respondent. Because individuals are expected to have different levels of Θ, a nonrepresentative sample of respondents is not necessary for estimating item properties such as difficulty or discrimination.

Several other points characterize IRT that make it different from CTT: response formats that differ (e.g., going from a three-point to a five-point response format) can be combined without difficulty; when initial scores on a pretest are different for different respondents, the change scores can be meaningfully interpreted; a process called full information factor analysis allows for the factor analysis of dichotomous items; and the item's stem or stimulus features can be assessed for their impact using IRT.

Practical Advantages of Modern Test Theory

The practical advantages of IRT over CTT are particularly salient at the item level. Specifically, items can be tested as to whether or not they fit a particular model. Items can be assessed as to whether or not they advantage or disadvantage certain demographic groups, holding constant the latent trait. New items can be added to tests and assessed as to whether or not their characteristics are functioning as expected. Tests administered in different languages can be assessed at the item level for differential functioning. Items can be deleted or added that have certain characteristics (e.g., more discriminating at specific levels of the latent trait). How respondents are using a neutral point can be modeled appropriately and thus the meaning of a neutral point on a response scale can be determined. Detection of unusual response styles by an individual can be readily determined in IRT. Computer adaptive testing uses IRT extensively to estimate the individual respondents' Θ level using as few items as possible.

Limitations of Modern Test Theory

Clearly, there are many advantages to using IRT. There are drawbacks, however. The three largest are the restrictive assumptions of using the model, the large sample sizes (both in terms of items and respondents) needed, and the lack of user-friendly computer programs. Although the latter is becoming less of an issue, the newer, more complex models are still not yet easily analyzed.

In addition, at the conceptual level we are often interested not just in how each item functions but also in how the items as a unit (most frequently as a total score) function. IRT is generally silent on this issue, except for the specific instance of the test information function. Therefore, it is useful to know both what classical and modern test theories have to offer to the scale building and assessment process. The two approaches answer very different types of questions. Both are necessary and neither, by itself, is sufficient for complete psychometric assessment.

Computer Programs

Several programs are available for running IRT analyses. By the time this book goes to print, the information contained in this section will likely be out of date. Thus, check the Web sites of the software firms to obtain the most up-to-date information on the capabilities of the various programs.

Three such software firms, in alphabetical order, are Assessment Systems Corporation (www.assess.com), the RUMM laboratories (www.rummlab.com.au), and Scientific Software Inc. (www.ssicentral.com). All have IRT packages that run in a Windows® environment. All have various strengths and weaknesses, including how the output is presented. These will not be detailed here and by now you should have an idea of what types of analyses you will likely want to use the software for and select the program that best suits your needs.

From Assessment Systems, the XCALIBRE and DIFPAK programs are available. The XCALIBRE program allows for 2PL and 3PL models to be estimated on dichotomous data. The DIFPAK is actually a series of five subtests that allow for the assessment of differential functioning for both items and persons.

From the RUMM laboratories, the RUMM2010 is available. RUMM stands for Rasch Unidimensional Measurement Models. It allows for analyses of data with two or more ordered categories. Differential analyses for persons is also part of the package.

Scientific Software provides four different IRT programs. MULTILOG 7 allows for the assessment of one-, two-, and three-parameter models. It handles dichotomous or polytomous response formats. Nominal, graded response, and partial credit models are also allowed for with this program. BILOG-MG 3 is used with dichotomous data and allows for the assessment of one-, two-, and three-parameter models. Differential item functioning for persons and items is a prime feature of this package. PARSCALE 4 for the assessment of one-, two-, and three- parameter models is most useful for graded response and partial credit models. TESTSFAC 4 allows for exploratory factor analysis using dichotomously scored items.

Practical Considerations

Although IRT approaches are elegant, they come at a fairly high cost. Most IRT computer programs are not as user-friendly as many common statistical packages, and thus there is a steep curve in learning the programming syntax. Fortunately, the ease of use continues to increase and the costs for such programs are not prohibitive. Now that personal computers are so powerful, stand-alone packages are quite common.

Tests of 20 or more items that assess one construct and are completed by several hundred respondents are by far the most suited to IRT models. Reise and Yu (1990) recommend 500 cases for the more complex graded response models. However, Drasgow (1989) found that reasonable estimates could be obtained with tests as short as five items with 200 simulated examinees. This was the case unless the item parameters were not extreme.

Summary

This chapter reviewed the basic tenets of modern test theory (known commonly as IRT) and also the types of analyses that can be used to assess items within IRT. The chapter covered

1. one-, two-, and three-parameter logistic models for dichotomous IRT models,

2. nominal response models;

3. graded response models;

4. partial credit models;

5. parameter estimation procedures;

6. assessment of fit;

7. practical considerations;

8. advantages and limitations of IRT compared to classical test theory; and

9. a brief description of some of the computer packages associated with IRT and the vendor Web sites as a starting point for readers interested in purchasing an IRT package.

Next Steps

The focus of the last two chapters has been at the micro (item) level. For many purposes, total test scores are used and are the focus of interest. However, it was worth spending time examining the items, as the total score can only be as useful as the sum of its parts. In the next chapters, the focus turns to the macro (test) level. Specifically, the stability of tests scores, more commonly referred to as *reliability*, will be introduced.

Problems and Exercises

1. What does the symbol theta (Θ) represent in item response theory (IRT)?

2. What is the critical linkage in IRT?

3. Why is the pattern of an individual's responses to a set of items so important in IRT?

4. How is the standard error of measurement of a test interpreted across multiple individuals' test scores in IRT?

5. What item parameter is estimated in the one-parameter logistic (1PL) model?

6. Would an item with a $b = -0.02$ be easier or more difficult than an item with a $b = -0.20$ in a 1PL model?

7. What is the probability that someone with an ability level of 1.2 will pass an item that has a difficulty level of 0.08 in a 1PL model?

8. What does it mean to have the steepest part of the slope at the *b* level in a 1PL IRT model?

9. What item parameters are estimated in the two-parameter logistic (2PL) model?

10. What is the probability that someone with an ability level of 1.2 will pass an item that has a difficulty level of 0.08 and a discrimination value of 1.3 in a 2PL model?

11. What item parameters are estimated in the three-parameter logistic (3PL) model?

12. What is the probability that someone with an ability level of 1.2 will pass an item that has a difficulty level of 0.08, a discrimination value of 1.3, and a guessing parameter of 0.25 in a 3PL model?

13. Using the functions for 1PL, 2PL, and 3PL IRT models, create item characteristic curves by plotting the probability (*Y*) against 5–6 levels of theta (*X*) manipulating the values of the *a*, *b*, and *c* parameters (Microsoft Excel® has an easy-to-use graphing program).

14. What is the benefit of analyzing multiple-choice items using a nominal analysis rather than a dichotomous analysis?

15. What do the *a* and *c* parameters in a nominal IRT analysis represent?

16. Why are graded response analyses of particular interest to those assessing attitudes?

17. Why is the graded response model presented as a two-step model?

18. Under what circumstances is it useful to use a partial credit IRT model?

19. What does it mean to have person and item parameters estimated simultaneously?

20. What are the two major types of item estimation procedures used in IRT programs?

21. What are three major types of person scoring estimation procedures used in IRT programs?

22. If my estimated latent trait on a scale is 0.12, what would be my estimated ability level on a test that had a mean of 100 and standard deviation of 15?

23. I want to determine if a simpler IRT model (1PL) will fit a set of 30 items as well as a more complex IRT model (2PL). The −2 log likelihood for the more complex model is 4000. The −2 log likelihood for the simpler model is 4040. What would I conclude?

24. How are the standard errors of the Θ values estimated in IRT models?

25. How is the test information generated in IRT analyses?

26. What is meant by local independence?

27. What are some limitations that make IRT unattractive as a way to assess items in a test?

CHAPTER 7

Reliability of Test Scores and Test Items

n this chapter, the bane of test developers will be presented. This is the reliability of the test instrument. *Reliability* is an umbrella term under which different types of score stability are assessed. It is up to the test developer and producer to ensure that the appropriate reliability indices are reported. It is up to test consumers to know how to interpret the presented reliability information.

In essence, the reliability index of a test score indicates its stability. That may mean stability of test scores over time (test-retest), stability of item scores across items (internal consistency), or stability of ratings across judges, or raters, of a person, object, event, and so on (interrater reliability). The focus of this chapter will be on the stability of test scores and test items.

These approaches to reliability stem from models of classical test theory (CTT). One of the critical features of reliability from this perspective is that it is concerned solely with random measurement error. Before presenting the various reliability indices, recall that classical testing approaches assume that the raw score (X) on a test is made up of a true component (T) and a random error (E) component:

(7–1) $$X = T + E.$$

The less random error, the more the raw score represents the true score. Because true scores are theoretical, a formula is needed that will allow for the calculation of the reliability without a true score component. We reviewed in Chapter 5 how a sample of raw scores can be used to get to the formula:

(7–2) $$\text{Reliability} = 1 - [\text{VAR}(E)/\text{VAR}(X)].$$

That is, the reliability is equal to the ratio of random error variance to total score variance.

In addition to the theory of true and error scores, we will also be adopting the domain-sampling model of CTT. This model assumes that the test is made up of a selection of a sample of parallel items from the universe of possible items. That is, there are assumed to be an infinite number of possible items that could be designed to assess any construct. A single test of 20 items, for example, is a sample from that universe.

Different ways to assess reliability using CTTs will be presented. Examples of how to calculate the various types of reliability indices and computer program printouts and their interpretations will be provided.

Test-Retest Reliability

This index of reliability assesses the stability over time for a set of scores on a particular test for a given sample. This means that the same test is given to the same sample at a point in time (T1) and then again at a later point in time (T2). The approach has some obvious advantages. First, only one test is needed, reducing the cost of test item development. In addition, the items (stimuli) are the same from T1 to T2. This ensures that the same construct is measured exactly the same way both times.

The test-retest reliability index is simply the zero-order correlation between the test scores at T1 and T2. If one were to obtain exactly the same scores from the entire sample of respondents at both times, then the correlation would be perfect (1.0). Inevitably, measurement error comes into play, and scores will vary from T1 to T2. This might be due to random error, such as some participants having been feeling poorly on the day of the test at T1 and feeling well at T2 or the room having been overly warm at T2 compared to T1. Table 7.1 shows 20 scores obtained from a sample of employees on the 10-item Team Player Inventory (TPI) at T1 and T2. The resulting correlation between these two vectors of scores is 0.91. This indicates that the scores are quite stable from T1 to T2.

When interpreting any reliability index, it is important to note that the generated value is a *squared* value. That is, it is usually the case that if two variables are correlated with one another (say at 0.40), then the square of that value is equal to the shared variance between the two variables (i.e., $0.40^2 = 0.16$; the variables share 16% of their variance), but because of the manner in which the reliability index is derived, the zero-order correlation is already a squared value. Thus, it is concluded that 91% of the variance of the scores at T1 on the TPI is shared with the variance at T2. The output for the analysis is shown in Box 7.1.

The fluctuation that occurs in scores from T1 to T2 may be due to systematic change rather than random fluctuation. A systematic change would occur in the following example. Assume that at T1, a sample of employees is given an honesty test. These employees are now sensitized to the types of questions asked on the test (such as, Do you ever take office supplies home for personal use?). Then, when the test is given six weeks later at T2, some people's scores might be changed from T1 not because they changed in honesty but because they were sensitized to the honesty issue at their place of work. This phenomenon is called reactivity. Another

Table 7.1   Data for Calculating the Test-Retest Reliability of the Team Player
Inventory for a Group of 20 Employees

Case Number	Time 1 Scores[a]	Time 2 Scores
1	40	42
2	30	41
3	20	26
4	17	18
5	45	39
6	27	23
7	15	22
8	32	28
9	33	33
10	45	41
11	41	37
12	30	32
13	25	22
14	12	11
15	49	43
16	48	47
17	34	30
18	36	32
19	26	29
20	22	20

a. Scores can range from 10–50.

example of this might occur in the following scenario. Assume a test of reading skill
is given at T1 to a group of students. Then the students take a four-week reading
skills course. They take the test again at T2 after the course is completed. Most of
the scores would be expected to be different from T1 (in this case, increase, if the
skills course does its work). This systematic change in scores is not considered to be
error in CTT because it is not random.

So, one practical question that is often asked is, How long should one wait
between test administrations to gather the T2 data? Because the exact same test
is administered at T1 and T2, the potential for practice or carryover effects is
substantial and this would artificially inflate the reliability index. Individuals not

Box 7.1 Test-Retest Correlation SPSS Output

		Time 1	Time 2
Time 1	Pearson Correlation	1	0.910
	Sig. (two-tailed)	—	0.000
	N	20	20
Time 2	Pearson Correlation	0.910	1
	Sig. (two-tailed)	0.000	—
	N	20	20

Note: Correlation is significant at the 0.01 level (two-tailed).

The printout shows that the correlation between Time 1 and Time 2 is 0.910 and is significant (0.000), and the sample size (N) is 20.

used to taking tests may do better at T2 simply because they have had an opportunity to practice taking the test at T1. In addition, there may be specific questions on the test that a respondent did not know the answer to at T1 (e.g., What is the meaning of *sanctimonious?*). The person may have looked up the answer after taking the test and therefore know the correct response at T2. Respondents may also remember what they gave as a response at T1 to particular items (e.g., Rate how much you like chocolate ice cream) and respond the same way at T2. All of these examples are problems that face test-retest reliability estimates.

Ghiselli, Campbell, and Zedek (1981) say, "It is desirable to maximize the interval between testing occasions to minimize the effects of memory" (p. 249). On the other hand, if the test assesses a construct that may be affected by historical/situational events (e.g., feelings toward a political party, levels of anxiety) or maturation/learning (e.g., cognitive ability) test-retest intervals that are overly long will likely produce reliability indices that are lower than would have been the case had the interval been shorter. This raises the issue of whether or not the test-retest reliability index should even be used in instances where the construct is susceptible to change.

So it seems that the test-retest method is most appropriate for tests that assess traits, such as intelligence or personality, that are assumed to be stable over time. In such instances, the maximal interval possible without undue cost is the rule of thumb to follow for the time interval between test administrations.

Clearly, there are some problems with the test-retest methodology. One is simply that there will likely be attrition in the sample—that is, there will be fewer individuals taking the test at T2 than T1. Participants will drop out, not show up, expire, be sick on the day of the second testing session, and so forth. Second, it is expensive to administer a test two times. Administration and scoring costs for some tests run into the hundreds of dollars. Third, the reactivity or sensitization discussed earlier can potentially negatively affect the reliability index. Fourth, the time interval may be inappropriate, unduly inflating or attenuating the reliability index.

Alternative Forms Reliability

To overcome, primarily, the problem of carryover effects and situational changes to test takers, the alternative forms approach to assessing reliability was developed. This is a much more costly approach in that two versions of the test must be developed. Extreme care must be taken to make sure that items are actually parallel, or equal, across test versions.

Specifically, alternative forms reliability data is collected first by one form of a test (Form A) when it is given to a sample at a point in time, T1. Then, at a later point in time (about two weeks), T2, the alternative form (Form B) is given to the same participants. The zero-order correlation between the test scores on Form A and Form B provides the index of alternative forms reliability.

The question of equality of items is of primary concern with alternative forms reliability. In the past, expert opinion and comparisons of pass rates were the only ways to really demonstrate that two forms of the test were equivalent. However, IRT produces item parameters that much more definitively answer the question of item and test equality. The onus is on the test developer to ensure that the alternative forms are equivalent and, thus, the reliability index associated with them is reasonable.

Another concern, although mitigated somewhat by the shorter time period between testing sessions, is attrition; the sample is likely to be smaller at T2 than at T1 for a variety of reasons. And, as with test-retest reliability, the test needs to be administered on two separate occasions, which may be very costly, depending on the specific test in question.

Interpretation of the index follows similarly from that of test-retest reliability. In this instance, however, the stability of the scores is from one test form to another test form.

Measures of Internal Consistency

There are several measures of internal consistency. All of them assess the stability, or consistency, of responses across items and are primarily based on the inter-correlations between items. The stability indices are not across total test scores but across items. Tests that are speeded, or where the items are ordered in terms of difficulty, should not be subjected to internal consistency assessments of reliability as the correlations among items are directly affected by time constraints and difficulty, rendering them spuriously high (Nunnally & Bernstein, 1994).

One of the most useful features of measures of internal consistency is that they can be calculated based on a single sample with just one test administration. This is a very desirable feature and has encouraged their use.

Split-Half. The split-half correlation between halves of tests was the first measure of internal consistency. That is, the test was divided into two equal parts, the scores on the two halves were calculated, and then the correlation between the two halves provided the split-half reliability. One problem with the split-half method has been, Where should the test be split? Usually, items are randomly split or all even numbers and all odd numbers make up the two halves. It is not wise to use the first and second halves, as the test taker may be more nervous on the first half or fatigued on the second half.

An example of a data set of 15 people taking the TPI is shown in Table 7.2. Recall that there are 10 items, so we decide that Half 1 will be the total of items 1, 3, 5, 7, and 9, whereas Half 2 will be the total of items 2, 4, 6, 8, and 10. The resulting split-half reliability for this data set is 0.825. The output for this analysis is shown in Box 7.2.

One problem spotted early on with the split-half method was that it underestimated the actual reliability index. This is because, under CTT, tests that are longer (i.e., have more items) are more reliable (assuming items that are similar are added). Note that the split-half reliability index was calculated on just five items for each half in our example. The length of the whole test, which respondents did complete, was actually 10 items. A formula to estimate the reliability of a test that is longer than the one on which the split-half coefficient was generated is called the

Table 7.2   Data for Calculating the Split-Half Reliability of the Team Player Inventory for a Group of 15 Employees

Case Number	Half 1 Scores[a]	Half 2 Scores*
1	12	12
2	16	16
3	6	8
4	9	13
5	18	15
6	13	14
7	12	17
8	11	14
9	10	10
10	23	20
11	11	14
12	7	10
13	12	10
14	19	15
15	20	17

a. Scores range from 5–25.

Box 7.2   Split-Half Correlation and Reliability SPSS Output

		Half 1	Half 2
Half 1	Pearson Correlation	1	0.825
	Sig. (two-tailed)	—	0.000
	N	15	15
Half 2	Pearson Correlation	0.825	1
	Sig. (two-tailed)	0.000	—
	N	15	15

Note: Correlation is significant at the 0.01 level (two-tailed).

The printout shows that the correlation between Half 1 and Half 2 is 0.825 and is significant (0.000), and the sample size (N) is 15.

If you analyze the data in the Reliability program of SPSS, you can indicate that you want to use the split-half method. In this case, the printout would indicate the following:

Reliability Coefficients

N of Cases = 15.0; N of Items = 2

Correlation Between Forms = 0.8249

Equal-Length Spearman-Brown = 0.9040

Note that the equal-length Spearman-Brown value of 0.9040 from the output is equal to the Spearman-Brown calculation done by hand.

Spearman-Brown prophesy formula. Whereas this is a general formula that can be used to assess a variety of different questions about test length and reliability, it is presented here because it is used extensively in calculating the "corrected" split-half reliability. The formula is

$$(7\text{–}3) \qquad\qquad r_{cc'} = k r_{xx}/[1 + (k - 1)(r_{xx})],$$

where $r_{cc'}$ = the expected reliability, k = the proportion the test is changed (e.g., 2 if it is doubled in length, 0.5 if it was halved), and r_{xx} = the original reliability index.

So, in our example, the original reliability index was 0.825. The expected reliability if the number of items on the test was doubled would be

$$r_{cc'} = 2(0.825)/[1 + (2 - 1)(0.825)],$$
$$= 1.65/1.825,$$
$$= 0.904.$$

Thus, our corrected split-half reliability for this set of data is 0.904.

The general formula can be used in some instances to shorten a test by a fixed amount and estimate the loss in reliability. For example, suppose a test is 100 items in length and has a reliability index of 0.90. However, it is too long for test takers to complete without complaining of fatigue. If the test is shortened to 75 items, there will be a loss in the reliability. The amount of that loss can be calculated using the following:

$$r_{cc'} = 0.75(0.90)/[1 + (0.75 - 1)(0.90)]$$
$$= 0.675/0.775,$$
$$= 0.871.$$

Thus, if 25 items are dropped from the test (i.e., 0.75 is used for the proportion the test is shortened), the reliability is expected to drop from 0.90 to 0.87. It must be decided if the fatigue experienced by the test takers is worth giving up the higher reliability.

One other useful way to use the formula is to rearrange the terms to estimate how much a test must be lengthened to achieve a desired level of reliability. This formula is

(7–4) $$k = [(r_{cc})(1 - r_{xx})]/[(r_{xx})(1 - r_{cc})].$$

For example, assume a 50-item test has a reliability of 0.70 and increasing the reliability to 0.80 is desired. Using the formula, the proportion increase needed can be calculated:

$$k = [(0.80)(1 - 0.70)]/[(0.70)(1 - 0.80)],$$
$$= 0.24/0.14,$$
$$= 1.71.$$

The test would need to increase by 1.71 times. This means the test would have to be 86 items in length to achieve the desired reliability (i.e., $50 \times 1.71 = 85.7$).

Cronbach's alpha (α). The α coefficient (Cronbach, 1951) is probably the most pervasive of the internal consistency indices. In fact, it is so pervasive that it has almost become synonymous with reliability. Its correct classification, however, is as a measure of internal consistency. The formula for α is

(7–5) $$\alpha = (N)(r_{mean})/[1 + (r_{mean})(N - 1)],$$

where N = the number of test items and r_{mean} = the average intercorrelations among the items.

Assume that there is a 20-item test where the average of the correlations of each item with all other items is 0.30. To find the α for this test, the formula would be

$$\alpha = (20)(0.30)/[1 + (0.30)(20 - 1)],$$
$$= 6/6.7,$$
$$= 0.896.$$

Thus, the α for the test is 0.896. Novick and Lewis (1967) demonstrated that α is the average of all possible combinations of split-half reliabilities. They also showed that, in general, α is the lower bound for a test of parallel items; that is, it is a conservative measure of internal consistency.

The equation shows that the value of α is dependent not only on the intercorrelations among the items but also on the length of the test. Note that if the test on which α was calculated was 10 items in length and not 20, the resulting α would be

$$(10)(0.30)/[1 + (0.30)(10 - 1)],$$
$$= 3/3.7,$$
$$= 0.810.$$

This is much lower than the original value despite the fact that the intercorrelations remained constant.

An example output for Cronbach's α is shown in Box 7.3. The data for this are 72 responses by employees to an Innovation Market Strategy scale that assesses employee perceptions about the market strategy being pursued by their organization (Kline, 2003). Interpretation of the results is also provided.

Coefficient Theta (θ). One little-used index of internal consistency is that of coefficient theta (θ; not to be confused with the theta of IRT). Theta is based on a principal components analysis of the test items. It differentially weights items that correlate more with each other than does θ. As a result, it is a special case of θ where a "weighting vector has been chosen so as to make alpha a maximum" (Carmines & Zeller, 1979, p. 61).

The formula for coefficient θ is

(7–6) $$\text{coefficient } \theta = [(N/(N-1)] \, [1 - (1/\lambda)],$$

where $N =$ the number of items in the test and $\lambda =$ the eigenvalue of the first principal component. For the moment, exactly where the eigenvalue comes from will be set aside as it will be discussed extensively in Chapter 10. At this point, just note that it is a measure of the variance shared between the items and it will be given in the examples in this chapter.

Assume that the responses by a sample of participants to the 10-item TPI scale is subjected to a principal components analysis. The eigenvalue for the first principal component is 6.7.

Coefficient θ for this data set can thus be calculated as follows:

$$\theta = [20/(20 - 1)][(1 - (1/6.7)],$$
$$= 1.053(0.851),$$
$$= 0.896.$$

The internal consistency for this set of items based on theta is 0.896. Coefficient θ is less conservative than α and is also less likely to be low if a test has a small number of items. It provides an alternative to α that can be readily computed.

Box 7.3   Cronbach's α SPSS Output

Item	Scale Mean if Item Deleted	Scale Variance if Item Deleted	Corrected Item-Total Correlation	Alpha if Item Deleted
M1	20.8750	26.1673	0.6350	0.8524
M4	22.2639	25.6336	0.6072	0.8545
M7	22.3611	26.1213	0.5756	0.8578
M10	21.1289	25.1354	0.7334	0.8422
M13	21.3889	23.8748	0.7396	0.8392
M16	21.5972	23.9059	0.6886	0.8452
M19	21.4306	25.0374	0.6293	0.8521
M22	21.6111	26.6072	0.4162	0.8770

Reliability Coefficients

N of Cases = 72.0; N of Items = 8

Alpha = 0.8689

Note that there are eight items and 72 cases used in this analysis. This scale has an internal consistency of 0.87, which is quite high. Examining the last column, notice that the α would drop if any of the items except the last one were to be deleted from the scale. That is, if M1 were deleted, then the α would drop from 0.8689 to 0.8524. This means that M1 contributes to making the internal consistency of the scale high. Note, however, that if the last item, M22, were to be deleted, then the α level would increase to 0.8773 (just slightly higher than the original 0.8689). Although this increase is not much and may very well be due to sampling error, it is useful to examine this column to see if any of the items can be deleted that would substantially increase the α level.

An example of the output for a principal components analysis that is used in calculating coefficient θ is shown in Box 7.4. The same data were used as that in demonstrating the Cronbach's α output. Interpretation of the results is provided.

Kuder-Richardson 21 (KR21). Kuder and Richardson introduced a measure of internal consistency for dichotomous items in 1937. They provided several formulae, the most notable one for our purposes being the KR21. It is as follows:

(7–7) $$\text{KR21 internal consistency} = [N/(N-1)] [1 - (\Sigma p_i q_i / \sigma^2)],$$

where N = the number of items, $p_i q_i$ = the proportion of individuals who pass (p) multiplied by the proportion of people who fail (q) each item (and then summed across all of the items), and σ^2 = the variance of the total test.

Box 7.4   Coefficient Theta Analysis: Total Variance Explained

---

First, a principal components analysis is carried out and the following SPSS output is generated.

Extraction Method: Principal Component Analysis

Component	Initial Eigenvalues	% of Variance
1	4.274	53.423
2	0.931	11.642
3	0.775	9.686
4	0.588	7.346
5	0.477	5.964
6	0.392	4.897
7	0.300	3.748
8	0.264	3.294

Note that the first eigenvalue is equal to 4.274. With eight items, the theta coefficient would be equal to $(8/7)(1 - 1/4.274) = (1.143)(1 - 0.234) = (1.143)(0.766) = 0.876$. This internal consistency value of 0.876 is just slightly higher than the one calculated using Cronbach's α.

There are several other parts to this output that we will be going over in the next chapter on validity.

So, for example, if 40 workers respond to a 10-item honesty test where individuals respond to statements as true (pass) or false (fail), the KR21 index can be calculated. Assume the variance of the test as a whole is 0.974 and the item pass and fail values are set up as in Table 7.3. The $\Sigma p_i q_i = 1.326$. So, substituting,

$$KR21 = [10/9] \ [1 - (1.326/0.974)],$$
$$= (1.111)(0.3614),$$
$$= 0.40.$$

Thus, it would be concluded that the internal consistency of this 10-item scale is very low. The KR21 is provided as an option in most computer programs. Interpretation of the magnitude of the KR21 is similar to other measures of internal consistency.

Setting Confidence Intervals

Once the reliability coefficient is calculated (by whatever means), it can be used to set confidence intervals around a given score. This is particularly important in

Table 7.3   Item *p* and *q* Values for Calculating the Kuder-Richardson 21

Item	p	q	pq
1	0.175	0.825	0.1444
2	0.200	0.800	0.1600
3	0.125	0.875	0.1094
4	0.825	0.175	0.1444
5	0.925	0.075	0.0694
6	0.175	0.825	0.1444
7	0.175	0.825	0.1444
8	0.100	0.900	0.0900
9	0.125	0.875	0.1094
10	0.700	0.300	0.2100
			$\Sigma pq = 1.326$

applied settings where a decision-maker should have a particular level of confidence in the accuracy of the score that the respondent obtained and report that value. This process is called setting a confidence interval around a score. To set the confidence interval, the raw score of an individual (X), the reliability of the test (R), and the standard deviation of the test (SD) all must be known.

While most confidence interval setting procedures use the raw score around which the interval is set, Nunnally and Bernstein (1994) argue that the interval should be set about the individual's estimated true score (T'), which is determined by

(7–8)
$$T' = (R)(X).$$

The more reliable the test, the less likely the individual's estimated true score is to regress toward the mean of the distribution. Suppose a score of 120 on an IQ test is obtained, and the test has a reliability of 0.95 and a standard deviation of 12. The T', then, would be $(0.95)(120) = 114$.

To set the confidence interval around the score of 114, the standard error of measurement (SE) is required. It is calculated by

(7–9) $SE = SD \sqrt{(1 - R)}$. In this case, the SE would equal
$$SE = 12 \sqrt{(1 - 0.95)},$$
$$= 2.68.$$

Then, if I want to be 90% confident that the score will fall within a certain range, the z value associated with the 90% confidence interval (1.65) will be multiplied with the value of the SE ($1.65 \times 2.68 = 4.42$). Then this value is added to and subtracted from the estimated true score (i.e., 114 ± 4.42). This leads to the following two equations:

$$114 - 4.42 = 109.58 \text{ and}$$

$$114 + 4.42 = 118.42.$$

Thus, I can be 90% confident that if the test was administered to the test taker 100 times, 90 times out of 100, the true score would fall between 109.58 and 118.42.

In this example, the 90% confidence interval was set. If the 95% or 99% confidence intervals were desired, the z values to use would have been 1.96 or 2.58, respectively.

Reliability of a Composite

Sometimes it is of interest for test users to want to create a composite score from a variety of tests. For example, scores on four math subtests (components), addition, subtraction, multiplication, and division, could be added together to obtain a composite score of basic math fact mastery. The process for determining the reliability of the composite follows the same logic as does adding test items to a single test. That is, the more the components (whether they be items or whole tests) are correlated with one another, the higher the reliability of the composite when these components are added. The general formula for the reliability of a composite measure is

(7–10) $$r_{comp} = 1 - [k - (kr_{iimean})]/[k + (k^2 - k)\ r_{ijmean}],$$

where r_{comp} = the reliability of the composite, k = number of components, r_{iimean} = mean reliability of the components, and r_{ijmean} = mean correlation between components.

Now, assume that the mean average reliability for the four component tests of addition, subtraction, multiplication, and division is 0.80, and the mean average correlation among the tests is 0.60. Substituting into the equation,

$$
\begin{aligned}
r_{comp} &= 1 - [4 - (4 \times 0.80)]/[4 + (16 - 4)0.60], \\
&= 1 - (0.80/11.2), \\
&= 0.93.
\end{aligned}
$$

Thus, the composite has a reliability that is higher than the average of the individual components (0.80). If the components were not highly intercorrelated, then the composite reliability would not have been much improved. For example, assume the mean correlation among the tests was 0.10 rather than 0.60. In this case, the resulting reliability of the composite would be 0.85.

This brings up the issue of whether or not to create a composite score from components that are heterogeneous in nature versus homogeneous. There is certainly a case to be made that if the components are homogeneous (have reasonably high intercorrelations), then creating a composite will provide a more reliable score and the meaning of the composite remains easily interpretable. The same is not true when combining heterogeneous scales. First, the reliability of the composite may be lower than each component alone, and second, interpreting a composite made up of a set of unrelated variables is "complicated if not impossible" (Allen & Yen, 1979, p. 224).

General intelligence tests often combine scores into a composite based on diverse constructs such as verbal fluency, pattern recognition, and spatial skills. Whether or not the resulting total score is really representative of "general intelligence" has been questioned. One positive aspect of these types of composite scores is that they tend to be related to other criterion variables that are also multidimensional (such as job or scholastic performance). In the end, make sure that the purpose of creating a composite score and the implications of doing so are known before going ahead to create such a variable.

Difference Scores—A Reliability Concern

A common event in research and practice with scores on items, or tests, is to calculate difference or change scores. For example, a training program for managers may be designed so that they learn to be good team leaders. To assess the effectiveness of the program, a team leadership scale is administered to them before training and then after training. Then the differences between the scores are calculated. These may then be used to relate to other variables of interest (such as subordinate satisfaction), presuming that those managers that changed the most should have better ratings of satisfaction by their subordinates. Another example is that employees might be asked to rate the actual culture of their organization on a supportiveness inventory and then asked to rate the desired supportiveness. The difference between them, then, is calculated and used.

A problem with this occurs in the CTT paradigm in that the reliability of difference scores is almost inevitably lower than the reliability of either of the component measures. The formula for the reliability of difference scores is as follows:

(7–11) $$r_{\text{diff}} = \{[(r_{xx} + r_{yy})/2] - r_{xy}\}/(1 - r_{xy}),$$

where r_{diff} = the reliability of the difference score, r_{xx} = the reliability of the first test, r_{yy} = the reliability of the second test, and r_{xy} = the correlation between the two tests.

Assume that the test of actual supportiveness from the example above had a reliability of 0.80 and the test of desired supportiveness had a reliability of 0.90. Further assume that the correlation between them was 0.50. Substituting in the formula,

$$r_{\text{diff}} = \{[(0.80 + 0.90)/2] - 0.50\}/(1 - 0.50),$$
$$= 0.35/0.50,$$
$$= 0.70.$$

The difference score reliability is 0.70—much lower than the reliability of either of the two component tests. This is because the two tests are moderately correlated. If the correlation between them was lower (e.g., 0.20 rather than 0.50), then the reliability of the difference score would be 0.81. If they were not correlated at all, then the resulting reliability would simply be the average of the two component reliabilities, in this case, 0.85.

This problem of difference score reliability occurs because of assumptions made in CTT. Theoretically, if two measured variables, X and Y, are highly correlated, then the "true scores" of X and "true scores" of Y are also assumed to be overlapping. If X and Y are measures of actual and ideal supportiveness, they will likely be correlated—that is, their true scores will overlap. What is not overlapping in the true scores is random error.

Assume the difference scores between actual and desired organizational supportiveness (the ones with the 0.70 reliability) are to be used by correlating them with employee intentions to leave the organization. The relationship between the difference scores and intentions to leave the organization will be attenuated due to the unreliability of the difference score. If a statistically significant relationship between the variables of interest is not found, it might be attributable to the unreliability of the difference score measure. It is worth noting that some researchers have provided explanations suggesting that the concern over the unreliability of difference scores is not as problematic as once thought (e.g., Rogosa, Brandt, & Zimowski, 1982; Rogosa & Willett, 1983; Williams & Zimmerman, 1996a, 1996b).

It is also important to examine the distributions of the scores on the two components. For example, assume one group of managers is sent into team training Program A and another group into team training Program B. Pretest and posttest measures on how much they learned from the training are obtained and the difference scores for each person are generated. Then the utility of Program A versus Program B is assessed by doing a t test on the difference scores of the two. It is assumed that the one with the greatest change is better. However, what if the group of managers that went into Program A all had relatively high scores on the pretest? If this was the case, then there was very little room for change for this group in advance of the training. Thus, Program A is disadvantaged for change.

It has been suggested in cases such as these that rather than difference scores, an analysis of covariance be used. In this instance, the covariate would be the pretest score, the dependent variable would be the posttest score, and the independent variable would be the training program group (Arvey & Cole, 1989).

Cribbie and Jamieson (2000) offer a compelling case for using structural equation modeling to assess difference score relationships with other variables of interest. The take-home message is simple: be wary of using difference scores as they can lead to potential problems in analysis and interpretation of findings.

Regardless of your own sentiments about difference scores, it is important to make cautious use and interpretation of results where they are used. If the two components are not strongly correlated and justification can be made for the difference score being a psychologically meaningful construct, then using difference scores might be warranted. It is also possible to correct the correlation between the difference score and the variable of interest using the correction for attenuation due to the unreliability of the difference score (Allen & Yen, 1979).

Practical Questions

There are a couple of practical questions that commonly occur regarding calculating reliability coefficients. One is, How many people should be in the sample? There really is not an answer to this question because the reliability index is descriptive, not inferential. Only in inferential statistical tests are issues of sample size important to test a statistic for significance. Rather, the question should be phrased, Is the sample on which the reliability coefficient is calculated representative of the samples on which I will want to use the test? Some test publishers provide reliability estimates for various samples (e.g., by gender, race, age), and this is very useful information as a consumer. As a test developer, you will want to assess reliability on samples of relevant populations. It makes no sense to develop a test of cognitive impairment for preschool children and test its reliability on elementary school children. So, sample size is less a concern than sample characteristics.

Another common question is, How high should the reliability index be to be considered "good"? This question is different for different test uses as well as for different types of reliability indices. Tests that will be used for making decisions about individuals (e.g., employee or student selection tests, tests that identify special needs students, tests that are used to determine treatment protocols) are expected to have very high reliability (0.90 at a bare minimum, as suggested by Nunnally and Bernstein, 1994). When individuals' lives are at stake, it is good practice not to accept any measurement error. One the other hand, in the early stages of research or where the test results will not be used for making decisions about people that affect their lives (sometimes called *low stakes*), modest reliability (0.70) of tests is acceptable (Nunnally & Bernstein, 1994). Another issue in reliability magnitude is the type of index used. For example, indices generated via the test-retest method are typically lower than are internal consistency methods for homogeneous sets of items.

Another question commonly presented is, What type of reliability analysis should I conduct? If the test contains homogeneous items, at the very least an internal consistency analysis needs to be conducted, unless it is a speeded test. In the latter case, alternative forms should be used. Test-retest is useful if the construct is not susceptible to historical, maturational, learning, or situational effects. Because of the potential problems with carryover, a long time should pass between test taking sessions. If the option for generating an alternative forms reliability index presents itself, then this would be a better way to assess reliability over time.

Each of the reliability estimate options has pros and cons associated with it. The test developer and test consumer should be testwise enough to know what type of reliability should be conducted and presented.

Summary and Next Steps

This chapter has focused on what is the primary concern for many psychometricians—reliability of the test scores. The topics that were covered included the following:

a. methods to assess reliability: test-retest, alternative forms, internal consistency, and composite scores;

b. applications of the reliability index in setting confidence intervals;

c. the potential problem of reliability with regard to difference scores; and

d. practical issues such as interpretation of indices, test length, sample sizes, and reliability standards.

In the next chapter, the discussion of reliability is extended to rater consistency. In addition, a note about modern test theory and how it differs from classical test theory in its approach to test reliability will be covered, as well as the issue of reliability generalization.

Problems and Exercises

1. Describe an example of test-retest reliability.

2. If the correlation between test scores at Time 1 and Time 2 is 0.85, how would this be interpreted?

3. What are some problems associated with reliability assessed via the test-retest method?

4. Under what circumstances is reliability assessed via the test-retest method most appropriate?

5. What are the strengths and drawbacks of alternative forms reliability?

6. Why is internal consistency such an easy way to assess reliability from a methodological perspective?

7. If a split-half reliability on a test is calculated to be 0.70, what would be the corrected split-half?

8. If a reliability of 0.60 is obtained on a test that is 10 items in length and the developer wants to increase it to 0.80, how many more items would need to be added to it?

9. If the average intercorrelation among all of the items on an eight-item test is 0.50, what is the Cronbach's alpha (α)?

10. If a principal components analysis on a set of six items is run and the first eigenvalue is equal to 4.0, what is the coefficient theta (θ)?

11. What would the KR21 be for a set of 20 dichotomous items where the overall test variance is 0.80 and the $\Sigma p_i q_i = 1.5$?

12. Set the 95% confidence interval around the true score of someone who obtained a raw score of 50 on a test that has a reliability of 0.90 and a standard deviation of 10.

13. What is the composite reliability of two tests that have a mean reliability of 0.70 and where the correlation between them is 0.50?

14. What would be the reliability of the difference score between two tests where the tests both had reliabilities of 0.80 and the correlation between the tests was 0.30?

15. If you obtained a reliability estimate of 0.80 on a test, how would you interpret it and use the test?

CHAPTER 8

Reliability of Raters

T his chapter continues to address the issue of test reliability. Recall that the reliability index of a test score indicates its stability. The types of stability that were demonstrated in the previous chapter were those of test scores over time and of item scores across items. In this chapter, the focus is on the stability of ratings across judges, or raters, of a person, object, event, and so forth (interrater reliability). The issues of reliability generalization and the modern test theory to test reliability are also presented.

Interrater Reliability Indices

Reliability indices that describe consistency of judgments, or ratings, across individuals or raters/judges are called interrater reliability indices. For example, we may be interested in knowing if judges of an ice dancing competition are consistent and, if so, how consistent. There are many types of these indices available and the one to use will depend on the type of data collected.

Observer Agreement Percentage. One of the most commonly used measures of observer agreement is simply the percentage of observations on which two or more judges agree (Mitchell, 1979). In observational studies, it may be the percentage of time units (say 1-minute intervals) in which there is agreement by two or more judges that a certain behavior has occurred. For example, suppose that two or more judges are observing cooperative play between children over a 10-minute period and the time intervals are 1 minute each. Each is to note whether or not cooperative play behavior occurred after each interval. If the two judges agree in 8 of the 10 intervals, then there would be an 80% observer agreement rate.

Alternatively, two judges might be coding a transcript of an interaction between a student and supervisor about the student's thesis. The "intervals" here might be sentences, of which there may be 100. Each judge indicates if each sentence is task based. Then they compare their ratings of the sentences and find they agreed on 95% of the sentences. This would provide an observer agreement rate of 95%.

Problems with this index have been noted by Mitchell (1979). First, it is insensitive to degrees of agreement—it is either there or not in the interval, and there is no way to code the degree of cooperative play or task-based sentence. Second, there is some level of agreement expected just by chance alone. This will artificially inflate the agreement value.

Interobserver Correlations. One index of agreement across raters is simply to calculate the Pearson or Spearman correlation coefficient if the ratings by judges are continuous or ranked, respectively. For example, two faculty members may be asked to rate, on a five-point scale, the quality of 10 different journal articles. The Pearson correlation of the 10 ratings would then be calculated and this would represent the interobserver correlation. Alternatively, if 10 graduate students in a department are rank ordered on some dimension (say scholarly output) by one faculty member, and another faculty member does the same, their rankings can be compared by calculating the Spearman rank-order coefficient on the rankings.

One problem with these methods of agreement is that the error reflects not only random error but also how the judge used or interpreted the scaling process. One judge may view a journal quality of "3" much differently than his or her colleague does. In addition, these correlations are based on ranked differences. To highlight the problem with this, assume that three journal articles are ranked 1, 2, and 3 by judge 1, and judge 2 rates the same articles 3, 4, and 5. Their interobserver correlation will be 1.0! Clearly, they don't agree much about the quality of these journal articles but this is not captured in the interobserver correlation.

Kendall's Coefficient of Concordance. This agreement index is used when multiple (more than one) judges rank order a series of stimuli. These stimuli may be people (e.g., ice skaters on a dimension of performance) or objects (e.g., cars on a dimension of utility) of any sort. As many judges as desired can rank order the stimuli.

The analysis is a nonparametric one, where it is a test of whether or not differences exist in the rankings across more than two judges. For example, if four instructors rank order a class of 10 students from best to worst, the reliability of their rankings can be calculated. Specifically, Friedman's two-way analysis of variance (judges as one variable and stimuli as the other variable) using ranked data is carried out. There is a significance level provided in this analysis. When it is significant, it indicates there are differences between the stimuli on the rankings. While this is not usually of interest from a reliability perspective (i.e., the 10 students were different in their rank-order), it is provided in the output. In addition to the Friedman's statistic, Kendall's coefficient of concordance is provided. It ranges from 0–1 and normalizes the Friedman's test statistic. Higher values indicate higher agreement across the judges.

Table 8.1   Data Set for Assessing Ranking Agreements of Six Job Applicants by
Four Judges

	App 1	App 2	App 3	App 4	App 5	App 6
Judge 1	1	3	4	5	6	2
Judge 2	2	3	5	4	6	1
Judge 3	1	2	5	6	4	3
Judge 4	2	3	4	5	6	1
Average Ranking	1.50	2.75	4.50	5.00	5.50	1.75

Table 8.1 shows an example of such a data set. Here, there are six applicants for a job and four "judges" (likely to be members of a hiring committee). The judges rank the six applicants as shown in the table. The resulting Friedman's test is significant, indicating there are differences between the applicants on the rankings. This is clear from the average rank shown in the last row, where Applicant 1 is ranked first and Applicant 5 is ranked last. In addition, Kendall's coefficient of concordance is 0.850, indicating a high level of agreement across the raters.

The SPSS nonparametric statistics program of k-related samples can be used to calculate the Friedman's and Kendall's tests. The output for the program for the data set in Table 8.1 is presented and interpreted in Box 8.1.

Cohen's Kappa Coefficient. The kappa coefficient calculates rater agreement in a fairly narrow circumstance. Specifically, two judges place a number of stimuli into nominal categories. For example, two supervisors in an organization might be asked to classify 20 members of a team into one of three behavioral categories (achievement oriented, helpful to others, and aggressive). The data could then be set up in a 3×3 table (Table 8.2).

Basically, large values on the diagonal and small values off the diagonal indicate better agreement. There is a t test for significance to assess if the values on the diagonal are higher than expected by chance. In this table, it is significant. In addition to the t test, a Cohen's kappa value ranging from 0 (low agreement) to 1 (perfect agreement) is generated, where "values of kappa less than 0.40 reflect poor agreement. With kappa between 0.40 and 0.75 agreement is fair to good. Values of kappa above 0.75 indicate strong agreement" (Dixon, Brown, Engelman, & Jennrich, 1990, p. 271). In this case, Cohen's kappa is 0.549, indicating fair to good agreement between the two supervisors' perceptions of how the team members should be grouped.

The SPSS crosstabs statistics program can be used to calculate Cohen's kappa coefficient. The output for the program for the data set in Table 8.2 is presented and interpreted in Box 8.2.

Any stimuli can be used for classification by the raters—such as persons, objects, statements, and so forth. The kappa coefficient, though, can only be calculated using two judges, and agreement is assessed based on the nominal categorization of stimuli.

Box 8.1 Friedman's and Kendall's Tests of Rank Consistency

Applicant	Mean Rank
Applicant 1	1.50
Applicant 2	2.75
Applicant 3	4.50
Applicant 4	5.00
Applicant 5	5.50
Applicant 6	1.75

Friedman's Test: Test Statistics	
N	4
Chi-Square	17.00
df	5
Asymp. Sig.	0.004

Kendall's W Test: Test Statistics	
N	4
Kendall's W	0.850

Note that the Friedman Test is significant, indicating that there are significant differences in the average applicant rankings. Clearly, Applicant 5 has the highest ranking and Applicant 1 has the lowest. In addition, the Kendall's W statistic of 0.850 indicates a high level of agreement between the raters.

Table 8.2 A Two-Dimensional Table for Assessing Agreement Via Cohen's Kappa Coefficient

		Supervisor 1		
		Achievement	Helpful	Aggressive
Supervisor 2	Achievement	5	1	1
	Helpful	1	5	1
	Aggressive	1	1	4

Box 8.2   Cohen's Kappa Coefficient Using SPSS Crosstabs

SUP1 × SUP2 Cross-Tabulation Counts					
			Supervisor 2		Total
		Achieve.	*Helpful*	*Aggress.*	
Supervisor 1	*Achieve.*	5	1	1	7
	Helpful	1	5	1	7
	Aggress.	1	1	4	6
Total		7	7	6	20

Symmetric Measures			
Value	Asymp. Std. Error	Approx. T	Approx. Sig.
Kappa = 0.549	0.154	3.467	0.001
N of valid cases	20		

Note that the crosstabulation table shows the two supervisor ratings placing 20 team members in three different categories of behaviors. The kappa coefficient, 0.549, is not high but it is statistically significant, indicating more agreement than would be expected by chance on the diagonal of the crosstabulation table.

r_{wg}. One commonly occurring need to assess consistency across raters is when there are multiple judges rating a single target. For example, let's say that in a study of teams, all members of 10 different teams are asked to rate their performance using a single item. Further assume that the researcher wants to aggregate the scores of each member into a "team-level team performance" score by taking the average of all five team members' scores on the performance measure. A question comes up as to whether or not it is reasonable to assume that all team members have enough agreement on the measure to warrant using the average.

This thorny problem was addressed by James, Demaree, and Wolf (1984, 1993). The r_{wg} is an estimate of the reduction in error variance of a group of raters/judges. That is, the expected variation of a set of ratings under the assumption that there is random rating is equal to σ_e^2. The calculated variance of a set of raters/judges for a single stimuli is S_x^2. If S_x^2 is considerably smaller than σ_e^2, then the r_{wg} will be high. Conversely, if S_x^2 is similar to σ_e^2, then the r_{wg} will be low. This relationship is captured in the equation for r_{wg}:

(8–1) $$r_{wg} = (\sigma_e^2 - S_x^2)/\sigma_e^2.$$

A couple of examples should help in clarifying how to use this equation. Assume that the variance on one item (e.g., How does your team perform compared to other teams in this organization?) for a team made up of five members is equal to 1.5. Further assume that the responses to this item were made using a five-point Likert-type scale. The population σ_e^2 for a five-point Likert-type scale is equal to 2.0. Using the equation we see that

$$r_{wg} = (2.0 - 1.5)/2.0,$$
$$= 0.25.$$

The r_{wg} value of 0.25 is low, indicating that there is quite a bit of variability in the agreement of team members on their performance. Assume that another team of four members were much more homogenous in their ratings and the variance of their ratings was equal to 0.25. The equation to calculate their agreement is

$$r_{wg} = (2.0 - 0.25)/2.0,$$
$$= 0.875.$$

This value indicates this team's agreement is quite high.

Table 8.3 shows 10 teams' variance on the performance item and the resulting r_{wg} indices for each. Two of the 10 teams (Teams 1 and 8) have very low agreement, rendering the average score for those teams on the item to be quite unreliable.

Generating the sample variance (S_e^2) to calculate r_{wg} is a simple exercise; estimating population variance (σ_e^2) has to be justified. As James, Demaree, and Wolf (1984) noted, a five-point Likert-type response format is represented by a discrete

Table 8.3   The Variance and r_{wg} for 10 Teams on Performance Item

Team	Team-Level Item Variance	Team r_{wg}	Number of Raters	Corrected[a] Team r_{wg}
1	1.50	0.250	5	0.075
2	0.25	0.875	4	0.834
3	0.30	0.850	6	0.820
4	0.40	0.800	7	0.766
5	0.22	0.890	6	0.868
6	0.16	0.920	5	0.900
7	0.37	0.815	8	0.789
8	1.63	0.185	9	0.081
9	0.19	0.905	10	0.895
10	0.20	0.900	7	0.887

a. (as per Lindell, Brandt, & Whitney, 1999)

uniform distribution and thus the population variance is equal to 2.0. This value is generated from the following equation:

(8–2) $$(A^2 - 1)/12,$$

where A equals the number of alternatives in the Likert-type scale.

For the five-point scale, the equation is

$$(25 - 1)/12,$$
$$= 24/12,$$
$$= 2.0.$$

for a six-point Likert-type scale, the population variance is expected to be

$$(6^2 - 1)/12,$$
$$= 35/12,$$
$$= 2.92.$$

James, Demaree, and Wolf (1984) also point out that the estimated variance for a continuous uniform distribution can be generated using the following formula:

(8–3) $$(A - 1)^2/12,$$

where A is equal to the number of points on the continuum. For example, if the continuum had a range of 40 points (scores from 10–50), then the estimated variance would be equal to

$$(40 - 1)^2/12, \text{ or } 126.75.$$

Lindell, Brandt, and Whitney (1999) suggested that S_x^2 is underestimated and should be corrected by a factor of

(8–4) $$[K/(K - 1)],$$

where $K =$ the number of raters in the sample. Referring to the data in Table 8.3, the first team's correction for item variance is

$$1.5 \times (5/4),$$
$$= 1.5 \times 1.25,$$
$$= 1.875.$$

Using this value, the corrected $r_{wg} = (2.0 - 1.875)/2.0$, or 0.075. For the second team, the correction is:

$$0.25 \times (4/3),$$
$$= 0.25 \times 1.33,$$
$$= 0.3325.$$

Using this value, the corrected $r_{wg} = (2.0 - 0.3325)/2.0$, or 0.834.

The revised r_{wg} values are listed in the final column of Table 8.3 for all 10 teams. Note that they are all smaller than the uncorrected values. As the number of raters increases, the effect of making the correction decreases.

When the raters rate more than one item (e.g., a whole series of items), the multi-item measure of rater agreement formula suggested by James, Demaree, and Wolf (1984) has been predominantly used:

$$(8-5) \qquad r_{mwg} = \{J[1 - (\bar{s}_x^2/\sigma_e^2)]\}/(\{J[1 - (\bar{s}_x^2/\sigma_e^2)]\} + (\bar{s}_x^2/\sigma_e^2)),$$

where J = the number of items being rated and $\bar{s}_x^2$ = the mean average across all of the items' variances (i.e., not the variance for all items together). As an example, consider a 10-item measure of a five-point Likert-type rating scale where the mean average of the item variances (i.e., $\bar{s}_x^2$) is 1.0. Recall that for a five-point Likert-type scale, the $\sigma_e^2 = 2$. Using formula 8–5, the resulting interrater agreement index is

$$\begin{aligned} r_{mwg} &= \{10[1 - (1.0/2.0)]\}/(\{(10[1 - (1.0/2.0)]\} + (1.0/2.0)), \\ &= 5/(5 + 0.5), \\ &= 0.91. \end{aligned}$$

If the mean item variance is higher (say 1.7), it is quite close to the expected variance, given no agreement among raters. The interrater agreement index is

$$\begin{aligned} r_{mwg} &= \{10[1 - (1.7/2.0)]\}/(\{10[1 - (1.7/2.0)]\} + (1.7/2.0)), \\ &= 1.5/(1.5 + 0.85), \\ &= 1.5/2.35, \\ &= 0.64. \end{aligned}$$

However, using the same mean item variance but with a 20-item scale, the interrater agreement index is

$$\begin{aligned} r_{mwg} &= \{20[1 - (1.7/2.0)]\}/(\{20[1 - (1.7/2.0)]\} + (1.7/2.0)]), \\ &= 3/(3 + 0.85), \\ &= 3/3.85, \\ &= 0.78. \end{aligned}$$

The interrater agreement is certainly in the acceptable range of reliability with the 20-item scale. This is true despite the fact that the actual mean item variance is quite high. Because of this issue, Lindell, Brandt, and Whitney (1999) demonstrated that the James, Demaree, and Wolf (1984) formula produced inadmissible values. They then suggested that the best way to assess interrater agreement across a number of items is given by the formula

$$(8-6) \qquad r_{mwg}^* = (\sigma_e^2 - \bar{s}_x^2)/\sigma_e^2.$$

Next, the interrater agreements are calculated using formula 8-6, where the mean item variances are 1.0 and 1.7, respectively,

$$r^*_{mwg} = (2 - 1.0)/2,$$
$$= 0.50, \text{ and}$$

$$r^*_{mwg} = (2 - 1.7)/2,$$
$$= 0.15.$$

It can be seen that the resulting indices are more conservative. However, they do seem to be more indicative of the actual agreement among the raters.

Because unreliable measures adversely affect any relationships of the measure with other variables that might be of interest (say team performance), the researcher may want to consider removing the two teams with low r_{wg} values from the analysis and collect data on two more teams to increase the sample size back to 10 teams, hoping that the new teams will show more agreement. Alternatively, the researcher may examine the individual responses to determine if there was coding error in entering the data, or remove an individual that may have an outlying score. Whatever approach is used, it must be justified.

Average Deviation Index. A variation on the approach used by James, Demaree, and Wolf (1984) is called the average deviation index (AD; Burke, Finkelstein, & Dusig, 1999). Specifically, a set of judges rates a single stimulus on a single rating scale (e.g., a five-point Likert-type scale). The mean of these ratings is calculated, and then the difference between each judge's rating and the mean is calculated. These differences are then averaged to produce the AD for the item. The smaller this value is, the more agreement there is among the judges.

Burke and Dunlap (2002) further demonstrated that an AD could be calculated for a single stimulus over a number of items by simply averaging the ADs associated with each item. They also demonstrated that $c/6$ (where c is equal to the number of response options of a Likert-type scale) could be used as a rule of thumb for an acceptable upper-level cutoff for interrater agreement. So, for example, five-, seven-, and nine-point Likert-type scales would have acceptable agreement levels of 5/6 (0.83), 7/6 (1.17), and 9/6 (1.50). Their operational definition of acceptability is predicated on the assumption that 0.70 is an appropriate lower limit of measurement consistency. They also provide easy-to-follow equations for calculating the AD for percentages, proportions, and two-category responses.

Generalizability Theory and the Intraclass Correlation Coefficient. Another method for assessing the interrater agreement uses generalizabiltiy theory (Cronbach, Gleser, Nanda, & Rajaratnam, 1972). Generalizability theory extends classical test theory (CTT) by not making the stringent assumption that a raw score has two parts— a systematic part score (all of which is true score) and error. Generalizability theory allows for a finer "carving up" of the systematic and error terms into relevant parts.

For example, it may be of interest to assess the reliability of three different judges' ratings of aggressive behavior displayed by 2nd-graders at three different times, each separated by 6 weeks. These students might be in four different teachers' classrooms. The ratings provided may differ due to a number of possible sources (or facets): (a) individual 2nd-grader differences on aggression (say there are 100 of them), (b) judges (there are three), (c) classrooms (there are four), and (d) occasions (there are three). Generalizability theory allows for the assessment of the effects of each of these facets on the variation on the ratings provided. This multifaceted approach is explained very well by Cardinet, Tourneur, and Allal (1976), who examine the generalizability of reading comprehension student test scores using author (three levels) and occasions (two levels).

In the following example, the simpler case where there are just two facets (persons [p] and judges [j]) as sources of variation in rating assessment will be used. Specifically, assume that five judges rate the quality of ten students' English essays. The judges use a scale of 1–10 where higher ratings mean better scores (for the raw data, see Table 8.4).

There is likely to be variance among the students' essays, with some students writing better essays than others—this is true variance, some of which will be captured in the judges' ratings of the essays, with some students receiving higher marks than others. In addition, however, there may be systematic variance in the judges' ratings. For example, Judge 5 may be particularly lenient in scoring so that he or she always gives higher scores to the essays than do the other judges. This systematic variance should not become part of the true score variance as it belongs to the judges.

In fact, generalizability theory is used to provide an estimate of how well the sample of judges' ratings that have been collected will *generalize* to the potential universe of judges. This is captured in a statistic called the intraclass correlation coefficient, symbolized ρ^2, and ranges from 0 to 1.0, where 0 indicates no generalizability and 1.0 indicates perfect generalizability. ρ^2 is equal to the ratio of true

Table 8.4   Data Set for Assessing the Intraclass Correlation Coefficient

	Judge 1	Judge 2	Judge 3	Judge 4	Judge 5
Essay 1	3	4	5	3	6
Essay 2	5	6	7	6	8
Essay 3	3	2	1	2	3
Essay 4	7	8	6	9	9
Essay 5	10	9	8	7	9
Essay 6	3	2	4	3	5
Essay 7	4	5	6	5	6
Essay 8	5	6	7	5	8
Essay 9	3	3	3	2	3
Essay 10	6	7	7	8	8

score variance across persons ($\sigma^2_{persons}$) divided by the sum of $\sigma^2_{persons}$ plus random error variance (σ^2_{error}) (Lord & Novick, 1968):

(8–7)
$$\rho^2 = \sigma^2_{persons}/(\sigma^2_{persons} + \sigma^2_{error}).$$

There are several variations on this basic formula, depending on how many facets are included in the study as well as the study's purpose. Regardless of purpose and facet, the $\sigma^2_{persons}$ term remains constant but the σ^2_{error} term will vary. Some of these variations are reviewed shortly, but first, let's return to our study of judges and essays.

It is usually not the case that we would be interested in any specific group of particular judges; rather, we would usually be more interested in generalizing to the population of judges. In this case, the judges are called a *random effect*. There are some instances where we might indeed be interested in the specific judges and their ratings. For example, assume we are training a group of managers to be better raters of their subordinates' performance. These managers attend a training program, and we expect that their ratings are going to be more accurate after having attended the program. If this were the case, we would have a *fixed effect* for the judges. Whether the effect is fixed or random affects the magnitude of the σ^2_{error} term.

There are two types of studies that employ generalizability theory; they are called G and D studies. G studies are general studies where the sample statistics are assessed as to their generalizability to a population. D studies are those used to make decisions about the most appropriate treatment or intervention. D studies follow G studies because G studies provide information about the relative reliability of various facets and thus how best to increase the reliability of the entire study. For example, we might be interested in using judges' ratings of English essays for awarding scholarships, and thus, eventually, we want to carry out a D study. So, we might then extend our G study of judges (facet J) rating English essays to include five different occasions (facet O), so that the judges rate five different essays from the 10 students that were written on five different occasions. We could even extend it to examining differences between four different schools (facet S). After we conduct our G study, we may find that the judges were not very consistent but that, over occasions and over schools, there was a high level of consistency. This would suggest that we need to either train the judges to be more consistent in their ratings or add many more judges to ensure that sampling error of judges is minimized in the D study.

For our purposes, we will be considering a G study using a single random-effect facet (the five judges) and one effect facet (the 10 student essays). In a G study, each judge rates each and every essay. The more judges there are and the more essays there are for them to rate, the better the reliability. This is the case because the stability of the estimates improves as the square root of the sample size increases (Nunnally & Bernstein, 1994).

Some theoretical computations need to be reviewed first before calculating the intraclass correlation coefficient. Note that any one judge's rating of an essay will be equal to (a) the difference between the students' mean rating across all the judges and the mean of all the other judges' ratings of all the essays ($\mu_{person} - \mu$), (b) the difference between that particular judges' mean ratings across all essays and the mean of all the judges' ratings of all the other essays ($\mu_{person} - \mu$), and (c) error for the specific rating ($e_{person \times judge}$). Repeated measures analysis of variance (ANOVA) to solve the equations is used. The resulting ANOVA summary table provides the variances and mean square error terms needed to allocate the true and error variances appropriately. Specifically, for a sample of judges rating all essays, the intraclass formula simplifies to

$$(8–8) \qquad\qquad \rho^2 = (MS_{persons} - MS_{residual})/MS_{persons},$$

where $MS_{persons}$ = mean squares for the *persons* effect and $MS_{residual}$ = mean square for the *residual* effect. This is the reliability formula proposed by Hoyt in 1941.

If the data in Table 8.4 are analyzed, the resulting repeated measures ANOVA summary tables shown in Table 8.5 are generated. The $MS_{persons}$ = 24.089 and the $MS_{residual}$ = 0.794.

Substituting into the formula, the reliability of the judges is

$$\rho^2 = (24.089 - 0.794)/24.089,$$
$$= 0.967.$$

Thus, we would conclude that the average ratings by our sample of judges correlates very well to the population of potential ratings from the universe of judges (i.e., they are highly consistent). This is likely the statistic we want for our purposes of interrater reliability.

In addition to the estimated intraclass correlation coefficient, confidence intervals can be set around the composite rating of an essay because the standard error (SE) of the intraclass is simply the square root of $MS_{residual}$ divided by the number of judges:

$$(8–9) \qquad\qquad SE = \sqrt{MS_{residual}/\# \ judges.}$$

Thus, in our example, the standard error is

$$SE = \sqrt{(0.795/5)},$$
$$= 0.399.$$

To set 95% confidence interval around the mean rating for the essay, 0.398 is multiplied by 1.96 (the *z* value associated with the 95% confidence interval) resulting in the value, 0.78. The average rating for the first essay in the sample was $(3 + 4 + 5 + 3 + 6)/5 = 4.2$. We can be 95% confident that the true score on the essay is 4.2 ± 0.78, or between 3.42 and 4.98.

Another inference using the intraclass correlation coefficient that one may want to make is whether these judges' overall reliability (0.967) is representative of any

Table 8.5   Calculating the Intraclass Correlation Coefficient Via Repeated Measures ANOVA

Tests of Within-Subjects Effects					
Source	Type III Sum of Squares	df	Mean Square	F	Sig.
Judges	15.600	2	4.150	– – –	– – –
Judges x Essays	28.600	36	0.794	– – –	– – –
Error (Judges)	0.000	0			

The essays are considered a between-subjects effect and the judges (1–5) are the repeated measure and 0.794 is the MS residual.

Tests of Within-Subjects Contrasts						
Source	Judges	Type III Sum of Squares	df	Mean	F	Sig.
Judges	Linear	9.000	1	9.000	– – –	– – –
Judges x Essays	Linear	10.400	9	1.156	– – –	– – –

Tests of Between-Subjects Effects					
Source	Type III Sum of Squares	df	Mean Square	F	Sig.
Intercept	1458.000	1	1458.000	– – –	– – –
Essays	216.800	9	24.089	– – –	– – –
Error	0.000	0			

The mean square for essays in this between-subjects effects table is the MS effect for persons.

one judge. If we want to make a generalizability statement about any one judge, we use this formula:

(8–10) $\rho^2 = (MS_{persons} - MS_{residual})/[MS_{persons} + (\#judges - 1)(MS_{residual})]$.

Substituting the data into this formula,

$$\rho^2 = (24.089 - 0.794)/[24.089 + (4)(0.794)]$$
$$= 23.295/27.265$$
$$= 0.854.$$

Table 8.6   Generating the Intraclass Correlation Coefficient Via the SPSS Reliability Program

Intraclass Correlation Coefficient Two-Way Random Effect Model (Consistency Definition): People and Measure Effect Random
Single Measure Intraclass Correlation = 0.8543 95.00% C.I.: Lower = 0.6907, Upper = 0.9549 $F = 30.3217$, $df = (9,36.0)$, Sig. = 0.0000 (Test Value = 0.0000)
Average Measure Intraclass Correlation = 0.9670 95.00% C.I.: Lower = 0.9178, Upper = 0.9906 $F = 30.3217$, $df = (9,36.0)$, Sig. = 0.0000 (Test Value = 0.0000)

It can be seen that the generalizability of one judge's rating to the universe of judges' ratings is lower than that of five judges' ratings to the universe of judges' ratings. This makes theoretical sense in that the mean ratings of five judges better represent the population than does one judge's ratings.

In the past, repeated measures ANOVA was used to generate the relevant MS terms needed to calculate the intraclass coefficient. In the Reliability program of SPSS, the intraclass can be generated by requesting the "intraclass" option and specifying the judges as "items" (see Table 8.6).

Note that the model indicates a "Two-Way Random Effect Model." This means that "People," which corresponds to the essays, and "Measure," which corresponds to the judges, are both random effects (i.e., sampled from a population to which we wish to generalize). It is optional to request fixed effects for either variable.

The "Single Measure Intraclass Correlation" is equal to the calculated value obtained from the repeated measures ANOVA table, assuming there was only one judge. The "Average Measure Intraclass Correlation" is equal to the calculated value obtained from the repeated measures ANOVA table, assuming a sample of five judges. The C.I. values are the lower and upper boundaries of the 95% confidence intervals around the calculated intraclass coefficient.

The F test values calculate whether the judges' consistency ratings are significantly different from 0. Although not apparent from this output, the degrees of freedom (9,36) correspond to the degrees of freedom for the MS essays and MS residual from the repeated measures ANOVA table.

As noted earlier, there are many more uses to generalizability theory than have been presented here. The interested reader should see Cardinet, Tourneur, and Allal (1976); Nunnally and Bernstein (1994); and Shrout and Fleiss (1979) for other examples.

Reliability Generalization

Tests per se are not reliable or unreliable. Rather, test scores have an index of reliability. While the philosophy in the preceding sentences may seem to be just a semantic issue, it is not—it is quite substantive. Many intelligent people are wont to say, "This test is reliable" or "This test is not reliable." Both statements are inappropriate, as it is the test scores on which the reliability estimate is calculated that are more or less reliable. However, is there a way to use reliability estimates generated from other sample settings to generalize to a setting of interest? The answer is yes.

Semantics out of the way, Vacha-Haase (1998) provided a cogent argument for the use of "reliability generalization." She bases her arguments on the following argument: Reliability generalization uses the mean measurement error of a test used across a number of different studies, as well as the sources of variability in variances across studies, to generate an index of reliability that can be generalized.

In Vacha-Haase's study (1998), she used the Bem Sex Role Inventory (Bem, 1974, 1981) as an example of carrying out a reliability generalization study. She found in her literature search (from 1984–1997) 87 reliability coefficients that had been reported in 57 studies for the masculinity and femininity scales of the inventory separately. She then coded the coefficients on the following dimensions: type of reliability (internal consistency vs. test-retest), type of study (substantive vs. measurement), gender of study participants, sample type (student vs. non student), test length (short vs. long form), and response format (five-point vs. seven-point Likert-type scale). These other variables, then, were assessed as to their effects on the reliability coefficient. She subjected the data to a meta-analysis and her findings suggested that there is a wide range of reliability of the masculinity and femininity scales, and these were primarily dependent on the sample size, the type of reliability index calculated, and test length.

Caruso (2000) reported on the reliability generalization of the five different NEO personality scales (Costa & McCrae, 1985, 1992). His literature search found 51 samples on which the meta-analysis could be calculated. The variables he used in detecting sources of variability in the reliability index were (a) referent (self vs. peer), (b) version of the NEO (one of three), (c) language administered (English vs. non-English), (d) sample type (student, nonstudent, clinical, other), (e) gender, and (f) type of reliability (internal consistency vs. test-retest). Means and medians of the reliability indices were reported. He found that, again, there was quite a bit of variation in reliability indices and also under what conditions the test scores would be more or less reliable.

These two studies were able to define under what conditions the tests under investigation would be most reliable and least reliable. This has been just a brief introduction to the notion of reliability generalization. It is very useful to have access to a study such as the ones cited above for a particular test that may be of interest. However, this technique is still relatively new, and often this type of data is difficult to come by. However, it is brought up here because, as wise test consumers and as test developers, it is important to recognize that reliability is not inherent in the test itself, but rather is a function of the test items, the sample, the situation, and so forth.

Modern Test Theory Approaches to Reliability

Thus far the discussion of reliability has assumed the CTT paradigm. Modern test theory (item response theory, or IRT) uses somewhat different indices of reliability based on patterns of responses to the test items and item parameters. Specifically, IRT provides information for each item and with the test as a whole in terms of its accuracy in estimating an individual's trait level. The empirical reliability of the test, then, is generated based on the standard errors of individual respondents' scores. This was described at length in chapter 6, using examples, so it will not be repeated here.

Summary and Next Steps

This chapter has focused on

a. interrater methods to assess reliability,

b. reliability generalization, and

c. how modern test theory approaches reliability in a very different manner than does classical test theory.

The next chapter covers what is nearest and dearest to the hearts of test developers and users—the validity of the inferences we want to make about test scores. If tests scores are not valid for the purpose for which the tests are developed, then what good are they? Conversely, test scores that are valid for the use to which they are put can be very useful tools, indeed, in many areas of our lives.

Problems and Exercises

1. If a Kendall's coefficient of concordance of 0.70 is obtained, what type of data has been analyzed and what can be concluded about the reliability?

2. If a Cohen's kappa of 0.70 is obtained, what type of data has been analyzed and what can be concluded about the reliability?

3. What would be the r_{wg} and corrected r_{wg} values for a 10-member team's rating of a single-item measure of their performance on a scale of 1–5? Assume that the variance of the item across the 10 members was 0.70. What would be the team's reliability on a six-item scale of their performance (again using a five-point scale) if the mean variance across all six items was 0.60 using the Lindell, Brandt, and Whitney (1999) formula?

4. Assume ratings (on a 10-point scale) of job performance by three supervisors of ten employees are collected. A repeated measures analysis of variance is run on the data and the following information from the summary table is obtained: mean square for persons = 20, and mean square residual = 2.0. Calculate the intraclass correlation coefficient and interpret it.

5. What is reliability generalization?

CHAPTER 9

Assessing Validity Using Content and Criterion Methods

O nce the test has been deemed reliable enough to use, it is time to begin the lengthy validation process. Often the analyses to assess an instrument's psychometric soundness will provide evidence for both reliability and validity. In many instances, the two issues are strongly tied. However, from a pedagogical perspective, it is useful to separate those analyses most closely linked with reliability from those most closely linked with validity. Keep in mind, though, that the two psychometric properties are not mutually exclusive.

The term *test validity* is a misnomer. Tests are not valid in and of themselves. The inferences made about a test score are more or less valid. For example, if I have a higher score on a need for achievement scale than does my colleague, then I want to infer that I am higher on the trait of need for achievement. Validity also is concerned with how the scores are used. For example, if I use the need for achievement scores for determining who gets a raise—myself or my colleague—this may not be a valid use of the test scores. This way of conceptualizing validity flies in the face of how validity is typically described, which is to indicate that there are different kinds of validity: face, content, criterion-related, and construct. These have been convenient categories that imply that there are various types of validity and that a test can have some of one category and none of another. This assumption is simply untenable.

The approach to test score validity that will be used in this and the next chapter does not assume there are different kinds of validity. Instead, there are different methods used to assess various aspects of test score validity for certain contexts. This chapter will cover the processes and analyses associated with assessing the wording and content of the items on the test and how test scores are related to other variables. The next chapter will cover the processes and analyses associated with assessing the internal structure of the test items.

Asking the Test Takers

A group of individuals that will provide valuable input in terms of what the test items ask is the test takers themselves. Test takers are important stakeholders in the testing process. If test takers find the items believable, they are more likely to respond appropriately. In the past, this has been called *face validity*. For example, if a group of employees is told that they will be assessed on their "propensity to want to be involved in teams," and they are administered a questionnaire with items such as, How often do you take office supplies home? the employees will likely have very negative reactions to the testing process.

While this is an extreme example of poor face validity, it is not uncommon for test items to seem irrelevant to test takers. This may be because the test items are poorly designed, the use to which the scores will be put is not of interest to or runs counter to the interest of test takers, or because the test items do not meet the expectations of test takers.

Thus, it is critical that items on a test appear both relevant and clear to the test takers. Pilot testing with the instrument using a small sample of test takers from the population of test takers is a great time-saving exercise. For example, with the Team Player Inventory (TPI), employees who have worked in team environments are the most appropriate ones from whom to solicit feedback as to the utility of the items. Usually after they take the test, extensive debriefing with the test takers as to the clarity of the items and their relevance is carried out. The information gathered assists developers and administrators in knowing whether or not it will even be worthwhile to administer the test to a larger sample.

Test taker comments and suggestions are completely subjective and are made by laypeople. Thus they do not have the aura of being "scientific." However, skipping this step may have dire consequences for using the test. If the test items fail to have adequate face validity, then rewriting the items or selecting a different instrument is warranted.

Asking the Subject Matter Experts

Another perspective that also falls under the "completely subjective" category is that of Subject Matter Experts (SMEs). SMEs can be grouped into two types for purposes of validation; one is for content and one is for process. Content SMEs were used as part of the initial item-creation exercise. Another group of content SMEs are now needed to determine if, from their perspective, the items capture the construct. As with the test takers, input from SMEs at the front end of test development or administration will save lots of problems later in the validation process.

To get the best feedback from the content SMEs, tell them very clearly what is being measured. By doing so, they will be better informed and able to indicate if the items are deficient (i.e., missing some aspect of the construct that should be included) or are contaminated (i.e., contain items that will solicit information not in the construct).

The process SMEs are the ones who will provide feedback on test administration procedures. They will help to ensure that the questions are clear and unambiguous. They will help decide what would be the most appropriate responding approach to use that will allow for making valid inferences from the test scores. These individuals should also help with administrative issues such as test length, compliance with legal issues, test presentation format, etc. For example, if a test is 400 items long, it may be wonderful in capturing the construct, but respondent fatigue would be at least as important an issue to consider as is item content. If the test is to be used with a special population, such as the elderly, handicapped, children, adolescents, and so forth, then how best to administer the test (one on one, electronically, paper and pencil, etc.) might be a consideration. If the test is speeded, scores on such tests are valid only if the construct being measured has speed as a primary characteristic (e.g., data entry, filing). These are the types of potential problems the process SMEs will help you to avoid.

This type of SME input in the past has been called *content validity.* It is obvious why content validity is subjective in nature and is present in any testing situation to some degree—it does not either exist or not exist. Rather, it is up to test administrators to ensure that they have exercised due diligence in constructing and/or selecting the most appropriate test to use on their particular sample for their particular purpose. SMEs are an invaluable resource and should be used to the fullest extent in test development, design, and administration. Their input should assist in efficiently administering a high-quality test under optimal conditions.

Assessments Using Correlation and Regression: Criterion-Related Studies

One common way to assess the utility of tests scores is to use them to predict other variables of interest. For example, it might be expected that teams with higher ratings of being team players (using team-aggregated scores on the TPI) would also have higher ratings on their willingness to work together in the future compared to teams with lower TPI scores. It might also be expected that individuals with higher TPI scores would like working on teams and thus have worked on more teams in the past than individuals with lower scores on the TPI. Relationships such as these are called *criterion-related* in that one variable, the predictor (e.g., TPI scores), is being used to predict another variable of interest, the criterion (e.g., number of teams worked on in the past two years). Thus, it follows that this type of validity assessment technique has been called in the past *criterion validity* and the correlations produced are called *validity coefficients* (although this is quite strong language considering much more is associated with validity than just a correlation coefficient!).

Many assessments, such as the type just described, of the validity of test scores use correlation or regression analyses. In Chapter 1, these analyses were described and thus will not be reviewed here again. Table 9.1 shows the TPI items and Table 9.2 the TPI scores for 25 individuals, the number of work teams they had been involved in over the past two years, and their ages.

Table 9.1   Team Player Items (Kline, 1999)

1. I enjoy working on team/group projects.*
2. Team/group project work easily allows others to <u>not</u> "pull their weight". (R)*
3. Work that is done as a team/group is better than the work done individually.*
4. I do all the work in team/group projects, while others get the credit. (R)
5. Others on the team/group benefit from my input.
6. I do my best work alone rather than in a team/group. (R)*
7. My experiences working in team/group situations have been primarily positive.
8. Working with others in a team/group situation slows my progress. (R)
9. My personal evaluation should be based on my team/group's collective work.
10. Team/group work is overrated in terms of the actual results produced. (R)*
11. Working in a team/group gets me to think more creatively. *
12. Team/groups are used too often, when individual work would be more effective. (R)*
13. A benefit of working in a team/group situation means that I get to meet new people.
14. A problem with working in a team/group situation is that some team members may feel "left out." (R)
15. A benefit of working in a team/group situation is that it gives the members a sense of common purpose.
16. Working in a team/group situation fosters conflict between the teams/groups. (R)
17. My own work is enhanced when I am in a team/group situation.*
18. My experiences working in team/group situations have been primarily negative. (R)*
19. More solutions/ideas are generated when working in a team/group situation than when working alone. *
20. I work harder alone than when I am in a team/group situation. (R)

Note: (R) = reverse coded items, * = retained items

If a simple correlation is done between TPI scores and number of work teams involved in over the past two years, the resulting correlation is 0.75. This is significant and indicates that the overlapping variance between TPI scores and work teams involved in is 56%. Table 9.3 shows the output of the SPSS correlation between the two variables.

If the question was phrased in more predictive terminology, the number of work teams involved in over the past two years would be regressed on TPI scores. The results would be the same in terms of the magnitude of the relationship, with a $b = 0.119$ and $\beta = 0.747$. The latter analysis is more directional than the former in that the researcher makes clear which variable is the predictor and which is the criterion. Box 9.1 shows regression output of the data in Table 9.1.

The issue of which analysis to use would be more relevant if there were two or more variables as predictors in the analysis. If this was the case, then regression would be the most appropriate technique to use. For example, assume that both

Table 9.2   Data for Assessing the Criterion-Related Association Between Team Player Inventory Scores and Number of Work Teams Involved in Over the Past Two Years

Case	TPI Score	Number of Teams	Years of Age
1	10	2	50
2	12	3	30
3	14	4	40
4	15	1	45
5	16	2	46
6	18	3	47
7	22	2	48
8	24	4	35
9	25	3	34
10	27	2	36
11	28	4	35
12	29	3	34
13	31	5	30
14	33	2	29
15	35	6	30
16	37	4	33
17	40	7	35
18	41	3	26
19	42	6	23
20	43	5	24
21	44	8	26
22	46	6	27
23	47	8	29
24	47	6	27
25	49	5	26

TPI scores and age are predictors of the number of teams worked on in the past two years. It is anticipated that older workers will be less likely to have been brought up with teams as typical work units, and, thus, as a conservative scientist, the effects of age need to be controlled for before assessing the predictive utility of the TPI scores.

Table 9.3   Correlation Between Team Player Inventory Scores and Number of
Work Teams Involved in Over the Past Two Years Using SPSS

	TPI	*Number of Work Teams*
TPI Sig. (two-tailed) *N*	1.00 25	0.747 0.000 25
Number of Work Teams Sig. (two-tailed) *N*	0.747 0.000 25	1.0 25

Note: The correlation between the two variables is 0.747 and is significant at an α of < 0.01. The two variables are positively and significantly correlated.

In this case, a hierarchical regression analysis is run where number of work teams involved in over the past two years is first regressed on age (resulting in an R^2 of 0.40, indicating that 40% of the variance of number of teams is accounted for by age). Then number of work teams involved in is regressed on age *and* TPI scores. The resulting R^2 is 0.560 and is significant, indicating that age and TPI scores together account for 56% of the variance in number of work teams involved in. Our question of interest, however, is whether the increased percentage (56% − 40% = 16%) by adding TPI scores is significant or not. This change upward in the R^2 value is indeed significant, indicating that TPI scores add significantly to predicting number of work teams involved in above and beyond that of age.

Box 9.2 shows the hierarchical regression analyses of the number of work teams involved in regressed on age and TPI scores based on the data in Table 9.2. This hierarchical approach is a more conservative test of the TPI scores in that age is first allowed to account for its shared variance in number of teams worked, and then any variance accounted for by TPI scores in addition to age is assessed for significance.

The examples reviewed above are relatively simple (one or two predictors and one criterion). It is easy to add more predictors, and thus the interpretation becomes more complex. For example, let's say cognitive skill scores, honesty scores, conscientious personality scores, and TPI scores are used to predict job performance ratings by supervisors (see Table 9.4).

In this case, job performance of 50 employees (using supervisor ratings of job performance) is regressed on all four predictor variables simultaneously (termed a simultaneous or direct solution). (See Box 9.3 for a detailed description of the analyses and output associated with this example.)

The overall R^2 value in this analysis is 0.641, indicating that all four variables together account for 64% variance in job performance. However, which of the four predictors add incremental information to knowledge of job performance above and beyond the other three variables is also of interest. In this case, the *b* values and their significance as well as the β values are examined to assess the relative contribution of each variable in predicting job performance. In this particular data set, the variables that account for significantly unique variance above and beyond the others are cognitive skills and TPI scores.

Box 9.1   Bivariate Regression of Number of Work Teams Involved in Over the Past Two Years Regressed on Team Player Inventory Scores Using SPSS

Model Summary				
Model	R	R-Square	Adjusted R-Square	Std. Error of the Estimate
1	0.747	0.558	0.538	1.33996

ANOVA					
Model	Sum of Squares	df	Mean Square	F	Sig.
Regression	52.064	1	52.064	28.997	0.000
Residual	41.296	23	1.795		
Total	93.360	24			

Coefficients					
	Unstandardized Coefficients		Standardized Coefficients	t	Sig.
Model	B	Std. Error	Beta		
Constant TPI	0.467	0.736		0.634	0.532
	0.119	0.002	0.747	5.385	0.000

Note that the model summary indicates that the variance accounted for by TPI scores is 0.558, or about 56%. The ANOVA table indicates that this is a significant amount of variance (F of 28.997 with 1 and 23 degrees of freedom). Additionally, the beta value (standardized regression weight) in the coefficients table is equal to 0.747, the same as the zero-order correlation between TPI scores and number of work teams involved in. The B (unstandardized regression weight) associated with the TPI scores is 0.119 with a standard error of 0.002. This yields a t value of 5.385, and it is significant. The other B (0.467) is that of the intercept value in the regression equation.

Criterion studies can be conducted concurrently or predictively. There is no difference in the analysis or interpretation of the magnitude of the relationship between the variables using one or the other. The difference between the two methods is when the data for the criterion variable are collected. For concurrent studies, the predictor and criterion variables are collected at the same time. Thus, a study

(Text continues on page 212)

Box 9.2 Hierarchical Regression of Number of Work Teams Regressed First on Age, and Then Age and TPI Scores Using SPSS

		Model Summary		
Model	R	R-Square	Adjusted R-Square	Std. Error of the Estimate
1	0.634	0.402	0.376	1.55824
2	0.749	0.560	0.520	1.36599

		Change Statistics		
R-Square Change	F Change	df1	df2	Sig. F Change
0.402	15.450	1	23	0.001
0.158	7.930	1	22	0.010

	Coefficients				
Model	Unstandardized Coefficients		Standardized Coefficients	t	Sig.
	B	Std. Error	Beta		
1 (Constant)	9.439	1.379		6.85	0.000
Age	−0.156	0.040	−0.634	−3.93	0.001
2 (Constant)	1.542	3.054		0.505	0.619
Age	−0.0215	0.059	−0.087	−0.363	−0.720
TPI	0.108	0.038	0.676	2.816	0.010

Note that in the Model Summary, for Model 1 overall, age accounts for 40.2% of the variance in number of work teams. For Model 2 overall, age and TPI scores account for 56.0% percent of the variance in number of work teams. The change statistics indicate that Model 1 significantly changes the variance accounted for from 0% to 40.2% (F of 15.450, sig. 0.001). Model 2 adds an additional 15.8% variance and it, too, is significant (F of 7.930, sig. 0.010). The coefficients assess both Models 1 and 2 separately. For Model 1, we can see that age is negatively related to number of work teams ($B = -0.156$) and it is significant ($t = -3.93$, sig. 0.001). Examining the coefficients for Model 2, we can see that TPI scores are significant predictors of number of work teams above and beyond age ($t = 2.816$, sig. 0.010), but age does not significantly predict number of work teams over and above TPI scores ($t = -0.363$, sig. 0.720).

Table 9.4   Data Set for Simultaneous Multiple Regression of Performance on Cognitive Skill, Honesty, Conscientiousness, and TPI

Case	Cognitive Skill	Honesty	Conscientiousness	TPI	Performance
1	20	1	6	10	1
2	25	2	5	12	2
3	26	3	4	14	3
4	24	1	3	42	2
5	26	2	7	50	3
6	27	3	8	16	2
7	30	4	9	29	3
8	33	3	12	27	2
9	35	5	13	26	3
10	26	4	3	25	4
11	25	3	5	30	3
12	24	2	6	33	4
13	28	5	18	24	3
14	23	5	16	25	3
15	24	6	14	26	2
16	25	9	20	30	4
17	28	8	3	35	5
18	30	3	4	34	3
19	35	6	5	18	5
20	36	5	20	14	4
21	34	9	19	20	5
22	37	4	18	22	4
23	38	7	4	23	5
24	39	6	6	19	4
25	35	7	8	27	5
26	40	3	4	26	4

(Continued)

Table 9.4 (Continued)

Case	Cognitive Skill	Honesty	Conscientiousness	TPI	Performance
27	41	6	6	35	5
28	40	2	3	40	6
29	42	7	8	41	4
30	43	4	9	42	5
31	44	8	9	43	6
32	45	9	10	46	5
33	43	4	12	47	6
34	45	9	13	48	7
35	46	4	13	43	5
36	47	5	14	45	7
37	47	7	15	46	6
38	46	3	20	47	6
39	45	8	16	48	5
40	42	9	17	39	6
41	41	6	14	38	7
42	35	5	13	37	8
43	39	8	12	47	7
44	38	4	18	45	8
45	37	6	18	46	8
46	40	3	17	36	7
47	47	8	16	38	9
48	48	8	20	41	6
49	49	3	20	42	7
50	49	6	19	49	8

Box 9.3   Simultaneous Solution Multiple Regression Using Cognitive Skills, Honesty, Conscientious Personality, and TPI Scores to Predict Job Performance Using SPSS

		Model Summary		
Model	R	R-Square	Adjusted R-Square	Std. Error of the Estimate
1	0.801	0.641	0.609	1.20768

		ANOVA			
Model	Sum of Squares	df	Mean Square	F	Sig.
Regression	117.088	4	29.272	20.070	0.000
Residual	65.632	45	1.458		
Total	182.720	49			

	Coefficients				
	Unstandardized Coefficients		Standardized Coefficients		
Model	B	Std. Error	Beta	t	Sig.
(Constant)	−1.678	0.770		−2.18	0.035
Cognitive	0.106	0.029	0.460	3.68	0.001
Honesty	0.105	0.083	0.127	1.26	0.213
Conscien.	0.0453	0.034	0.136	1.35	0.185
TPI	0.0483	0.019	0.284	2.51	0.016

Using a simultaneous (direct) solution, a number of indicators can be assessed at once regarding each one's usefulness in accounting for overall and unique variance in job performance. Note that the model using all four variables as predictors of job performance allows us to account for 64% of the variance in job performance scores. The ANOVA table indicates that this is significantly different from 0% ($F = 20.070$, sig. 0.000). In the coefficients table, we can see that the only variables that predict job performance above and beyond that of any of the other three predictors are cognitive skills ($t = 3.68$, sig. 0.001) and TPI ($t = 2.41$, sig. 0.016). This is also demonstrated in the magnitude of the beta values (0.460 for cognitive skills and 0.284 for TPI). Honesty (0.136) and conscientious personality (0.136) are relatively less useful in predicting job performance.

where both TPI scores and number of teams worked on in the past two years is collected at the same time from a group of employees would be a concurrent criterion-related study. If TPI scores on a group of employees is collected at Time 1, and then, after two years go by, that same group of employees is asked how many teams they had worked on, then the criterion data are gathered at Time 2. This is called a predictive criterion-related study.

There are *post*dictive studies, where one gathers a criterion variable from the past. For example, a group of workers might be asked how many teams or clubs they were involved in during their high school years. Then they would be asked to complete the TPI scale, and their scores would be used to predict, retroactively, the number of teams or clubs those individuals were involved in during their high school years.

One issue that comes up in criterion-related studies is that, if there are multiple predictors, should some of them be weighted more than others when making a decision? For example, if a test of cognitive ability and test of a work sample are both used to predict job performance, should one be given more weight in the decision-making process than the other? The evidence suggests that using complex weighting schemes for the predictors does not offer much improvement over not doing so (i.e., unit weighting; Aamodt & Kimbrough, 1985).

Convergent/Divergent Assessment. Validation via convergent and divergent assessment was first introduced by Campbell and Fiske (1959) almost 50 years ago. This process has to do with relationships between the construct of interest and other similar or dissimilar constructs. For example, it would be expected that TPI scores should be somewhat positively related to other variables that assess sociability. It would be expected that TPI scores would be negatively related to variables such as independence or autonomy.

As a concrete example, suppose TPI scores were correlated with social interaction and social relation values scores (Macnab, Fitzsimmons, & Casserly, 1987; as was done in Kline, 1999). There should be a significant amount of shared variance between the constructs. This provides convergent information that the TPI construct is indeed assessing what it purports to assess. However, if the correlations were very high (0.80 or more), then the TPI construct would be considered to be too redundant with social interaction and social relation. To ensure that the construct diverges enough from the others to be considered unique, the correlations between such similar constructs should be moderate (between 0.30 and 0.50).

In addition, it is also expected that correlations of the similar constructs (social interaction and social relation) with other criteria (e.g., team cohesion) acted similarly in terms of strength and direction as did TPI scores. Again, this helps to provide convergent evidence about the validity of the TPI construct.

Upper Bounds of Validity and Correction for Unreliability. As just reviewed, criterion-related validity studies depend on assessing the relationship between a test (predictor) and outcome (criterion), usually with a correlation or regression coefficient. Both the predictor and criterion should be assumed to be fallible (unreliable) measures. Almost no test (predictor) has a reliability coefficient of 1.0, and the outcomes (criteria) are often even more plagued by unreliability. While test developers and users are quite cognizant of the issues associated with the reliability of the predictor variable, the criterion may not even be subjected to any type of reliability assessment. This "criterion problem" was cited many years ago (Ghiselli, 1956), but continues to plague those using criterion measures for purposes of test score validation (e.g., Binning & Barrett, 1989).

While this may seem to be of only theoretical importance, note that the maximum value of a validity coefficient (r_{xy}) is

(9–1)
$$r_{xy} = \sqrt{(r_{xx})(r_{yy})},$$

where r_{xx} is the reliability of the X variable and r_{yy} is the reliability of the Y variable. That is, the upper limit of any criterion-related validity coefficient, r_{xy}, is equal to the square root of the product of the reliabilities of the predictor (r_{xx}) and criterion (r_{yy}). For example, if test scores and criterion scores with reliabilities of $r_{xx} = 0.50$ and $r_{yy} = 0.50$, respectively, are correlated with each other, the upper limit of their relationship (the validity coefficient) is

$$r_{xy} = \sqrt{(0.50)(0.50)},$$
$$= \sqrt{0.25},$$
$$= 0.50.$$

If the predictor and criterion are much more reliable, let's say $r_{xx} = 0.90$ and $r_{yy} = 0.80$, the upper limit of their relationship is

$$r_{xy} = \sqrt{(0.90)(0.80)},$$
$$= 0.85.$$

The lower the reliability of either, the less likely it is that a validity coefficient will be significant. Therefore, the practical implications of the relationship between reliability and validity are extremely important. This is the case because, even at the best of times, the validity coefficient will not get close to its upper limit.

So, what some individuals do to get around this issue is engage in a process called *correction for reliability attenuation.* This means that first an observed validity coefficient is calculated. Then the question is asked: What would the corrected validity coefficient be if the predictor, criterion, or both were perfectly reliable? For example, if $r_{xy} = 0.28$, $r_{xx} = 0.70$, and $r_{yy} = 0.80$, what would the corrected $r_{x'y}$ be if $r_{xx} = 1.00$ (i.e., r_{xt})? The formula for correcting the validity coefficient for unreliability in the predictor is

(9–2)
$$r_{x'y} = r_{xy}/\sqrt{r_{xx}}$$
$$= 0.28/\sqrt{0.70},$$
$$= 0.28/0.84,$$
$$= 0.33.$$

Thus, if it could be assumed that the test scores were perfectly reliable, then the validity coefficient would go up from 0.28 to 0.33. The formula for correcting the validity coefficient for unreliability in the criterion is

(9–3)

$$r_{xy'} = r_{xy}/\sqrt{r_{yy}}$$
$$= 0.28/\sqrt{0.80},$$
$$r_{xy'} = 0.31.$$

Thus, if could be assumed that the criterion values were perfectly reliable, then the validity coefficient would go up from 0.28 to 0.31. Now assume that both predictor and criterion were corrected for attenuation. This formula for this correction is

(9–4)

$$r_{x'y'} = r_{xy}/\sqrt{(r_{xx})(r_{yy})},$$
$$= 0.28/\sqrt{(0.70)(0.80)},$$
$$= 0.37.$$

Now the validity coefficient has jumped from 0.28 to 0.37! Be cautious in interpreting such corrected values. Note that the more unreliable the variable is to start with, the more this "correction" will boost the validity coefficient.

It is more reasonable to correct the predictor for unreliability than it is to correct the criterion. This is because test content can be changed to enhance its reliability. It is less defensible to correct the criterion for unreliability unless it, too, can be made more reliable.

Range Restriction and Correction. One common problem in correlational studies is that one or both of the variables have a *restricted range.* For example, assume I was interested in seeing the relationship between accident rates and driver's scores on a paper-and-pencil driving test to predict accidents during the first year of driving. If the driver's test can be assumed to be useful, there should be a negative relationship between test scores and accident rates. Assume that a data set based on 30 individuals is collected. All of them were given the test and all of them were given a driver's license regardless of their test score. The data for this example is shown in Table 9.5.

If a correlation analysis is run on the data, the resulting correlation is −0.72, which is very high. The scatterplot of the data is shown in Figure 9.1. However, if a decision rule had been invoked where only those with driving test scores of 80 or more pass and get a license, then those scoring less than 80 would not have been on the roads and getting into accidents. The correlation based only on those who did pass would be very low ($r = 0.13$) and nonsignificant. The scatterplot of these scores is shown in Figure 9.2.

This is a rather extreme example. However, it is not uncommon to have restricted ranges in the data. If either or both of the variables to be correlated have restricted ranges, be cautious in assuming the relationship between them is nonsignificant.

There is a correction one can make to estimate what the correlation would be if the range was not restricted. If it is to be used, the population variance needs to be known or estimated in advance. Often this can be determined by using information contained in past studies or by using the distributions calculated for the r_{wg} in Chapter 8. In the driving test example, assume that the 30 cases actually represented

Table 9.5 Data for Assessing the Relationship Between Driver's Test Scores and First-Year Accident Rates

Case	Test Score	Accidents in First Year Driving
1	50	2
2	60	1
3	45	2
4	58	2
5	62	1
6	72	1
7	70	2
8	66	1
9	83	1
10	77	2
11	76	1
12	72	1
13	55	3
14	47	3
15	83	1
16	92	1
17	67	2
18	77	1
19	95	1
20	87	1
21	88	0
22	85	0
23	79	1
24	86	0
25	91	0
26	90	1
27	87	0
28	76	2
29	70	1
30	72	2

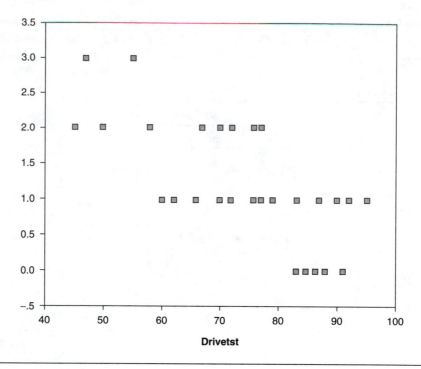

Figure 9.1   Scatterplot of Driving Test Scores and Accidents

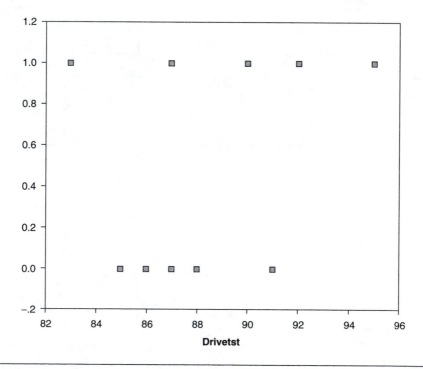

Figure 9.2   Scatterplot of Driving Test Scores and Accidents With a Restricted Range

the population. In this case, the standard deviation of their scores on the driving test scores was 13.87. When the sample was restricted to only those scoring 80 or more on the test, the standard deviation of these individuals was 3.78. The correction for attenuation due to range restriction formula is given by Guilford and Fruchter (1973):

$$(9\text{--}5) \qquad r_{xy'} = [r_{xy}(\sigma_{pop}/\sigma_{sample})]/\sqrt{1 - r_{xy}^2 + r_{xy}^2\,(\sigma_{pop}^2/\sigma_{sample}^2)},$$

where $r_{xy'}$ = the corrected validity coefficient, r_{xy} = the calculated validity coefficient, σ_{pop} = the population standard deviation, and σ_{sample} = the sample standard deviation.

So, substituting in the driving test example,

$$r_{xy'} = [0.13(13.87/3.78)]/\sqrt{(1 - 0.0169) + 0.0169\,(192.38/14.29)},$$
$$= 0.48/\sqrt{0.9831 + 0.2275},$$
$$= 0.48/1.10,$$
$$= 0.43.$$

The estimate of the correlation between driving test and accident rates based on the cases who scored 80 or more on the test and corrected for range restriction is 0.43. This is substantially higher than 0.13, so the restricted range on the driving test variable clearly attenuated the correlation. Thus, it is very important to assess both predictor and criterion variables for range restriction and take steps to deal with the problem if it is appropriate to do so.

Sample Size. Sample sizes are sometimes a problem in criterion-related validity studies. A simple examination of a table to test the significance of a correlation coefficient will drive home this point. For example, if the relationship between GRE test scores and graduate school performance is calculated, there may only be 10 students to supply the data for the analysis if one department was used. A validity coefficient of 0.632 will be needed to be considered statistically significant with that number of cases. However, assume that information on graduate students was pooled across several departments; by doing so, the analysis could be conducted on 30 students. Now a validity coefficient of only 0.361 is needed to be considered statistically significant. Assume a sample size of more than 100 cases. It will be possible to have a statistically significant relationship if the validity coefficient is less than 0.20.

Thus, it is important in interpreting studies that report validity coefficients to examine both the size and representativeness of the sample on which the data were collected.

Making Decisions: Cutoffs and the Roles of the Standard Error of Estimate and the Standard Error of Measurement. The outcomes of criterion-related validity studies are often used to set standards by invoking a cutoff score below which individuals are not selected. For example, assume that a criterion-related validity coefficient suggests that there is a significant and positive relationship between children's IQ scores and success in a gifted scholastic program. The relationship is strong enough that IQ scores are now going to be used to make decisions about which children to allow into the program and which to exclude. How strong is "strong enough" has to do with the standard error of estimate. The standard error of estimate was briefly introduced in Chapter 1 as part of the output of a regression analysis, and it plays a large role in the accuracy of predicting criterion scores. An example will assist in demonstrating the centrality of the standard error of estimate.

Assume that in a pilot study of the usefulness of IQ scores in predicting performance in gifted programs, 100 students with a wide range of IQ scores were all allowed into a gifted program. The criterion variable was the teacher's rating of the success of each student on a 10-point scale where 4 was the cutoff for "successful completion."

Now, IQ scores are regressed on ratings of success. Assume the calculated R^2 value was 0.35, indicating that 35% of the variance in success is predicted by IQ scores. Further assume that the calculated standard error of estimate was 0.50. The standard error of estimate is equal to the standard deviation of the criterion score (success in this example) for individuals with the same score on the predictor (IQ in this example).

So, assume that students with an IQ score of 120 have a predicted success score of 2.5. The standard error of estimate can be used to set a confidence interval around the predicted score of 2.5. To set the 95% confidence interval, the relevant t value is needed. Because a 95% confidence interval is desired, the α is 0.05, and because there were 100 participants, the degrees of freedom are 98 (i.e., $100 - 2$). The t value at $\alpha = 0.05$ with 98 degrees of freedom is equal to 1.99. Then the standard error of estimate is multiplied by that t value ($0.50 \times 1.99 = 0.995$). Finally, the confidence interval is set by subtracting 0.995 from and adding 0.995 to the estimated score (i.e., $2.5 - 0.995 = 1.505$ and $2.5 + 0.995 = 3.495$).

It is concluded that an individual with an IQ of 120 will have a predicted success score between 1.505 and 3.495 with 95% confidence. In more practical terms for this example, those with IQ scores of 120 or less would not meet the success criterion of 4 because the highest they would be expected to obtain on the criterion would be 3.495, 95 times out of 100. The IQ score where the 95% confidence interval upper bound includes the success criterion (4 in this example) could appropriately be used as the cutoff score.

This is a simplification of the process by which cutoff scores are set. It should be obvious that in such pilot studies, the larger and more representative the sample, the better the future decisions will be. Unrestricted range in the predictor and excellent training of the teachers in making their criterion ratings would also be critical to the process being above reproach. In such high stakes decision making, the process for setting cutoffs is always under scrutiny. Often, several different pilot studies of the type described are carried out and the results pooled and interpreted. Ultimately, a judgment call is made about where to set the cutoff, but it should be based on the results of methodologically and statistically sound studies.

In Chapter 7, the standard error of measurement was used to set confidence intervals around an estimated true score for any one individual. This process is particularly salient when the scores are being used for decision making. Continuing with the IQ and gifted program example, assume for the sake of argument that, based on a series of studies, it has been shown that children must score statistically above 125 on a measure of IQ to be successful, and therefore that is the test cutoff score to be used before being admitted into the program. Now suppose there is a child seeking admission, and she has an obtained test IQ score of 125.

Let's assume that the population mean and standard deviation for this test are 100 and 15, respectively. Further assume that the reliability of the test is 0.95, and therefore her estimated true score is 118.75 (i.e., 125×0.95). Further assume that the standard error of measurement for the IQ test is 3.35. The 95% confidence interval around her score, then, is

$$118.75 + (1.96 \times 3.35),$$
$$= 118.75 + 6.57,$$
$$= 112.18 <\!\!-\!\!> 125.32.$$

Now the question is a practical one: How much "above 125" does the score have to be? In this case, it is above 125 (by 0.32) but it rounds to 125. Interpretation of such differences can become a legal nightmare. This is why it is critical that more than just one indicator be used to make such decisions. It would not be appropriate to base the judgment on a single test score alone. Other pieces of information that might be useful in this example would be test scores on classroom work, portfolios of work samples, interviews with teachers, and so forth. Then the preponderance of the evidence can be used to make a final decision about the appropriateness of admission.

There are situations where cutoff scores are the only indicator used (e.g., licensing examinations for professionals), and therefore information about the standard error of estimate, test reliability, and standard error of measurement becomes essential in defending decisions based on test scores.

Multiple Criteria

To this point, it has been assumed that the criterion is a single variable. However, most variables of interest are multivariate. Job performance, scholastic performance, social adjustment, marital satisfaction, and so forth have several facets, or elements. A question arises from this phenomenon: How should facet information be combined to come up with a single criterion?

The process of dealing with this issue often juxtaposes a multiple hurdle/multiple cutoff model versus a compensatory model. It will depend on the context as to which makes most sense. For example, if the criterion is the skill set needed to be a pizza delivery person, then there might be several predictors: (a) a valid driver's license so that the person can deliver the pizza, (b) quantitative skills for collecting the correct amount owed, (c) map-reading skills for getting around the city, and (d) interpersonal skills for interacting with the customer in the hope of obtaining repeat business. Tests might be used for some of these predictors. In the end, it really is up to the pizza store managers to decide how to weight these various facets.

Some of the facets may be critical and stop or continue the process (e.g., if the job applicant does not have a valid driver's license, then the individual cannot do the job). Other facets may be more difficult to decide upon, and some sort of decision process needs to be used where facets b, c, and d described above are differentially weighted as 2, 2, and 1, respectively. This gives twice as much weight to the quantitative and map-reading skills than to interpersonal skills. However, these more complex weighting schemes are not always desirable, and it is recommended that when several criteria are combined, simple unit weighting is actually a better approach (Society for Industrial and Organizational Psychology, 2003).

Whether criteria facets are differentially weighted or not, the decision of doing so or not must be defensible. Again, SMEs are invaluable in making these determinations. In employment or other high stakes situations, the process by which the criterion is developed is as important as the test development. Unfortunately, not nearly as much care goes into the development of sound criteria as goes into sound test development.

In the end, like it or not, a decision must be made, and therefore the information is combined somehow. Such decisions include hire or not, promote or not, give a license or not, stream a student or not, and deliver a course of treatment or not. Multiple pieces of information will go into such overall decisions and those making the decisions will often invoke their own decision rules for doing so. The more solid statistical information that can be provided to these decision makers about how to combine the information and the better the predictors, the more likely their decisions are going to be of high quality.

Classification Approaches to Test Score Validation

Sometimes it is not of interest to be as fine-grained as many of the criterion-related validity studies described thus far allow for. For example, from a practical perspective, the specific score an individual gets on a criterion measure may not be as important as whether the individual succeeds or meets expectations. In such cases, classification approaches to assessing criterion-related validity studies are appropriate.

Predictive Accuracy With a Dichotomous Predictor and Criterion. When one dichotomous predictor (e.g., pass/fail) and one dichotomous criterion (e.g., succeed/fail) form the data set to be analyzed, they can be placed in a 2×2 matrix such as those used in signal detection theory (see Table 9.6). Here, A = hits (pass on the predictor and successful on the criterion), B = correct rejections (fail on the predictor and unsuccessful on the criterion), C = false alarms (pass on the predictor and unsuccessful on the criterion), and D = misses (fail on the predictor

Table 9.6   Predictive Accuracy When the Predictor and Criterion Are Dichotomized

Successful	D Misses	A Hits
Unsuccessful	B Correct Rejections	C False Alarms
	Fail	Pass

and successful on the criterion). False alarms can be very costly because if one hires or accepts someone but that person turns out to be unsuccessful on the job, then recruiting costs, training time, salary, and so forth are lost. Misses are also expensive in terms of lost opportunities. Good predictors will maximize the number of individuals in cells A and B while minimizing the number in cells C and D.

It is clear from this table that the stronger the relationship between predictor and criterion, the better the predictive accuracy. In this case, more of the cases will cluster around an imaginary line that cuts across the square diagonally. That means fewer cases will be in the C and D quadrants. In addition, given that all else remains constant, one can shift around the cutoff score on the predictor to change the numbers in the quadrants. So, if the line was moved from the center to the left, more cases would be in the A and C quadrants. If the line was moved to the right, more cases would be in the B and D quadrants. Finally, when the successful/unsuccessful split is 50%/50%, the predictor is most powerful (i.e., has the opportunity to be of most value). To understand this concept, visualize an example where there are very few cases in the A and D quadrants or, alternatively, where there are very few cases in the B and C quadrants. If this was the case, then correct decisions (hits and correct rejections) would be harder to make.

The base rate for success can only be determined if one were to not use any predictors at all. For example, suppose 100% of the 50 applicants for being a registered psychologist over the next six months were licensed. Then, a year later, it is determined that 50% of them were unsuccessful (by what means *unsuccessful* was determined is not relevant to this discussion, although it would be, of course, in another context). Then the question can be asked: What would be the improvement in the accuracy of judgments (increases in quadrants A and C) if a predictor such as "applicants have to pass an examination" is added to the decision process? To answer this, another group of 100 applicants is given the test, but only those who pass the test (i.e., obtain a score of 70% or more) are licensed ($n = 80$), and then it is determined a year later how many were unsuccessful. Assume, in this example, that 25% were unsuccessful. Is the 25% reduction in unsuccessful psychologists significant?

The test for differences between two proportions can be used to answer this question:

$$(9\text{-}6) \qquad z = (P_{\text{success1}} - P_{\text{success2}})/\sqrt{(\overline{p})(1 - \overline{p})(\tfrac{1}{n_1} + \tfrac{1}{n_2})},$$

where P_{success1} = the proportion of successes in sample 1, P_{success2} = the proportion of successes in sample 2, n_1 = the number of cases in sample 1, n_2 = the number of cases in sample 2, and $\overline{p}$ = the pooled estimate of the population proportion of successes, $\overline{p} = (X_1 + X_2)/(n_1 + n_2)$, where X_1 and X_2 are the number of successes in samples 1 and 2, respectively.

In the example, $n_1 = 50$, $n_2 = 80$, $P_{\text{success1}} = 0.50$, $P_{\text{success2}} = 0.75$. Thus, $\overline{p} = (25 + 60)/(50 + 80)$, $\overline{p} = 85/130 = 0.65$. Now the question can be answered:

$$z = (0.50 - 0.75)/\sqrt{(0.65)(0.35)(0.02 + 0.0125)},$$
$$= (-0.25)/\sqrt{(0.65)(0.35)(0.0325)},$$
$$= -0.25/0.086,$$
$$= -2.91.$$

The significance level that needs to be exceeded for the proportional difference to be considered significant is ± 1.96. Because -2.91 does exceed this value, it can be concluded that there is a significant improvement in the proportion of successful psychologists after implementing the new test.

In a selection context (whether it be for employment, graduate school, educational programming, treatment programs, etc.) where the relationship between the predictor and criterion is known, the success base rate is known, and the selection ratio (proportion taken in versus rejected) is known, Taylor-Russell (1939) tables can be used to determine the improved accuracy by changing the selection ratio. For example, assume that the success base rate for students to survive the first year of medical school is 0.60, and we want to improve that by instituting a test as a selection device that has been used in other medical schools. Studies have shown that the validity coefficient between the test and medical school success in the first year is about 0.40. It is decided that in the upcoming year, 20% of the applicants will be selected (selection ratio of 0.20). Using the Taylor-Russell tables (example is in Table 9.7), it is determined that the proportion of students who will be successful the first year will now be 0.81. This is an improvement of 21% ($0.81 - 0.60$) and is likely to be of practical importance given the cost of educating students in medical schools.

Discriminant Function Analysis. It is possible to have multiple predictors, some of them continuous and others dichotomous, for a given criterion of success. If this is the case, then an assessment of predictive accuracy can be carried out using discriminant function analysis (DFA). DFA answers two questions: (a) Do the predictors help to classify individuals as successful or not better than chance? and (b) Which of the predictors are most relevant in that prediction?

Table 9.7   Taylor-Russell Table: Base Rate = 0.60

	Selection Ratio										
r	.05	.10	.20	.30	.40	.50	.60	.70	.80	.90	.95
.00	.60	.60	.60	.60	.60	.60	.60	.60	.60	.60	.60
.05	.64	.63	.63	.62	.62	.62	.61	.61	.61	.60	.60
.10	.68	.67	.65	.64	.64	.63	.63	.62	.61	.61	.60
.15	.71	.70	.68	.67	.66	.65	.64	.63	.62	.61	.61
.20	.75	.73	.71	.69	.67	.66	.65	.64	.63	.62	.61
.25	.78	.76	.73	.71	.69	.68	.66	.65	.63	.62	.61
.30	.82	.79	.76	.73	.71	.69	.68	.66	.64	.62	.61
.35	.85	.82	.78	.75	.73	.71	.69	.67	.65	.63	.62
.40	.88	.85	**.81**	.78	.75	.73	.70	.68	.66	.63	.62
.45	.90	.87	.83	.80	.77	.74	.72	.69	.66	.64	.62
.50	.93	.90	.86	.82	.79	.76	.73	.70	.67	.64	.62
.55	.95	.92	.88	.84	.81	.78	.75	.71	.68	.64	.62
.60	.96	.94	.90	.87	.83	.80	.76	.73	.69	.65	.63
.65	.98	.96	.92	.89	.85	.82	.78	.74	.70	.65	.63
.70	.99	.97	.94	.91	.87	.84	.80	.75	.71	.66	.63
.75	.99	.99	.96	.93	.90	.86	.81	.77	.71	.66	.63
.80	1.0	.99	.98	.95	.92	.88	.83	.78	.72	.66	.63
.85	1.0	1.0	.99	.97	.95	.91	.86	.80	.73	.66	.63
.90	1.0	1.0	1.0	.99	.97	.94	.88	.82	.74	.67	.63
.95	1.0	1.0	1.0	1.0	.99	.97	.92	.84	.75	.67	.63
1.00	1.0	1.0	1.0	1.0	1.0	1.0	1.0	.86	.75	.67	.63

Note: From Taylor & Russell (1939).

DFA classifies individuals into their respective groups based on a linear combination of predictor variables. Like the regression equation, a DFA equation can be written as follows:

$$(9\text{--}7) \qquad D' = a + w_1\, V_1 + w_2\, V_2 + w_3\, V_3 \cdots + w_x\, V_x,$$

where D' = the discriminant function score for any individual, a = the constant, w_1–w_x = the weights assigned to each variable (predictor), and V_1–V_x = the predictors.

The weights assigned to each predictor maximize the differences between the criterion groups. In a DFA, a series of discriminant functions will be generated from the computer program; however, not all of them will be significant. The maximum number that will be generated is equal to either (a) the number of criterion groups minus 1 or (b) the number of predictor variables, whichever is smaller. Each function must be orthogonal (uncorrelated) to the previous functions, and each subsequent function accounts for less and less variance in criterion. In the example used here for demonstration purposes, there will be two groups, successful and unsuccessful, so the maximum number of functions will be $2 - 1$, or 1. It is worth noting here, though, that DFA can be used with a criterion that is made up of more than two groups.

In the first part of the DFA, there is a significance test for how well each function is able to place cases into the correct group (successful or unsuccessful). The test follows a χ^2 distribution, and thus this statistic is used for assessing the significance of each function.

If the function is significant, then determining the contributions of each of the predictors (if there are more than one) is the next step. This information is found in the structure coefficients. The structure coefficients are equal to the zero-order correlations between the each of the predictors (V_1-V_x) and the discriminant function scores (D').

Finally, the classification table provides an overall summary of the correct classification of individuals. The percentages on the diagonal are correct decisions and the off-diagonal percentages are incorrect decisions (i.e., the computer misclassified them).

In addition, a *jackknife*, or *cross-validation*, table is provided. To generate this table, each case one at a time is excluded from the analysis; a new DFA is generated and the excluded case is classified using the new discriminant function. Then a different case is excluded, another DFA run, and the case is classified using the new discriminant function. This proceeds until all the cases have been excluded and subsequently classified. In a way, it is like cross validating without having to gather data on another sample.

As an example, assume that we have a data set of 20 individuals; 10 of them are successful on the job and 10 are not. They are administered three tests to ascertain if their success is related to these instruments. The first is the TPI, the next is a cognitive skills test (IQ), and the third is an assessment of personal adaptability (ADAPT). A DFA analysis is run and the resulting discriminant function helps to classify the cases into "successful" and "unsuccessful" to a greater degree than chance (80% versus 50%). In addition, all of the predictors are useful in classifying the cases, although the TPI scores are most useful. Box 9.4 shows the output for this example using the discriminant program from SPSS.

Group Differences and Test Bias

A potential problem using tests in high stakes environments is that the relationship between predictor and criterion act differently for identifiable subgroups.

(Text continues on page 228)

Box 9.4 Discriminant Function Analysis: Using SPSS

In this analysis, a *direct* solution was requested, meaning that all three variables were forced into the analysis. Note, though, that it is possible to use a stepwise or hierarchical process in DFA.

Table 9.8 DFA Group Statistics

Success	Mean	Standard Deviation
0 Unsuccessful	TPI = 20.3 IQ = 101.2 ADAPT = 4.2	TPI = 4.19 IQ = 3.52 ADAPT = 1.81
1 Successful	TPI = 27.2 IQ = 105.9 ADAPT = 6.0	TPI = 5.63 IQ = 8.90 ADAPT = 2.31

Table 9.8 shows the means for each group on the predictor variables. From the information, we see that the successful group is higher on all three scales than the unsuccessful. Our next question is whether these can be used to discriminate between the two groups.

Table 9.9 DFA Eigenvalues

Function	Eigenvalue	% Variance	Cumulative %	Canonical Correlation
1	0.965	100.0	100.0	0.701

Note in Table 9.9 that there is only one function generated. The eigenvalue is a measure of shared variance (although the actual value of 0.965 is not relevant to us at this point). The percent variance is found by taking the eigenvalue for the function and dividing it by the total of all the eigenvalues for all the functions together. Because there is only one function, the percent variance is $0.965/0.965 \times 100$, or 100%. If there was more than one function generated, the relative contributions of each could be determined by examining this information. Because there is only one function, it is irrelevant. The canonical correlation represents the relationship between the discriminant function scores (D') and the original grouping (successful vs. unsuccessful). The higher this is, the more the function separates the groups.

Table 9.10 DFA Wilks's Lambda

Test of Function (s)	Wilks's Lambda	Chi-Square	df	Sig.
1	0.509	11.149	3	0.011

(Continued)

Box 9.4 (Continued)

In Table 9.10, the function is tested for significance. The Wilks's lambda is an assessment of "badness of fit"—the lower value the better (it ranges from 0–1). There is no distribution to test the Wilks's lambda for significance, and to do so we convert it to a chi-square (formula shown shortly). The chi-square of 11.149 with 3 degrees of freedom is significant. The degrees of freedom are equal to (# of groups on the criterion − 1) (# predictors); in our case, 1 × 3 = 3. If we had three groups and four predictors, we would have generated two functions before running out of degrees of freedom: the first would be (# groups − 1)(# predictors), or 2 × 4 = 8; the second would be (# groups − 2)(# predictors − 1), or 1 × 3 = 3. Degrees of freedom, then, are based on the number of groups and number of predictors. When either one becomes 0, there are no more degrees of freedom available to test the significance of the function. The significance level is 0.011, indicating that the function is significant in being able to correctly classify our 20 cases.

For completeness, the equation for converting the Wilks's lambda to chi-square is provided:

(9 – 8) $\text{Chi-square} = -[N - 1 - 0.5\,(p + q + 1)]\,[\log_n \text{Lambda}],$

where N = the sample size (20 in our case), p = the number of criterion variables (always 1 in DFA), q = the number of predictors (3 in our case), and $\log_n$ Lambda = the natural log of the Wilks's lambda value ($\log_n 0.509$). So,

$$\text{chi-square} = -[20 - 1 - 0.5\,(1 + 3 + 1)]\,[-0.6753],$$
$$= -(19 - 2.5)(-0.6753),$$
$$= -16.5 \times -0.6753,$$
$$= 11.14.$$

Table 9.11   DFA Structure Coefficients Matrix

	Function 1
TPI	0.745
ADAPT	0.465
IQ	0.372

The cell entries in Table 9.11 are the zero-order correlations of each variable with the discriminant function scores (D'), and they help to determine which of the variables are most important in the function. These are always placed in descending order. There are no tests of significance for these coefficients, so we use a rule of thumb of 0.30 to determine if the coefficients are substantive. In this case, all three predictors contribute to the function, but the TPI scores do so more than the others.

Table 9.12   DFA Canonical Discriminant Function Coefficients

	Function 1
TPI	0.178
ADAPT	0.060
IQ	0.196
(Constant)	−11.415

Table 9.12 reports the unstandardized weights used to calculate the D' scores. For example, if Case 1 had a score of 20 on TPI, 9 on ADAPT, and 100 on IQ, the D' score, then, would be:

$$D' = -11.415 + (0.178 \times 20) + (0.060 \times 9) + (0.196 \times 100),$$
$$= -11.415 + 3.56 + 0.54 + 19.6,$$
$$= -12.285$$

A D' score for each case is created using this function, and these are used, then, for calculating the canonical correlation and the structure coefficients.

Table 9.13   DFA Group Centroids

Success	*Function1*
0	−0.932
1	0.932

The values in this matrix (Table 9.13) are equal to the mean average D' values for each group. Thus, we can see that the average D' score for those in the unsuccessful group was −0.932, and those in the successful group had mean D' scores of 0.932. For each function, these sum to zero, although they are weighted by the sample size for each group. Because we had equal numbers in each group (10 in each), simply adding the centroids will give a value of 0. If there were two times as many cases in one group, the centroid for that group would be weighted twice as much before summing.

Table 9.14   DFA Prior Probabilities for Groups

Success	*Prior*
0	0.50
1	0.50

(Continued)

Box 9.4 (Continued)

Before calculating the classification statistics for each case, the prior probabilities of belonging to each group are reported (Table 9.14). Because we had equal numbers of cases in each group, the prior probability would be 0.50 for each. If there were 15 in one group and 5 in the other, the prior probabilities would be 0.75 and 0.25, respectively. You can also change the prior probabilities yourself in the command syntax. For example, if you knew in the population that prior probabilities were 0.33 and 0.67, then you could specify these values.

Table 9.15 DFA Classification Results

| | | | Predicted Group Membership | | |
		Success	0	1	Total
Original	Count	0	8	2	10
		1	2	8	10
	%	0	80.0	20.0	100.0
		1	20.0	80.0	100.0
Cross Validated	Count	0	7	3	10
		1	2	8	10
	%	0	70.0	30.0	100.0
		1	20.0	80.0	100.0

The first half of Table 9.15 (Original) shows the original group to which the cases belonged and the predicted group to which they belonged. We can see that 80% of the cases were correctly classified. This is 30% better than the prior chance probability of 50%. The second half of the table (Cross Validated) shows the results of the jackknife procedure. In this case, 75% of the cases were correctly classified. This half is helpful in letting you know to what extent you may be capitalizing on chance with the sample-specific characteristics. In this case, the cross validation shows that 75% of the cases would be correctly classified with another sample of similar size, which is still much better than chance.

Depending on the instrument, differences based on gender, race, language, culture, ethnicity, and so forth may or may not be expected. If test score differences emerge based on these types of demographic groups, it will limit the unrestricted use of norms generated for the test. When those subgroups are protected in the legal system, there is the opportunity for litigation issues to arise. The statistical issues and the relationship between predictor and criterion can provide some insight into whether or not the test is discriminatory.

Table 9.16   Scores of 15 Males (Group = 1) and 15 Females (Group = 2) on Two
Variables, X and Y

Group	X	Y
1	1	3
1	2	4
1	3	5
1	4	4
1	5	6
1	1	2
1	2	3
1	3	3
1	4	7
1	5	8
1	1	4
1	2	5
1	3	6
1	4	8
1	5	9
2	1	2
2	2	9
2	3	1
2	4	8
2	5	7
2	1	4
2	2	5
2	3	3
2	4	7
2	5	2
2	1	8
2	2	6
2	3	7
2	4	4
2	5	5

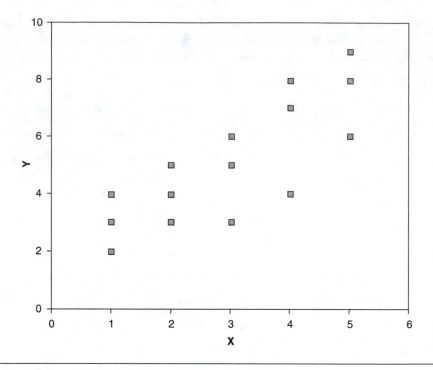

Figure 9.3   Scatterplot of *X* and *Y* Scores for 15 Males

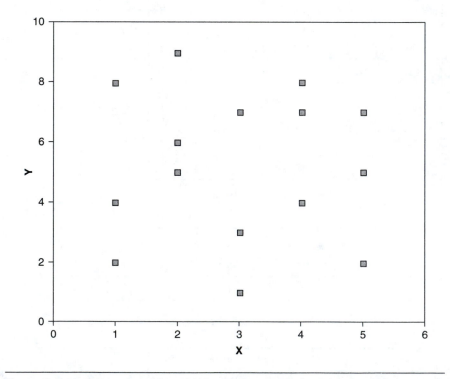

Figure 9.4   Scatterplot of *X* and *Y* Scores for 15 Females

Assume the following example where the scatterplots (Figures 9.3 and 9.4) of two different groups look quite different, and notice what happens to the validity coefficient. The data for this example are given in Table 9.16; there are 15 males and 15 females. For males, the validity coefficient between X and Y is equal to 0.80. The validity coefficient for females is equal to −0.02.

Examining the scatterplots and the magnitude of the validity coefficients would lead us to conclude that X predicts Y for males but not for females. Take care to ensure that the test being used reports validity coefficient information on demographic subgroup differences. This will ensure that the scores are interpreted appropriately. In cases such as these, where there is a difference between the slopes of the regression lines for one group versus the other (which can be tested for statistical significance), differential validity is said to occur (Cleary, 1968) and this would be considered "unfair." This makes sense in the example; if the test (X) was used for females, there is no evidence to suggest that it predicts the criterion (Y), but if the test was used for males, there is evidence to suggest it predicts the criterion.

Groups can also differ only on the intercept. That is, the slopes of the regression equations are not statistically different from one another, but the lines for the two groups cross the y-axis in different locations (see Figure 9.5). In this case, the difference in criterion scores would be directly proportional to the difference in predictor scores, and the test would be considered unfairly used to predict the criterion. Specifically, the score on the criterion variable systematically differs at a given level of the predictor.

The line that is above the other in this example is the group that is "unfairly treated" because their predicted Y scores are consistently underestimated when

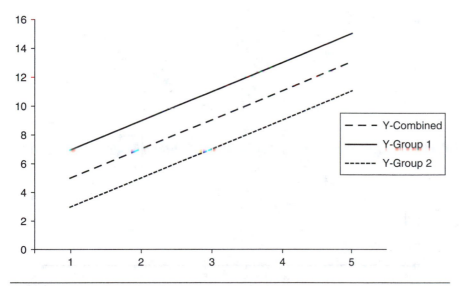

Figure 9.5   Regression Lines With Two Different Intercepts for Focal and Reference Groups

using a regression line based on the entire sample, whereas those with the line below have consistently overestimated predicted scores. An example may clarify this idea. Assume that one regression equation is used for both groups:

$$Y' = 3 + 2.0(X).$$

If an individual gets a score of 2 on X, his or her predicted Y score will be 7. The appropriate regression approach would have been, however, to generate two separate lines because there are different intercepts for the two groups:

Group 1 (Focal): $Y' = 5 + 2.0(X)$ and

Group 2 (Reference): $Y' = 1 + 2.0(X)$.

Thus, if an individual in Group 1 has a score of 2 on X, the predicted score would be 9 (2 more than would have been the case if one regression equation had been used). For an individual in Group 2 with a score of 2 on X, the predicted score would be 5 (2 less than would have been the case if one regression equation had been used).

It can also be the case that there are no differences in slopes or intercepts, but there are differences where the group scores fall on the same line (see Figure 9.6). In the regression sense, the relationship between X and Y for the two groups would not be considered unfair. Some do argue that this is unfair if the focal group scores lower than the reference group on both the test (X) and on the criterion (Y). For example, individuals from lower socioeconomic status

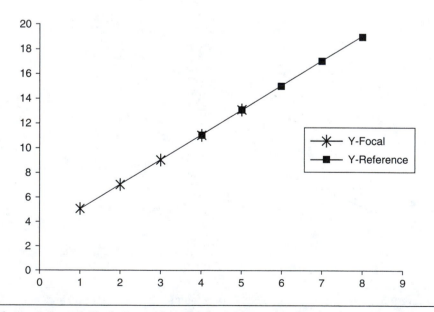

Figure 9.6   A Single Regression Line for Both Focal and Reference Groups

families usually do more poorly on achievement tests than do those from higher socioeconomic status families. In addition, individuals from lower socio-economic status families may also be more likely to be rated lower on a criterion measure (such as job performance). Those who claim that the process is unfair base their argument on systematic bias in both the test and criterion. However, this is an argument that has to be made on social or political grounds, not statistical grounds.

In general, tests are better if they do not result in differential validity coefficients for different identifiable subgroups. Usually, researchers and practitioners are interested in generalizing their knowledge claims about test scores as widely as possible.

Extending the Inferences of Criterion-Related Validity Studies

For many small organizations, it is extremely difficult to conduct local validation studies. Assume, for example, that a company with 50 employees would like to institute a test as part of the selection system for new employees. However, gathering the needed data for a reasonable validity study to be carried out might take years before the sample size of new employees brought in is large enough to make any statistical inferences about the use of the test.

Validity Generalization. Many organizations face similar situations, where accountability for decisions must be demonstrated but practical constraints do not allow for appropriate statistical inferences to be generated. Some examples of these organizations would include (a) small firms wanting to use a test for employment selection purposes, (b) small social agencies interested in demonstrating that a particular program is more effective than another, and (c) small treatment centers wanting to demonstrate the use of a test in selecting appropriate treatment.

In such cases, the validity coefficient findings of previous studies are heavily relied on and generalized to the local context. The appropriateness of reliance on these findings, however, is based on the extent to which the local context (sample and criterion) can be assumed (and perhaps demonstrated to others) to be similar to the context in which the previous research was conducted. As Ghiselli pointed out some years ago (1959), validity coefficients for the same job in different contexts often give highly disparate validity coefficients.

Meta-Analysis. A meta-analysis attempts to generalize these disparate validity coefficients by summarizing a number of them across many contexts into a single index. Schmidt and Hunter (1977, 1990) popularized meta-analysis, where the results of many criterion-related studies using a predictor and criterion are pooled. Although it is beyond the scope of this book to describe in detail the meta-analysis processes, it is helpful to review the general process and understand the logic involved.

1. Calculate the desired descriptive statistic for each study available and average that statistic across studies.

2. Calculate the variance of the statistic across studies.

3. Correct the variance by subtracting out the amount due to sampling error.

4. Correct the mean and variance for study artifacts other than sampling error.

5. Compare the corrected standard deviation to the mean to assess the size of the potential variation in results across studies in qualitative terms. If the mean is more than two standard deviations larger than zero, then it is reasonable to conclude that the relationship considered is always positive. (Hunter & Schmidt, 1990, p. 82)

Thus, the first step is to identify all of the relevant published or unpublished validity coefficients. Then these are corrected for a number of artifacts. Schmidt and Hunter (1990) report no fewer than 11 sources of artifactual error in these coefficients that they recommend be corrected. They include sample size, unreliability of the predictor and criterion, range restriction, attrition, invalid measures of the predictor and criterion, transcription errors, and variance due to extraneous variables that are not controlled for. After making some or all of these corrections to the validity coefficients and then combining them (weighting some coefficients more than others), a single true validity coefficient emerges. This coefficient, then, represents the true magnitude of the relationship between predictor and criterion. The inference that can be drawn is that the predictor is related to the criterion at a certain level and is transportable across situations *(validity generalization)*. By using validity generalization (i.e., quoting a meta-analytically derived validity coefficient), one seemingly does not need to carry out an expensive, time-consuming local validation study in a specific context.

A critical feature of the meta-analytic process is in finding the results to use as fodder for the meta-analysis. The predictor has to be identified (e.g., measure of leadership style) as well as the criterion (e.g., task performance). An extensive search of both published and unpublished results is expected. The literature review is usually constrained over a certain time period (say the last 10 or 20 years). In addition, more constraints can be placed on the literature search that will make the results more specific to a particular context (such as the workplace).

As has been noted, the purpose of a meta-analysis is to generate a single corrected mean effect size that characterizes the relationship between two variables. For example, there may be an effect size in the population between intelligence and salary of, let's say, 0.25. This mean effect size has a standard deviation around it. A credibility interval can be set around the mean effect size using the corrected standard deviation. A credibility interval around the mean effect size that is large or contains zero suggests that the mean effect size (in our example, 0.25) is actually the mean of more than one subpopulation. For example, the relationship between intelligence and salary may be different for males compared to females (e.g., for males it may be 0.35 and for females 0.00). A credibility interval that is small or does not contain zero suggests that the mean effect size is the mean of one population. Thus, credibility intervals provide information about whether moderator effects (such as gender in our example) need to be taken into account when interpreting the results.

The mean effect size also has a standard error around it reflecting sampling error. The standard error is used to set confidence intervals around the effect size. As in prior discussions about confidence intervals, these assist in determining the accuracy of the corrected mean effect size. Confidence intervals that do not include zero indicate the effect is significantly different from zero. Whitener (1990) provides a cogent and detailed review of credibility and confidence intervals.

While meta-analytic results are popular in the published research these days, and have their usefulness, meta-analysis is not without detractors. Nunnally and Bernstein (1994) say,

> Meta-analysis is extremely useful in aggregating the well-done studies hampered by small sample size. . . . Consequently, it can be a useful tool to integrate the literature. . . . Meta-analysis is no substitute for careful evaluation of individual studies' procedures and results, and was never intended as a "meat grinder" to average out results of studies that vary in their quality of execution. (p. 101)

Algera, Jansen, Roe, and Vijn (1984) say,

> Our critical comments on the Schmidt-Hunter approach to validity generalization do not imply that their work is not relevant for the theory and practice of personnel selection. . . . However, the ways in which they have worked out their ideas on validity generalization show fundamental shortcomings, needing correction in the future. As a consequence, their conclusions should be considered as premature. (pp. 208–209)

Informed consumers of meta-analytic results and users of validity generalization should be clear that the final true validity coefficient is only as good as the quality and completeness of the data (i.e., results from other studies) that went into generating the coefficient. As has been demonstrated, some of the corrections carried out as routine in meta-analysis (e.g., correction for unreliability) can have dramatic effects on the magnitude of the validity coefficients. The appropriateness of the corrections and weighting scheme should be readily apparent. Simply quoting the findings of a meta-analysis does not absolve the test user of being diligent in assessing the utility of the test for any specific context.

Synthetic Validity. Synthetic validity had been proposed as a potential alternative to local validation studies many years ago (Balma, 1959; Lawshe, 1952). Synthetic validity assumes that at least two tests, called a test battery, will be used as predictors. Basically, the process is as follows. First, an analysis of the criterion (e.g., job performance, scholastic performance, social adjustment, etc.) is carried out such that the elements that make up the criterion are clearly articulated. Second, a test battery is compiled where each test is selected because it is expected to correlate with one or more of the elements. Third, the synthesis of the test battery validity coefficients into a single overall coefficient provides a *synthetic validity coefficient.* There are various ways to generate the synthetic coefficient. In this chapter, a couple of them will be described.

A simple but concrete example will help put all of these points in perspective. Assume we are interested in predicting who will successfully pass a driver's training course. The task is broken down into its elements: A = driver knowledge, B = psychomotor coordination, C = visual acuity, D = conscientious personality. Now, four tests are selected to create a battery: 1 = a paper and pencil test of driver knowledge, 2 = a test of psychomotor coordination, 3 = a test of acuity, and 4 = a test of conscientious personality.

The next step requires judgments to be made to determine the combinatorial rules for these tests. One of these is the *J* coefficient (Primoff, 1957; 1959). Generally, this process requires either ratings by SMEs or some empirically derived values to estimate the linkages between (a) the criterion and elements (R_{ye}) and (b) the tests and the elements (B_{xe}). These are then multiplied together over the elements and summed.

Continuing with the driving example, the R_{ye} values were generated by having a group of 10 driver trainers weight each element in terms of its contribution to the overall criterion. They did this task under the restriction that the total value must add to 1.0. Their weightings were averaged, providing the R_{ye} values.

Next, the B_{xe} values have to be generated using one of a number of different ways. The literature can be searched and the average validity coefficient in previous studies between each test and the associated element found. Alternatively, concurrent criterion-related validity analyses with a sample of current successful and unsuccessful driver training students, correlating test scores with element scores can be carried out. Another way to generate the B_{xe} values would be to have SMEs (e.g., driver trainers) estimate the validity coefficients given their knowledge of the test and the elements. Other techniques are also possible. However, regardless of which is used, the generated values now become our B_{xe} values. The R_{ye} and B_{xe} values for each of the four elements for successful driving are as reported in Table 9.17.

Next, the R_{ye} and B_{xe} values for each element are multiplied and summed, providing the synthetic validity coefficient. In this example, the resulting coefficient of 0.35 leads to the conclusion that the test battery will predict driver success at a validity coefficient level of 0.35.

Hollenbeck and Whitener (1988) put a bit of a twist on the usual *J* coefficient procedure. They assessed several (13) jobs in terms of their elements. Although, across all jobs, 14 elements were identified, each job had only a few elements associated with it. Each element was rated as irrelevant, minor, or major for each job

Table 9.17   The R_{ye} and B_{xe} Values to Generate the J Coefficient in Synthetic Validity

Element	R_{ye}	B_{xe}	$R_{ye} \times B_{xe}$
A (driver knowledge)	0.50	0.30	0.15
B (psychomotor coordination)	0.20	0.25	0.05
C (visual acuity)	0.15	0.80	0.12
D (conscientious personality)	0.15	0.20	<u>0.03</u>
			$\Sigma\, R_{ye} \times B_{xe} = 0.35$

by SMEs, where the values for each job were to total 1.0. Thus, if a job had two elements, one major and one minor, the weightings for that job would be 0.667 and 0.333 respectively. If a job had five elements, all rated as major, then they would be equally weighted at 0.20 each. These were called *element importance indices*.

Then employees in each job were given the tests associated with the elements that had been identified as relevant to their jobs. Next, supervisors rated each employee's performance on the elements. Individual test scores and individual ratings of performance were then standardized. Next, they created two matrices, with a row devoted to each employee. In the test matrix, each employee's standardized test value was multiplied by each element importance index. These were then summed to provide what will be called a test value. In the criterion matrix, each employee's standardized performance rating value was multiplied by each element importance index. These were then summed to provide what will be called a criterion value.

The synthetic validity index was calculated by correlating the test values with the criterion values across all 83 employees. It was 0.22, which is statistically significant based on a sample size of 83. This approach used synthetic validity for the entire population of employees in the firm. Because of the small number of employees in each job, it would have been impossible to carry out a traditional criterion-related validity study.

Synthetic validity is a very content-oriented approach to validity assessment and relies heavily on SMEs' opinions. The integrity of the synthetic validity approach hangs very much on how accurately the elements have been identified. If important ones are missed, then there will be a serious shortcoming in the synthetic validity coefficient. The links between element-criterion and test-element must be demonstrated to be reasonably and reliably representative of the true values for the synthetic validity coefficient to be believable (see Mossholder & Arvey, 1984, for a review of the various techniques). Synthetic validity has been used primarily in the context of employee selection testing and job performance. Given the move away from small job elements and toward broader job competencies in the job analysis literature, synthetic validity may play a more prominent role than in the past. However, broadening its use with examples using predictors and criteria from other domain areas, such as scholastic performance or mental health, will be needed to generalize the use of this technique.

Summary

The chapter was devoted to some of the methods used to assess the degree to which the inferences made from test scores are valid. Specifically, those methods that used the subjective assessment of item content and the relationships of the test scores to a criterion were reviewed. Many validation techniques were covered, including using

a. information from test-takers,

b. information from SMEs,

c. correlation and regression,

d. convergence and divergence, and

e. discriminant function analysis.

Other topics covered were

a. upper bounds of validity,

b. dealing with multiple criteria,

c. the standard error of measurement,

d. validity generalization, and

e. synthetic validity.

In the next chapter, the validity of inferences made from test scores will continue to be discussed. However, the primary focus will be on the internal structure of the test items.

Problems and Exercises

1. Why is it important to ask test takers to provide feedback on test items?

2. Why is it important to ask SMEs to provide feedback on test items?

3. Suppose I have a Primary Grade Adjustment Test that I am interested in using to predict social adjustment in primary grade school (PGAT). Teacher assessments to social adjustment for a group of 50 students is regressed on age first (obtained R^2 value of 0.15,) and then on test score (obtained R^2 value of 0.40). What would the conclusions be?

4. What is the difference between predictive and concurrent criterion-related validity studies?

5. What are convergent and divergent assessment useful for?

6. What is the upper bound on my validity coefficient for a test with a reliability of 0.70 and a criterion with a reliability of 0.80?

7. What would be the corrected validity coefficient (uncorrected is 0.20) if the unreliability of the test and the criterion from the previous exercise (Item 6) is corrected?

8. Assume the correlation between GRE score and performance in first year of graduate school (measured via GPA) is calculated to be 0.15. Further assume that the range on GRE for the sample is restricted (standard deviation of the sample is 25 and standard deviation in the population is 100). What would be the corrected validity coefficient?

9. You are interested in seeing if a new test will help to determine who will be successful in a training program. The current rate of success is 70% for 200 students. When the new test is implemented, the rate increases to 85% for the 50 students who pass the test and are allowed into the program. Is this difference significant?

10. Assume that the base rate for success in a clinical psychology graduate program is 0.60. We want to improve this by using a test that is known to correlate with the criterion of graduate school success at 0.30. Then, in the next year, 30% of the applicants are allowed into the program. What is the proportion of students that will be successful given the new testing procedure?

11. Suppose that I want to use a test to help predict who will quit their jobs before the end of the three-month probation period. One hundred new applicants are hired and the test is administered to all of them the first day. Half of them quit before the end of the 3-month probation period. Discriminant function analysis is used to determine if the test is useful. The chi-square is significant and the success rate of predicting the "quitters" versus "stayers" is 80%. What would be the conclusion?

12. If the slopes of two regression lines are significantly different for two identifiable subgroups, what would be concluded?

13. Two identifiable subgroups have regression lines between the predictor and criterion that have equal slopes but different intercepts. Group 1 has an intercept of 5 and Group 2 has an intercept of 3. Which group will be unfairly treated?

14. What is the reason for wanting to use validity generalization?

15. What is meta-analysis?

16. Why is synthetic validity so dependent on the expertise of SMEs?

CHAPTER 10

Assessing Validity Via Item Internal Structure

I n the last chapter, some methods to assess the validity of making inferences from test scores were reviewed. These included asking test takers and experts their subjective opinions about the content of the test items. Then, processes that focused on predictors and criteria were covered. Clearly, there have been many efforts devised to assess the validity of test scores indexed by their utility in predicting a criterion. In this chapter, the focus shifts to several other methods for assessing the validity of test scores. In this instance, however, the methods center on assessing the internal structure of an instrument. The question that these methods answer is, How do the items relate to one another?

This question is quite different from the analyses discussed previously, where there was an external, or criterion, variable by which to assess test scores. The topics that will be covered are principal components analysis, common factor analysis, and analysis of covariance structures. All of these analyses provide information about the interrelationships among the items. These methods have often been grouped together and called construct validity in the past, but this is not an appropriate way to think about the validity of test scores.

In all cases, the input to the analyses is the correlation, or the variance-covariance matrix, between all items. The majority of the inter-item correlations should be at least 0.30 to consider subjecting them to these types of analyses. The correlation matrix is useful as input to all the various types of analyses. The variance-covariance matrix is most useful as data if the purpose is to compare the results of the internal structure of the items for two different groups.

Principal Components Analysis

If a set of items can account for the variance in some underlying construct, then there should be an analysis that will tell us if that is a reasonable knowledge claim.

That analysis is principal components analysis (PCA). Like DFA, a set of equations (called components rather than functions in this analysis) is generated. Instead of scores on some set of predictors, however, the "predictors" in PCA are test items. Instead of D' scores based on group belonging as the criteria, a set of principal components (PCs) are the criteria. The primary formula for PCA is

(10–1)
$$PC = bX_1 + bX_2 + bX_3 \cdots + bX_n.$$

The formula is a weighted (the weights are the b values in the equation) linear combination created from the items (X_1–X_n) generated to account for as much variance as possible in a variable labeled PC. This PC is not a truly existing variable but is made up of the variance associated with the original set of items. The PCs are the constructs in which the items are supposed to account for variance. That is, if a test of social adjustment had been created, the component (construct) the developer wants to call social adjustment should share a lot of variance with the items.

As noted earlier, a set of these component equations will be generated. Specifically, the number of component equations that will be generated equals the number of items in the test. Like DFA, subsequent component equations are generated (or extracted, in PCA jargon) such that each is orthogonal to the previous equations, and each subsequent one shares less and less variance with the original items.

So, if a test is three items in length, then three component equations will be generated from the analysis, each sharing less and less variance with the original test items:

$$PC1 = b_{11} X_1 + b_{12} X_2 + b_{13} X_3,$$
$$PC2 = b_{21} X_1 + b_{22} X_2 + b_{23} X_3, \text{ and}$$
$$PC3 = b_{31} X_1 + b_{32} X_2 + b_{33} X_3.$$

PC1 shares the most variance, PC2 shares the next largest amount of variance, and PC3 shares the least amount of variance with the items. Notice that the b values in the component equations are different from component to component (e.g., b_{11}, b_{21}, b_{31}). This means that the bs are weighting each item differently across components. Recall that the components must be orthogonal to one another, and this restricts the bs to be orthogonal to one another across equations.

As in DFA, once again a determination will need to be made about which of the components is worth further consideration. This is called the extraction question: How many components should be extracted before the interpretation is stopped? The answer is not as easy as in DFA, where a χ^2 test with a significance attached to it was available to assist in making a decision. Instead, in PCA theory, rules of thumb, or practical considerations, are used to finally arrive at a decision.

A theoretical approach would work as follows. If the test developer believes that there is only one component (i.e., one construct) that will share most of the variance in the test items, then this can be specified in the analysis. If the test developer expects two constructs, then two principal components can be specified in the analysis. The most common rule of thumb when no theory is there as a guide for interpreting components is eigenvalues greater than 1.0 (Guttman, 1954; Kaiser, 1960, 1970). Each component generated has an eigenvalue associated with it. If the eigenvalue is divided by the number of items in the analysis and multiplied by 100, this gives the percent of variance that component shares with *all items in the test.*

Suppose I have a 10-item scale and the items are subjected to a PCA. In total, 10 components will be generated. Assume that the first one has an eigenvalue of 6.0. This means that the first component shares $6/10 \times 100$, or 60%, of the variance across all 10 items. If the second component has an eigenvalue of 1.0, then it accounts for 10% of the variance $(1/10 \times 100)$. It is important to note that depending on the number of items, the eigenvalues greater than 1.0 rule of thumb makes more or less sense.

Assume a test that is 25 items in length is subjected to a PCA, and the first four components have eigenvalues of 5.0, 4.0, 3.0, and 1.0, respectively (subsequent components have eigenvalues less than 1.0). The rule of thumb suggests that the first four components are all important enough to interpret. However, the variance accounted for by these four are 5/25, 4/25, 3/25, and 1/25—20%, 16%, 12%, and 4%, respectively. It may be that there is no practical use in interpreting a component that accounts for only 4% of the variance in all 25 items.

Here is another example. Assume a test that is five items in length is subjected to a PCA. The first component has an eigenvalue of 0.90 and the rest have lower values. The rule of thumb suggests that not even the first component is important enough to interpret. However, the variance it shares with the items is $0.90/5 \times 100$, or 18%. It might be of practical use to interpret the first component despite the fact that it does not meet the rule of thumb.

Another way to use the eigenvalues rule of thumb is to combine it with a standard of practical utility where the cutoff eigenvalue point for interpreting PCs is, let's say, 10%. This means that, regardless of the actual number associated with the eigenvalue, for a PC to be considered relevant or of practical use, it has to share at least 10% of its variance with all the items. Thus, for a test of 40 items, a rule could be invoked such that eigenvalues less than 4.0 would not be interpreted $(4/40 \times 100 = 10\%)$. In addition to the eigenvalue approach to determine if a PC is worth interpreting, each component should have at least three items that load on it for it to be conceptually relevant (Comrey, 1973; Thurstone, 1947). This is another piece of evidence that one should look for in making a decision about how many components one should interpret.

Another way to try to assess the number of components relevant for interpretation is to use the scree plot that is usually printed out as part of a computer program (although one can do it by hand). The y-axis on the scree plot is the eigenvalue and the x-axis is the component number. Because the eigenvalues decrease in value as the components increase, the line will be an accelerated curve downward. The point at which there is a sharp bend in the curve at a low eigenvalue indicates nonsubstantive components. Figure 10.1 shows a scree plot of some data showing that there are two components with fairly high eigenvalues. At Component 3, there is a sharp bend and the eigenvalues become very low, and thus it could be argued that there are two relevant components for these data.

Once the extraction problem has been solved (i.e., how many components/constructs are useful in sharing variance in the items), the next question is, How do we interpret those components? Basically, the interpretation of components is based on how the items are related to them. Therefore, the next step focuses on an examination of the *b*s associated with each PC. These *b*s are called component loadings (although they are

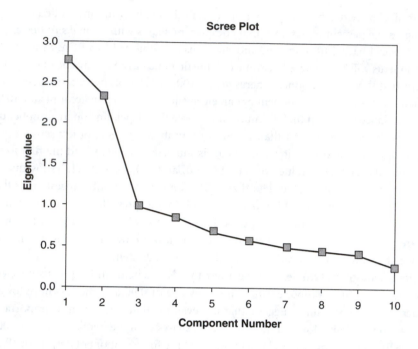

Figure 10.1   A Scree Plot That Shows Two Relevant Components

commonly misnamed factor loadings). The bs represent the zero-order correlations between the item and the PC. High b values indicate that the item shares a lot of variance with the PC. For example, a b (loading) for Item 1 on PC1 of 0.50 means that PC1 shares 25% ($0.50^2 \times 100$) of its variance with Item 1. A loading for Item 2 on PC1 of 0.20 means that PC1 shares 4% ($0.20^2 \times 100$) of its variance with Item 2.

There are no tests of significance for the component loadings. Again, rules of thumb are invoked, or some practical significance level, to decide if a PC shares a substantive or meaningful amount of variance with each item. The most common rule of thumb is a loading of 0.30 to be considered substantive. This means a given PC has to share at least 9% ($0.30^2 \times 100$) of the variance with the item to be considered meaningful. Some suggest a more strict value of 0.40 as the magnitude of loadings to be considered meaningful if the sample size is 5–10 participants per item (e.g., Floyd & Widaman, 1995).

Assume that for a 10-item test, two PCs are extracted that share 17.4% and 14.9% of the variance with the items, respectively. The remaining eight PCs are deemed nonsubstantive. A matrix of loadings by PCs as in Table 10.1 can be created. This helps to determine which PC shares variance with which items. The items that cluster together with high loadings on the PCs, then, would assist in understanding the construct sharing variance with those items. Notice, in Table 10.1, that two columns of PCs have been created where the loadings have been squared ($PC1^2$ and $PC2^2$). If the squared loadings are summed, they equal the eigenvalues for the PC.

In addition, if the squared loadings across for each item are summed, the communalities for the items are obtained. Their meaning is that for the PC solution, in total, X% of variance is accounted for in each item. For example, 26% of the variance in Item 1 is accounted for by the two-component solution. Very low communalities (lower than 0.20) indicate that the item is not well accounted for in the solution. This information may play a role in determining which items to retain and which to delete in scale development.

In a PCA, if all of the PCs extracted were used and the loadings across each item were squared and summed, they would all have communalities of 1.0, meaning that 100% of the variance in all of the items has been accounted for. Obviously, no one does this as it defeats the purpose of the PCA, but we do want communalities to be as high as possible.

The PC solution reported in Table 10.1 is easily interpretable (called a simple solution in PC jargon). PC1 shares a lot of the variance with items 1–5 but very little with items 6–10. Conversely, PC2 shares a lot of the variance with items 6–10 but very little with items 1–5. Therefore, one would be fairly comfortable making the claim that there are two constructs being assessed with these 10 items. The first is associated with items 1–5 and the second with items 6–10.

It is not often the case, however, that the solution is so simple. Instead, there may be items that have meaningful loadings (greater than 0.30) on more than one PC. There may be PCs with only one or two items that load on it, making it not very interpretable. There may be items with loadings of 0.29, which is just below the rule of thumb cutoff of 0.30. Very high or very low loadings are desirable so that it is clear that the item either does or does not belong with the PC. There may be items

Table 10.1   A Theoretical Principal Components Loadings and Loadings Squared by Components Matrix

Item	PC1	PC2	PC1^2	PC2^2	PC1^2 + PC2^2 [a]
1	0.50	0.10	0.25	0.01	0.26
2	0.60	0.02	0.36	0.0004	0.3604
3	0.70	0.01	0.49	0.0001	0.4901
4	0.60	0.04	0.36	0.0016	0.3616
5	0.50	0.10	0.25	0.01	0.26
6	0.10	0.60	0.01	0.36	0.37
7	0.05	0.50	0.002	0.25	0.2525
8	0.03	0.50	0.000	0.25	0.2509
9	0.10	0.60	0.01	0.36	0.37
10	0.10	0.50	0.01	0.25	0.26
			$\Sigma = 1.74$	$\Sigma = 1.49$	

a. Otherwise communalities.

that have negative loadings on PCs. This may or may not be a problem, depending on the items in question. For example, if a test has both negatively and positively worded items, there may be positive loadings for the positively worded items and negative loadings for the negatively worded items on the component. Negative loadings need to make sense in light of the other item loadings. All of these conditions make for a difficult-to-interpret solution. This leads to the third question in PC analysis: Can the PCs be rotated to create a simple solution?

So what is meant by *rotate*? It means that the PCs are literally rotated in space so that the loadings will become easier to interpret. Let's back up a bit. Each PC is like a line (axis) in space. So, let's say the first PC is a horizontal axis. The next PC has to be orthogonal to the first, and therefore is a vertical axis that perpendicularly intersects the first PC. For pedagogical purposes, this discussion is confined to a solution with two components only, but note that more than two components would just extend the idea. Once the two intersecting PC axes are generated, each component loading can be plotted in space along those axes (see Figure 10.2).

Notice that the data points, while clustering together in this example, do not fall directly on the PC axes. So, axes are rotated in space to make the items fall as closely as possible on the axis lines. The new loadings can be read off from the new axes placement and these, then, are the rotated loadings (see Figure 10.3). This process forced the loadings to be high on one axis (PC1) while being low on the other axis (PC2). Table 10.2 shows the unrotated and rotated loadings of the 10 items shown in Figures 10.2 and 10.3.

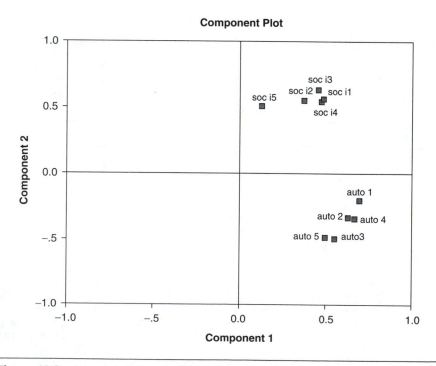

Figure 10.2   Unrotated Plot of 10-Item Component Loadings

Table 10.2   Unrotated and Orthogonally Rotated Component Loadings for a 10-Item Measure

Item	Unrotated Loadings		Orthogonally Rotated Loadings	
	PC1	PC2	PC1	PC2
1	0.705	−0.206	0.705	0.206
2	0.667	−0.333	0.741	0.078
3	0.555	−0.483	0.728	−0.109
4	0.643	−0.334	0.722	0.065
5	0.502	−0.481	0.682	−0.135
6	0.488	0.558	0.110	0.733
7	0.370	0.556	0.013	0.668
8	0.451	0.635	0.038	0.778
9	0.472	0.552	0.101	0.719
10	0.130	0.510	−0.165	0.499

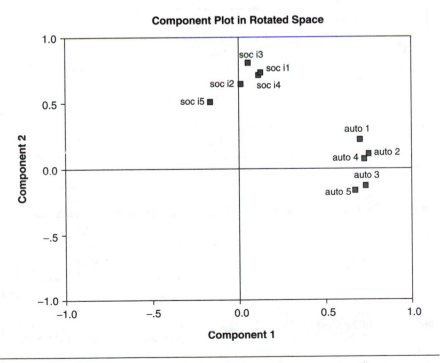

Figure 10.3   Orthogonally Rotated Plot of 10-Item Component Loadings

Examining the rotated loadings shows quite clearly that there are two components, whereas the unrotated loadings do not show that to be the case. It can be concluded from the rotated matrix that Items 1–5 form one construct and Items 6–10 form another. The output from this analysis is provided and described in Box 10.1.

Box 10.1   Principal Components Analysis: Orthogonal Rotation Using SPSS

In this analysis, 10 items that assess two aspects of work values—autonomy (AUTO1–AUTO5) and social interactions (SOCI1–SOCI5)—are analyzed. Each construct is assessed with five items. A total of 180 individuals completed the items. Because two separate scales were being assessed, a constraint on the "number of factors = 2" was specified. Table 10.3 shows the communalities for the items. Note the Initial column, which shows the initial communality estimates (always 1.0 in PCA) and the Extraction column, which shows the communalities after the PCs have been extracted.

Table 10.3   PCA Communalities of a Principal Components Analysis

Item	Initial	Extraction
AUTO1	1.000	0.540
AUTO2	1.000	0.555
AUTO3	1.000	0.541
AUTO4	1.000	0.525
AUTO5	1.000	0.483
SOCI1	1.000	0.550
SOCI2	1.000	0.446
SOCI3	1.000	0.607
SOCI4	1.000	0.527
SOCI5	1.000	0.277

Note that the communalities are all moderate (0.277–0.607).

Table 10.4 summarizes the number of PCs extracted and the variance they account for in the items. The default was used in that eigenvalues less than 1.0 were not interpreted.

Table 10.4   Initial Eigenvalues Associated With Each Component in the Principal Components Analysis

	Initial Eigenvalues		
Component	Total	% Variance	Cumulative %
1	2.733	27.329	27.329
2	2.318	23.175	50.504
3	1.151	11.515	62.019
4	0.889	8.885	70.905
5	0.739	7.385	78.290
6	0.595	5.955	84.245
7	0.517	5.173	89.418
8	0.446	4.462	93.880
9	0.334	3.340	97.220
10	0.278	2.780	100.00

Note that there are three eigenvalues greater than 1.0. However, there were expected to be only two components, and, thus, only two components were specified and analyzed. You will also notice that the eigenvalues decrease in value as the PCs increase and that, in the end, 100% of the variance in all the items is accounted for by all the PCs.

Table 10.5 shows the initial solution and how much variance is accounted for by just the first two PCs.

Table 10.5   Initial Solution for First Two Components in the Principal Components Analysis

	Extraction Sums of Squared Loadings		
Component	Total	% Variance	Cumulative %
1	2.733	27.329	27.329
2	2.381	23.175	50.504

(Continued)

Box 10.1 (Continued)

Table 10.6 shows the variance accounted for after the varimax rotation. Notice that although the variance changes for each component, the total variance accounted for is the same as before rotation (50.504%).

Table 10.6   Variance Accounted for After Orthogonal Rotation in the Principal Components Analysis

Component	Extraction Sums of Squared Loadings		
	Total	% Variance	Cumulative %
1	2.613	26.13	26.126
2	2.438	24.378	50.504

Table 10.7 shows the unrotated component loadings.

Table 10.7   Unrotated Principal Component Loadings

Item	PC1	PC2
AUTO1	0.705	−0.206
AUTO2	0.667	−0.333
AUTO3	0.555	−0.483
AUTO4	0.643	−0.334
AUTO5	0.502	−0.481
SOCI1	0.488	0.558
SOCI2	0.370	0.556
SOCI3	0.451	0.635
SOCI4	0.472	0.552
SOCI5	0.130	0.510

Table 10.8 shows the rotated loadings. Varimax rotation was used, which is the most commonly used orthogonal method.

Table 10.8   Orthogonally Rotated Principal Component Loadings

Item	PC1	PC2
AUTO1	0.705	0.206
AUTO2	0.741	7.842E-02
AUTO3	0.728	−0.109
AUTO4	0.722	6.502E-02
AUTO5	0.682	−0.135
SOCI1	0.110	0.733
SOCI2	1.292E-02	0.668
SOCI3	3.834E-02	0.778
SOCI4	0.101	0.719
SOCI5	−0.165	0.499

Notice in the rotation that the PC axes remained at 90 degrees (orthogonal) to one another. This means that although the actual loadings shifted, the components remained uncorrelated with one another and also that the total variance accounted for by the PCs remained constant (although it was distributed between the two PCs differently). The communalities of each item remained the same as in the initial solution. This is called an *orthogonal rotation.*

It was also possible to carry out an *oblique rotation.* This means that the PC axes are not constrained to be at 90 degrees to one another. The ramifications of this are (a) the loadings are now correlated and (b) the PCs are now correlated. If the loadings for this rotated solution are squared and summed for each PC and then added across PCs, the total will no longer equal the total variance accounted for originally by the uncorrelated PCs as it was in the orthogonal rotation. Thus, when an oblique rotation is conducted, the variance accounted for before rotation is reported.

So why would one carry out an oblique rotation? It is worth doing if the PCs (constructs) are indeed correlated in real life. This is not uncommon. For example, in items about satisfaction with coworkers and items about satisfaction with day-to-day job tasks, the constructs are likely to be related. This is because job tasks may often cause employees to interact quite a bit with their coworkers.

Take a look at Figure 10.4. This is an example of where an oblique rotation of loadings for the 12 items would be more appropriate than an orthogonal rotation. The unrotated loadings are not at 90 degrees to one another. When the PC axes are obliquely rotated, they are allowed to be correlated with each other, and the resultant loadings are simplest to interpret. Figure 10.5 shows the rotated items and Table 10.9 reports the unrotated and rotated loadings.

Table 10.9   Unrotated and Obliquely Rotated Component Loadings for a 12-Item Measure

	Unrotated Loadings		Obliquely Rotated Loadings	
Item	PC1	PC2	PC1	PC2
1	0.674	0.388	0.070	0.735
2	0.636	0.462	−0.0317	0.804
3	0.568	0.483	−0.100	0.800
4	0.710	0.371	0.112	0.730
5	0.600	0.327	0.082	0.633
6	0.775	−0.157	0.694	0.150
7	0.648	−0.245	0.697	−0.006
8	0.737	−0.211	0.723	0.072
9	0.706	−0.281	0.774	−0.023
10	0.766	−0.304	0.838	−0.024
11	0.758	−0.198	0.724	0.095
12	0.740	−0.366	0.883	−0.107

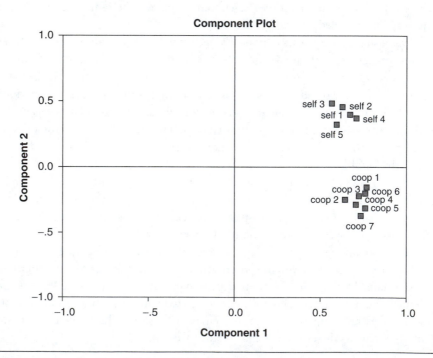

Figure 10.4   Unrotated Plot of 12-Item Component Loadings

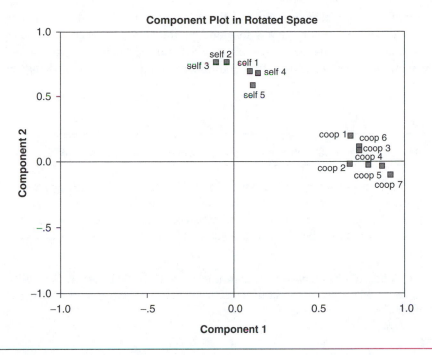

Figure 10.5   Obliquely Rotated Plot of 12-Item Component Loadings

The rotated loadings show a simple solution. Items 1–5 load on PC2 and Items 6–12 load on PC1. Therefore, it is concluded that there are two constructs underlying these 12 items. However, the constructs are correlated with one another. In fact, the correlation between the PCs will be printed out if an oblique solution is requested. Again, there are no statistical tests to assist in determining if the correlations between the PCs are significant or not. In this example, the PCs are correlated at 0.58, which would be considered moderate to high. The output from this analysis is discussed in more detail in Box 10.2.

Interpretation of oblique solutions is more complicated than interpretation of orthogonal solutions because there needs to be a theoretical reason for why the two constructs should be correlated. Thus, there is debate as to whether or not orthogonal versus oblique is the best rotation to use. Clearly, theory has to be the guide. If the components are likely to be correlated, then an oblique rotation is warranted. If there is no reason to expect the components to be correlated, then an orthogonal rotation can be tried first. If the test developer has no idea what will happen, an oblique rotation can be run first to examine the correlations between components. If they are low, then an orthogonal solution would be easier to interpret. If they are high, then the oblique solution would be more reasonable. As Nunnally and Bernstein (1994) point out with regard to this issue, "any results should make theoretical sense" (p. 483).

One of the assumptions in PCA is that the items are measured without error. After the previous lengthy discussion about reliability, it is obvious that this assumption is untenable in most situations. However, dealing with fallible items was not manageable until a way to model in the error was available. Analyses that could incorporate these errors into the structure of the inter-relationships of the items were developed after PCA and under a model known as *common factor analysis*.

Box 10.2   Principal Components Analysis: Oblique Rotation Using SPSS

In this analysis, five items that assess self-sufficiency (SELF1–SELF5) and seven items that assess preference for cooperative learning environments (COOP1–COOP7) are analyzed. A total of 180 individuals completed the items. Because two separate scales were being assessed, a constraint on the "number of factors = 2" was specified.

The extracted communalities are shown in Table 10.10. They are all fairly high (0.467–0.681). This indicates that the PC solution was able to account for a good portion of the variance in the items.

Table 10.10   Initial Item Communalities for a Two-Component Solution

Item	Initial	Extraction
SELF1	1.000	0.604
SELF2	1.000	0.618
SELF3	1.000	0.556
SELF4	1.000	0.641
SELF5	1.000	0.467
COOP1	1.000	0.625
COOP2	1.000	0.481
COOP3	1.000	0.588
COOP4	1.000	0.578
COOP5	1.000	0.680
COOP6	1.000	0.613
COOP7	1.000	0.681

Next, the initial eigenvalues are generated before rotation. Note that two are above the rule of thumb of 1.0 (see Table 10.11).

Table 10.11   Initial Component Eigenvalues for a Two-Component Solution

Component	Total	% Variance	Cumulative %
1	5.816	48.469	48.469
2	1.316	10.969	59.437
3	0.917	7.643	67.080
4	0.756	6.302	73.382
5	0.625	5.210	78.592
6	0.554	4.621	83.213
7	0.468	3.898	87.111
8	0.416	3.463	90.574
9	0.353	2.944	93.518
10	0.321	2.674	96.191
11	0.258	2.147	98.338
12	0.199	1.662	100.000

Table 10.12 shows the initial solution and how much variance is accounted for by just the first two PCs before oblique rotation (59%) and after rotation. Notice that after the oblique rotation, the total variance accounted for is $(5.275 + 4.400)/12 \times 100$, or 81%. It is inappropriate to use this value as the PCs are correlated—it would be like adding all of the zero-order correlations together in a multiple regression analysis. You are not allowed to count the same variance twice. So make sure, in writing up any oblique rotation, you report the variance associated with the unrotated solution.

Table 10.12   Variance Accounted for in the Unrotated and Obliquely Rotated Solutions of the Principal Components Analysis

Component	Extraction Sums of Squared Loadings			Rotation
	Total	% Variance	Cumulative %	Total
1	5.816	48.469	48.469	5.275
2	1.316	10.969	59.437	4.400

(Continued)

Box 10.2 (Continued)

Table 10.13 shows the unrotated component loadings.

Table 10.13   Unrotated Component Loadings in the Two-Component Principal Components Analysis

Item	PC1	PC2
SELF1	0.674	0.388
SELF2	0.636	0.462
SELF3	0.568	0.483
SELF4	0.710	0.371
SELF5	0.600	0.327
COOP1	0.775	−0.157
COOP2	0.648	−0.245
COOP3	0.737	−0.211
COOP4	0.706	−0.281
COOP5	0.766	−0.304
COOP6	0.758	−0.198
COOP7	0.740	−0.366

Table 10.14 is the *pattern matrix*: the rotated loadings that are reported and interpreted. A *direct oblimin* oblique rotation was used. This is the most frequently used of the oblique rotations. The loadings in this matrix take into account that the components are correlated. It is clear from the loadings that there are two components.

Table 10.14   Rotated Component Loadings in the Two-Component Principal Components Analysis (Pattern Matrix)

Item	PC1	PC2
SELF1	6.993E-02	0.735
SELF2	−3.171E-02	0.804
SELF3	−0.100	0.800
SELF4	0.112	0.730

Item	PC1	PC2
SELF5	8.165E-02	0.633
COOP1	0.694	0.150
COOP2	0.697	−6.427E-03
COOP3	0.723	7.157E-.02
COOP4	0.774	−2.308E-02
COOP5	0.838	−2.375E-02
COOP6	0.724	9.459-02
COOP7	0.883	−0.107

The *structure matrix* is shown in Table 10.15. It is not usually reported nor interpreted. The loadings are equal to the zero-order correlations between items and PCs and do not account for the correlation between them.

Table 10.15   Correlations Between Items and Components in the Two-Component Principal Components Analysis (Structure Matrix)

Item	PC1	PC2
SELF1	0.497	0.775
SELF2	0.436	0.785
SELF3	0.365	0.741
SELF4	0.537	0.796
SELF5	0.450	0.680
COOP1	0.781	0.553
COOP2	0.693	0.399
COOP3	0.764	0.492
COOP4	0.760	0.437
COOP5	0.824	0.464
COOP6	0.779	0.516
COOP7	0.821	0.407

(Continued)

Box 10.2 (Continued)

Last, the correlation matrix between the PCs is shown in Table 10.16. Notice that the PCs are highly correlated (0.582), suggesting that an oblique rotation is warranted.

Table 10.16   Principal Component Correlation Matrix

Component	1	2
1	1.000	0.300
2	0.582	1.000

Common Factor Analysis

Common factor analysis (CFA) is actually a family of different analyses. This discussion will be confined to the ones typically used in scale development and assessment. One of the most important differences between PCA and CFA is that CFA assumes that the items are measured with error. These errors are assumed to be uncorrelated with each other across items.

The fundamental equations in CFA, then, are quite different from those used in PCA. Assume, for a set of 10 items, that there are two factors underlying the relationship of the items. The equation for each item is as follows:

(10–2)   Item $X = wF1 + wF2 +$ error.

Therefore, for each item,

$$\text{Item } 1 = wF1 + wF2 + \text{error,}$$
$$\text{Item } 2 = wF1 + wF2 + \text{error,}$$
$$\cdots$$
$$\text{Item } 9 = wF1 + wF2 + \text{error, and}$$
$$\text{Item } 10 = wF1 + wF2 + \text{error.}$$

These equations look very different from those of PCA, where the PCs were on the "left" side and were a weighted linear combination of the items. Each of the ws in the CFA equations represents the weight assigned to each factor that is expected to account for variance in each item. These ws are called factor loadings.

The variance that items share with the underlying factors is called *common variance* and that associated with the error is *unique variance*. This is the reason the model is called common factor analysis. The analysis is designed to determine what the common factors are that account for variance in the items. It is important to note that the unique variance is not just random variance, as in classical test theory (CTT). Instead, this unique variance includes both systematic and random error.

Note that all factors have a *w* for all items. Graphically, the way CFA would be modeled is as follows (see Figure 10.6). As can be seen, this is rather a complicated model. However, it does show quite clearly that each item has variance associated with it, some due to Factor 1, some due to Factor 2, and some due to unique variance.

One of the indeterminacies in CFA is how many factors will be extracted. In PCA, the answer was simple—the number of items was the number of PCs. In CFA, the estimate of the number of factors is the number of principal components that are substantive (i.e., eigenvalues greater than 1.0 unless otherwise specified). So the initial estimates of the eigenvalues in a CFA is actually a principal components solution! Based on the number of components greater than 1.0, the CFA will proceed using that same number of common factors. The programmer can override this and request a

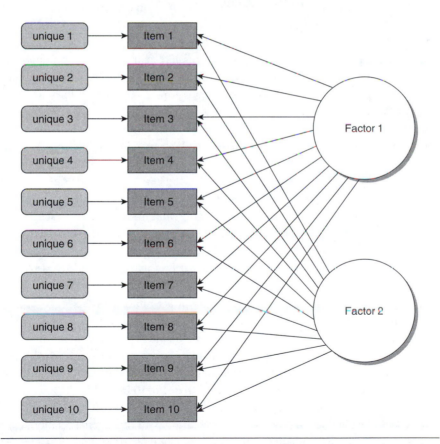

Figure 10.6 Graphic Representation of 10 Items and Two Common Orthogonal Factors in "Exploratory" Factor Analysis

certain number of factors to be extracted. Unlike PCA, CFA does not presume to account for all of the variance in the items. CFA is only programmed to account for the common, or shared, variance in the items. Therefore, the eigenvalues associated with a CFA analysis are smaller than those associated with a PCA of the same data.

Another indeterminacy in CFA is finding the final communalities for the items. In PCA, these were always equal to 1.0 if all the loadings from all the PCs were used. In CFA, the initial estimate is most often the squared value of the item regressed on all of the other items in the data set. This means that the initial estimate of the common variance of the item (i.e., that shared with the other items) is based on how much variance in it can be accounted for by all the other items in the data.

In CFA, there is less chance that most of the variance will be apportioned to the first factor. This is another difference from PCA, where the first component eigenvalue usually is much higher than the subsequent components.

Other than these differences, the interpretation of communalities, eigenvalues, unrotated factor loadings, rotated factor loadings, orthogonal and oblique solutions, factor pattern and structure matrices, and factor correlation matrices all are similar to those of a PCA.

As noted earlier, CFA is really a family of methods and so there are several options for conducting a CFA. One of the most common is principal axis factoring (PAF). Another common one is the maximum likelihood estimation (ML) procedure. Both produce similar results, and the differences in their analytical algorithms are beyond the scope of this book. ML is "fussier" than PAF in that one of the assumptions in factor analysis is that all of the items have normally distributed data. In addition, items are all assumed to have similar variances. If these assumptions are violated, ML may not converge on a final solution. PAF is less affected by violations of these assumptions and thus will converge more rapidly.

ML provides the only inferential statistic available in CFA. Specifically, a χ^2 value is given at the end of the analysis. This is an index of how well the factor solution was able to reproduce the correlations between the items. If the χ^2 is significant, it means that there are significant differences between the original correlations of the items and the correlations of the items based on what information the factor solution was able to provide. Conversely, if the χ^2 is not significant, it means that there are no significant differences between the original correlations of the items and the correlations of the items based on what information the factor solution was able to provide. So a nonsignificant χ^2 at the end of the analysis is usually desired. The χ^2 can also be used to help in assessing the appropriate number of factors to extract. For example, if the χ^2 is significant when two factors are extracted but not when three are extracted, then it would be best to report the three-factor solution.

Next, an example of a CFA using a PAF analysis is presented. Only cursory descriptions are provided here as the more detailed descriptions of the output have already been discussed in the context of PCA. Assume there are 10 items (five TPI items and five measuring the workplace value of social relationships). Three different PAF analyses will be conducted: (a) a two-factor solution with orthogonal rotation, (b) a two-factor solution with oblique rotation, and (c) a one-factor solution. The specifics of each output are shown in Box 10.3, and the highlights are reported as follows.

(Text continues on page 267)

Box 10.3   Common Factor Analysis: Orthogonal Rotation Using SPSS

In this analysis, five team player Items (TPI1–TPI5) and five items that assess social relations (SOCR1–SOCR5) are analyzed. A total of 180 individuals completed the items. A CFA requesting two factors is carried out using PAF with orthogonal (varimax) rotation. Table 10.17 shows the initial estimated communalities (equal to the squared multiple correlation of each item with all the other items) as well as the communalities after the extraction. Interpretation of the communalities is the same as that of PCA.

Table 10.17   Initial Communalities in a Principal Axis Analysis

Item	Initial	Extraction
TPI1	0.292	0.333
TPI2	0.490	0.585
TPI3	0.364	0.430
TPI4	0.392	0.455
TPI5	0.475	0.585
SOCR1	0.163	0.191
SOCR2	0.328	0.428
SOCR3	0.217	0.237
SOCR4	0.366	0.492
SOCR5	0.401	0.526

Table 10.18 shows the initial extraction of common factors. Note that the intial extraction is really a PCA. The number of common factors extracted will be equal to the number of components extracted with eigenvalues greater than 1.0 unless the software is programmed to do otherwise. In our case, two factors would be extracted based on the PC information (i.e., Component 1 has an eigenvalue of 3.373 and Component 2 has an eigenvalue of 1.989. Component 3 has an eigenvalue of 0.862 and thus does not meet the default value).

Table 10.18   Initial Extraction of Common Factors in a Principal Axis Analysis

Initial Eigenvalues			
Factor	Total	% of Variance	Cumulative %
1	3.373	33.733	33.733
2	1.989	19.890	53.622

(Continued)

Box 10.3 (Continued)

Table 10.18 (Continued)

Initial Eigenvalues			
Factor	Total	% of Variance	Cumulative %
3	0.862	8.619	62.241
4	0.768	7.677	69.918
5	0.687	6.866	76.785
6	0.542	5.420	82.204
7	0.504	5.044	87.248
8	0.482	4.818	92.066
9	0.431	4.309	96.375
10	0.363	3.625	100.000

Table 10.19 shows the eigenvalues based on the PAF with two factors requested. Note that the total percentage of variance accounted for will be less than that with a PC solution. This is typical, as CFAs account only for common variance but PCA accounts for all variance.

Table 10.19 Initial Eigenvalues in a Principal Axis Analysis With Two Factors Requested

Factor	Total	% of Variance	Cumulative %
1	2.851	28.506	28.506
2	1.411	14.108	42.614

Table 10.20 shows the eigenvalues associated with the orthogonally rotated factors. Note that the cumulative percentage is equal to that of the unrotated solution (42.614).

Table 10.20 Eigenvalues After the Orthogonal Rotation in a Principal Axis Analysis with Two Factors Requested

Factor	Total	% of Variance	Cumulative %
1	2.377	23.769	23.769
2	1.885	18.845	42.614

Tables 10.21 and 10.22 show the unrotated and rotated factor loadings, respectively.

Table 10.21   Unrotated Factor Loadings in a Principal Axis Analysis With Two Factors Requested

	Factor	
Item	1	2
TPI1	0.476	−0.327
TPI2	0.734	−0.215
TPI3	0.573	−0.318
TPI4	0.590	−0.327
TPI5	0.700	−0.309
SOCR1	0.250	0.358
SOCR2	0.442	0.482
SOCR3	0.373	0.312
SOCR4	0.422	0.560
SOCR5	0.586	0.427

Table 10.22   Orthogonally Rotated Factor Loadings in a Principal Axis Analysis With Two Factors Requested

	Factor	
Item	1	2
TPI1	0.577	5.298E-03
TPI2	0.725	0.244
TPI3	0.652	6.827E-02
TPI4	0.671	7.018E-02
TPI5	0.751	0.148
SOCR1	−3.598E-04	0.437
SOCR2	8.595E-02	0.648

(Continued)

Box 10.3 (Continued)

Table 10.22 (Continued)

	Factor	
Item	1	2
SOCR3	0.127	0.470
SOCR4	2.435E-02	0.701
SOCR5	0.235	0.686

The rotated matrix clearly shows two distinct factors, team player (Factor 1) and social relations (Factor 2).

Common Factor Analysis: Oblique Rotation Using SPSS

The same data were analyzed using PAF, this time with oblique (direct oblimin) rotation.

Only where there are differences in the output will the information be presented. The first difference is that the rotated sums of squared loadings (eigenvalues) are higher that those in the orthogonal rotation (Table 10.23). They cannot be added to obtain a value of "total variance accounted for" due to the fact that the factors are correlated.

Table 10.23   Obliquely Rotated Sums of Squared Loadings in a Principal Axis Analysis

Rotation Sums of Squared Loadings	
Factor	Total
1	2.544
2	2.068

The pattern matrix (Table 10.24) suggests the same conclusion as the orthogonal rotation did—that there are two factors, team player and social relations. The structure matrix is not presented as it is not interpreted.

Table 10.24   Pattern Matrix of Factor Loadings in an Obliquely Rotated Principal Axis Analysis

	Factor	
	1	2
TPI1	0.592	−7.277E-02
TPI2	0.711	0.153

Table 10.24 (Continued)

	Factor	
	1	*2*
TPI3	0.660	−1.828E-02
TPI4	0.679	−1.887E-02
TPI5	0.751	5.009E-02
SOCR1	−5.946E-02	0.448
SOCR2	5.384E-04	0.654
SOCR3	6.673E-02	0.465
SOCR4	−6.978E-02	0.716
SOCR5	0.149	0.672

The factor correlation matrix (Table 10.25) indicates that the factors are somewhat correlated. This suggests that the construct of team player is positively associated with the construct of social relations.

Table 10.25 Factor Correlation Matrix

Factor	*1*	*2*
1	1.000	0.259
2	0.259	1.000

Common Factor Analysis: A One-Factor Model Using SPSS

The same data were analyzed using PAF, this time requesting a one-factor solution. Only where there are differences in the output will the information be discussed. The extracted communalities (Table 10.26) with a one-factor solution are lower than those in the two-factor solution.

Table 10.26 Extracted Communalities in a One-Factor Principal Axis Analysis

Item	*Initial*	*Extraction*
TPI1	0.292	0.230
TPI2	0.490	0.565
TPI3	0.364	0.331

(Continued)

Box 10.3 (Continued)

Table 10.26 (Continued)

Item	Initial	Extraction
TPI4	0.392	0.348
TPI5	0.475	0.492
SOCR1	0.163	5.347E-02
SOCR2	0.328	0.157
SOCR3	0.217	0.128
SOCR4	0.366	0.132
SOCR5	0.401	0.288

The total variance accounted for by the one factor is more than that of the first factor in the two-factor solution but not as much as the two factors together, as shown in Table 10.27.

Table 10.27   Eigenvalue in a One-Factor Principal Axis Analysis

Factor	Total	% of Variance	Cumulative %
1	2.725	27.249	27.249

The factor matrix of loadings (Table 10.28) suggests that the TPI items generally load better than the SOCR items.

Table 10.28   Factor Loadings in a One-Factor Principal Axis Analysis

Item	Factor 1
TPI1	0.479
TPI2	0.752
TPI3	0.576
TPI4	0.590
TPI5	0.702
SOCR1	0.231
SOCR2	0.396
SOCR3	0.357
SOCR4	0.363
SOCR5	0.537

In the two-factor solution with orthogonal rotation, the initial estimates of the communalities are all slightly lower than the extracted communalities. The extracted communalities range from 0.19 (low) to 0.585 (moderate). The two orthogonally rotated factors account for 23.8% and 18.8% of the variance in the items (42.6% in total). The unrotated and rotated factor loadings are reported in Table 10.29. The loadings suggest that there are indeed two factors with the TPI items loading on Factor 1 and the social relations items loading on Factor 2.

Table 10.29   Unrotated and Orthogonally Rotated Factor Loadings for a 10-Item Measure (Five TPI Items and Five Social Relations Items)

Item	Unrotated Loadings		Orthogonally Rotated Loadings	
	Factor 1	Factor 2	Factor 1	Factor 2
TPI1	0.476	−0.327	0.577	0.005
TPI2	0.734	−0.215	0.725	0.244
TPI3	0.573	−0.318	0.652	0.068
TPI4	0.590	−0.327	0.671	0.070
TPI5	0.700	−0.309	0.751	0.148
SOCR1	0.250	0.358	0.000	0.437
SOCR2	0.442	0.482	0.086	0.648
SOCR3	0.373	0.312	0.127	0.470
SOCR4	0.422	0.560	0.024	0.701
SOCR5	0.586	0.427	0.235	0.686

The final two-factor solution with oblique rotation is similar to that of the orthogonal solution other than minor changes in the factor loadings. These are shown in Table 10.30. The correlation between the factors is 0.259, suggesting that the two factors are somewhat correlated. However, this is not extremely high and so it is still ambiguous as to whether or not an oblique or orthogonal solution is more appropriate.

Finally, a one-factor solution was conducted. The communalities for this solution are all lower than with the two-factor solution. The one factor did account for more variance than the first factor in the orthogonal solution (27.2% versus 23.8%). The factor loadings are moderate to high for the TPI items but low to moderate for the SOCR items (see Table 10.31). This suggests that a two-factor solution is a better representation of the data than a one-factor.

Table 10.30   Obliquely Rotated Factor Loadings for a 10-Item Measure (Five TPI Items and Five Social Relations Items)

Item	Obliquely Rotated Loadings	
	Factor 1	Factor 2
TPI1	0.592	−0.073
TPI2	0.711	0.153
TPI3	0.660	−0.018
TPI4	0.679	−0.019
TPI5	0.751	0.050
SOCR1	−0.059	0.448
SOCR2	0.000	0.654
SOCR3	0.067	0.465
SOCR4	−0.070	0.716
SOCR5	0.149	0.672

Table 10.31   Factor Loadings for a One-Factor Solution for a 10-Item Measure (Five TPI Items and Five Social Relations Items)

Item	Factor
TPI1	0.479
TPI2	0.752
TPI3	0.576
TPI4	0.590
TPI5	0.702
SOCR1	0.231
SOCR2	0.396
SOCR3	0.357
SOCR4	0.363
SOCR5	0.537

There are a number of rules of thumb and much intuitive decision making that must go on in interpreting PCA and CFA solutions. Fortunately, another type of analysis has been created so that many of the rules of thumb can give way to statistical assessment. In addition, more control over the nature of the factor structure is allowed. This process is commonly called *confirmatory factor analysis* but is more aptly named *analysis of covariance structures*. It is that to which we now turn our attention.

Common Factor Analysis Using Analysis of Covariance Structures

Frustration with the limitations of PCA and CFA procedures led researchers to solve some of the indeterminacies of the earlier attempts to identify the factor structure that underlies a set of items. The general class of analyses that do so are called analysis of covariance structures (ACS). Joreskog and Sorbom (1979) were the first to create a computer program (called Linear Structural Relations, or LISREL) to handle the new approach. There are several others now available, including Bentler's EQS (1989), AMOS, and SAS CALIS, that have gained much popularity.

The equations that assess the ACS are very complex, beyond the scope of this book, and are explained well elsewhere (e.g., Kline, 1998; Long, 1983). Thus, the discussion will be confined to the conceptual improvements of ACS over PCA and CFA, as well as an example of the application of one of the programs (LISREL).

As noted earlier, one of the shortcomings of CFA is that variances of all of the items are specified to be accounted for by all factors. This shortcoming is solved in ACS by the user defining which factors are expected to account for variance in which items. Another shortcoming in CFA is that the choice for orthogonal versus oblique rotation is an all-or-none decision. That is, if there are more than two factors, all of them have to be specified to be correlated (oblique) or none of them (orthogonal). ACS allows the user to specify which (if any) factors are expected to be correlated. Yet another shortcoming of CFA is that the measurement error terms (unique variances) for each item in CFA are assumed to be uncorrelated. Because unique variances include both systematic as well as random error, there may very well be correlations between the unique variances in the systematic error portions (e.g., respondents may exhibit a socially desirable response bias). ACS allows the user to specify any expected correlations between the unique variances. The shortcoming of no statistical tests of factor loadings or correlations between factors in CFA is not a problem in ACS.

It is easy to see why ACS is inappropriately called *confirmatory factor analysis*. However, in science, we never confirm anything—we find support for our hypotheses or we fail to disconfirm them. Thus, the term ACS, rather than confirmatory factor analysis, will be used throughout the discussion.

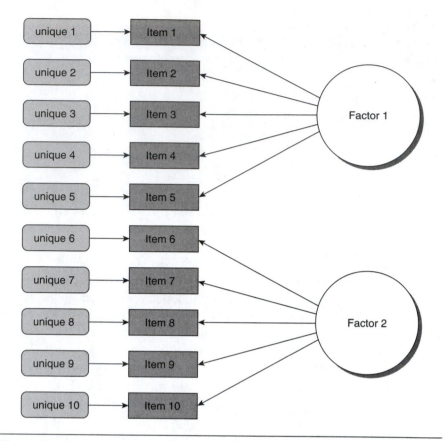

Figure 10.7   Graphic Representation of 10 Items and Two Common Orthogonal
Factors Using the Restrictions Allowed in Structural Equation
Modeling

An example is the best way to show the utility of ACS. The same data and
models that were used for the PFA example will be used to demonstrate ACS. This
time, however, constraints will be placed on the model of the factor structure.
Figure 10.7 shows the model that is to be tested. The constraints are that (a) the
unique variances are not correlated with one another, (b) the factors are not correlated with one another, and (c) the first factor is specified to account for variance
in only the first five items whereas the second factor is specified to account for
variance in only the last five items.

Three analyses were conducted that parallel those of the PAF analyses. These
were (a) solutions using two factors with the factors uncorrelated, (b) two factors
with the factors correlated, and (c) one factor. A full description of the output
is contained in Box 10.4, but conceptually relevant points are reported here for
interpretation.

Box 10.4   Common Factor Analysis Using Structural Equation Modeling With LISREL (8.54)

In the program we have 10 items, the first five (all TPI items) loading on a team player construct and the second five (all social relations items) loading on a social relations factor. The measurement errors associated with each item are assumed to be uncorrelated with one another, and the factors are specified to be uncorrelated as well (i.e., an orthogonal solution). In addition, as specified by Joreskog and Sorbom (1993), one of the item loadings for each factor was set to 1.0 to set the scaling for the rest of the items. The item in each factor set to 1.0 cannot be tested for significance, but its magnitude can be examined in relation to the other loading estimates. The correlations between the items are used as the raw data input for this analysis.

Common Factor Analysis Using Structural Equation Modeling
With LISREL (8.54), Assuming No Correlations Between Constructs

The first matrix (called lambda-X) in the output that we'll examine is the one that assesses the significance of the loadings. Recall that, in earlier analyses, we used a rule of thumb of 0.30 or 0.40 to determine substantiveness. In ACS, these loadings are tested for statistical significance. Note that they are *not* standardized values. They are, instead, scaled to the item that was set to 1.0. The first entry for each item is the LISREL estimate of the parameter. The second (in parentheses) is the standard error of the parameter estimate. The third is the first divided by the second and is equal to the *z* test of significance. Values that are ±1.96 (or, conventionally, 2.0 for ease of interpretation) are statistically significant. Note that all of the items load significantly on their respective constructs (Table 10.32).

Table 10.32   Lambda-X: Uncorrelated Factors

	Team Play	Soc. Rel.
TPI1	1.0000	
TPI2	1.3248	
	(0.1924)	
	6.8866	
TPI3	1.1464	
	(0.1806)	
	6.3491	
TPI4	1.1936	
	(0.1834)	
	6.5075	
TPI5	1.3513	
	(0.1945)	
	6.9485	

(Continued)

Box 10.4 (Continued)

Table 10.32 (Continued)

	Team Play	*Soc. Rel.*
SOCR1		1.0000
SOCR2		1.5154
		(0.3209)
		4.7226
SOCR3		1.1034
		(0.2689)
		4.1036
SOCR4		1.6150
		(0.3357)
		4.8114
SOCR5		1.6483
		(0.3410)
		4.8343

The next matrix (phi; Table 10.33) is the variance/covariance matrix of the relationships between the factors. We specified no correlation between them, so the entries represent only the variance of the factors.

Table 10.33   Phi Matrix: Uncorrelated Factors

Team Play	*Soc. Rel.*
0.3216	0.1863
(0.0852)	(0.0704)
3.7761	2.6451

The next matrix (theta-delta; Table 10.34) reports the measurement error associated with each item and a test of each one's significance levels. The results indicate that a significant amount of variance is *not* accounted for in each of the items. This is a very usual finding in ACS.

Table 10.34   Theta-Delta Matrix: Uncorrelated Factors

TPI1	TPI2	TPI3	TPI4	TPI5	SOCR1	SOCR2	SOCR3	SOCR4	SOCR5
0.6784	0.4356	0.5774	0.5418	0.4128	0.8137	0.5721	0.7732	0.5141	0.4938
(0.0798)	(0.0643)	(0.0725)	(0.0701)	(0.0634)	(0.0926)	(0.0798)	(0.0900)	(0.0786)	(0.0784)
8.5038	6.7742	7.9682	7.7289	6.5159	8.7826	7.1682	8.5883	6.5402	6.2983

Next, the squared multiple correlations for the items are shown (Table 10.35). These are equal to the amount of variance that is accounted for in each item by the solution and are thus similar to communalities.

Table 10.35   Squared Multiple Correlations of Items: Uncorrelated Factors

TPI1	TPI2	TPI3	TPI4	TPI5	SOCR1	SOCR2	SOCR3	SOCR4	SOCR5
0.3216	0.5644	0.4226	0.4582	0.5872	0.1863	0.4279	0.2268	0.4859	0.5062

Next, some of the goodness-of-fit indices are reported in Table 10.36. There are actually 33 of them in the output. In this instance, the chi-square is significant, indicating that the model *does not* fit the data. The RMR and standardized RMR are equal in this case because we used a correlation matrix as input rather than a covariance matrix. The value is 0.11, which is higher than desirable but still indicates a reasonable fit. The GFI indicates that, of the variance that is shared between the items, the model captures 94% of it. The AGFI is also high, at 0.91.

Table 10.36   Goodness-of-Fit Statistics: Uncorrelated Factors

Degrees of Freedom = 35

Minimum Fit Function Chi-Square = 54.8930 ($P = 0.01856$)

Root Mean Square Residual (RMR) = 0.1063

Standardized RMR (SRMR) = 0.1063

Goodness-of-Fit Index (GFI) = 0.9436

Adjusted Goodness-of-Fit Index (AGFI) = 0.9113

Normed Fit Index = 0.9255

Non-Normed Fit Index = 0.9630

Comparative Fit Index = 0.9712

(Continued)

Box 10.4 (Continued)

Next, the modification indices are reported for each parameter that was constrained to be 0 (i.e., was not estimated) in Table 10.37. Values are interpreted to mean that freeing the parameter to be estimated will reduce the chi-square value by the amount of the modification index. Values greater than 5.0 are considered worthy of examination for improving the fit of the model to the data. This is because, for every parameter estimated, there is a loss of a degree of freedom. To counterbalance the degree of freedom lost, the reduction of the chi-square should be at least 5.0. It is strongly advised not to modify more than one parameter at a time in subsequent LISREL analyses. In the first matrix, the modification indices suggest that the social relations factor should be allowed to account for variance in TPI2 and the team play factor should be allowed to account for variance in SOCR5.

Table 10.37   Modification Indices for Lambda-X: Uncorrelated Factors

	Team Play	*Social Relations*
TPI1		0.8581
TPI2		8.2786
TPI3		0.0006
TPI4		0.0195
TPI5		1.3624
SOCR1	0.2177	
SOCR2	0.2079	
SOCR3	1.5721	
SOCR4	0.4252	
SOCR5	11.4016	

The modification index in Table 10.38 indicates that the team play and social relations factors should be allowed to be correlated. In the next LISREL run, we will allow for an *oblique* solution, meaning that the team play and social relations factors will be allowed to be correlated.

Table 10.38   Modification Indices for Phi: Uncorrelated Factors

	Team Play	*Social Relations*
Team Play		
Social Relations	13.5172	

The modification indices in Table 10.39 suggest that allowing the correlation between the TPI2 and SOCR3 measurement error terms would improve the fit of the model.

Table 10.39   Modification Indices for Theta-Delta: Uncorrelated Factors

	TPI1	TPI2	TPI3	TPI4	TPI5	SOCR1
TPI1						
TPI2	1.6753					
TPI3	0.0018	1.0982				
TPI4	0.0747	1.0041	1.0555			
TPI5	1.1385	1.0984	3.7394	0.0148		
SOCR1	0.0379	0.1568	1.8725	1.7329	0.0055	
SOCR2	2.2080	1.0960	0.7697	1.8172	0.0500	0.0414
SOCR3	0.1560	6.7174	0.0247	2.9755	0.0152	0.0020
SOCR4	3.8524	0.0270	0.5564	1.4168	0.5125	1.2618
SOCR5	0.2159	0.5677	0.7174	0.0535	2.8499	0.8948
	SOCR2	SOCR3	SOCR4	SOCR5		
SOCR2						
SOCR3	1.0292					
SOCR4	0.2113	1.7041				
SOCR5	0.0460	0.0953	0.4927			

Next shown is the completely standardized solution (Table 10.40). This means that the parameter estimates from the LISREL analysis are converted to standardized values (ranging from 0 to ± 1). Here, it is easy to determine the relative loading of the items that had "lambdas set to 1.0." In this case, all loadings would be considered substantive in the usual CFA procedures.

Table 10.40   Standardized Lambda-X (Equivalent to Factor Loadings): Uncorrelated Factors

	Team Play	Social Relations
TPI1	0.5671	
TPI2	0.7513	

Box 10.4 (Continued)

Table 10.40 (Continued)

	Team Play	Social Relations
TPI3	0.6501	
TPI4	0.6769	
TPI5	0.7663	
SOCR1		0.4316
SOCR2		0.6541
SOCR3		0.4763
SOCR4		0.6971
SOCR5		0.7115

The next matrix (Table 10.41) is equivalent to the correlations between factors. Because we specified no correlation between the factors, this is a diagonal matrix with 1.0s along the diagonal.

Table 10.41 Standardized Phi: Uncorrelated Factors

Team Play	Social Relations
1.0000	1.0000

Next shown are the standardized error terms in measuring the items (Table 10.42).

Table 10.42 Standardized Theta-Delta: Uncorrelated Factors

TPI1	TPI2	TPI3	TPI4	TPI5	SOCR1	SOCR2	SOCR3	SOCR4	SOCR5
0.6784	0.4356	0.5774	0.5418	0.4128	0.8137	0.5721	0.7732	0.5141	0.4938

*Common Factor Analysis Using Structural Equation Modeling
With LISREL (8.54), Assuming Correlations Between Constructs*

Only the portions of the output that are different from the one above will be discussed at any length. In this analysis, the only change from the previous one is that the two factors are allowed to be correlated. The first matrix (Table 10.43) indicates again that each item loaded significantly on its respective factor. The phi matrix is where the change was specified and shows that the covariation between the factors is significant (z value of 2.8615).

Table 10.43   Phi Matrix: Correlated Factors

	Team Play	Social Relations
Team Play	0.3113	
	(0.0838)	
	3.7154	
Social Relations	0.0837	0.1753
	(0.0292)	(0.0681)
	2.8695	2.5742

The theta-delta matrix again show significant variance was not accounted for in each item. The goodness-of-fit indices result in a nonsignificant chi-square value, indicating that the model fits the data. The other fit indices show a better fit of this model compared to the previous model (Table 10.44).

Table 10.44   Goodness-of-Fit Statistics: Correlated Factors

Degrees of Freedom = 34

Minimum Fit Function Chi-Square = 40.2622 ($P = 0.2127$)

Root Mean Square Residual (RMR) = 0.05259

Standardized RMR = 0.05259

Goodness-of-Fit Index (GFI) = 0.9567

Adjusted Goodness-of-Fit Index (AGFI) = 0.9300

Normed Fit Index = 0.9454

Non-Normed Fit Index = 0.9880

Comparative Fit Index = 0.9909

None of the modification indices for the lambda-X or the theta-delta matrices were greater than 5. The completely standardized solution (Tables 10.45 and 10.46) shows that the factor loadings are all high and that the correlation between the constructs is 0.3585, which was significant. Recall that in the principal axis factor analysis, we were not able to test the correlation between the factors for significance.

(Continued)

Box 10.4 (Continued)

Table 10.45   Completely Standardized Lambda-X Matrix: Correlated Factors

	Team Play	Social Relations
TPI1	0.5579	
TPI2	0.7640	
TPI3	0.6461	
TPI4	0.6700	
TPI5	0.7669	
SOCR1		0.4187
SOCR2		0.6464
SOCR3		0.4825
SOCR4		0.6754
SOCR5		0.7396

Table 10.46   Completely Standardized Phi Matrix: Correlated Factors

	Team Play	Social Relations
Team Play	1.0000	
Social Relations	0.3585	1.0000

Overall, the data support the model that the ten items load on their respective factors and that the factors are correlated.

Common Factor Analysis Using Structural Equation Modeling
With LISREL (8.54): A One-Factor Model

In this analysis, a one-factor solution was requested. The findings (Tables 10.47 and 10.48) indicated that SOCR1 did not significantly load on the one factor, but the other items did. The goodness-of-fit indices suggested that a one-factor model is a very poor fitting model. The standardized solution suggested that several of the SOCR items did not have substantive loadings on the factor. Thus, the two-factor oblique solution fits the data best.

Table 10.47   Goodness-of-Fit Statistics: One Factor Model

Degrees of Freedom = 35

Minimum Fit Function Chi-Square = 172.6112 (P = 0.0)

Root Mean Square Residual (RMR) = 0.1321

Standardized RMR = 0.1321

Goodness-of-Fit Index (GFI) = 0.7920

Adjusted Goodness-of-Fit Index (AGFI) = 0.6732

Normed Fit Index = 0.7644

Non-Normed Fit Index = 0.7427

Comparative Fit Index = 0.7997

Table 10.48   Standardized Lambda-X Matrix: One Factor Model

TPI1	0.5322
TPI2	0.7773
TPI3	0.6271
TPI4	0.6420
TPI5	0.7499
SOCR1	0.1536
SOCR2	0.2967
SOCR3	0.2913
SOCR4	0.2561
SOCR5	0.4382

Table 10.49 shows the factor loadings from the LISREL analyses. In addition to the factor loading magnitudes reported, the significance of each was tested. In all instances, the loadings were significant except for SOCR1 in the one-factor model. However, SOCR1 to SOCR4 all had weak loadings compared to the other items. In addition to the loadings, the correlation between the factors for the two-factor oblique solution was 0.36, and this was statistically significant.

One assessment of the fit of the model is the AVE index. The interpretation of AVE is the amount of item variance extracted in the solution relative to its

Table 10.49 Standardized Factor Loadings for a Two-Factor Orthogonal, Two-Factor Oblique and One-Factor Solution for a 10-Item Measure (Five TPI Items and Five Social Relations Items) Using LISREL

| Item | Orthogonal Factors | | Oblique Factors | | One Factor |
	Factor 1	Factor 2	Factor 1	Factor 2	Factor
TPI1	0.567		0.558		0.532
TPI2	0.751		0.764		0.777
TPI3	0.650		0.646		0.627
TPI4	0.677		0.670		0.642
TPI5	0.766		0.767		0.750
SOCR1		0.432		0.418	0.154
SOCR2		0.654		0.646	0.300
SOCR3		0.476		0.483	0.291
SOCR4		0.697		0.675	0.256
SOCR5		0.712		0.740	0.438

measurement error. For newly developed scales, values above 0.45 are reasonable (Netemeyer, Bearden, & Sharma, 2003). The calculation for this index is

$$(10\text{–}3) \quad \left[\sum_{i=1}^{p} \lambda^2\right]/p,$$

where p = number of items. In the two-factor oblique solution, five items were hypothesized to be related to each underlying construct. The AVE value for the first factor can be calculated as

$$= [(0.558)^2 + (0.764)^2 + (0.646)^2 + (0.670)^2 + (0.767)^2]/5$$
$$= [(0.311 + 0.584 + 0.417 + 0.449 + 0.588)]/5$$
$$= 0.4698.$$

There are several other fit indices reported in the analysis (33 to be exact). However, only the most common will be reported and discussed. The first is the minimum fit χ^2. It is a test of whether or not the correlations between the items can be replicated using the information in the model. The degrees of freedom associated with the test are the number of parameters in the model that have been constrained to be equal to 0. It is easy to have the minimum fit χ^2 value be significant with large sample sizes and large models due to the distribution of the χ^2 in relation to degrees of freedom. Therefore, a ratio of χ^2/df of 2:1 is considered a good fit (Tabachnick & Fidell, 2001) and 3:1 is considered a reasonable fit (Kline, 1998).

The minimum fit χ^2 is the only fit index that has a distribution associated with it to assess statistical significance. The others all use rules of thumb. The root mean residual (RMR) is a measure of "badness of fit," and the lower the value the better. It is a summary statistic of how much deviation there is between each of the observed correlations and the reproduced correlations. The RMR is unstandardized, though, and so interpretation is difficult. The standardized RMR ranges from 0 to 1.0, with lower values indicating better fit. The standardized RMR should be less than 0.10 for "good-fitting" models.

The goodness of fit (GFI) indicates that, of the variance that is shared between the items, the model captures a certain percentage of it. The GFI is expected to be 0.90 or more for good-fitting models. The adjusted goodness of fit (AGFI) adjusts the GFI for the number of parameters estimated. If there are relatively few degrees of freedom compared to parameters estimated, the AGFI will be substantially lower than the GFI. If there are many degrees of freedom compared to the number of parameters estimated, then the AGFI will not be much lower than the GFI. AGFI values greater than 0.90 indicate models that fit the data well. The normed (NFI), non-normed (NNFI), and comparative fit indices (CFI) are all incremental fit indices (Bentler, 1990; Bentler & Bonnett, 1980). The NFI indicates how well the specified model improves the fit to the *null* model (no relationships between the observed variables). If the NFI is 0.90, then this means there is a 90% improvement in fit. The NNFI adjusts the NFI for the number of parameters estimated, as did the AGFI. The CFI also compares the fit of the specified model to other models but is not as affected by sample size. The indices for all three models are reported in Table 10.50.

Table 10.50   Fit Indices for a Two-Factor Orthogonal, Two-Factor Oblique, and One-Factor Solution for a 10-Item Measure (Five TPI items and Five Social Relations Items) Using LISREL

Fit Index	Two-Factor Orthogonal	Two-Factor Oblique	One-Factor
χ^2	55 (35 df)[a]	40 (34 df)	172 (35 df)[a]
Standardized RMR	0.11	0.05	0.13
GFI	0.94	0.96	0.79
AGFI	0.91	0.93	0.67
NFI	0.93	0.95	0.76
NNFI	0.96	0.99	0.74
CFI	0.97	0.99	0.80

a. Denotes statistical significance.

The χ^2 can also be used to test *nested* models. A model that is nested within another model means that it has at least one parameter fewer than the more fulsome model. For example, in the data analyses reviewed thus far using LISREL, the two-factor model with orthogonal factors is nested within the oblique model that allows for correlation between the underlying factors. The χ^2 can be used to test if the additional parameter estimated significantly improves the fit of the model. Specifically, the χ^2 for the orthogonal solution is 55 with 35 degrees of freedom; the χ^2 for the oblique solution is 40 with 34 degrees of freedom. The drop in χ^2 by adding the path between factors is 15, and the degrees of freedom for testing this drop is 1 (i.e., 35 − 34). This χ^2 (1) = 15 is significant ($p < 0.001$), indicating that the oblique solution is a significantly better fit of the model to the data than the orthogonal solution.

All of the fit indices reviewed are best for the two-factor solution with oblique rotation. In addition, it is the only one of the three with a nonsignificant χ^2 value. Thus, it is the model that best fits the data and that is also theoretically defensible.

Some Other Issues in Factor Analysis

A few issues in factor analysis deserve mention. The first is that of factor-based scales. A factor-based scale is one that is based on a factor analysis. Assume that a set of 20 items is factor analyzed and two distinctive factors emerge (one where items 1–10 load and the other where items 11–20 load). If two separate subscale scores are generated by adding the scores on items 1–10 and then 11–20, the two subscales would be called factor-based scales because they are based on a factor analysis.

In factor-based scales, the items are unit weighted, meaning that each response to each item is counted fully. Some techniques for factor-based scales use the factor loadings to weight the items and thus create factor scores for each person. In this instance, an individual's response to each item is multiplied by the factor loading of that item for each factor, and factor scores can then be generated for each factor. This approach has the effect of weighting items more heavily that have higher loadings on the factor.

There are problems with factor scores in that factor loadings change from sample to sample. Weighting items based on the factor analysis on the same sample as that used to generate the loadings in the first place capitalizes on the unique characteristics of the sample. We have already seen, in Chapter 5, that differential item weighting does not improve the predictive utility of a set of items, with the correlation between weighted and unit-weighted scores being nearly perfect (Ghiselli, Campbell, & Zedek, 1981). Thus, creating and using factor scores is questionable.

Factor structures may differ across different demographic groups or between samples. For example, respondents from individualistic countries may respond differently to a questionnaire on group cohesion than do respondents from a collectivist culture. One may be interested in seeing if the factor analysis produces similar results for both groups. Separate analyses for the two groups would be run and then the results compared. Only ACS procedures allow for a statistical test of differences in the factor structure. They are beyond the scope of this book but are useful because they do provide those statistical assessments. However, simply examining the number of components, or factors; communalities; and loadings for both groups in a CFA or PCA may be sufficient to make some claims about similarity or differences of factor structure.

Higher-order factor analysis can occur when correlated factors are, in turn, factor analyzed. That is, the correlation matrix of correlated factors is used as input to determine if there are second-order factors that underlie the constructs found in the first-order factor analysis. This process is only appropriate if the factors are indeed correlated. In addition, the second-order factors are more complex to interpret. Higher-order factor analyses have been used in assessments of personality and intelligence where the number of items is very large (say 200) and the supposed underlying constructs quite small (fewer than 10).

The factor analysis procedures discussed throughout this chapter have assumed that the analysis was based on items. This is called an R factor analysis. It is sometimes of interest to use the cases or participants as the basis of the analysis rather than the items. This is called a Q analysis. In a Q analysis, the data is transposed—cases are in columns and items are in the rows of the data set. The purpose of a Q analysis is to group respondents together; that is, clusters of cases are the end result. This might be useful if, for example, it was of interest to see if one factor comprised females and the other factor comprised males.

Practical Issues

One of the most frequently asked questions about analyses of internal structure is, Which one should I use? The answer is, it depends. PCA makes some untenable assumptions about measurement error, but is the most likely to provide a very large eigenvalue on the first component. Because of the assumptions, the eigenvalues and communalities associated with a PCA are going to be higher than those in a CFA. Thus, if a single underlying construct is hypothesized, then PCA might be the most appropriate. If more than one construct is hypothesized to account for the variance in the items, then a CFA is likely to spread the variance across the factors more than a PCA. Regardless, if the underlying constructs of the items are strong (no matter how many there are), then the overall conclusions will be very similar between the two analyses.

The other question in this domain is whether an ACS is warranted. ACS usually requires a fairly large sample. In addition, it is susceptible to violation of normality of item distributions. Thus, it is sometimes not an option. The other issue with ACS is that the computer programs needed to execute the operations are sometimes user-unfriendly and expensive. This is becoming less and less the case as program publishers respond to the needs of clients. Given the control that the operator can execute over the model, ACS approaches are the best alternative if the conditions can be met.

Another common question is, How many cases do I need in the analysis? This depends on the number of items in the analysis. The more items, the more cases are needed for a replicable solution. That is, while the analysis will converge on a solution with as few as two cases per item, the likelihood of replicating the same factor structure with another sample is very poor. Thus, a rule of thumb such as about 10 cases per item for PCA and CFA is usually quoted as being appropriate (e.g., Nunnally, 1978). For example, a 20-item scale would require about 200 cases to converge on a stable factor structure. Comrey (1973) states that 200 cases would only be a "fair" sample size. However, this statement does not make any reference to the number of items nor the number of factors. Lawley and Maxwell (1971) suggest that a sample of $N - n - 1 > 50$ ($N =$ sample size and $n =$ number of items) is appropriate for an ML solution and the associated significance test. Thus, for a 20-item scale, a sample of 71 would be sufficient ($71 - 20 - 1 = 50$). Guadagnoli and Velicer (1988) have reported that using a sample size to items ratio is inappropriate. However, their Monte Carlo study used PC analysis only and also assumed that component loadings are known in advance in order to estimate the sample size needed. Thus, for most general applications, the rule of thumb that ensures non-capitalization on the chance characteristics of the sample suggests that a reasonable number of cases per item is appropriate.

For ACS, about 10 cases per estimated parameter is a reasonable expectation (Kline, 1998). The number of parameters estimated includes common and unique variances for each item and variances of the factors. Thus, a 20-item measure with two underlying factors requires 42 parameter estimates and thus about 420 cases. In addition to sample size issues, sample representativeness is also very important in terms of generalizing results. The sample that the analysis is conducted on should be representative of the population on which the test is to be used.

Another question that comes up is whether dichotomously scored items should be factor analyzed, given the assumption of a normal distribution of items. Generally, the answer is no, unless just general clusterings of items is desired and the correlations between the items are less than 0.6 or 0.7 (Kim & Mueller, 1978). If the dichotomous items are true dichotomies, then the phi-coefficients correlations are appropriate to use as data points for such an analysis. If the dichotomies are false, then tetrachoric correlations should be used in the analysis. Most computer programs do not calculate the tetrachoric correlations so that the interrelationships between the items are underestimated.

Concluding Comments on Internal Structure and Validity

Much of the time and effort spent by those developing and assessing tests is taken up with attempts to defend the internal structure of test items. The importance of this exercise cannot be underestimated. However, although these approaches have been equated with construct validity, clearly these types of analyses only provide one piece of a much larger puzzle about the validity of test scores. To make the knowledge claim that a test measures what it purports to measure requires more than an assessment of its internal structure.

Threats to the Validity of Scores

Test scores can be contaminated by a number of constructs. These constructs contribute to the error in assessment. They are often systematic and thus are not captured readily by traditional measures of reliability, which only assess random error. Some of the most common include response bias or response tendency.

There are several response biases that may systematically affect the true score of an individual. For example, some respondents may tend to select options in the mid-range of a Likert-type scale (central tendency). Some may prefer the extreme ends of the scale (extreme tendency). One way to try to ensure that these effects are minimized is to give directions that encourage respondents to use all levels of the responses. Correctly anchor the options with good descriptors to encourage respondents to select the most appropriate one for them.

Respondents may not be motivated to partake in the testing process. In this case, careless or random responding may occur. Try to provide an incentive for participants to pay attention and be motivated to read the items and respond honestly. This incentive may be an actual reward but can also be a statement by the administrator about why their participation and appropriate responding are important.

Respondents may be having a bad day and feel negatively toward everything and this will affect their responses (negative affect). Conversely, some may be having a great day and this will positively influence how they respond to each item (positive affect). These types of biases will inflate the inter-item correlations, but do so artificially. One way to assess and remove this source of contamination is to also give measures of positive or negative affectivity. Then, when the scores on the test are related to a criterion, positive or negative affectivity scores can be accounted for first and thus removed from the relationship between the test and criterion.

Another potential bias is that individuals may be conscious of the social demands of the test (say a survey on attitudes toward minorities) and therefore respond to items in a way that their responses show that they are socially acceptable. This socially desirable response style affects some scales (such as attitudes) more than others (such as cognitive skills). Dealing with this potential problem follows a similar approach as that taken to deal with positive or negative affectivity. That is, give a measure of social desirability as well as the test and remove this source of contamination prior to analysis of the test with other variables.

Some scales are affected by individuals' faking their responses. For example, if I give an honesty test to job applicants as part of the selection process, they may respond to items in a way that their scores show they are very honest (faking good). Clearly, respondents would do so in order to improve their chances of being offered the position. In situations where respondents may feel compelled to fake, it is very important to assure them of anonymity. It is hoped that they will give more candid responses if they know the information will not be traced back to them. When the situation is such that the administrator knows the respondent, then some other mechanism needs to be used to assess those who might be faking.

One other problem in validity studies arises when the methods used to collect data on both the predictor and criterion measures are similar. This problem is called *common method variance*. For example, a paper-and-pencil self-report measure of job satisfaction is given to a group of employees. Then another paper-and-pencil self-report measure on work commitment is given to them. Then work commitment scores are predicted using job satisfaction scores. Assume there is a strong correlation between the two measures. Part of that correlation is likely due to the fact that a common method (i.e., self-report paper-and-pencil measures) was used in the data collection. This may artificially inflate the correlation between the measures (cf. Spector, 1994; Spector & Brannick, 1995; Williams & Brown, 1994).

The best way to avoid the problem of common method variance is to use a different method to collect one of the variables. For example, the employees might provide their ratings of job satisfaction, but their supervisors may rate the employees' work commitment. Then the relationship between the two variables will not be contaminated by common method variance.

Multitrait-Multimethod Assessment

In tandem with the common method variance concern, but also contributing to the assessment of test score construct validity, is the multitrait-multimethod assessment approach put forward by Campbell and Fiske (1959). This was introduced in Chapter 9 in conjunction with determining convergent and discriminant validity of test scores. In the present context, this approach is used to assess common method variance as well. The logic is as follows: Convergent validity examines the extent to which different methods of measuring the same construct (trait) show high correlations; discriminant validity examines the extent to which similar methods of measuring different constructs (traits) show low correlations.

A simple example will help to demonstrate this procedure. Assume that we want to assess two constructs (such as being a team player and need for achievement) with four different measures (two for each): TeamScale1, TeamScale2, Achievement1, and Achievement2. To gather the data, a group of employees fill out TeamScale1 and Achievement1 (Method 1), and then one coworker for each participant completes similar questionnaires rating the participant on TeamScale2 and Achievement2 (Method 2). Now, assessments of two traits (multitrait) and two methods for assessment (multimethod) have been gathered. All four scores are correlated with each other and the matrix in Table 10.51 is obtained.

In the best-case scenario, TeamScale1 and TeamScale2 (both supposedly measuring being a team player) should have high correlations *across* methods (i.e., convergence). Similarly, Achievement1 and Achivement2 should have high correlations *across* methods. Table 10.51 shows that both are high at 0.40. There should be low correlations (i.e., discrimination) of TeamScale1 and Achievement1 *within* method (self-report). There should also be low correlations of TeamScale2 and Achievement2 *within* method (peer rating). Table 10.51 shows that both are low at 0.15. Different traits measured with different methods should have (and do in this example) the lowest correlations (0.05).

Table 10.51   A Multitrait-Multimethod Matrix

	Team Player Self-Report	Achievement Need Self-Report	Team Player Peer-Report	Achievement Need Peer-Report
Team Player Self-Report				
Achievement Need Self-Report	0.15			
Team Player Peer-Report	0.40	0.05		
Achievement Need Peer-Report	0.05	0.40	0.15	

Closing Comments on Test Score Validity

As promised at the beginning of these last two chapters, we now return to what validity means. Hopefully it is clear that the trinitarian (Guion, 1980) view of test validity is outdated. This view has been attributed to Cronbach and Meehl (1955), who proposed that validity could be placed into four separate categories (predictive, concurrent, content, and construct) with two (predictive and concurrent) being collapsed into criterion-related. While this was a convenient way to divide test score validation strategies into pedagogically meaningful groupings, it also had an unintended consequence—that the groupings became separate validities.

For example, it would be very unusual indeed to find a test that had been demonstrated to have excellent content validity and was able to predict criteria in expected ways, but was not construct valid. As another example, if a set of items is factor analyzed and all load on a single factor, this is not enough to claim the test is construct valid. Taken as a whole, it is the preponderance of evidence that suggests how much faith should be put into the inferences made about test scores. The trinitarian versus unitarian debate is described very well by Landy (1986). While the effects of the trinitarian view are waning, they still are very much a part of the language used in the testing field.

Instead of the artificial division of validity into three types, the way testing actually occurs is that test scores for various samples are collected and used in different types of analyses. Test scores that nicely represent a single construct can be used appropriately or inappropriately. For example, an excellent set of items that assess being a team player can be developed. However, if scores on the test are used to predict how well someone could drive a vehicle, it would be nonsensical. Thus, it is appropriate to say that the use to which test scores are put is more or less valid; it is not appropriate to say that a test without a context is or is not valid.

Summary

The chapter was devoted to the methods used to assess the degree to which the inferences we make from test scores are valid, focusing primarily on the internal structure of the items using principal components and factor analytic approaches.
Other topics covered were:

a. threats to validity,

b. multimethod-multitrait analyses,

c. practical considerations, and

d. the trinitarian versus unitarian framework of validity.

In the next chapter, the discussion moves to the issues associated with appropriate use of tests. Specifically, it is devoted to ethical, professional, and legal issues surrounding test use.

Problems and Exercises

1. If a test of 20 items is subjected to a principal components analysis and the first eigenvalue is 5.0, what does this mean?

2. What do the component loadings represent in an orthogonal principal components analysis?

3. What is a communality?

4. What is meant by a simple solution in factor or component analysis?

5. What does it mean to rotate a solution?

6. What are the differences between an orthogonal and an oblique rotated solution?

7. What are the differences between principal components and common factor analysis?

8. What does the χ^2 in maximum likelihood factor analysis represent and how is it interpreted?

9. What are some of the advantages of using analysis of covariance structures over common factor analysis?

10. What is the AVE index and how is it interpreted?

11. What is the minimum fit χ^2 and how is it interpreted?

12. What is a factor-based scale?

13. What is a higher-order factor analysis?

14. What is meant by contamination of constructs?

15. What is common method variance?

16. What are the arguments for adopting a unitarian framework for validity?

CHAPTER 11

Ethics and Professional Issues in Testing

Taking a test is often a stressful experience for most people. This is especially true when the scores on the test will be used for making important decisions such as being accepted into a university, hired for a job, or placed into a particular treatment group. Therefore, it is absolutely essential that the administration and use of test scores follow ethical and professional guidelines.

Because test scores are used for making all types of decisions where the quality of people's lives are at stake, this chapter is devoted to describing some of the professional issues about which anyone in the testing business should be aware. The previous ten chapters in this book have focused almost exclusively on the test itself. Thus, it is not surprising that the psychometric characteristics of the instrument itself are of primary importance in test use.

There are, however, other considerations in test use that go beyond the instrument itself. These include who is going to be tested, who is to administer the test, who is going to score the test, who will interpret the score, who gets the information, and for what purpose the information is to be used. All of these latter issues are separate from the issues associated with the test itself, but they are nonetheless extremely important considerations.

First, then, some of the ethical guidelines that have been developed in and around the testing industry are reviewed. Next, the ethical protocols associated with the test taker, test administrator, test publisher, and test situation are covered. Integrity testing has become popular, so this topic is then reviewed, followed by a brief description of computer adaptive testing. Following that, some of the evidence about coaching and retaking tests is presented. Then, as society often has a stake in the use to which tests have been put, relevant U.S. court rulings and civil interests in testing are reviewed. Some statistical techniques that have been used to address some of these societal concerns are also presented. Finally, with increased globalization and technological sophistication, the issues of translating tests from one language to another and administering tests electronically are becoming more of a concern for test developers. Thus, a discussion about these topics is included.

Professional Standards and Guidelines

Several governing bodies have a vested interest in ensuring ethical and professional compliance with testing. A number of professional associations have made clear the responsibilities of test administrators and users. Documentation that outline these include the *Standards for Educational and Psychological Testing* (American Educational Research Association, American Psychological Association, National Council on Measurement in Education, 1999), *Guidelines for Computer-based Tests and Interpretations* (American Psychological Association, 1986), *Principles for the Validation and Use of Personnel Selection Procedures* (Society for Industrial and Organizational Psychology, 2003), *Uniform Guidelines on Employee Selection Procedures* (United States Equal Employment Opportunity Commission, Civil Service Commission, Department of Labor and Department of Justice, 1978), and *Test User Qualifications: A Data-Based Approach to Promoting Good Test Use* (Eyde, Moreland, Robertson, Primoff, & Most, 1988).

The *Ethical Principles of Psychologists and Code of Conduct* (American Psychological Association, 1992) clearly indicates that any evaluation and diagnosis of an individual should be conducted only by someone adequately trained to do so. In addition, the Code states, "Psychologists respect and protect human and civil rights, and do not knowingly participate in or condone unfair discriminatory practices" (p. 1599). However, just because there are guidelines in existence does not mean that tests are administered, scored, and interpreted appropriately in all cases. The potential for abuse is high, and thus test users should be quite careful about what inferences are made from test scores.

Ethical Procedures and Protocols

The individuals taking a test have the right to be informed about the testing process. They (or their guardian, for those not capable) should clearly understand (a) the purpose of the test, (b) what the scores on the test mean, (c) any implications of the scores, (d) who will have access to the results of the test, and (e) how confidentiality and/or anonymity of the test scores is being handled. They should be provided a full interpretation of their scores with the opportunity to ask questions and seek clarification. Test taking is often stressful, and test takers should be aware that scores can be adversely affected by feeling unduly anxious, under high stress, or physically ill or fatigued.

Test users must be competent in administering, scoring, and interpreting test scores. One of the earliest systems developed by the American Psychological Association for test qualifications was to rate the test itself in terms of who should have access to the material. A Level A test can be administered by an individual who may not be a psychologist but is responsible, has read the testing manual, and follows the manual's directions for test administration, scoring, and interpretation. Most achievement tests fall into this category. Level B tests require that the user have extensive psychometric knowledge. Persons using these tests have technical knowledge in test construction and validation as well as familiarity with the ethical and professional codes of conduct. Many vocational, personality, and standardized achievement tests fall into the Level B category. Level C tests require the qualifications associated with Level B, but also require specific training in the particular test administration. They usually require that the user be a licensed professional and a member in good standing of a professional association that oversees member conduct. These tests are often individually administered, such as the Wechsler Intelligence Scales and the Minnesota Multiphasic Personality Inventory. While these levels are convenient groupings for tests, they are not always followed. Generally, the test user needs to know how to use the test. For some tests, much in-depth information or training is needed for appropriate use, whereas for other tests, not as much is required.

Most test publishers require that a test purchaser provide professional information (e.g., education, training, professional affiliations, etc.) before selling a test to any individual. The test publishers should also provide all psychometric information available about the test to potential users. Typically, a test manual accompanies a test so that correct administration, scoring, and interpretation are carried out. Any concerns about the test should be clearly indicated in the testing manual.

Test Administration

Tests are administered individually or in groups. For individually administered tests, the administrator is an integral part of the testing process. The administrator often spends time with the test taker to develop a rapport with the person and ensure that the test taker is prepared to take the test. These types of tests are often fairly lengthy and may have follow-up probe questions and/or require that the test administrator determine when to quit asking test questions. For example, the Wechsler Intelligence Scale for Children requires several hours to administer, and the administrator may decide that two sessions are appropriate if the child becomes fatigued.

Most of us are much more familiar with group tests. *Group* tests are somewhat of a misnomer in that the test does not necessarily have to be administered with a group of people. Instead, it refers to the procedures of administration. In these testing situations, the administrator is there primarily to ensure that appropriate procedures are followed. Generally, the test-taking environment should be comfortable and free from distraction. If there is a time limit on the test, then the administrator should ensure that all tests are completed within the allotted time. The administrator is responsible for collecting and securely storing any test materials such as booklets or answer sheets. The administrator proctors the test situation to ensure no cheating occurs and is there to clarify test directions. Achievement tests are often group tests, whether they are high school tests of history, or the Scholastic Assessment Tests, or the Graduate Record Exam. Some of these tests are now administered online by computer.

Integrity Testing

Integrity testing is a burgeoning industry. Employers are interested in hiring the most honest employees possible. As a result, part of the employee selection process may include some form of integrity or honesty testing. There are, however, reasons to have strong reservations about such processes.

The first is that the terms *integrity* and *honesty* are often used interchangeably, but they are not the same construct. Integrity is a broad construct that implies that individuals will follow through on their promises and act according to their beliefs. Honesty is a subset of integrity that involves not telling lies and upholding the truth. Measurement tools used in selection processes should be clear about what they actually are measuring, and this has not generally been the case in integrity testing.

The second issue about integrity testing is that a wide variety of methods have been devised to assess this construct that provide very different types of information. Polygraph tests are commonly used in criminal investigations, but their use as an employee-screening device is unique to the U.S. However, in 1988, this practice was banned by the Employee Polygraph Protection Act and is no longer used except in highly specialized security jobs or in situations where there has been demonstrated evidence that the employee has likely been involved in criminal activity. The assumption in polygraph testing is that physiological reactions can be used to infer whether or not the person taking the test is lying.

Paper-and-pencil tests are another method used to assess integrity. They come in two primary varieties: clear (overt) and veiled (covert) purpose. Clear purpose tests of integrity ask directly about past illegal behaviors (e.g., Have you stolen $50 worth of merchandise in the last two years?), opinions about illegal behaviors (e.g., If a man steals a loaf of bread to save his family from starving, is this wrong?), and thinking about illegal activities (e.g., I have often thought about taking office supplies home for personal use.). The purpose of such questions is obvious to a potential employee, and thus faking on such tests is a concern. In addition, potential employees may form negative impressions of organizations that use such tests in their screening process. Veiled tests of integrity assess characteristics that are supposedly related to honest behaviors, such as conscientiousness and dependability, or dishonest behaviors, such as impulsiveness or hostility to rules.

The third issue in integrity testing is the degree of predictive validity of such procedures. The use of the polygraph as a valid screening device has not been demonstrated (Murphy, 1993). Most early reviews of the validity of paper-and-pencil integrity tests were highly critical (e.g., Sackett & Decker, 1979; Sackett & Harris, 1984), but later reviews have been more positive (e.g., Ones, Chockalingam, & Schmidt, 1995). It seems that these paper-and-pencil tests are useful in predicting the broad construct of overall job performance but not necessarily the narrow constructs of honesty or theft in the workplace.

The fourth issue is the administration and use of integrity tests. These are perhaps the most odious of the problems with integrity testing. Ethical standards of test use have stressed the importance of informed consent as well as informing test takers of the scores and the use to which those scores will be put. However, organizations are not always honest (surprising, given that these are honesty tests!) with job applicants about what is being assessed, how the applicant did on the test, and whether or not a hiring decision was based on the test performance.

Be cautious in overinterpreting the results of integrity tests. The marketing of such tools is often far too zealous, with promises made that cannot be met (e.g., Kay, 1991), and there are many remaining questions about the proper use of such instruments (Lilienfeld, Alliger, & Mitchell, 1995). It is wise to adhere to appropriate testing standards when developing or considering using such instruments, and a good source of information for these guidelines as they pertain to this issue is the *Model Guidelines for Preemployment Integrity Testing Programs* (Association of Personnel Test Publishers, 1990).

Computerized Testing

Computers have had a large impact on how tests can be administered. An important contribution of the computer is called computer adaptive testing (CAT). CAT is being widely adopted in tests of achievement and aptitude. In a CAT situation, often a small set—perhaps two or three—of midlevel difficulty locator items are given to all test takers. Depending on whether the individual passes or fails the items, subsequent items are presented that better match the test taker's ability level. So, if I fail all of the first locator items, the next item I get will be easier than the locator items. If I pass them all, I will be presented with a harder item. If I pass one and fail the others, I will be presented with an item at about the same difficulty as the locator items. Thus, whereas traditional tests present all test takers with the same items, in CAT, each test taker gets, in essence, a different test, one that is customized to his or her own ability level.

One valuable outcome of the CAT process is that a computer adaptive test is often shorter than a traditional test because fewer items are needed to determine test taker ability level. Thus, computer adaptive tests also take less time to administer. The ability level of the test taker is often very precisely determined using CAT because more items are presented at the test taker's individual capability level. In a more traditional testing situation, the test taker is presented with items that will be too easy and too difficult.

Developing such tests takes tremendous amounts of resources. Item characteristics must be determined, and each item must be highly reliable to be included in the test item bank. To carry out the item analyses properly, thousands of cases are needed to have stable item parameter estimates. Therefore, it is not surprising that the large testing corporations are the ones most likely to develop CAT capacity in test delivery.

Coaching, Testwiseness, and Retakes

Because of the high stakes involved in the results of test scores (e.g., acceptance into a particular university, entrance into medical school, obtaining of employment, etc.), questions arise as to whether or not intensive training courses for improving test scores are worth the resources. These courses focus on providing exposure to similar types of items as those found on the test. There have been many studies examining this issue, and the preponderance of the evidence suggests that short-term, intense training does not significantly improve achievement test scores (Bond, 1989; College Entrance Examination Board, 1971; Donlon, 1984; Owen, 1985; Powers, 1986, 1993; Slack & Porter, 1980; Wigdor & Garner, 1982a, 1982b). Murphy and Davidshofer (2001) summarize this debate well by stating, "Those individuals who are most apt to benefit from coaching or tutoring are those whose academic skills are rusty or nonexistent" (p. 409). Instead, those who want to do well on tests of general verbal and math abilities should hone those skills over several years of challenging courses in formal school settings.

Setting aside coaching for the moment, there is a construct of "testwiseness" that should not be overlooked. For students in typical high school, college, or university settings, tests are part of their everyday world. As students become familiar with taking tests, they become "wise" as to how to prepare for and perform on the test. Some ways to be testwise include the following suggestions. If old tests are available for reviewing, get hold of them as they will provide an excellent preview of what types of questions will likely be on the next test. Take your time to carefully read the instructions to make sure that you answer what is being asked. Make sure you know how much time is being given. Be informed about whether there will be a penalty for guessing. If an item is too difficult, skip over it and come back to it later. If there is extra time left at the end, take time to review your answers. Make sure you have had enough sleep and feel well on the day of the test.

Suppose someone does not do well on a test, such as the Graduate Record Examination (GRE) and wants to get into graduate school. Is it worth it to retake the test to improve the score? First, make sure that the source of the problem has been determined. If the person was ill, fatigued, or overly stressed on testing day, then the answer is, yes—take the test again as the score will likely improve when one feels one's best. Also, if the testing situation was very unfamiliar (e.g., the person had not taken a paper-and-pencil test for many years), he or she will likely do better the next time (American College Test Program, 1995). However, if none of the above is the case, and the person just thinks he or she will do better next time, the evidence suggests it would not be a useful way to spend time and money (Wilson, 1989).

Testing Legislation

Title VII of the Civil Rights Act passed in 1964 is one of the most important pieces of legislation as it pertains to testing. It was revised in 1972 as the Equal

Employment Opportunity Act, and the Equal Employment Opportunity Coordinating Council (EEOCC) was created. The EEOCC released a set of guidelines in 1973 that dealt with fair employment selection procedures. These were revised in 1978 and state that the procedures used to select employees cannot include any practice that has adverse impact on any identifiable demographic subgroup.

So what is adverse impact? It is operationally defined as the four-fifths rule. This rule states that a selection rate that is less than 4/5 (80%) of the rate for the group with the highest selection rate will be regarded as adverse impact. So, for example, if 50% of all female applicants are hired, then at least 4/5 of 50% (40%) of the male applicants must also be hired. Assume that 100 women applied for nursing positions and 50 were hired. Now assume that 10 men applied for the nursing positions. Using the 4/5 rule, at least 4 of them (40% of 10) would need to be hired to ensure that adverse impact was not occurring.

The EEOCC has also put forward guidelines regarding their expectations of demonstrating test validity. They outlined them as content validity, construct validity, and criterion-related validity. In addition, in 1980, sexual harassment guidelines were added. In 1991, the Civil Rights Act was updated and passed into law, which reaffirmed the intentions of the original Act. In this update, the burden of proof for use of tests in personnel decision making clearly rested with the employer. In addition, this Act effectively outlawed the use of differential cutoff scores for minority groups and thus shifted organizations away from using quota hiring systems.

In 1975, the Education for All Handicapped Children Act was passed. In doing so, the law guaranteed that all handicapped children have a publicly funded education (e.g., local schools). What this means is that individual educational plans have to be developed for each handicapped child. To determine whether an individual plan is warranted, tests have been used to assess the child's ability. These tests have to be reliable and valid and cannot discriminate against any group.

The Americans with Disabilities Act (1991) was passed to ensure that disabled individuals had access to workplaces and public areas. While not allowing for preferential treatment, it does require schools and employers to provide reasonable accommodation to those with physical and mental handicaps to allow them to compete for jobs and placements. Developing testing procedures that reasonably accommodate handicaps of varying types will continue to pose challenges for test developers and publishers.

The National Skills Standards Act was incorporated into the 1994 Goals 2000: Educate America Act. The purpose was to address the declining achievement test scores across the U.S. in the preceding two decades. This spurred debates about the utility of a national testing program in schools.

The New York Truth in Testing Law was passed in 1979. This law requires that testing companies provide all studies on test validation (both the positive and negative ones); provide information on how test scores are calculated and what the test scores mean; and also provide a copy of the test questions, correct answers, and student answers to their test. While the first two are not a concern for test developers, the third compromises the security of any test bank. After having just spent many hours reviewing the first ten chapters of this book, you have some idea of how much time and effort goes into test item creation. When items are compromised, then new ones must be created and the cost is passed on to the test takers.

While laws and acts codify the political desires of the day, it is in court decisions where interpretation comes into play, and these have long-ranging consequences for subsequent court decisions. Most often, these cases occur when definable demographic subgroups or individuals from a definable demographic subgroup bring legal action against an organization or institution.

While all the cases associated with these interpretive decisions cannot be discussed here, a listing of some of the more relevant ones for education and employment settings are provided in Tables 11.1 and 11.2. The take-home messages from the rulings are that the court rulings vary from jurisdiction to jurisdiction, vary across time, and vary depending on the political climate of the day. Given the recent dates of some of the cases, it seems that the legal battles are far from being over. Thus, hard-and-fast rules are not easy to come up with regarding test use. Instead, it is best to be prudent in ensuring that the tests one uses have been demonstrated to have good psychometric properties and the scores are being used appropriately for the situation.

Due diligence and a careful, thoughtful decision-making process goes a long way in defending one's position in using a particular test score. It is part of the professional responsibility of those working in the testing industry in any capacity to remain current on relevant legislation and court rulings.

Test Item Bias and Adverse Impact

From the preceding information about laws, acts, and court rulings, there is a clear need for test developers to be sensitive to the potential problem of adverse impact. While statistics are brought to bear on differences, the overall test scores or the differential selection rates of individuals from identifiable subgroups by themselves do not constitute a biased test. If the items, however, behave differently across groups, then measurement bias is said to occur and the items are not equivalent for different groups.

The demonstration of test item bias must occur by first taking into account the ability level of the test taker. For example, let's say three of my family members and I want to try out for the Olympic Team in the sport of 100-meter dash. We all continually fail to meet the minimum requirement for speed. Should we then claim that the test (time and the timer) is unreliable or invalid and thus discriminates against the Kline clan? Probably not. The reason we can't get on the 100-meter dash team is because we do not have the ability to do so.

This is quite a blatant example that may seem far-fetched. However, the principle is the same in a testing situation; group differences in test scores are not in and of themselves indications of test bias. First, the ability level of the test takers must be partialled out. So, how does one do this? Two techniques will be demonstrated. The first uses χ^2 statistics. This is suitable with small samples and a small set of items. The calculations are straightforward and are easily explained and understood. The other approach uses the item response theory (IRT) and item

Table 11.1   Educational Legislation Affecting the Testing Community

Case	Date	Issue
Plessy v. Ferguson	1896	Schools could remain segregated but the quality of the schools must be equal.
Brown v. Board of Education	1954	Overturned the Plessy v. Ferguson decision by ruling schools must provide nonsegregated schools for African American and white children.
Stell v. Savannah-Chatham County Board of Education	1963	Because IQs of black children were lower than white children, requiring them to integrate in the same schools would be disadvantageous to both groups. This ruling was later overturned.
Hobson v. Hansen	1967	Group ability tests discriminate against minority children and thus could not be used to assign children to different learning tracks.
Diana v. State Board of Education	1970	Traditional testing procedures could not be used to place Mexican American children in educable mentally retarded classes in California. Special procedures (i.e., bilingual) had to be used to test these minority children.
Guadalupe v. Mesa Elementary School District	1972	Minority children must be tested in their primary language. In addition, IQ scores have to be at least two standard deviations below the mean and there must be other indicators (e.g., behavioral measures) corroborating the decision as to the mental capacity of the child.
Regents of the University of California v. Bakke	1978	Minority group members with lower test scores were admitted to medical school under a quota system; the university had to admit Bakke. The ruling implied that the use of differential cutoff scores was not appropriate, but it acknowledged that race could be taken into account in selection decisions.
Larry P. v. Wilson Riles	1979	IQ tests denied five black plaintiffs equal protection under the law. In 1986, all black children were banned from being tested with IQ tests to place them in educable mentally retarded classes in California. Note that this did not include a ban on testing for white, Latino(a), Asian American, or Native American children. In 1992, the same judge lifted the ban, in effect reversing his earlier decision.

(Continued)

Table 11.1 (Continued)

Case	Date	Issue
Debra P. v. Turlington	1979	Ruled that an absolute minimum standard was expected for obtaining a high school diploma and the test was not discriminatory. However, the ruling suspended use of high school competency exit examinations for four years until those minority students who had attended segregated high schools had graduated.
Parents in Action on Special Education (PASE) v. Joseph P. Hannon	1980	IQ tests, when used in conjunction with the statutorily mandated other criteria for determining an appropriate educational program for a child, do not discriminate against black children.
Brookhart v. Illinois State Board of Education	1983	Disabled students were not passing minimum competency examinations. Ruling that students be provided more time, but that the test content did not have to be modified.
Marchall v. Georgia	1984, 1985	Allowed the use of tests to assist in determining whether students should be placed into educable mentally retarded or learning disabled classes.
Georgia State Conferences Branches of NAACP v. State of Georgia	1985	Ruled that intelligence tests do not discriminate against black children.
Crawford et al. v. Honig et al.	1994	Black child denied access to IQ testing for possible placement into an educable mentally retarded class in California based on race.
Barbara Grutter v. Lee Bollinger et al.	2003	White female applicant to the University of Michigan's law school was denied entry and challenged the legality of using race and ethnicity for admission decisions. Supreme Court ruled that race was taken into account appropriately as individualized assessment for each case was carried out.
Jennifer Gratz et al. v. Lee Bollinger et al.	2003	White applicants to the University of Michigan's College of Literature, Science and Arts were denied entry and challenged the legality of using race and ethnicity for admission decisions. Supreme Court ruled that race was taken into account inappropriately without enough emphasis on a case-by-case, individualized assessment.

Table 11.2   Employment Legislation Affecting the Testing Community

Case	Date	Issue
Griggs v. Duke Power Company	1971	Employment practices (e.g., selection tests) have a demonstrated relationship to job performance.
Albemarle Paper Co. v. Moody	1975	Company's testing program was inadequate because although the test was valid, it still had adverse impact.
Washington v. Davis	1976	Expanded the validation criteria for tests to include performance in job training programs.
Detroit Police v. Young	1979	Supported the use of race as an important part of the selection decision-making process.
Connecticut v. Teal	1982	All parts of a selection process must be valid.
Golden Rule Insurance Company et al. v. Washburn et al.	1984	Insurance company sued Educational Testing Service (ETS) because the test they developed had a cultural bias. It was settled out of court. ETS did change the test items.
Allen v. Alabama State Board of Education	1985	Board of Education agreed to use only test items where the black vs. white proportion of correct answers did not differ by more than 0.05.
Watson v. Fort Worth Bank and Trust	1988	Not just tests but other, less objective, selection processes (e.g., job interviews) also must be validated and be free of adverse impact.
Wards Cove Packing Co. v. Antonio et al.	1989	Burden of proof shifted from employer to employee to demonstrate tests used are not reliable and valid. This led to the Civil Rights Act of 1991, which overruled the decision but did outlaw use of differential cutoff scores.
Adarand Constructors, Inc. v. Pena, Secretary of Transport, et al.	1995	Ended the practice of giving primary contractors an economic incentive (through federal contracts) to subcontract to small businesses controlled by minority group members.
Association of Mexican-American Educators v. California	1996	Allowed the use of a well-constructed test that had the effect of excluding a disproportionate number of minority teachers from being certified.
Petit v. City of Chicago	2003	Supported the use of race as an important part of the promotion decision-making process.

characteristic curve approach. It is complex to use, needs hundreds of cases and at least 20 or so items to generate stable estimates of item differences, and requires care in the interpretation of the computer printouts. However, in the end, it is very elegant and parsimonious.

Although test-item bias may be of interest for some attitudinal tests, by far the most common interest of researchers, practitioners, and policy decision-makers has to do with the potential of bias in tests of ability where the stakes are high. Most of these tests are of the correct/incorrect variety, so for both examples presented, tests that require a dichotomous (correct or incorrect) response will be used.

χ^2 *Approach to Item Bias Assessment.* The probability that a particular group of test takers, within a defined band of ability, will pass an item forms the basis of the most common χ^2 method of assessing test item bias (Marascuilo & Slaughter, 1981). An item is considered unbiased if those from definable demographic sub-groups (e.g., male/female, English-speaking/non-English speaking, etc.) have equal probabilities of passing an item if they have equal ability levels. A χ^2 goodness-of-fit index is used to determine whether there is a significant difference in the pass rates of different groups with similar ability levels.

The procedure is relatively straightforward. First, the group takes all of the test items. Then the ability levels are defined by using the total number of items correct. Those with more items correct are defined to have more ability.

Once the levels are established, each participant falls into an overall ability level. Depending on the distribution of passing rates for each item, the ability levels may have to be shifted to ensure that there are a reasonable number of cases for each cell. While it would be great to have each participant stay in the same ability level for all item analyses, this is usually only possible when the sample size is fairly large.

Tables for each item are then created, such that ability level is crossed with group and the cell entries are the number of individuals from each group and ability level that pass each item. Then χ^2 tests are run for each item at each ability level to determine if there is a significant difference between observed and expected frequencies of those expected to pass the item. If the test is significant, then this is evidence of test item bias at a particular ability level or levels.

Some methodological issues in this type of analysis include how many participants are needed and how many ability levels there should be. The two issues are really interconnected. The number of ability levels is partly determined by logic and partly by administrative convenience. If the sample size of participants is large, then finer-grained ability levels can be created. However, a χ^2 is calculated at each ability level, and if there are many levels, this process can become tedious quite quickly. At the very least, four ability levels should be used. For the Pearson χ^2, usually it is helpful to have at least 10–20 entries per cell. If the sample size is small, then collapsing ability levels into a fewer number may be warranted to ensure stability of the results.

It will be most helpful to go through an example next. Let's say the demographic groups of males ($N = 400$) and females ($N = 600$) take a 10-item test of geography. Four ability levels are created: those who got 0–2 correct, 3–4 correct, 5–6 correct, and 7–10 correct (lowest, low, high, and highest). Table 11.3 shows the distribution of ability levels for each sex over the entire test.

Table 11.3   Ability Levels for the Entire Geography Test for 400 Males and 600 Females

Ability Level (Score Interval)	Males	Females	Row Total
Highest (7–10)	50	100	150
High (5–6)	200	150	350
Low (3–4)	100	250	350
Lowest (0–2)	50	100	150
Column Total	400	600	1000

The next step is to examine the performance of each of the demographic groups by ability level for Item 1 of the test. The number of individuals who made correct and incorrect responses to Item 1 is shown in Tables 11.4 and 11.5. In addition, the proportion of participants at each ability level, regardless of demographic group, who made a correct or incorrect response is also indicated.

Table 11.4   Obtained Frequencies of Males and Females Giving Correct Responses to Item 1 of the Geography Test

Ability Level (Score Interval)	Males	Females	Row Total	Overall Proportion Correct
Highest (7–10)	40	90	130	130/150 = 0.87
High (5–6)	120	140	260	260/350 = 0.74
Low (3–4)	80	100	180	180/350 = 0.51
Lowest (0–2)	5	30	35	35/150 = 0.23
Column Total	245	360	605	605/1000 = 0.605

Table 11.5   Obtained Frequencies of Males and Females Giving Incorrect Responses to Item 1 of the Geography Test

Ability Level (Score Interval)	Males	Females	Row Total	Overall Proportion In correct
Highest (7–10)	10	10	20	20/150 = 0.13
High (5–6)	80	10	90	90/350 = 0.26
Low (3–4)	20	150	170	170/350 = 0.49
Lowest (0–2)	45	70	115	115/150 = 0.77
Column Total	155	240	395	395/1000 = 0.395

Overall, these tables show that 60.5% of the individuals made a correct response to the item. Those with a higher percentage of correct responses are at the higher ability levels compared to the lower ability levels. The next step is to generate the expected frequencies for each sex and ability level for correct and incorrect responses. To do so, take the number of examinees in each group at each ability level and multiply that number by the overall proportion making a correct response. Then do the same thing but this time use the overall proportion making an incorrect response. In this way, 2×2 contingency tables for each ability level for this item can be built. Tables 11.6 and 11.7 show these generated expected frequencies.

Table 11.6   Expected Frequencies of Males and Females Giving Correct Responses to Item 1 of the Geography Test

Ability Level (Score Interval)	Males	Females
Highest (7–10)	$0.87 \times 50 = 43.5$	$0.87 \times 100 = 87$
High (5–6)	$0.74 \times 200 = 148$	$0.74 \times 150 = 111$
Low (3–4)	$0.51 \times 100 = 51$	$0.51 \times 250 = 127.5$
Lowest (0–2)	$0.23 \times 50 = 11.5$	$0.23 \times 100 = 23$

Table 11.7   Expected Frequencies of Males and Females Giving Incorrect Responses to Item 1 of the Geography Test

Ability Level (Score Interval)	Males	Females
Highest (7–10)	$0.13 \times 50 = 6.5$	$0.13 \times 100 = 13$
High (5–6)	$0.26 \times 200 = 52$	$0.26 \times 150 = 39$
Low (3–4)	$0.49 \times 100 = 49$	$0.49 \times 250 = 122.5$
Lowest (0–2)	$0.77 \times 50 = 38.5$	$0.77 \times 100 = 77$

The next step is to create four 2×2 tables with the observed and expected frequencies and calculate the χ^2 value associated with the table. The degrees of freedom for each test will be $(\text{rows} - 1) \times (\text{columns} - 1)$ and thus equal to 1. In addition, the alpha level must be set a priori using a Bonferroni correction for family-wise error rate. This means that if the conventional 0.05 α-level is used, and four contingency tables are going to the analyzed, the corrected familywise α-level will be 0.05/4, or 0.0125. With one degree of freedom at $\alpha = 0.0125$, the critical value for χ^2 to exceed is 6.25. Tables 11.8–11.11 show the 2 × 2 tables, and the calculation of observed versus expected frequencies. Recall that the formula for the χ^2 is

$$(3-2) \qquad \chi^2 = \Sigma[(O_{ij} - E_{ij})^2/E_{ij}]$$

where O_{ij} = the observed frequencies for each cell and E_{ij} = the expected frequencies for each cell.

Table 11.8 χ^2 Table for Highest Ability Level for Item 1 of the Geography Test

	Males	*Females*
Correct	Obtained = 40 Expected = 43.5	Obtained = 90 Expected = 87
Incorrect	Obtained = 10 Expected = 6.5	Obtained = 10 Expected = 13

$$\chi^2 = [(40 - 43.5)^2/43.5] + [(90 - 87)^2/87] + [(10 - 6.5)^2/6.5] + [(10 - 13)^2/13]$$
$$= 0.28 + 0.10 + 1.88 + 0.69$$
$$= 2.95 \text{ (not significant)}$$

Table 11.9 χ^2 Table for High Ability Level for Item 1 of the Geography Test

	Males	*Females*
Correct	Obtained = 120 Expected = 148	Obtained = 140 Expected = 111
Incorrect	Obtained = 80 Expected = 52	Obtained = 10 Expected = 39

$$\chi^2 = [(120 - 148)^2/148] + [(140 - 111)^2/111]^2 + [(80 - 52)^2/52] + [(10 - 39)^2/39]$$
$$= 5.30 + 7.58 + 15.08 + 21.56$$
$$= 49.52 \text{ (significant)}$$

The results indicate that this item is biased at three of the four ability levels. Interestingly, at the high ability level, females were advantaged insofar as there were more females in the correct category than would be expected by chance and, conversely, more males were in the incorrect category than would be expected by chance. At the low ability level, males were advantaged, and at the lowest ability level, females were advantaged.

Table 11.10 χ^2 Table for Low Ability Level for Item 1 of the Geography Test

	Males	Females
Correct	Obtained = 80 Expected = 51	Obtained = 100 Expected = 127.5
Incorrect	Obtained = 20 Expected = 49	Obtained = 150 Expected = 122.5

$$\chi^2 = [(80 - 51)^2/51] + [(100 - 127.5)^2/127.5] + [(20 - 49)^2/49]$$
$$+ [(150 - 122.5)^2/122.5]$$
$$= 16.49 + 5.93 + 17.16 + 6.17$$
$$= 45.75 \text{ (significant)}$$

Table 11.11 χ^2 Table for Lowest Ability Level for Item 1 of the Geography Test

	Males	Females
Correct	Obtained = 5 Expected = 11.5	Obtained = 30 Expected = 23
Incorrect	Obtained = 45 Expected = 38.5	Obtained = 70 Expected = 77

$$\chi^2 = [(5 - 11.5)^2/11.5] + [(30 - 23)^2/23] + [(45 - 38.5)^2/38.5] + [(70 - 77)^2/77]$$
$$= 3.67 + 2.13 + 1.10 + 0.64$$
$$= 7.54 \text{ (significant)}$$

Item Bias Detection Using IRT. DIF stands for differential item functioning and uses IRT as a starting point. Because much of the IRT terms and programming were covered in previous chapters, this material will not be reviewed here again. Only the additional information pertinent to DIF analysis is presented. DIF is said to occur when individuals who have the same underlying trait level but come from different subgroups do not have the same probability of obtaining a correct response on the item.

The approach begins by running the DIF routine, which requests that item difficulty (*b* level) parameters be specified for each subgroup separately. The slopes (discriminations) are held constant across groups, and no guessing parameters are estimated. That is, a 1PL model as described in Chapter 6 will be used. In addition, one group is named the *reference* group (usually the majority group) and the other group is the *focal* group. After the analysis is run, the overall fit value is noted; this is the −2 log likelihood value.

Then, another 1PL model IRT analysis is run with all subgroups combined. Another fit value (−2 log likelihood) is generated for this second analysis. The fit will be degraded (i.e., the −2 log likelihood value will be larger) in the second analysis because the same item parameters are used for all subgroups combined rather than separately. If the difference between the likelihood values is not significant, then this means overall the fit across all items is not degraded significantly, and the conclusion is that no DIF occurs. The difference between the fit indices is distributed as a χ^2, and the degrees of freedom used to test the difference is the number of constrained parameters. In the case of a one-parameter model, the degrees of freedom will be equal to the number of items.

If there is evidence of DIF, the next step is to reexamine the output from the first analysis in more detail to determine if all of the items are biased or just some of them. In addition, check whether the bias favors one group consistently or favors one group with some items and the other group with other items.

A fictitious example is presented next to demonstrate how DIF would be carried out based on an output of the computer program BILOG-MG 3 (Zimowski, Muraki, Mislevy, & Bock, 2003). Assume a 20-item test of adult world geography knowledge is administered to a group of 1,000 randomly selected 20- to 30-year-old people in the United States. Further assume that, of these 1,000, 300 did not speak English as their first language. So, the referent group is the 700 English-as-first-language test takers and the focal group is the 300 non-English-as-first-language test takers.

The data would be set up in as in Table 11.12. Note that each row represents one case. The first four columns of each row comprise the case identification number. This is followed by a space, which is then followed by a 1 when the case belongs to the referent group and a 2 when the case belongs to the focal group. The data must be entered this way into the program, with all cases that make up the referent group listed sequentially together followed by a listing of all cases of

Table 11.12   Data For DIF Analysis

```
0001 1 11111100001111000101
0002 1 11110101001100100101
0003 1 10011100001001000001
0004 1 10100101001100100101
0005 1 11111100111010001011

              .

              .

              .

              .

              .


              .

0996 2 10011100001111011101
0997 2 10110101000111100101
0998 2 11111101101111000101
0999 2 10110101001100100101
1000 2 11001100000111001101
```

the focal group. There is another space, followed by the 20 test items. Note that the default approach is used, where 1 means a correct response and 0 is an incorrect response.

The control language from the programs where the group item parameters are estimated separately and then combined is shown in Box 11.1. The final –2 log likelihood value for the separate estimation was equal to 17561.027. The output for the entire sample combined yielded a final –2 log likelihood value of 17673.573. The difference between this value and the value obtained when the groups were estimated separately is 112.546 (17673.573 – 17561.027) and is distributed as a χ^2. With 20 degrees of freedom at an alpha level of 0.05, the critical value to exceed is 31.410. Thus, the difficulty parameters estimated separately for each group provide a significantly better fit of the model to the data than combining the groups (i.e., DIF is occurring).

Now, return to the first output where the groups were analyzed separately, and DIF was run to determine which of the items are functioning differentially and in favor of which group. Selected parts of this output are shown in Box 11.2. It is interesting to note that, of the six items that were shown in the output, one was significantly biased in favor of the English group and one in favor of the non-English group.

This highlights the importance of investigating each item before claiming that there is bias if the overall difference in the –2 log likelihood value suggests DIF is occurring. In addition, Drasgow and Hulin (1990) advise against rejecting or revising biased items out-of-hand just because evidence of DIF has been found. An examination of all the items needs to be carried out and, if they are consistently biased in favor of one group, then revisions may be necessary. However, if the biased items "cancel each other out," then serious measurement bias is not a reasonable conclusion. They argue that evaluation of measurement bias be made at the overall test level, as that is the level at which decisions about individuals are made.

Translation Issues

Translating scales into other languages has become more and more of an issue as globalization and cross-cultural awareness continues to grow. A good review of various test translation procedures has been written by Buchner and Mayr (1999). The quality of the translation of a scale has dramatic effects on how valid the scores are that are attached to that translated version. There have been guidelines published about translation, but they are rather abstract. For example, van de Vijer and Hambleton (1996) say, "Instrument developers/publishers should implement systematic judgmental evidence, both linguistic and psychological, to improve the accuracy of the translation/adaptation process and compile evidence of the equivalence of all language versions" (p. 94).

The easiest, most frequently used, and worst approach is to simply translate the scale from one language into another (e.g., from English to Spanish)—called direct translation (van de Vijver & Tanzer, 1997). A better approach is to use back-translation. In this instance, the original scale (English) is translated by one person

(Text continues on page 311)

Box 11.1 Control Language and Selected Output for DIF Analysis Using BILOG-MG

DIF Analysis of 20 Geography Items With 1,000 Cases

300 did not learn English as their first language

> Global Nparm = 1, Dfname = 'Geography.Dat';

> Length Nitems = (20);

> Input Ntot = 20, Ngroups = 2, Dif, Nidchar = 4;

> Items Inames = (Geog1(1)Geog20), Inum = (1(1)20);

> Test Tname = Geography;

> Group1 Gname = English;

> Group2 Gname = Nonenglish;

(4a1,1×,I1,1×,20a1)

> Calib Reference = 1;

The control language used for multiple group DIF analysis is shown first. The first two lines are the title lines. The third line is the *global* command and indicates that this is a one-parameter model (item difficulty only), and that the data can be found in a file called "geography.dat" that is in the same directory (folder) as the control language. The *length* command indicates that there are 20 items in the data set to be analyzed. The *input* command line indicates the number of items in total, how many groups there are, that a DIF analysis is to be carried out, and that there are four columns that identify each case. The *items* command indicates that the items are to be named Geog1 to Geog20 and that the numbers are to be 1 to 20, respectively. The *test* command indicates what the test as a whole is to be called. The two *group* commands indicate that the first group is the English language group and the second group is the non-English language group. The next line is a fortran statement that indicates to the program how to read the data—4A1 means that the first four columns are the ways to identify each case, 1X indicates a space, I1 indicates that the next column is the place to find the group to which each case belongs, 1X again indicates a space, and, finally, 20A1 indicates that the next 20 columns are the data for the item responses. Last, the *calib* command indicates that the reference group is the one coded 1 (English speakers). Note that there is no *score* command as there was in Chapter 6. This is because no scoring is carried out with the DIF analysis.

Control Language For Combined Analysis

Combined Analysis of 20 Geography Items With 1000 Cases

300 did not learn English as their first language

> Global Nparm = 1, Dfname = 'Geography.Dat';

> Length Nitems = (20);

> Input Ntot = 20, Nidchar = 4;

> Items Inames = (Geog1(1)Geog20), Inum = (1(1)20);

> Test Tname = Geography;

(4a1,1×,I1,1×,20a1)

> Calib;

Next, the control language is used for a single group analysis with the same data set. Recall that we need the −2 log likelihood value produced in this analysis. The differences are (a) a small change in the title line, (b) on the *input* line, Ngroups = 2 and *DIF* are removed, (c) there are no *group* command lines, and (d) on the *calib* line, there is no *reference = 1*. While there could have been a *score* command in this program, it will not serve our purpose here.

Box 11.2 Selected Output for DIF Analysis Using BILOG-MG

Model For Group Differential Item Functioning

Group 1: English; Item Parameters After Cycle: 11

Model For Group Differential Item Functioning Group 1: English; Item Parameters After Cycle: 11			
Item	Slope	Threshold	Asymptote
	S.E.	S.E.	S.E.
Geog01	0.875	0.321	0.000
	0.019*	0.124*	0.000*
Geog02	0.875	−0.080	0.000
	0.019*	0.122*	0.000*
Geog03	0.875	−0.231	0.000
	0.019*	0.313*	0.000*
Geog18	0.875	−1.004	0.000
	0.019*	0.214*	0.000*
Geog19	0.875	0.090	0.000
	0.019*	0.142*	0.000*
Geog20	0.875	−0.201	0.000
	0.019*	0.182*	0.000*

Note: The asterisk marks the standard error scores.

Group 2: Nonengl; Item Parameters After Cycle: 11			
Item	Slope	Threshold	Asymptote
	S.E.	S.E.	S.E.
Geog01	0.875	0.198	0.000
	0.019*	0.362*	0.000*
Geog02	0.875	−0.233	0.000
	0.019*	0.310*	0.000*
Geog03	0.875	0.211	0.000
	0.019*	0.223*	0.000*

Group 2: Nonengl; Item Parameters After Cycle: 11			
Item	Slope	Threshold	Asymptote
Geog18	0.875	−0.324	0.000
	0.019*	0.114*	0.000*
Geog19	0.875	0.080	0.000
	0.019*	0.212*	0.000*
Geog20	0.875	−0.614	0.000
	0.019*	0.132*	0.000*

Note: The asterisk marks the standard error scores.

Parameter	Mean	Stn. Dev.
Group: 1; Number Of Items: 20		
Threshold	−0.726	0.856
Group: 2; Number Of Items: 20		
Threshold	−0.318	0.998

Threshold Means	
Group	Adjusted Value
1	0.000
2	0.408

Model For Group Differential Item Functioning:

Adjusted Threshold Means		
Item	Group 1	Group 2
Geog01	0.321	−0.210
Geog02	−0.080	−0.641
Geog03	−0.231	−0.179
Geog18	−1.004	−0.732
Geog19	0.090	−0.328
Geog20	−0.201	−1.022

(Continued)

Box 11.2 (Continued)

Model For Group Differential Item Functioning:

Group Threshold Differences	
Item	Group 2 – 1
Geog01	–0.531
	0.482*
Geog02	–0.561
	0.223*
Geog03	0.052
	0.384*
Geog18	0.272
	0.109*
Geog19	–0.418
	0.231*
Geog20	–0.821
	0.532*

Note: The asterisk marks the standard error scores.

Means of the Latent (Ability) Distributions Of Groups	
Group	1
Mean	0.00000
S.D.	1.00000
Group	2
Mean	–0.32116
S.D.	0.93428

The item parameters for the two groups are estimated and printed separately. The slopes (*a*, item discrimination parameters) as well as their standard errors are all constrained to be equal across items and groups. In this example, all the slopes are 0.875 and their standard errors are 0.019. The asymptotes, or guessing parameters, are all constrained to equal zero.

The means and standard deviations for the two groups are then estimated. The difference between the means of these distributions is calculated. This step generates the difference in latent trait levels between the groups, and is used to adjust the item-level differences. In this example, the mean difficulty across items for the English group is – 0.726 and for the non-English group is – 0.318. This indicates that the English group is finding the items easier than the non-English group. The threshold mean for the reference group is adjusted to be equal to zero by adding + 0.726, and the focal group's threshold is adjusted by the same amount (+ 0.726) that was used to bring the reference group's threshold to zero. This makes the adjusted threshold for the focal group equal to 0.408 (– 0.318 + 0.726).

Then, each of the item's thresholds for the focal group is adjusted by the value of the latent trait adjusted threshold. In our case, this means that 0.408 is subtracted from each item threshold. For Geog01, the focal group's original item threshold was 0.198. When 0.408 is subtracted from that value, it results in an adjusted item threshold of −0.210. This same adjustment is made to each of the focal group's items. The original thresholds for the reference group and the adjusted thresholds for the focal group are reported. Although not shown, the standard errors of the item thresholds for each group remain the same regardless of being unadjusted and adjusted.

Next, each item's adjusted difficulty level for the focal group is subtracted from the unadjusted difficulty level for the reference group. The standard error of this difference is also calculated. For Geog01, the difference is − 0.210 − 3.21 = − 0.531. The items Geog01, Geog02, Geog19, and Geog20 are relatively easier for the non-English group than for the English group (i.e., the differences result in a negative value). Conversely, items Geog03 and Geog18 are relatively easier for the English group than for the non-English group (i.e., the differences result in a positive value).

To test whether the difference in item difficulties is significant is calculated by taking the difference and dividing it by its standard error. As these are parameter estimates, the significance level is based on the normal distribution, with ±1.96 (or 2 for rounding purposes) being the alpha level usually used. Thus, if the difference divided by its standard error is greater than 2.0, then DIF is said to occur for the item. In this example, Geog02 is significantly easier for the non-English group (−0.561/0.223 = 2.51) and Geog18 (0.272/0.109 = 2.49) is significantly easier for the English group. None of the other differences in the six items shown here are significant.

Finally, the estimated latent distributions of the groups' ability levels are given with the mean and standard deviation of the reference group being constrained to be 0 and 1 respectively. The difference between the means of the latent distributions of the participants provides an index as to whether the focal group demonstrates more or less of the latent trait than the reference group. In this example, the English group has a latent ability of 0.0 and the non-English group has a latent ability of −0.32, indicating that the English group has a higher group level of latent ability than does the non-English group.

into another language (Spanish), and then translated back from the other language (Spanish) into the original language (English) by a different person. Comparisons are made of the original and back-translated versions. Discrepancies in the translations have to be resolved and this may take considerable time and resources to carry out in a timely manner. In addition, the translators should have a clear idea of the construct of interest as well as excellent linguistic capabilities. A word used in some contexts for some samples may not be the same as another word in another context for another sample.

A double-translation process in back-translation occurs iteratively. That is, the back-translated version is modified to deal with the discrepancies, and then this new version is subjected to a translation–back-translation process. The iterations continue until equivalence has been met for not just one, but two versions of the scale. This is a very expensive and time-consuming process.

Merging is another process, where two bilingual individuals each produce a translation of a scale. Another bilingual person then merges the two translations into a single scale. This is more expensive than direct or back-translation.

Still another approach is a review, or group procedure, where a group of subject matter experts (SMEs) in the field examine the translation, discuss it with one another, and reconcile their differences until they come up with a single translated version that all of them agree on. Again, this is very expensive. Obviously, care must go into translating and adapting scales that will be used in other cultures.

Electronic Presentation and Capture

One issue facing many test developers and publishers is that of electronic capture—that is, the translation from traditional paper-and-pencil completion to online completion. The upsides are very obvious. There is a very fast turn-around time in the scoring and interpretation of scale scores for the respondents. Tests can be delivered to any geographic location as long as there is a computer hookup. Tests cannot get lost or go missing, and copying costs are reduced to almost zero. If the test is timed, this feature can be built into the computer program that administers the test. If the test is a power test, then people can take as much time as they need to complete the test without taking up an administrator's time. Computer-captured responses are less likely to suffer from errors such as misalignment of a response sheet to the question sheet or inaccuracies because the respondent used a pen rather than a pencil to complete the test. Double-responding (circling more than one answer) is not possible. The scale can be modified for some disabilities by changing font size.

The downsides are just as obvious. Because the test is taken in a nonproctored environment, the issue of who is actually taking the test is a concern. Hardware and software limitations may make some graphs and figures illegible or not appear at all. Simply getting the computer program to scroll through the test in a logical and coherent manner takes a lot of time and pilot testing. The decisions about whether the test taker can go back into past items has to be made and built into the program. Computer literacy variation may be an issue, depending on who will be taking the test.

Translation of a test into a different mode of responding requires a thoughtful and thorough review of the issues that may arise. Many of the concerns can be dealt with relatively quickly, and some may not be issues at all, depending on who will be taking the test and where. There has been a lot of research into the differences in mode of test taking (paper-and-pencil versus computer-based). In general, for power tests, mode of responding does not seem to have any systematic effects on test scores. However, it is worthwhile for test publishers to conduct equivalence research for their particular tests (American Educational Research Association, American Psychological Association, National Council on Measurement in Education, 1999; American Psychological Association, 2000). Test equivalence of traditional versus computer-administered tests can be shown by (a) having similar rank orders of test takers on both versions, (b) having similar means on both versions, and (c) having similar variances on both versions. Issues surrounding test taking on the Internet have been reviewed in several reports (Mead & Drasgow, 1993; Naglieri et al., 2004; Ployhart, Weekley, Holtz, & Kemp, 2003).

Summary

In this chapter, the issues that are of concern for professional test developers and users were reviewed. The topics included

1. codes of ethics and standards of practice for those involved in the testing profession;

2. issues in test administration, integrity testing, computerized testing, and coaching;

3. important legislation and court decisions for the testing community;

4. test item bias and examples of two alternative statistical methods for detecting item bias; and

5. the recently emerging issues of test translation into another language and/or electronic presentation.

Clearly, there are many issues that professionals in the testing business need to be aware of as they go about their day-to-day activities. Keeping abreast of the latest professional codes, relevant court decisions, and statistical technology are all part of being a competent psychometrician.

In the next and last chapter, several different tests will be described and evaluated. In addition, a summary of the topics covered and closing comments are made.

Problems and Exercises

1. Review the ethical standards associated with testing using the citations in the chapter.

2. What are the rights of the test taker?

3. What are the responsibilities of the test user?

4. What is meant by Level A, B, and C tests?

5. What are some of the ways that integrity has been measured?

6. What are some advantages of computer adaptive testing?

7. What is the general consensus on the findings regarding the usefulness of test coaching?

8. What does it mean to be testwise?

9. Why was Title VII of the Civil Rights Act such an important piece of legislation for the testing industry?

10. Assume 200 individuals applied for a job, and 20% of them were women. Of the men applicants, 30% were hired. How many women would have to be hired so that adverse impact against the women according to the 4/5 rule would not occur?

11. What did the 1991 Civil Rights Act do that had an impact on the testing industry?

12. What did the 1975 Education for All Handicapped Children Act do that had an impact on the testing industry?

13. What does the Americans with Disabilities Act of 1991 dictate?

14. Why was the National Skills Standards Act incorporated into the 1994 Goals 2000: Educate America Act?

15. Why are court decisions at least as important as legislation regarding the use of tests?

16. What is meant by a biased test?

17. Determine if the following test item (see Table 11.13) shows bias at the both the high and low ability levels using the χ^2 method.

Table 11.13   Number of Males and Females Giving Correct and Incorrect (in Brackets) Responses to an Item

Ability Level (Score Interval)	Males	Females	Row Total	Overall Proportion Correct (Incorrect)
High (6–10)	50(20)	50(10)	100(30)	100/130 = 0.769 (30/130 = 0.231)
Low (0–5)	10(50)	20(50)	30(100)	30/130 = 0.231 (100/130 = 0.769)
Column Total	60(70)	70(60)	130(130)	130/260 = 0.50 130/260 = 0.50

18. I want to use DIF analysis to determine if a 20-item test is biased based on respondent gender. The first analysis is run, which requests that the item parameters be estimated for each group separately, and a −2 log-likelihood value of 3,000 is obtained. A second analysis is run, which requests that the item parameters be estimated on both groups simultaneously, and a −2 log-likelihood value of 4,000 is obtained. What would be concluded?

Table 11.14 Sample Portions of a DIF Output for a 10-Item Test Where Item Bias Was Assessed for the Subgroups Males and Females

Threshold Means	
Group	Adjusted Value
1	0.000
2	0.300

Model For Group Differential Item Functioning:

Group Threshold Differences	
Item	Group 2 – 1
Item 01	−0.500
	0.400*
Item 02	−0.600
	0.390*
Item 03	0.070
	0.300*
Item 04	−0.700
	0.400*
Item 05	−1.700
	0.400*
Item 06	1.300
	0.500*
Item 07	−0.400
	0.408*
Item 08	0.500
	0.350*
Item 09	0.600
	0.400*
Item 10	0.500
	0.300*

Note: The asterisk marks the standard error scores.

Table 11.14 (Continued)

Means of the Latent (Ability) Distributions of Groups	
Group	1
Mean	0.00000
S.D.	1.00000
Group	2
Mean	−0.11000
S.D.	0.98765

19. Assume a 10-item test shows evidence of DIF. The preceding output (see Table 11.14) is generated. What would the conclusions be about the test item bias if Group 1 was men and Group 2 was women?

20. What is the back-translation method of translating test items?

21. What are the pros and cons of having traditional paper-and-pencil tests administered electronically?

CHAPTER 12

Brief Reviews of Some Selected Tests and Concluding Comments

Th   his chapter examines several different types of tests in different domains. Rather than the exhaustive approach to this task adopted by many traditional testing textbooks, the purpose here is to briefly review a few tests (with the expectation that interested readers will pursue examining tests that are of interest to them) rather than attempting to provide a summary of the hundreds of tests available for use. Specifically, where and how to extract test information will be reviewed. Then, some well-known tests of intelligence, achievement, structured personality, and career interest/guidance will be presented. Finally, a quick review of the book's topics and some concluding thoughts will wind up the chapter.

Information About Existing Tests

The *Mental Measurements Yearbook* (MMY) is one of the most utilized sources of information about existing tests. The first edition was written in 1938 by Oscar Buros. Over the next 40 years, Buros published seven additional such yearbooks. These set the standard for evaluation and critical assessment of tests and, in 1981, the Oscar K. Buros Center was established to continue the tradition of publishing the MMY. The most recent edition (*Fifteenth Mental Measurements Yearbook*) was edited by Plake, Impara, and Spies (2003). In addition, a Web site is available where reviews of specific tests can be accessed for a price (www.unl.edu/buros).

In each of the *Yearbooks,* several tests are evaluated by subject matter experts (SMEs) who have no conflict of interest regarding the test's use. Information such as administration time, cost, publisher, and so forth is also provided. The objectivity of the reviews provides the consumer of the information a powerful tool by which to assess the usefulness of a test for a specific purpose. Not all tests are evaluated in each MMY, and thus the Web site is of particular use insofar as reviews (both current as well as older ones) are available for perusal. Other test reviews are provided in *Test Critiques* (Keyser & Sweetland, 1984–1994). Journals that were noted in Chapter 2 often carry reviews and validation studies of specific tests.

Another source of information about tests is *Tests in Print* (the 6th edition is the most current, edited by Murphy, Plake, Impara, & Spies, 2002), which is also published by the Buros Center. It is a bibliography of all commercially available tests in the English language that are currently in print. This is helpful if you are looking for a test of a particular construct but do not have any leads on what tests might be available. The construct tested, administration issues, and where test reviews in the MMY can be found are all part of this catalogue.

Perhaps the fastest way to locate a test and/or obtain test reviews is through the World Wide Web. Test locator services can be accessed via www.unl.edu/buros, and www.ets.org. PsycINFO, PsycLIT, and ERIC searches pull up tests used in all types of research. The periodically updated *Directory of Unpublished Experimental Measures* (Goldman & Mitchell, 2002) provides another resource. The experimental measures in this source are not commercially available but have been used by researchers and are often available at low or no cost.

Next, reviews of some well-known tests that are commercially available are presented. This section might be particularly helpful to those who have been asked to write test reviews. How to organize such a review and the type of information expected in a review are provided through these examples.

Some Intelligence Tests

The term *intelligence* has caused much controversy in the literature. However, it is generally agreed that tests purporting to measure this construct assess general mental ability. An assumption of all general intelligence tests is that some individuals are better able to benefit and learn from experience than are others and that these individuals have higher levels of general mental ability. The reviews are confined to two major commercially available intelligence tests. Strong theoretical frameworks have guided the development of these tests and given rise to the administration and scoring procedures used.

Stanford-Binet Intelligence Tests. Alfred Binet was a psychologist who was contracted by the French government to develop a tool to identify mentally retarded children in the Paris public school system. He believed that intelligence was manifested by performance on tasks. He also emphasized reasoning, judgment, and understanding in the development of test items. Because the context in which he was working was the school system, most of the items he developed for the test were academic in nature. The term *items* is used loosely insofar as the items he created were tasks.

Binet and his colleague, Theodore Simon, created 30 tasks initially and, by 1908, had revised and added to the tasks so that they numbered 58. They arranged these from least to most difficult and grouped them into age-level tasks with the levels ranging from 3 to 13 years. A final version of the scale was created in 1911, with 54 tasks arranged in increasing order of difficulty for ages 3 to adult. Based on the number of tasks the test takers could complete, a "mental age" could be calculated for them. For example, tasks such as "shows right hand and left ear" is a task that is age-appropriate for a 7-year-old. Another example is that, by age 15, the respondent is expected to be able to repeat seven digits correctly in order.

In 1916, Lewis Terman at Stanford University translated and revised the 1911 version of the Simon-Binet tests; this version was called the Stanford-Binet Intelligence Scale. Like the previous tests, tasks were specific to an age level. The mental age of test takers was determined by how many of the tasks they could complete. The intelligence quotient (IQ) was calculated by taking the mental age (MA) and dividing it by the individual's chronological age (CA) and then multiplying by 100.

(12–1) $$IQ = MA/CA \times 100.$$

So, if a test taker were to pass at age 12 all the tasks associated with a 13-year-old, his or her IQ would be $(13/12) \times 100 = 108$. Those individuals with scores over 100 were presumed to have faster than average mental development and those with scores lower than 100 to have slower than average mental development. In this version of the test, the maximum mental age that could be assessed was 19.5, and thus anyone taking the test older than this age would, by definition, have an IQ of less than 100.

This early version was standardized on a nonrepresentative and small sample (1,000 white children and 400 adults in California), so, in 1937, the Stanford-Binet scale was revised. The new scale had new tasks added that extended the mental age range that could be determined from a low of 2 years to a high of 22 years and 10 months. New standards for normative performance were established using a much broader age sample (100 children at each 1/2 year age interval from ages 1-1/2 to 5-1/2, 200 children at each age year from 6 years to 14 years, and 100 children at each age year from 15 years to 18 years). The children came from 11 different states but again were native-born Caucasian. Two parallel forms of the test were developed (forms L and M), which was helpful in determining the psychometric properties of the test. Reliability coefficients were higher for older versus younger children and higher for those with lower rather than higher IQ scores. In addition, standard deviations of the IQ scores were greater at higher ages, making IQ scores non-equivalent across age groups.

A third edition was published in 1960 that updated the best items of the 1937 version. In 1972, another standardization occurred with a stratified national sample of 2,100 children that better reflected the U.S. population. A new manual for this third edition reported test-retest reliability coefficients of 0.90 and over, and moderate correlations with school grades and other achievement test scores (0.40–0.75; Terman & Merrill, 1973).

The fourth edition of the Stanford-Binet scale was published in 1986 (Thorndike, Hagen, & Sattler, 1986). While the editions to this point reflected a single "general intelligence" approach, the new edition was a sharp departure. Four content areas (verbal reasoning, abstract/visual reasoning, quantitative reasoning, and short-term memory) were assessed by 15 different subtests (e.g., vocabulary subtest of 15 items for the verbal reasoning area, and number series subtest of 26 items for the quantitative reasoning area).

The test continues to be an individually administered instrument taking about 75 minutes. Administrators are to establish a basal age for each subtest (the lowest level where two consecutive items of about equal difficulty are passed) as well as the ceiling for each subtest (level at which at least three out of four items are missed). Raw scores are converted to standard age scores (mean of 50 and standard deviation of 8). The subtest scores can be grouped into the four area scores, each with a mean of 100 and standard deviation of 16. Finally, the four area scores can be grouped into a single, overall global mental ability level—this time with a mean of 100 and standard deviation of 16.

The items of this newest version were standardized on a stratified sample (based on geographic region, community size, ethnic group, age, school class standing, and sex) of 5,013 people (aged 2 years to 23 years 11 months) in 47 states plus the District of Columbia. Items were subjected to two separate field trials for clarity and fairness.

Test-retest reliabilities for each subtest are reported by age range and were calculated based on time intervals of between 2 and 8 months. Whereas the overall global reliability is high (above 0.90), the subtest reliabilities are lower (generally about 0.80 with a few quite low values). Internal consistencies are higher, with the global composite and area scores all above 0.90. However, the individual subtests have lower coefficients, suggesting that caution should be taken in using the individual subtests for decision making. The four-factor structure underlying the test has not been unequivocally supported (e.g., Glutting, 1989; Kline, 1989; McCallum, 1990; Renolds, Kamphaus, & Rosenthal, 1988). There is support that the Stanford-Binet: Fourth Edition scores correlate with other measures of general mental ability (e.g., Carvajal, Gerber, Hewes, & Weaver, 1987; Carvajal, Hardy, Smith, & Weaver, 1988; Laurent, Swerdlik, & Ryburn, 1992; McCrowell & Nagle, 1994).

The Stanford-Binet test has been, and continues to often be, the standard to which other tests are compared. This is particularly true for younger children and those with lower cognitive ability (e.g., Kaplan & Alfonso, 1997). The theoretical framework, long history, careful creation and revision of the test items, and extensive research with the instrument over the years have contributed to its success.

Wechsler Intelligence Scales. The Wechsler-Bellevue Intelligence Scale (Wechsler, 1939) was a response by David Wechsler to what he believed were several shortcomings of the Binet approach to assessing intelligence. Wechsler argued that (a) the Binet tasks and items were inappropriate for use with adults, (b) the point system developed for scoring the Wechsler-Bellevue Intelligence Scale was superior to age-scaling, (c) performance was an important aspect of intelligence, and (d) speeded assessment penalized older individuals. For all these reasons, Wechsler embarked on the development of a new intelligence assessment tool specifically for use with adults.

The first edition (Wechsler-Bellevue Form I) and the second (Form II), published in 1947, were not standardized on a proper sample and thus were revised in 1955 and became known as the Wechsler Adult Intelligence Scale—or WAIS (Wechsler, 1955, 1958). It was revised again in 1981 (WAIS-R; Wechsler, 1981) to be used for testing adult intelligence for those aged 16 years to 74 years. The current version, revised in 1997 (WAIS-III; Tulsky, Zhu, & Ledbetter, 1997) was normed on 2,450 individuals ranging in age from 16 years to 89 years and stratified based on age, sex, educational level, and geographic region. The items were updated to more appropriate content for the era.

Wechsler believed that intelligence was manifested by the capability of acting purposefully and adaptively to the environment. Although individual elements that made up intelligence could be assessed separately, the elements were interrelated. The sum of the capability on these elements would represent general intelligence.

The WAIS-III scales are grouped into two major categories: verbal and performance. There are seven verbal subtests (e.g., vocabulary, arithmetic, comprehension) and seven performance subtests (e.g., picture completion, block design, object assembly), although only 11 are used in scoring (one fewer for the verbal and two fewer for the performance dimensions). The WAIS-III is an individually administered test but, like the group-administered tests, allows the test taker to attempt as many items as possible and earn points for each one completed correctly. After a certain number of items for each test is failed, the testing is completed. It takes about 75 minutes to administer all the tests.

Raw scores for each subtest are converted to standard scores with a mean of 10 and standard deviation of 3. Once the subtests are standardized, a table in the manual converts the verbal subtest scores into a Verbal IQ, the performance subtest scores into a Performance IQ, and all of the subtests scores into a Full IQ. Each of these IQ scores has a mean of 100 and standard deviation of 15. Research with these three IQ scores suggests that they do not adequately represent intelligence; instead, grouping the subtests differently into four indexes (verbal comprehension, perceptual organization, working memory, and processing speed) has more empirical support (Tulsky, Zhu, & Ledbetter, 1997).

The internal consistencies for the Verbal, Performance, and Full IQ scores are very high (above 0.95). Test-retest reliabilities are also quite high for these composite IQ scores. Internal consistencies for the four index scores are also very high, with most being above 0.90 across age ranges. However, like the Stanford-Binet scale, the subtest reliabilities are considerably lower. In addition, most of the subtests are correlated with one another quite highly. This poses a problem for the theoretical approach to the WAIS insofar as Wechsler assumed that the pattern of scores on the subtests would provide useful diagnostic information. Due to the psychometric characteristics of the subscales, such conclusions would be suspect. The WAIS-III Full IQ and Stanford-Binet IV global scores are correlated at 0.80.

The theoretical framework used to develop the test, extensive work that has been done to create the items, norms available, wide age range encompassed by this test, extremely reliable composite scores, and empirical work associated with the test all combine to make this one of the most popular adult intelligence scales available. Two other tests based on the same theory and approach as the WAIS are the Wechsler Intelligence Scale for Children (WISC-IV Integrated; Kaplan, Fein, Kramer, Delis, & Morris, 2004—the most current version) and the 3rd edition of the Wechsler Preschool and Primary Scale of Intelligence—WPPSI-III (Wechsler, 2002). All of these tests are published by the Psychological Corporation.

Academic Achievement Tests

While the two tests briefly reviewed thus far were developed to assess general mental ability, the next two described were developed specifically to assess knowledge or skill in the area of academic achievement. It is the case that measures of general intelligence correlate with measures of scholastic achievement. However, the two constructs are quite different. Scholastic achievement tests require students to indicate the knowledge they have obtained from a particular setting, usually a school system.

Their widespread use and machine (now computer) scoring makes them ubiquitous. The use of test scores of these types is unfortunately not always for educational improvement. Instead, they have been used for furthering the political agendas of various constituencies. Although a great many of these types of tests exist, two will be briefly reviewed here: the Scholastic Assessment Tests and Graduate Record Examination.

Scholastic Assessment Tests (SAT). The Scholastic Assessment Tests (known until 1994 as the Scholastic Aptitude Test) are administered by the College Entrance Examination Board to millions of college- and university-bound high school students each year. SATs have been in existence since 1926. Scores on the SAT make up part of many college/university entrance requirements and thus are part of the high stakes testing industry.

The SAT I: Reasoning Test is a measure of both verbal and mathematical reasoning. In addition to these general areas, specific subtests (SAT II) have also been developed (e.g., world history, chemistry, physics, biology, etc.).

The SAT I also contains items that are not used for scoring proper but are for refreshing the item bank, called an equating section. The SAT I takes 3 hours to administer, with 75 minutes devoted to each reasoning area. It is given seven times per year at testing centers that have been established specifically to administer the SAT.

The verbal reasoning test is made up of 78 items with analogies, sentence completion, and critical reasoning. The mathematical reasoning is made up of 60 items in the areas of regular mathematics, quantitative comparisons, and "student-produced" responses (i.e., they are not multiple choice).

The SAT I provides scores for both aspects of reasoning with means of 500 and standard deviations of about 110. In addition, the percentile score for each reasoning area is also provided. The scores represent where each participant's score is in relation to his or her 2–3 million peers of that year.

In 2005, the SAT will be changing its format to include a writing section (multiple-choice questions on grammar and usage and a student-written essay).

The critical reading (currently called the verbal section) test will include short as well as long reading passages and the analogies section will be eliminated. The math test will be changed to include topics from third-year college preparatory math and eliminate quantitative comparisons.

The SAT is revised each year because previously used forms are part of the public domain. Thus, item development is a constant issue for the test publisher. The SAT scales have high internal consistencies (above 0.90) and alternative forms reliabilities in the high 0.80s. The predictive validity of the SAT is moderate for college performance, with coefficients in the 0.40–0.60 range. Items are carefully assessed for potential sex and ethnic bias and for keeping the content current. Because of its importance in making college entrance decisions, a thriving industry has developed in coaching to increase SAT scores. However, the effects of improvements from coaching are about the same as for taking the tests a second time (i.e., practice). The College Board provides a detailed guide for preparing for the test, including testing tips, sample questions and answers, and a practice exam.

The original SAT mean of 500 and standard deviation of 100 norming scale was based on a 10,000-person sample of data collected in 1941. In the 1980s and 1990s, there was a definitive change downward in the scores of the test takers, with average scores on the SAT-Verbal being about 420 and SAT-Mathematical being about 480. While some ascribed this shift to a poorer school system and degeneration in society at large, instead it reflected a societal movement away from the 1940s, when only a highly select group of individuals went to college and therefore took the test, to an era where 50% of high school students have college aspirations and they all take the test.

Regardless of why the scores shifted, in 1994, new norms were created based on a sample of over a million test takers in 1989–1990. The new average score of 500 is based on this sample, and the new standard deviation is about 110. The result is that an average performer who took the test in 1995 would have Verbal and Mathematical scores of 500, but would have had scores of 420 for Verbal and 480 for Mathematical in 1994. The items did not get easier—the norming scale had changed. Although this has caused some confusion in correctly interpreting scores that come from years prior to and post-April 1995, the College Board has provided a conversion chart for scores obtained in 1994 or earlier. As time passes, this renorming will be less and less of a problem.

The SAT has come under fire for its utility (e.g., Gottfredson & Crouse, 1986) and concern over the different scores obtained by ethnic minorities (e.g., Lawlor, Richman, & Richman, 1997). However, there is evidence that the pattern of SAT scores is such that minority groups are not different from the majority on the SAT (e.g., Williams & Ceci, 1997). In addition, although high school grades are also part of the selection decisions for colleges, they are highly variable because high schools vary widely in their student body makeup, geographic location, ability to secure resources, and so forth. The SAT is common to all test takers and thus provides an index that is comparable across the nation. High school grades are useful in determining how well the student has done in the past. SAT scores add value in the selection decision in that they ask broad-based reasoning questions which may tap into something different than high school grades.

As with all test score uses, decisions about what the scores will be used for and why they are useful should be made before using the test, not as a justification after adopting it.

Graduate Record Examination. The Graduate Record Examination (GRE) is used as one of the selection indicators for entrance into many graduate programs—particularly those in the social and behavioral sciences. Other popular tests for admission to professional schools are the Law School Admissions Test (LSAT), the Medical College Admission Test (MCAT), and the Graduate Management Admission Test (GMAT).

The GRE is a test that purports to assess general scholastic ability and is administered via computer at many college or university campus testing centers year-round. Because the GRE results are also often used in awarding scholarships and fellowships as well as financial assistantships, the GRE is a high stakes test. There are three primary components to the General GRE—verbal (GRE-V), quantitative (GRE-Q), and analytic writing (GRE-A). The verbal test contains items of reasoning, analogies, and comprehension. Quantitative items include algebra, geometry, and arithmetic reasoning. The verbal and quantitative sections have multiple-choice-formatted items. The analytic writing section has two parts: a 45 minute "present your perspective on an issue" task and a 30-minute "analyze an argument" task.

The GRE-V and GRE-Q use computer adaptive technology in test administration. Test items are given to the test taker and, depending on the performance (pass or fail), other easier or harder items are presented. The writing component is done via computer but is scored by experts.

Advanced subject tests are also available in many college majors (e.g., psychology, history, physics, chemistry, sociology, biology, economics). These tests are sometimes required if an applicant is applying for a graduate program in one area but has a major in another (e.g., wants to go into a psychology graduate program but has a bachelor's degree in anthropology). The advanced subject tests are given via paper and pencil three times each year and take 3 hours to administer.

The three general components are each scaled to have a mean of 500 and standard deviation of 100. The reference group for this distribution was tested in 1952. Because the distributions for each component are not equivalent, it is not possible to directly compare the scaled scores of, say, the verbal and quantitative scores. The scores represent relative performance to a fixed reference group. In addition, percentile ranks are given for each of the general and subject tests. These percentiles represent the performance of the individual relative to those who took the test in the past 3 years. Because the Educational Testing Service allows the test taker to request GRE scores for up to 5 years, the scaled score will not change but the percentile rank very well might change over that period.

It appears that there is little value in taking coaching courses to enhance performance on the GRE. Instead, examining the manual, doing the practice questions, and generally abiding by good test-taking tips is the most cost-effective approach to getting good scores on the GRE.

The internal consistencies of the GRE general tests are very high (above 0.90). Items are carefully designed and screened regularly. Relationships between GRE scores and grades in graduate school have been less than overwhelming, ranging from 0.00 to moderate (about 0.35). Part of this is due to restriction of range. Recall that only the best applicants are selected into graduate school, and these individuals are likely to all have high GRE scores. Thus, the variance on the predictor is constrained. Given the extraordinary lengths applicants go through to be accepted into graduate school, they are also likely to be highly motivated to do well and thus restrict the range on grade point average (GPA) as well. Despite these problems, while the validity coefficients are less than spectacular for the GRE, the evidence suggests that it is still better to use it than not (e.g., Educational Testing Service, 1997; House, 1997; House & Johnson, 1998; Ji, 1998; Kuncel, Campbell, & Ones, 1998; Morrison & Morrison, 1995; Roznowski, 1998; Sternberg & Williams, 1997).

In addition, there is so much variation in grading systems at various colleges that it is not possible to make direct comparisons of college GPAs of applicants from two different schools. Given the Freedom of Information Act that gives students the right to examine the letters in their files, there is suspicion about the validity of letters of reference.

The GRE manual is clear that scores on the GRE should be only part of the decision-making process for graduate school admission. In fact, almost all graduate programs require transcripts of college courses, letters of recommendation, and sometimes interviews before making their final selection decisions. Other important selection criteria include research experience, volunteer work experience, and publication/presentation of scholarly work. However, abuse of GRE scores is not unheard of (e.g., applications with GRE-Q + GRE-V scores of less than 1200 are instantly rejected).

Structured Personality Tests

Personality is usually defined as relatively stable patterns of responding to environmental conditions that vary from individual to individual. Structured personality tests attempt to evaluate various personality traits by asking respondents to indicate the extent to which an item or statement characterizes them. The interest in measuring aspects of personality first became an issue for society during World War I, when suitability for being a soldier became an important question. Because of the huge numbers of recruits that needed to be assessed, individual psychiatric screening was not possible. Instead, self-report structured personality inventories were developed that primarily assessed emotional well-being and adjustment to the military.

Over the next 20 years, vast improvements in structured personality testing were developed. Various dimensions of personality were theoretically proposed, giving rise to multiscale inventories. Recognizing the problems inherent in self-reports, items were deliberately designed to assess faking good, faking bad, defensiveness, lying, and so forth. Most test development followed one of two general approaches: deductive and empirical. Deductive approaches used theory and common sense to develop items designed to assess various aspects of personality. Empirical approaches used statistics to guide test development and refinement. For example, items that discriminated between groups (e.g., psychopaths from nonpsychopaths) were kept regardless of the face and content validity of the item. Factor analysis was used to group items together that would then be used to infer a personality construct. Although, at their extremes, these two approaches caused some infighting in the personality literature, most scale developers use the best of both procedures for test development and refinement.

California Psychological Inventory. The California Psychological Inventory (CPI) is one of the most widely used structured personality inventories. It assesses 20 attributes of normal personality. Some examples of these attributes are dominance, independence, well-being, and intellectual efficiency. The 480-item instrument was first published by Harrison Gough in 1968 and was designed to assess normal personality in adolescents and adults. The scale was revised in 1987 (Gough, 1987) and reduced to 462 items. Norms for this version are based on more than 6,000 male and 7,000 female test takers. The revised inventory added several new scales, and some of the remaining items were updated. A third revision (Gough & Bradley, 1996) reduced by 28 the number of items. Norms for this version were based on 3,000 males and 3,000 females.

The CPI was intended to assess interpersonal behavior and social interaction. About half of the items on the original version were taken directly from the Minnesota Multiphasic Personality Inventory (MMPI), which was designed to differentiate individuals based on various psychiatric disorders. The CPI was developed emphasizing the empirical approach. Groups of individuals who had been identified as having a specific personality trait (e.g., high dominant or low dominant) would take the inventory. The items that the two groups scored significantly differently on were used to assess, for instance, the dominance trait. Thirteen of the 20 scales were developed this way. One of the criticisms of the CPI is that some of the criterion groups used in establishing the scales were identified by their friends as being high or low on the trait (for example, empathy or independent).

Four of the scales (Social Presence, Self-Acceptance, Self-Control, and Flexibility) were developed by selecting items that theoretically were designed to measure the construct. Then these scales were refined by assessing the intercorrelations among the items. Three scales—Well-Being (faking bad), Good Impression (faking good), and Communality (popular responding)—are used as validity scales. Individuals are expected to score in the normal range on these scales, and, if not, then the rest of the scale scores are suspect. Additionally, 13 special-purpose/ research scales are also available for use (e.g., Managerial Potential, Creative Temperament, Social Desirability).

The CPI is easy to administer and score. Individuals or groups read items and either indicate that they are true or false in terms of characterizing themselves. Scale score totals are generated by counting the number of true responses on each scale. The raw scores are then plotted on a profile sheet that automatically converts the raw scores to *T* scores with a mean of 50 and standard deviation of 10. The manual provides gender-specific norms as well as gender-combined norms.

The psychometric properties of the CPI are not stellar. Test-retest reliabilities range from 0.38 to 0.90, depending on the sample and length of time elapsed between tests. The intercorrelations among the scales are also high. These two problems make it unwise to differentiate among a single test taker's scores on the various scales. That is, "profile interpretation" for a single individual is not advised (e.g., Megargee, 1972). On the other hand, comparing the scale mean scores across various groups does not pose such problems. Factor analysis with earlier versions of the CPI suggests that most of the variance on the instrument can be captured with five or six factors (Crites, Bechtoldt, Goodstein, & Heilbrun, 1961; Mitchell & Pierce-Jones, 1960), whereas Gough (1987) indicated that a four-factor solution best captured the variance in the scales. The CPI has been used to predict job and scholastic performance and delinquency. Despite some of the shortcomings associated with the CPI, it remains one of the most researched structured personality inventories today.

NEO Personality Inventory. The NEO Personality Inventory (Revised) (NEO-PI-R; Costa & McCrae, 1985, 1992) was designed to measure five primary dimensions of personality (called the Big Five) in normal adults ranging from 20 years to 80 years of age. The five personality constructs assessed are Neuroticism (N), Extraversion (E), Openness to Experience (O), Agreeableness (A), and Conscientiousness (C). There are six facets that underlie each of the major constructs. *N* indicates the degree to which a person is anxious and insecure versus calm and self-confident; the six facets are anxiety, hostility, depression, self-consciousness, impulsiveness, and vulnerability. *E* indicates the degree to which a person is sociable and assertive versus quiet and reserved; the six facets are warmth, gregariousness, assertiveness, activity, excitement-seeking, and positive emotions. *O* indicates the degree to which a person is imaginative and curious versus concrete and narrow-minded; the six facets are fantasy, aesthetics, feeling, actions, ideas, and values. *A* indicates the degree to which a person is warm and cooperative versus unpleasant and disagreeable; the six facets are trust, modesty, compliance, altruism, straightforwardness, and tender-mindedness. *C* indicates the degree to which a person is persevering and responsible; the six facets are competence, self-discipline, achievement striving, dutifulness, order, and deliberation.

The full scale is 240 items (30 for each facet) with three additional validity-check items, and it takes about 30 minutes to complete. However, a short version of 60 items, the NEO-FFI (NEO Five Factor Inventory), assesses only the five major constructs and takes about 15 minutes to complete. Items on the scale are rated on a five-point scale with the ends anchored with strongly disagree and strongly agree. Forms allow for self-report (Form S) or observer-report (such as spouse, colleague, friend; Form R). The response sheets can be hand- or machine-scored.

Theory and factor-analytic approaches were used in the development of this inventory. The personality dimensions were derived using a lexical approach. Specifically, adjectives to describe individuals were determined by examining dictionaries and compiling lists of these words. They were then grouped and assessed as to the major constructs they assessed. Items were written both positively and negatively to create a balanced set. Items were revised and deleted after various psychometric analyses.

Test-retest and internal consistency reliabilities for the major construct scales are very good (in the high 0.80 to low 0.90 range) but for the facet scales are lower (in the 0.50 to 0.90 range). The shorter form (NEO-FFI) scales also have somewhat lower reliabilities (in the 0.70 to 0.80 range). Validity research suggests that the NEO is a good scale to use in assessing normal versus pathological personality and to predict interests, coping styles, job performance, and a host of other behaviors. Factor analyses of existing personality inventories also support the Big Five as underlying many of the longer lists of personality characteristics.

An encouraging feature of the NEO is that it seems to work across many cultures (e.g., Caprara, Barbaranelli, & Compey, 1995; Spirrison & Choi, 1998). It has been the most researched personality inventory since it came on the scene in the 1990s and is likely to continue to be the scale of choice in many situations. Research into the scale's properties includes the manuals themselves as well as Barrick and Mount (1991); Botwin (1995); Costa and McCrae (1995); Costa, McCrae, and Kay (1995); Digman (1990); Hess (1992); Juni (1995); and Widiger (1992).

Career Interest/Guidance Instruments

One of the oldest and most common uses to which psychological tests are put is to assist individuals in making vocational and career choices. High school and college counselors who see individuals who are making initial career choices use these instruments. As career progression is more and more punctuated by change, middle-aged individuals are also seeking assistance with career choices. Interest inventories do just that—they assess interests people have in various types of careers. They do not, however, purport to assess skills and abilities in those areas. Career guidance instruments provide a somewhat more fulsome picture of an individual's strengths, abilities, and interests.

Strong Inventories. An early career interest inventory appeared in 1927 with the Strong Vocational Interest Blank (SVIB; Strong, 1927). The theoretical basis for the SVIB was that different professional groups showed consistent differences in the things they liked versus things they did not like to do (e.g., work with people, perform repetitive tasks, engage in artistic work, etc.). Not only did this apply to work-related tasks but also to school subjects, hobbies, books, entertainment, and so forth. For years, Strong set out to differentiate men in one profession from men in other professions based on their likes and dislikes. Thus, the SVIB is primarily an empirically based scale. Items on the SVIB are activities and are responded to by the test taker with "like," "dislike," or "indifferent." Strong used items for each scale (e.g., the dentistry scale) where the professional group answered statistically differently from "men in general." When someone takes the SVIB, the interests that are most like certain professions form the basis of the career counseling process. In 1933, Strong created a form of the SVIB that included professions that were also populated by women. The 1966 version of the SVIB included 399 items that mapped onto 54 occupations for men.

Raw scores were converted to standard scores with a mean of 50 and standard deviation of 10. Each of the 54 groupings contained responses from about 300 people in that profession. Reliabilities were quite good (low 0.80 to low 0.90) for split-half and short-term test-retest. Long-term (some as long as 20 years) test-retest reliabilities were in the 0.60 range. Later versions of the SVIB have shown similar reliabilities. Strong and Campbell (1966) reported significant predictive utility of the SVIB with job satisfaction. Indeed, the inventory does not predict success in the occupation but does predict career exploration and satisfaction with and length of time in a chosen occupation (e.g., Borgen & Harper, 1973; Dolliver, Irvin, & Bigley, 1972; Randahl, Hansen, & Haverkamp, 1993; Spokane, 1979). While the SVIB has enjoyed widespread use and good psychometric characteristics, disenchantment with it for being gender-biased, as well as atheoretical, gave rise to a series of changes over the next twenty years.

A more recent version of the SVIB, called the Strong-Campbell Interest Inventory (SCII) was published in 1974 (Campbell, 1974). The men's and women's forms were merged into a single form and a theoretical basis for the interests was proposed. This theoretical linkage was based on the work of John Holland (1959, 1971), whose Self-Directed Search will be discussed next. The CSII was revised in 1977 (Campbell, 1977), in 1981 (Campbell & Hansen, 1981), and again in 1985 (Hansen & Campbell, 1985). The 1981 version attempted to use more up-to-date samples for norming purposes. The 1985 version attempted to expand the number and types of occupations represented in the inventory. This included adding non-professional vocations into the inventory.

The 1994 update (Harmon, Hansen, Borgen, & Hammer, 1994) was extensive and used responses to the Strong from over 50,000 people in 50 occupations. Item updating, coverage of new and emerging occupations, and norms for work groups not previously covered were all part of the 1994 improvements. The test is 317 items in length and individuals still respond with like, dislike, or indifferent. Automated scoring and profiling is offered by many agencies. The profile shows the test taker's score on 211 different occupational scales, 25 basic interests, and six occupational themes. There are also administrative scales to ensure from a clerical perspective that test taking and scoring were completed accurately.

Self-Directed Search. While most interest inventories were developed to be administered, scored, and interpreted by a professional, John Holland developed the Self-Directed Search (SDS; 1971, 1979) to be self-administered, self-scored, and self-interpreted. The SDS is based on Holland's theory of career choice. He defined personality types and work environments to be one of six: Realistic (R), Investigative (I), Artistic (A), Social (S), Enterprising (E), and Conventional (C). These six types are placed on a hexagon in the following order: R, I, A, S, E, C. Holland hypothesized that the types adjacent to one another (e.g., R and I, R and C) were more similar than those across from one another (e.g., R versus S, E versus I). The purpose of the SDS was to give the test taker an idea of his or her personality type and then to match that with the type of work environment that would be most congruent. This approach required Holland not only to define personality but also to define work environments.

Those who complete the SDS indicate their career aspirations, occupational interests, skills, and abilities in the six different areas by responding to a series of questions. Test takers then score their own sheets and calculate their scores on the six different areas. Let's say that, based on my responses, I score highest on the "E for enterprising" scale. In addition, I note that my next two highest scales are "A for artistic" and "S for Social." Then, going to the occupational finder, I can locate occupations that have been defined as being "EAS." These occupations, then, would most likely be compatible with my aspirations, interests, and skills.

Several revisions of the SDS occurred between 1971 and 1985. The 1994 revision (SDS Form R) was to make the SDS more useful for counselors and clients. Research in the 1990s ensured that the scales were reliable and valid (Holland, Fritzsche, & Powell, 1997). Internal consistencies are in the 0.70 to 0.90 range for activities, competencies, and occupations, with the summary scale in the low 0.90s. Test-retest reliabilities are in the range of 0.70 to 0.90 for the summary scales. The test is to be used by normally functioning individuals with minimal career advising needs (e.g., in high schools, colleges, adult centers, etc.). The SDS is not meant to replace career counselors for those who are uneducated, illiterate, or mentally disturbed. Evidence suggests that the SDS process benefits users engaged in career search decisions. In addition, men and women tend to select and remain in occupations consistent with their personality types (Holland, Fritzsche, & Powell, 1997).

The 1994 revision is very similar to the 1985. It has 228 items and takes about 40 minutes to complete. Because of its similarity to the 1985 version, many of the psychometric properties of the revised version are assumed to have been inherited from the earlier version. Changes in the accompanying support manuals also occurred in the 1990s. The Occupations Finder (Holland, 1996a), Educational Opportunities Finder (Rosen, Holmberg, & Holland, 1997) and Leisure Activities Finder (Holmberg, Rosen, & Holland, 1997) were created to help find an occupation (1,334 occupational titles), help find a postsecondary field (750 postsecondary fields of study), and assist in transition to retirement (700 leisure activities), respectively. There is an SDS Easy form (Form E) for those with limited reading ability (Holland, 1996b).

Summary

There are thousands of tests that have been developed and used over the years for various purposes. The ones reviewed in this chapter have some common features: they are widely available and have been used extensively for many years. Thus, they have plenty of psychometric information available on them. Not all tests have such a large information base on which to make a decision as to whether it will fit a particular purpose. Test users or administrators should proceed to use a test only if they are confident that the inferences made from the test scores are reliable and valid for the purpose intended. The topics covered were

1. where and how to extract test information,

2. the Stanford-Binet Intelligence Tests and Wechsler Intelligence Scales as measures of cognitive functioning,

3. the Scholastic Assessment Tests and Graduate Record Examination as measures of academic achievement,

4. the California Psychological Inventory and NEO Personality Inventory as structured measures of personality, and

5. the Strong Inventories and Self-Directed Search as measures of career interest/ guidance.

A Quick Book Review

The purpose of this book was to walk the reader through the process of developing and evaluating psychometric assessment tools. The first item of business was to remind the reader of the critical role of measurement in theory, research, and practice as well as review some common statistical procedures and protocols. The second chapter was devoted to the art and science of writing good items. This is a thoughtful and time-consuming process. Next, the types of responses that are available and appropriate for the specific items and the use to which the data will be put were outlined. After the scale has been constructed, it will need to be administered to a sample. Issues about sampling and the problems arising from sampling were covered in Chapter 4.

Once a scale's items and responses are constructed and the data have been collected, some thought as to the theoretical model or models that will be used to assess the scale and its items were presented in chapters 5 and 6. Chapters 7–10 were devoted to the statistical and interpretive issues of reliability and validity of use. Chapter 11 highlighted the importance of testing in people's everyday lives. As a result, professional, ethical, and legal concerns have to be part of the psychometrician's repertoire of knowledge. Finally, this last chapter very briefly reviewed a few existing, commercially available tests. Although this was not meant to be exhaustive, it should provide the reader with some ideas about what is important in evaluating the utility of a test in a particular setting, with a particular individual, and for a particular use.

This book should have provided an appreciation of the time and effort that goes into excellent test construction and validation work. It should assist in developing measuring instruments in those cases where research or practical questions cannot be assessed with currently existing tests. It should also assist in being an effective consumer and user of tests; it should point out what their good points are as well as their blemishes.

Concluding Comments

Testing and psychometrics have a long and respected history in the field of psychology. Without instruments that provide accurate and reliable information about the constructs of interest, we would certainly be without the tools needed to develop and test theory or to apply our knowledge in a thoughtful, competent manner. Much of the capacity of any science—psychology included—rests on the capability of its measurement tools.

For a construct to be scientifically admissible, Cronbach and Meehl (1955) outlined the process for building a *nomological net* around that construct. A simple beginning of such a net was shown in Figure 1.4 in chapter 1, where the links between the measurements of two constructs, between the constructs and their respective measures, and between the constructs themselves are noted. Cronbach and Meehl, as well other researchers since then (e.g., Bacharach, 1989; Binning & Barrett, 1989) have noted the importance of creating a large, complex, interlocking system of linkages around the construct in order for the construct to become a viable one.

In this example, one could imagine a number of ways to link the construct of "team player" with measures of that construct other than the Team Player Inventory (e.g., peer ratings, supervisor ratings, etc.). Similarly, one could imagine a number of ways to link the construct of "team effectiveness" with measures of that construct other than number of errors in a computer program (e.g., sales volume, customer satisfaction, etc.). The degree to which these are useful measures of the constructs must be demonstrated. Additionally, the empirical links between the various measures would provide evidence to support the nomological net around the construct of team player.

This book has demonstrated that developing a measure to represent a construct is a slow, iterative process. The critical role of measurement will not only grow as we proceed into this century but will likely become even more important as we begin to tackle questions of societal importance. These range from issues with the aging population; ethical concerns with the advances in biotechnology and computer use; the roles of work, education, and family; mental and physical well-being; cross-cultural and multicultural phenomena; and general social and personal adjustment. Tests and their use will be an integral part of how these problems can and should be dealt with effectively.

Problems and Exercises

1. What are some sources for obtaining test information?

2. Find a test of intelligence other than the Stanford-Binet and Wechsler Intelligence Scales. Review the test. Be sure to include issues of sampling, test theory, test item development, standardization, norms, reliability, validity, special characteristics of the test itself, and its scoring or its use.

3. Find a test of achievement other than the Scholastic Assessment Tests and Graduate Record Examination. Review the test. Be sure to include issues of sampling, test theory, test item development, standardization, norms, reliability, validity, special characteristics of the test itself, and its scoring or its use.

4. Find a test of personality other than the California Psychological Inventory and the NEO Personality Inventory. Review the test. Be sure to include issues of sampling, test theory, test item development, standardization, norms, reliability, validity, special characteristics of the test itself, and its scoring or its use.

5. Find a test of career interest or vocational guidance other than the Strong Inventories or the Self-Directed Search. Review the test. Be sure to include issues of sampling, test theory, test item development, standardization, norms, reliability, validity, special characteristics of the test itself, and its scoring or its use.

6. Find other tests that might be of interest to you (e.g., tests of special populations, psychomotor tests, tests of special interests or potentials). Review the test. Be sure to include issues of sampling, test theory, test item development, standardization, norms, reliability, validity, special characteristics of the test itself, and its scoring or its use.

References

Aamodt, M. G., & Kimbrough, W. W. (1985). Comparison of four methods for weighting multiple predictors. *Educational and Psychological Measurement, 45,* 477–482.

Adarand Constructors, Inc. v. Pena, Secretary of Transport et al., 115 U.S. 2097 (1995).

Albemarle Paper Co. v. Moody, 442 U.S. 405 (1975).

Algera, J. A., Jansen, P. G. W., Roe, R. A., & Vijn, P. (1984). Validity generalization: Some critical remarks on the Schmidt-Hunter procedure. *Journal of Occupational Psychology, 57,* 197–210.

Allen, M. J., & Yen, W. M. (1979). *Introduction to measurement theory.* Monterey, CA: Brooks/Cole.

Allen v. Alabama State Board of Education, 612 F. Supp. 1046 (1985).

American College Test Program. (1995). *Using the ACT assessment on campus.* Iowa City, IA: Author.

American Educational Research Association. American Psychological Association, National Council on Measurement in Education. (1999). *Standards for educational & psychological testing.* Washington, DC: American. Educational Research Association.

American Psychological Association. (1986). *Guidelines for computer-based tests and interpretations.* Washington, DC: Author.

American Psychological Association. (1992). Ethical principles of psychologists and code of conduct. *American Psychologist, 47,* 1567–1611.

American Psychological Association. (2000). *Guidelines for computer-based testing.* Washington, DC: Association of Test Publishers.

Anderson, N. H. (1991). *Contributions to information integration theory.* Hillsdale, NJ: Erlbaum.

Andrich, D. (1978a). Application of a psychometric model to ordered categories which are scored with successive integers. *Applied Psychological Measurement, 2,* 581–594.

Andrich, D. (1978b). A rating formulation for ordered response categories. *Psychometrika, 43,* 561–573.

Angus Reid Group. (1991). *Calgary Transit Stress Study: Identifying, measuring, and addressing stress among Calgary transit employees.* Calgary, Alberta: Author.

Arvey, R. D., & Cole, D. A. (1989). Evaluating change due to training. In I. Goldstein (Ed.), *Training and development in work organizations* (pp. 89–117). San Francisco: Jossey-Bass.

Association of Mexican-American Educators v. California, 836 F. Supp. 1534 (1996).

Association of Personnel Test Publishers. (1990). *Model guidelines for preemployment integrity testing programs.* Washington, DC: Author.

Bacharach, S. B. (1989). Organizational theories: Some criteria for evaluation. *Academy of Management Review, 14,* 496–515.

Balma, M. J. (1959). The development of processes for indirect or synthetic validity. *Personnel Psychology, 12,* 395–396.

Barbara Grutter v. Bollinger et al., US No. 02–241 (2003).

Barrick, M. R., & Mount, M. K. (1990). The Big Five personality dimensions and job performance: A meta-analysis. *Personnel Psychology, 44,* 1–26.

Bass, B. M., Cascio, W. F., & O'Connor, E. J. (1974). Magnitude estimations of expressions of frequency and amount. *Journal of Applied Psychology, 59,* 313–320.

Bem, S. L. (1974). The measurement of psychological androgeny. *Journal of Consulting and Clinical Psychology, 42,* 155–162.

Bem, S. L. (1981). *Bem Sex-Role Inventory: Professional manual.* Palo Alto, CA: Consulting Psychologists Press.

Bentler, P. M. (1989). *EQS structural equations program manual.* Los Angeles: GMDP Statistical Software.

Bentler, P. M. (1990). Comparative fit indexes in structural models. *Psychological Bulletin, 107,* 238–246.

Bentler, P. M., & Bonnett, D. G. (1980). Significance tests and goodness of fit in the analysis of covariance structures. *Psychological Bulletin, 88,* 588–606.

Berg, B. L. (1989). *Qualitative research methods for the social sciences.* Boston: Allyn & Bacon.

Binning, J. F., & Barrett, G. V. (1989). Validity of personnel decisions: A conceptual analysis of the inferential and evidential bases. *Journal of Applied Psychology, 74,* 478–494.

Birren, J. E., & Schaie, K. W. (Eds.). (2001). *Handbook of the psychology of aging.* San Diego, CA: Academic Press.

Block, J. (1978). *Q-sort method in personality assessment and psychiatric research.* Palo Alto, CA: Consulting Psychologist Press.

Bock, R. D. (1972). Estimating item parameters and latent ability when responses are scored in two or more nominal categories. *Psychometrika, 37,* 29–51.

Bock, R. D., & Aitken, M. (1981). Marginal maximum likelihood estimation of item parameters: Application of an EM algorithm. *Psychometrika, 46,* 443–459.

Bond, L. (1989). The effects of special preparation on measures of scholastic ability. In R. L. Linn (Ed.), *Educational measurement* (3rd ed., pp. 429–444). New York: American Council on Education/Macmillan.

Borgen, F. H., & Harper, G. T. (1973). Predictive validity of measured vocational interests with black and white college men. *Measurement and evaluation in guidance, 48,* 378–382.

Botwin, M. D. (1995). Review of the revised NEO Personality Inventory. In J. C. Conoley & J. C. Impara (Eds.), *The twelfth mental measurements yearbook* (pp. 862–863). Lincoln, NE: The Buros Institute of Mental Measurements.

Bowman, M. L. (1989). Testing individual differences in ancient China. *American Psychologist, 44,* 576–578.

Brookhart v. Illinois State Board of Education, 697 F.2d. 179 (7th Cir. 1983).

Brown v. Board of Education, 347 U.S. 483 (1954), 349 U.S. 294 (1955).

Buchner, A., & Mayr, S. (1999). *Cross-cultural normative assessment: Recommendations and methods for the adaptation of ILSS analytical problem solving tasks.* Washington, DC: U.S. Department of Education, National Center for Education Statistics.

Burke, M. J., & Dunlap, W. P. (2002). Estimating interrater agreement with the average deviation index: A user's guide. *Organizational Research Methods, 5,* 159–172.

Burke, M. J., Finkelstein, L. M., & Dusig, M. S. (1999). On average deviation indices for estimating interrater agreement. *Organizational Research Methods, 2,* 49–68.

Buros, O. (Ed.). (1938). *The 1938 mental measurements yearbook.* Lincoln, NE: University of Nebraska Press.

Campbell, D. P. (1974). *Manual for the Strong Campbell Interest Inventory.* Stanford, CA: Stanford University Press.

Campbell, D. P. (1977). *Manual for the SVIB-SCII Strong Campbell Interest Inventory,* Second Edition. Stanford, CA: Stanford University Press.

Campbell, D. P., & Hansen, J. C. (1981). *Manual for the Strong Campbell Interest Inventory, Third Edition.* Stanford, CA: Stanford University Press.

Campbell, D. T., & Fiske, D. W. (1959). Convergent and discriminant validation by the multitrait-multimethod matrix. *Psychological Bulletin, 56,* 81–105.

Caprara, G. V., Barbaranelli, C., & Compey, A. L. (1995). Factor analysis of the NEO-PI Inventory and Comprey Personality Scales in an Italian sample. *Personality and Individual Differences, 18,* 193–200.

Cardinet, J., Tourneur, Y., & Allal, L. (1976). The symmetry of generalizability theory: Applications to educational measurement. *Journal of Educational Measurement, 13,* 119–135.

Carmines, E. G., & Zeller, R. A. (1979). *Reliability and validity assessment.* Thousand Oaks, CA: Sage.

Cartwright, S., & Cooper, C. L. (1997). *Managing workplace stress.* Thousand Oaks, CA: Sage.

Caruso, J. C. (2000). Reliability generalization of the NEO personality scales. *Educational and Psychological Measurement, 60,* 236–254.

Carvajal, H., Gerber, J., Hewes, P., & Weaver, K. (1987). Correlations between scores on Stanford-Binet IV and Wechsler Adult Intelligence Scale-Revised. *Psychological Reports, 61,* 83–86.

Carvajal, H., Hardy, K., Smith, K., & Weaver, K. (1988). Relationships between scores on Stanford-Binet IV and Wechsler Preschool and Primary Scale of Intelligence. *Psychology in the Schools, 25,* 129–131.

Champney, H. & Marshall, H. (1939). Optimal refinement of the rating scale. *Journal of Applied Psychology, 23,* 323–331.

Chatman, J. A. (1989). Improving interactional organizational research: A model of person-organization fit. *Academy of Management Review, 14,* 333–349.

Clark, L. A., & Watson, D. (1995). Constructing validity: Basic issues in scale development. *Psychological Assessment, 7,* 309–319.

Cleary, T. A. (1968). Test bias: Prediction of grades of Negro and white students in integrated colleges. *Journal of Educational Measurement, 10,* 43–56.

Cohen, J. (1988). *Statistical power analysis for the behavioral sciences.* Hillsdale, NJ: Lawrence Erlbaum.

College Entrance Examination Board. (1971). *Report of the Commission on Tests.* New York: Author.

Collins, L. M. (1996). Is reliability obsolete? A commentary on "Are simple gain scores obsolete?" *Applied Psychological Measurement, 20,* 289–292.

Collins, L. M., & Sayer, A. G. (Eds.). (2001). *New methods for the analysis of change.* Washington, DC: American Psychological Association.

Comrey, A. L. (1973). *A first course in factor analysis.* New York: Academic Press.

Connecticut v. Teal, 102 S. Ct. 2525 (1982).

Cornwell, J. M., & Dunlap, W. P. (1994). On the questionable soundness of factoring ipsative data: A response to Saville & Willson (1991). *Journal of Occupational and Organizational Psychology, 67,* 89–100.

Costa, P. T., Jr., & McCrae, R. R. (1985). *The NEO Personality Inventory: Manual.* New York: Psychological Assessment Resources.

Costa, P. T., Jr., & McCrae, R. R. (1992). *NEO-PI-R manual.* Odessa, FL: Psychological Assessment Resources.

Costa, P. T., Jr., & McCrae, R. R. (1995). Domains and facets: Hierarchical personality assessment using the revised NEO Personality Inventory. *Journal of Personality Assessment, 64,* 21–50.

Costa, P. T., Jr., McCrae, R. R., & Kay, G. G. (1995). Persons, places, and personality: Career assessment using the revised NEO Personality Inventory. *Journal of Career Assessment, 76,* 123–139.

Crawford et al. v. Honig et al., 37 F.3d 485, 487 (9th Cir 1994).

Creswell, J. W. (1998). *Qualitative inquiry and research design: Choosing among five traditions.* Thousand Oaks, CA: Sage.

Cribbie, R. A., & Jamieson, J. (2000). Structural equation models and the regression bias for measuring correlates of change. *Educational and Psychological Measurement, 60,* 893–907.

Crites, J. O., Bechtoldt, H. P., Goodstein, L. D., & Heilbrun, A. B., Jr. (1961). A factor analysis of the California Psychological Inventory. *Journal of Applied Psychology, 45,* 408–414.

Cronbach, L. J. (1951). Coefficient alpha and the internal structure of tests. *Psychometrika, 16,* 297–334.

Cronbach, L. J., & Furby, L. (1970). How should we measure "change"—or should we? *Psychological Bulletin, 74,* 68–80.

Cronbach, L. J., Gleser, G. C., Nanda, H., & Rajaratnam, N. (1972). *The dependability of behavioral measurements: Theory of generalizability of scores and profiles.* New York: Wiley.

Cronbach, L. J., & Meehl, P. E. (1955). Construct validity in psychological tests. *Psychological Bulletin, 52,* 281–302.

Cureton, E. E. (1957). The upper and lower twenty-seven percent rule. *Psychometrika, 22,* 293–296.

Debra P. v. Turlington, 474 F. Supp. 244, 260 (M.D. Fla. 1979).

Denzin, N., & Lincoln, Y. S. (2000). *Handbook of qualitative research* (2nd ed.). Thousand Oaks, CA: Sage.

Detroit Police Officers v. Young 608 F.2d 671 (CA4 1979).

DeVellis, R. F. (2003). *Scale development: Theory and applications* (2nd ed.). Thousand Oaks, CA: Sage.

Diana v. State Board of Education, C.A. No. C-70 37 RFP (N.D. Cal., filed Feb. 3, 1970).

Digman, J. M. (1990). Personality structure: Emergence of the five-factor model. *Annual Review of Psychology, 41,* 417–440.

Dixon, W. J., Brown, M. B., Engelman, L., & Jennrich, R. I. (Eds.). (1990). *BMDP statistical software manual: Vol. 1.* Berkeley, CA: University of California Press.

Dodd, B. G. (1990). The effect of item selection procedure and stepsize on computerized adaptive attitude measurement using the rating scale model. *Applied Psychological Measurement, 14,* 355–366.

Dolliver, R. H., Irvin, J. A., & Bigley, S. E. (1972). Twelve-year follow-up of the Strong Vocational Interest Blank. *Journal of Consulting Psychology, 19,* 212–217.

Donlon, T. F. (Ed.). (1984). *The College Board technical handbook for the Scholastic Aptitude and Achievement Tests.* New York: College Entrance Examination Board.

Doyle, K. O., Jr. (1974). Theory and practice of ability testing in Ancient Greece. *Journal of the History of the Behavioral Sciences, 10,* 202–212.

Drasgow, F. (1989). An evaluation of marginal maximum likelihood estimation for the two-parameter logistic model. *Applied Psychological Measurement, 13,* 77–90.

Drasgow, F., & Hulin, C. L. (1990). Item response theory. In M. D. Dunnett & L. M. Hough (Eds.), *Handbook of industrial and organizational psychology* (Vol. 1, 2nd ed., pp. 577–636). Palo Alto, CA: Consulting Psychologists Press.

Educational Testing Service. (1997). *GRE: 1997–1998 guide to the use of scores.* Princeton, NJ: Author.

Edwards, A. L. (1959). *Manual for the Edwards Personal Preference Schedule.* New York: Psychological Corporation.

Edwards, J. R. (1993). Problems with the use of profile similarity indices in the study of congruence in organizational research. *Personnel Psychology, 46,* 641–665.

Edwards, J. R. (1994). Regression analysis as an alternative to difference scores. *Journal of Management, 20,* 683–689.

Edwards, J. R. (1995). Alternatives to difference scores as dependent variables in the study of congruence in organizational research. *Organizational Behavior and Human Decision Processes, 64,* 307–324.

Edwards, J. R., & Cooper, C. L. (1990). The person-environment fit approach to stress: Recurring problems and some suggested solutions. *Journal of Organizational Behavior, 11,* 293–307.

Embretson, S. E., & Reise, S. P. (2000). *Item response theory for psychologists.* Mahwah, NJ: Lawrence Erlbaum.

Eyde, L. D., Moreland, L. L., Robertson, G. I., Primoff, E. S., & Most, R. B. (1988). *Test user qualifications: A data-based approach to promoting good test use.* Washington, DC: American Psychological Association.

Fairclough, E. H. (1977). Personal interviews and postal questionnaires: Some observations and experiences. *Statistician, 26,* 259–268.

Floyd, F. J., & Widaman, K. (1995). Factor analysis in the development and refinement of clinical assessment instruments. *Psychological Assessment, 7,* 286–299.

Flanagan, J. C. (1954). The critical incident technique. *Psychological Bulletin, 51,* 327–358.

Georgia State Conferences Branches of NAACP v. State of Georgia, No. 84–8771 (11th Cir. Court of Appeals 1985).

Ghiselli, E. E. (1956). Dimensional problems of criteria. *Journal of Applied Psychology, 40,* 374–377.

Ghiselli, E. E. (1959). The generalization of validity. *Personnel Psychology, 12,* 397–402.

Ghiselli, E. E., Campbell, J. P., & Zedek, S. (1981). *Measurement theory for the behavioral sciences.* New York: W. H. Freeman.

Glaser, B., & Strauss, A. (1967). *The discovery of grounded theory: Strategies for qualitative research.* Chicago, IL: Aldine.

Glutting, J. J. (1989). Introduction to the structure and application of the Stanford-Binet Intelligence Scale, Fourth Edition. *Journal of School Psychology, 27,* 69–80.

Goldenberg, S. (1992). *Thinking methodologically.* New York: Harper Collins.

Goldman, B. A., & Mitchell, D. F. (2002). *Directory of unpublished experimental measures: Vol. 8.* Washington, DC: American Psychological Association.

Gosling, S. D., Vazire, S., Srivastava, S., & John, O. P. (2004). Sould we trust Web-based studies? A comparative analysis of six preconceptions about Internet questionnaires. *American Psychologist, 59,* 93–104.

Gough, H. G. (1968). An interpretive syllabus for the California Psychological Inventory. In P. McReynolds (Ed.), *Advances in personality assessment* (Vol. 1, pp. 55–79). Palo Alto, CA: Science and Behavior Books.

Gough, H. G. (1987). *The California Psychological Inventory administrator's guide.* Palo Alto, CA: Consulting Psychologists Press.

Gough, H. G., & Bradley, P. (1996). *The California Psychological Inventory manual, third edition.* Palo Alto, CA: Consulting Psychologists Press.

Greer, T., & Dunlap, P. (1997). Analysis of variance with ipsative measures. *Psychological Methods, 2,* 200–207.

Griggs v. Duke Power Company, 401 U.S. 424(a) (1971).

Gottfredson, L. S., & Crouse, J. (1986). Validity versus utility of mental tests: Example of the SAT. *Journal of Vocational Behavior, 29,* 363–378.

Guadagnoli, E., & Velicer, W. F. (1988). Relation of sample size to the stability of component patterns. *Psychological Bulletin, 103,* 265–275.

Guadalupe v. Mesa Elementary School District, Stipulation and order (January 24, 1972).

Guilford, J. P. (1952). When not to factor analyze. *Psychological Bulletin, 49,* 26–37.

Guilford, J. P. & Fruchter, B. (1973). *Fundamental statistics in psychology and education* (5th ed.). New York: McGraw-Hill.

Guion, R. M. (1980). On trinitarian doctrines of validity. *Professional Psychology, 11,* 385–398.

Gulliksen, H. (1950). *Theory of mental tests.* New York: Wiley.

Gurlanik, D. B. (Ed.). (1976). *Webster's new world dictionary of the American language* (2nd College Ed.). Cleveland, OH: William Collins and World Publishing.

Guttman, L. (1947). The Cornell technique for scale and intensity analysis. *Educational and Psychological Measurement, 7,* 247–249.

Guttman, L. (1954). Some necessary conditions for common factor analysis. *Psychometrika, 19,* 149–161.

Hansen, J. C., & Campbell, D. P. (1985). *Manual for the Strong Campbell Interest Inventory, Fourth Edition.* Palo Alto, CA: Consulting Psychologists' Press.

Harmon, L. W., Hansen, J. C., Borgen, F. H., & Hammer, A. L. (1994). *Strong Interest Inventory applications and technical guide.* Stanford, CA: Stanford University Press.

Hathaway, S. R., & McKinley, J. C. (1943). *Manual for the Minnesota Multiphasic Personality Inventory.* New York: Psychological Corporation.

Hess, A. K. (1992). Review of the NEO Personality Inventory. In J. J. Kramer & J. C. Conoley (Eds.), *The eleventh mental measurements yearbook* (pp. 603–605). Lincoln, NE: Buros Institute of Mental Measurements.

Hicks, L. E. (1970). Some properties of ipsative, normative, and forced-choice normative measures. *Psychological Bulletin, 74,* 167–184.

Hobson v. Hansen, 269 F. Supp. 401 (D.D.C. 1967).

Holland, J. L. (1959). A theory of vocational choice. *Journal of Consulting Psychology, 6,* 35–45.

Holland, J. L. (1971). *The counselor's guide to the Self-Directed Search.* Palo Alto, CA: Consulting Psychologists' Press.

Holland, J. L. (1979). *The Self-Directed Search: Professional manual.* Palo Alto, CA: Consulting Psychologists' Press.

Holland, J. L. (1985). *The Self-Directed Search: Professional manual.* Odessa, FL: Psychological Assessment Resources.

Holland, J. L. (1996a). *The Occupations Finder.* Palo Alto, CA: Consulting Psychologists' Press.

Holland, J. L. (1996b). *The Self-Directed Search (SDS): Form E.* Odessa, FL: Psychological Assessment Resources.

Holland, J. L., Fritzsche, B. A., & Powell, A. B. (1997). *The Self-Directed Search (SDS): Technical manual.* Odessa, FL: Psychological Assessment Resources.

Hollenbeck, J. R., & Whitener, E. M. (1988). Criterion-related validation for small sample contexts: An integrated approach to synthetic validity. *Journal of Applied Psychology, 73,* 536–544.

Holmberg, K., Rosen, D., & Holland, J. L. (1997). *The Leisure Activities Finder.* Odessa, FL: Psychological Assessment Resources.

House, D. J. (1997). Predictive validity of Graduate Record Examination scores and outcomes of American Indian/Alaska native students. *Psychological Reports, 81,* 337–338.

House, D. J., & Johnson, J. J. (1998). Predictive validity of the Graduate Record Examination for grade performance in graduate psychology courses. *Psychological Reports, 82,* 1235–1238.

Hoyt, C. J. (1941). Test reliability estimated by analysis of variance. *Psychometrika, 6,* 153–160.

Humphreys, L. G. (1996). Linear dependence of gain scores on their components imposes constraints on their use and interpretation: Comment on "Are gain scores obsolete?" *Applied Psychological Measurement, 20,* 293–294.

Hunter, J. E., & Schmidt, F. L. (1990). *Methods of meta-analysis: Correcting error and bias in research findings.* Newbury Park, CA: Sage.

Jackson, D. N. (1977). *Jackson Vocational Interest Survey manual.* London, Ontario: Research Psychologists Press.

James, L. R., Demaree, R. G., & Wolf, G. (1984). Estimating within-group interrater reliability with and without response bias. *Journal of Applied Psychology, 69,* 85–98.

James, L. R., Demaree, R. G., & Wolf, G. (1993). r_{wg}: An assessment of within-group interrater agreement. *Journal of Applied Psychology, 78,* 306–309.

Jennifer Gratz et al. v. Lee Bollinger et al., US No. 02–516 (2003).

Ji, C. C. (1998). Predictive validity of the Graduate Record Examination in education. *Psychological Reports, 82,* 899–904.

Johns, G. (1981). Difference score measures of organizational behavior variables: A critique. *Organizational Behavior and Human Performance, 27,* 443–463.

Jolliffe, F. R. (1986). *Survey design and analysis.* Chichester, UK: Ellis Horwood.

Joreskog, K. G., & Sorbom, D. (1979). *Advances in factor analysis and structural equation models.* Cambridge, MA: Abt Books.

Joreskog, K. G., & Sorbom, D. (1993). *LISREL 8 user's reference guide.* Chicago, IL: Scientific Software.

Juni, S. (1995). Review of the Revised NEO Personality Inventory. In J. C. Conoley & J. C. Impara (Eds.), *The twelfth mental measurements yearbook* (pp. 863–868). Lincoln, NE: Buros Institute of Mental Measurements.

Kaiser, H. F. (1960). The application of electronic computers to factor analysis. *Educational and Psychological Measurement, 20,* 401–417.

Kaiser, H. F. (1970). A second generation Little Jiffy. *Psychometrika, 35,* 141–151.

Kaplan, E., Fein, D., Kramer, J., Delis, D., & Morris, R. (2004). *WISC-IV integrated manual.* San Antonio, TX: Psychological Corporation.

Kaplan, S. L., & Alfonso, V. C. (1997). Confimatory factor analysis of the Stanford-Binet Intelligence Scale: Fourth edition with preschoolers and developmental delays. *Journal of Psychoeducational Assessment, 15,* 226–236.

Kay, G. G. (1991). Casting stones at integrity testing, not integrity tests. *Forensic Reports, 4,* 163–169.

Kelderman, H., & Rijkes, C. P. M. (1994). Loglinear multidimensional IRT models for polytomously scored items. *Psychometrika, 59,* 149–176.

Keyser, D. J., & Sweetland, R. C. (Eds.). (1984–1994). *Test critiques: Vols. 1–X.* Austin, TX: Pro-Ed.

Kim, J., & Mueller, C. W. (1978). *Factor analysis: Statistical methods and practical issues.* Beverly Hills, CA: Sage.

Kline, R. B. (1989). Is the Fourth Edition Stanford-Binet a four factor test? Confirmatory factor analyses of alternative methods for ages 2 through 23. *Journal of Psychoeducational Assessment, 7,* 4–13.

Kline, R. B. (1998). *Principles and practice of structural equation modeling.* New York: Guilford.

Kline, T. J. B. (1994). Measurement of tactical and strategic decision-making. *Educational and Psychological Measurement, 54,* 745–756.

Kline, T. J. B. (1999). The Team Player Inventory (TPI): Reliability and validity of a measure of predisposition toward organizational team-working environments. *Journal for Specialists in Group Work, 24,* 102–112.

Kline, T. J. B. (2001). The Groupware Adoption Scale: A measure of employee acceptance. *Human Systems Management, 20,* 59–62.

Kline, T. J. B. (2003). The psychometric properties of scales that assess market orientation and team leadership skills: A preliminary study. *International Journal of Testing, 3,* 321–332.

Kline, T. J. B., & Brown, D. (1994). *Eau Claire Estates Owner Opinion Survey.* Calgary, Alberta: Author.

Kline, T. J. B., & Brown, D. (1995). *Report to United Way: Results of employee survey on human resource issues.* Calgary, Alberta: Author.

Kline, T. J. B., & McGrath, J. L. (1998). Development and validation of five criteria for evaluating team performance. *Organization Development Journal, 16,* 19–27.

Kolb, D. A. (1985). *Learning Styles Inventory.* Boston: McBer.

Kuder, G. F. (1979). *Manual, Kuder Occupational Interest Survey 1979 revision.* Chicago: Science Research Associates.

Kuder, G. F., & Richardson, M. W. (1937). The theory of the estimation of test reliability. *Psychometrika, 2,* 151–160.

Kuncel, N. R., Campbell, J. P., & Ones, D. S. (1998). Validity of the Graduate Record Examination: Estimated or tacitly known? *American Psychologist, 53,* 567–568.

Landy, F. J. (1986). Stamp collecting versus science: Validation as hypothesis testing. *American Psychologist, 41,* 1183–1192.

Larry P. v. Wilson Riles, 343 F. Supp. 1306 (N.D. Cal. 1972), aff'd, 502 F.2d 963 (9th Cir. 1979).

Latham, G. P., & Wexley, K. N. (1977). Behavioral observation scales for performance appraisal purposes. *Personnel Psychology, 30,* 255–268.

Laurent, J., Swerdlik, M., & Ryburn, M. (1992). Review of validity research on the Stanford-Binet Intelligence Scale: Fourth edition. *Psychological Assessment, 4,* 102–112.

Lawley, D. N., & Maxwell, A. E. (1971). *Factor analysis as a statistical method.* London: Butterworth.

Lawlor, S., Richman, S., & Richman, C. L. (1997). The validity of using the SAT as a criterion for black and white students' admission to college. *College Student Journal, 31,* 507–515.

Lawshe, C. H. (1952). Employee selection. *Personnel Psychology, 5,* 31–34.

Levine, M. V., & Drasgow, F. (1983). The relation between incorrect option choice and estimated ability. *Educational and Psychological Measurement, 43,* 675–685.

Likert, R. (1932). A technique for the measurement of attitudes. *Archives of Psychology, No. 140.*

Lilienfeld, S. O., Alliger, G., & Mitchell, K. (1995). Why integrity testing remains controversial. *American Psychologist, 50,* 457–458.

Lindell, M. K., Brandt, C. J., & Whitney, D. J. (1999). A revised index of interrater agreement for multi-item ratings of a single target. *Applied Psychological Measurement, 23,* 127–135.

Long, J. S. (1983). *Confimatory factor analysis.* Beverly Hills, CA: Sage.

Lord, F. M. (1980). *Applications of item response theory to practical testing problems.* Hillsdale, NJ: Erlbaum.

Lord, F. N., & Novick, M. R. (1968). *Statistical theories of mental test scores.* Reading, MA: Addison-Wesley.

Madow, W. G., Nisselson, H., & Olkin, I. (Eds.). (1983). *Incomplete data in sample surveys volume 1: Report and case studies.* New York: Academic Press.

Marascuilo, L. A., & Slaughter, R. E. (1981). Statistical procedures for analyzing possible sources of test item bias based on χ^2 statistics. *Journal of Educational Measurement, 18,* 229–248.

Marchall v. Georgia, CV482–233 (U.S. District Court for the Southern District of Georgia June 28, 1984), *aff'd*, No. 84–8771 (11th Cir. Oct. 29, 1985).

Masters, G. N. (1982). A Rasch model for partial credit scoring. *Psychometrika, 47,* 149–174.

McCallum, R. S. (1990). Determining the factor structure of the Stanford-Binet: Fourth Edition: The right choice. *Journal of Psychoeducational Assessment, 8,* 436–442.

McCrowell, K. L., & Nagle, R. J. (1994). Comparability of the WPPSI-R and the S-B:IV among preschool children. *Journal of Psychoeducational Assessment, 12,* 126–134.

McKinley, R. L., & Mills, C. N. (1985). A comparison of several goodness-of-fit statistics. *Applied Psychological Measurement, 9,* 49–57.

Mead, A. D., & Drasgow, F. (1993). Equivalence of computerized and paper-and-pencil cognitive ability tests: A meta-analysis. *Psychological Bulletin, 114,* 449–458.

Megargee, E. I. (1972). *The California Psychological Inventory handbook.* San Francisco: Jossey-Bass.

Meijer, R. R., & Sijtsma, K. (2001). Methodology review: Evaluating person fit. *Applied Psychological Measurement, 25,* 107–135.

Mitchell, J. V., & Pierce-Jones, J. (1960). A factor analysis of Gough's California Psychological Inventory. *Journal of Consulting Psychology, 24,* 453–456.

Mitchell, S. K. (1979). Interobserver agreement, reliability, and generalizability of data collected in observational studies. *Psychological Bulletin, 86,* 376–390.

Morrison, T., & Morrison, M. (1995). A meta-analytic assessment of the predictive validity of the quantitative and verbal components of the Graduate Record Examination with grade point average representing the criterion of graduate success. *Educational and Psychological Measurement, 55,* 309–316.

Mossholder, K. W., & Arvey, R. D. (1984). Synthetic validity: A conceptual and comparative review. *Journal of Applied Psychology, 69,* 322–333.

Muraki, E. (1990). Fitting a polytomous item response model to Likert-type data. *Applied Psychological Measurement, 14,* 59–71.

Muraki, E. (1992). A generalized partial credit model: Application of an EM algorithm. *Applied Psychological Measurement, 16,* 159–176.

Muraki, E. (1993). Information functions of the generalized partial credit model. *Applied Psychological Measurement, 17,* 351–363.

Muraki, E., & Bock, D. (2003). *PARSCALE 4.* Lincolnwood, IL: Scientific Software.

Muraki, E., & Carlson, J. E. (1995). Full-information factor analysis for polytomous item responses. *Applied Psychological Measurement, 19,* 73–90.

Murphy, K. R. (1993). *Honesty in the workplace.* Pacific Grove, CA: Brooks/Cole.

Murphy, K. R., & Davidshofer, C. O. (2001). *Psychological testing: Principles and applications* (5th ed.). Upper Saddle River, NJ: Prentice Hall.

Murphy, L. L., Plake, B. S., Impara, J. C., & Spies, R. A. (Eds.). (2002). *Tests in print VI.* Lincoln, NE: University of Nebraska Press.

Myers, I., McCaulley, M., Quenck, N., & Hammer, A. (1998). *Manual: A guide to the development and use of the Myers-Briggs Type Indicator, Third Edition.* Palo Alto, CA: Consulting Psychologists' Press.

Naglieri, J. A., Drasgow, F., Schmit, M., Handler, L., Prifitera, A., Margolis, A., & Velasquez, R. (2004). Psychological testing on the Internet: New problems, old issues. *American Psychologist, 59,* 150–162.

Nandakumar, R. (1993). Assessing essential dimensionality of real data. *Applied Psychological Measurement, 17,* 29–38.

Nandakumar, R. (1994). Assessing dimensionality of a set of items: Comparison of different approaches. *Journal of Educational Measurement, 31,* 17–35.

Nandakumar, R., & Stout, W. F. (1993). Refinement of Stout's procedure for assessing latent trait dimensionality. *Journal of Educational Statistics, 18,* 41–68.

Netemeyer, R. G., Bearden, W. O., & Sharma, S. (2003). *Scaling procedures: Issues and applications.* Thousand Oaks, CA: Sage.

Novick, M., & Lewis, G. (1967). Coefficient alpha and the reliability of composite measurements. *Psychometrika, 32,* 1–13.

Nunnally, J. C. (1978). *Psychometric theory* (2nd ed.). New York: McGraw-Hill.

Nunnally, J. C., & Bernstein, I. H. (1994). *Psychometric theory* (3rd ed.). New York: McGraw-Hill.

Ones, D. S., Chockalingam, V., & Schmidt, F. L. (1995). Integrity tests: Overlooked facts, resolved issues, and remaining questions. *American Psychologist, 50,* 456–457.

Owen, D. (1985). *None of the above: Behind the myth of scholastic aptitude.* Boston: Houghton-Mifflin.

Parents in Action on Special Education (PASE) v. Joseph P. Hannon, USCD N111 J. Grady Pub. (July 7, 1980).

Petit v. City of Chicago, 90 C 4984, 91 C 668 (CA7 2003).

Plake, B. S., Impara, J. C., & Spies, R. A. (Eds.). (2003). *Fifteenth mental measurements yearbook.* Lincoln, NE: University of Nebraska Press.

Ployhart, R. E., Weekley, F. A., Holtz, B. C., & Kemp, C. (2003). Web-based and paper-and-pencil testing of applicants in a proctored setting: Are personality, bio-data, and situational judgment test comparable. *Personnel Psychology, 56,* 733–752.

Powers, D. E. (1986). Relations of test item characteristics to test preparation/test practice effects: A quantitative summary. *Psychological Bulletin, 100,* 67–77.

Powers, D. E. (1993). Coaching for the SAT: A summary of summaries and an update. *Educational Measurement Issues and Practice, 12,* 24–30.

Primoff, E. S. (1957). The J-coefficient approach to jobs and tests. *Personnel Administration, 20,* 31–40.

Primoff, E. S. (1959). Empirical validation of the J-coefficient. *Personnel Psychology, 12,* 413–418.

Randahl, G. H., Hansen, J. C., & Haverkamp, B. E. (1993). Instrumental behaviors following test administration and interpretation: Exploration validity of the Strong Interest Inventory. *Journal of Counseling and Development, 71,* 435–439.

Rasch, G. (1960). *Probabilistic models for some intelligence and attainment tests.* Chicago: University of Chicago Press.

Ravlin, E. C., & Maglino, B. M. (1987). Effect of values on perception and decision-making: A study of alternative work measures. *Journal of Applied Psychology, 72,* 666–673.

Regents of the University of California v. Bakke, 438 U.S. 265, 17 Fair Empl. Prac. Cas. (BNA) 1000 (1978).

Reise, S. P. (1990). A comparison of item- and person-fit methods of assessing model-data fit in IRT. *Applied Psychological Measurement, 14,* 127–137.

Reise, S. P., & Yu, J. (1990). Parameter recovery in the graded response model using MULTILOG. *Journal of Educational Measurement, 27,* 133–144.

Renolds, C. R., Kamphaus, R. W., & Rosenthal, B. L. (1988). Factor analysis of the Stanford-Binet Fourth Edition for ages 2 years through 23 years. *Measurement and Evaluation in Counseling and Development, 21,* 52–63.

Rogers, G., Finley, D., & Kline, T. (2001). Understanding individual differences in university undergraduates: A learner needs segmentation approach. *Innovative Higher Education, 25,* 183–196.

Rogosa, D., Brandt, D., & Zimowski, M. (1982). A growth curve approach to the measurement of change. *Psychological Bulletin, 92,* 726–748.

Rogosa, D. R., & Willett, J. B. (1983). Demonstrating the reliability of the difference score in the measurement of change. *Journal of Educational Measurement, 20,* 335–343.

Rosen, D., Holmberg, K., & Holland, J. L. (1997). *The Educational Opportunities Finder.* Odessa, FL: Psychological Assessment Resources.

Roznowski, M. (1998). The Graduate Record Examination: Testing. *American Psychologist, 53,* 570-572.

Rudas, T. (1997). *Odds ratios in the analysis of contingency tables.* Thousand Oaks, CA: Sage.

Sackett, P. R., & Decker, P. J. (1979). Detection of deception in the employment context: A review and critique. *Personnel Psychology, 32,* 487–506.

Sackett, P. R., & Harris, M. M. (1984). Honesty testing for personnel selection: A review and critique. *Personnel Psychology, 37,* 221–245.

Samejima, F. (1969). Estimation of latent ability using a response pattern of graded scores. *Psychometrika Monograph Supplement, 34*(4), 100–114.

Saville, P., & Willson, E. (1991). The reliability and validity of normative and ipsative approaches in the measurement of personality. *Journal of Occupational Psychology, 64,* 219–238.

Schmidt, F. L. & Hunter, J. E. (1977). Development of a general solution to the problem of validity generalization. *Journal of Applied Psychology, 62,* 529–540.

Shrout, P. E., & Fleiss, J. L. (1979). Intraclass correlations: Uses in assessing rater reliability. *Psychological Bulletin, 86,* 420–428.

Slack, W. V., & Porter, D. (1980). The Scholastic Aptitude Test: A critical appraisal. *Harvard Educational Review, 50,* 154–175.

Society for Industrial and Organizational Psychology. (2003). *Principles for the validation and use of personnel selection procedures* (4th ed.). Bowling Green, OH: Author.

Spector, P. E. (1976). Choosing response categories for summated rating scales. *Journal of Applied Psychology, 61,* 374–375.

Spector, P. E. (1994). Using self-report questionnaires in OB research: A comment on the use of a controversial method. *Journal of Organizational Behavior, 15,* 385–392.

Spector, P. E., & Brannick, M. T. (1995). The nature and effects of method variance in organizational research. In C. L. Cooper & I. T. Robertson (Eds.), *International review of industrial and organizational psychology* (Vol. 10, pp. 249–274). Chichester, UK: Wiley.

Spirrison, C. L., & Choi, S. (1998). Psychometric properties of a Korean version of the revised Neo-Personality Inventory. *Psychological Reports, 83,* 263–274.

Spokane, A. R. (1979). Occupational preference and the validity of the Strong-Campbell Interest Inventory for college women and men. *Journal of Consulting Psychology, 26,* 312–318.

Stell v. Savannah-Chatham County Board of Education, 210 F. Supp. 667, 668 (S.D. Ga. 1963), *rev'd* 333 F.2d 55 (5th Cir 1964), *cert denied* 397 U.S. 933 (1964).

Sternberg, R. J., & Williams, W. M. (1997). Does the Graduate Record Examination predict meaningful success in the training of psychologists? *American Psychologist, 52,* 630–641.

Stout, W. (1987). A nonparametric approach for assessing latent trait unidimensionality. *Psychometrika, 52,* 589–617.

Stout, W. (1990). A new item response theory modeling approach with applications to unidimensional assessment and ability estimation. *Psychometrika, 55,* 293–326.

Strauss, A., & Corbin, J. (1998). *Basics of qualitative research: Techniques and procedures for developing grounded theory.* Thousand Oaks, CA: Sage.

Strong, E. K. (1927). Vocational Interest Test. *Educational Record, 8,* 107–121.

Strong, E. K. (1933). *Strong Vocational Interest Blank for Women.* Stanford, CA: Stanford University Press.

Strong, E. K., & Campbell, D. P. (1966). *Manual for Strong Vocational Interest Blank.* Stanford, CA: Stanford University Press.

Symonds, P. M. (1924). On the loss of reliability in ratings due to coarseness of the scale. *Journal of Experimental Psychology, 7,* 456–461.

Tabachnick, B. G., & Fidell, L. S. (2001). *Using multivariate statistics.* Boston, MA: Allyn & Bacon.

Taylor, H. C., & Russell, J. T. (1939). The relationship of validity coefficients to the practical validity of tests in selection: Discussion and tables. *Journal of Applied Psychology, 23,* 565–578.

Tenopyr, M. L. (1988). Artifactual reliability of forced-choice scales. *Journal of Applied Psychology, 73,* 749–751.

Terman, L. M., & Merrill, M. A. (1973). *Stanford-Binet Intelligence Scale: 1972 norms edition.* Boston: Houghton Mifflin.

Thissen, D., Chen, W. H., & Bock, D. (2002). *MULTILOG 7.* Lincolnwood, IL: Scientific Software.

Thissen, D., & Steinberg, L. (1988). Data analysis using item response theory. *Psychological Bulletin, 104,* 385–395.

Thorndike, R. L., Hagen, E. P., & Sattler, J. M. (1986). *Technical manual: Stanford-Binet Intelligence Scale: Fourth Edition.* Chicago: Riverside.

Thurstone, L. L. (1929). Theory of attitude measurement. *Psychological Bulletin, 36,* 222–241.

Thurstone, L. L. (1947). *Multiple-factor analysis: A development & expansion of the vectors of the mind.* Chicago: University of Chicago Press.

Tisak, J., & Smith, C. (1994). Defending and extending difference score methods. *Journal of Management, 20,* 675–682.

Tisak, J., & Tisak, M. S. (1996). Longitudinal models of reliability and validity: A latent curve approach. *Applied Psychological Measurement, 20,* 275–288.

Tulsky, D., Zhu, J., & Ledbetter, M. (1997). *WAIS-III WMS-III technical manual.* San Antonio, TX: Psychological Corporation.

United States Equal Employment Opportunity Commission, Civil Service Commission, Department of Labor and Department of Justice. (1978). *Uniform guidelines on employee selection procedures.* 29 CFR 1607.

Vacha-Haase, T. (1998). Reliability generalization: Exploring variance in measurement error affecting score reliability across studies. *Educational and Psychological Measurement, 58,* 6–20.

van de Vijer, F., & Hambleton, R. K. (1996). Translating tests: Some practical guidelines. *European Psychologist, 1,* 89–99.

van de Vijver, F. J. R., & Tanzer, N. K. (1997). Bias and equivalence in cross-cultural assessment: An overview. *European Review of Applied Psychology, 47,* 263–279.

Wards Cove Packing Co. v. Antonio et al., 490 U.S. 642 (1989).

Washington v. Davis, 96 U.S. 2040(c) (1976).

Watson v. Fort Worth Bank and Trust, 487 U.S. 977 (1988).

Wechsler, D. (1939). *The measurement of adult intelligence.* Baltimore: Williams & Wilkins.

Wechsler, D. (1955). *Manual for the Wechsler Adult Intelligence Scale.* New York: Psychological Corporation.

Wechsler, D. (1958). *The measurement and appraisal of adult intelligence* (4th ed.). Baltimore: Williams & Wilkins.

Wechsler, D. (1981). *Wechsler Adult Intelligence Scale-Revised.* New York: Psychological Corporation.

Wechsler, D. (2002). *Wechsler Preschool and Primary Scale of Intelligence, 3rd. ed. (WPPSI-III).* San Antonio, TX: Psychological Corporation.

Whitener, E. M. (1990). Confusion of confidence intervals and credibility intervals in meta-analysis. *Journal of Applied Psychology, 75,* 315–321.

Widiger, T. A. (1992). Review of the NEO Personality Inventory. In J. J. Kramer & J. C. Conoley (Eds.), *The eleventh mental measurements yearbook* (pp. 605–606). Lincoln, NE: Buros Institute of Mental Measurements.

Wigdor, A. K. & Garner, W. R. (1982a). *Ability testing: Uses, consequences, and controversies, part I: Report of the committee.* Washington, DC: National Academy Press.

Wigdor, A. K. & Garner, W. R. (1982b). *Ability testing: Uses, consequences, and controversies, part II: Documentation section.* Washington, DC: National Academy Press.

Williams, L., & Brown, B. (1994). Method variance in organizational behavior and human resources research: Effects on correlations, path coefficients, and hypothesis testing. *Organizational Behavior and Human Decision Processes, 57,* 185–209.

Williams, R. H., & Zimmerman, D. W. (1996a). Are simple gain scores obsolete? *Applied Psychological Measurement, 20,* 59–69.

Williams, R. H., & Zimmerman, D. W. (1996b). Commentary on the commentaries of Collins and Humphreys. *Applied Psychological Measurement, 20,* 295–297.

Williams, W. M., & Ceci, S. J. (1997). Are Americans becoming more or less alike? Trends in race, class, and ability differences in intelligence. *American Psychologist, 52,* 1226–1235.

Wilson, K. M. (1989, Spring). A study of the long-term stability of GRE test scores. In J. Pfleiderer, *GRE Board Newsletter* (Vol. 5, Report No. 86–18R.). Princeton, NJ: Graduate Records Examination Board.

Wonderlic. (1999). *Wonderlic Personnel Test & Scholastic Level Exam User's Manual.* Libertyville, IL: Author.

Yen, W. M. (1993). Scaling performance assessments: Strategies for managing local item dependence. *Journal of Educational Measurement, 30,* 187–213.

Zimowski, M., Muraki, E., Mislevy, R., & Bock, D. (2003). *BILOG-MG 3.* Lincolnwood, IL: Scientific Software.

Zuckerman, M. (1979). *Sensation seeking: Beyond the optimal level of arousal.* Hillsdale, NJ: Lawrence Erlbaum.

Zuckerman, M., Gagne, M., Nafshi, I., Knee, C. R., & Kieffer, S. C. (2002). Testing discrepancy effects: A critique, a suggestion, and an illustration. *Behavior Research Methods, Instruments, & Computers, 34,* 291–303.

Zumbo, B. D. (1999). The simple difference score as an inherently poor measure of change. *Advances in Social Science Methodology, 5,* 269–304.

Index

About the Author

Theresa J. B. Kline (Ph.D., 1990) is a Professor of Industrial-Organizational Psychology at the University of Calgary. She has an active research program in the areas of psychometrics, team performance, organizational effectiveness, and work attitudes. Theresa has published two books on teams, *Teams That Lead* (2003) and *Remaking Teams* (1999), and has published over 50 peer-reviewed journal articles.

Theresa teaches psychometrics, statistics, methods, and organizational psychology at both the undergraduate and graduate levels. She has an active organizational consulting practice with projects ranging from individual and organizational assessment to strategic alignment. She has made presentations and run workshops on topics that range from statistics and methods to how to use assessment tools for personnel decision making in an ethical manner to executive team development practices.

Theresa has supervised more than a dozen research-based theses. She encourages her students to take an active role in deciding what they will study, and, as a result, she has learned at least as much from them as they have from her, as they have drawn her into research areas such as organizational learning, lifelong learning, organizational citizenship, fairness, leadership, job change, workplace stress, and performance appraisal.